Veena R. Howard is _____ Department of Philosophy at California State University, Fresno. She is the author of *Gandhi's Ascetic Activism: Renunciation and Social Action* (2013).

"*Dharma* is an ambitious volume that dares to teach Indian traditions of practice, inquiry, and spiritual insight in ways not governed solely by categories already familiar in the English language. Once 'dharma,' 'dhamma,' and 'dharam' seize the space usually occupied by 'religion,' then the Dharmic traditions—Hindu and Buddhist, Jain and Sikh, and South Asian Sufi—can be appreciated for characteristics not predictably shared with the Abrahamic religions, and for continuities among themselves that might slip by unnoticed when the categories of analysis are imposed from afar. If *Dharma*'s good example is followed by scholars studying and teaching still other traditions globally, then the achievement of this helpful and original book will be all the greater."

– Francis X. Clooney, SJ, Parkman Professor of Divinity, Harvard University

"In the diverse landscape of medieval India, the founder of the Sikh tradition pronounced that 'there is only one *dharam*'. Veena Howard's excellent introductory volume explores the complex and multifarious definitions of this one 'dharma', and urges us to reflect on our spiritual identities across cultures. Written by eminent scholars, the volume brings together accessible and comprehensive chapters on the different 'religious' traditions of India, disclosing both their shared patterns and their distinct impressions. The appendix on 'Sufism in India' is particularly useful in contextualizing how a West Asian tradition worked out in South Asia. Sikhism emerged of course between these two cultures. In our dangerously divided world, *Dharma* makes a splendid contribution to the academy and is moreover an ideal resource for better understanding and appreciating our South Asian neighbors."

– Nikky-Guninder Kaur Singh, Crawford Family Professor of Religious Studies, Colby College, Waterville, Maine

dharma

The
Hindu, Jain,
Buddhist and Sikh
Traditions of India

Edited by
VEENA R. HOWARD

BLOOMSBURY ACADEMIC
LONDON • NEW YORK • OXFORD • NEW DELHI • SYDNEY

BLOOMSBURY ACADEMIC
Bloomsbury Publishing Plc
50 Bedford Square, London, WC1B 3DP, UK
1385 Broadway, New York, NY 10018, USA
29 Earlsfort Terrace, Dublin 2, Ireland

BLOOMSBURY, BLOOMSBURY ACADEMIC and the Diana logo are
trademarks of Bloomsbury Publishing Plc

First published in Great Britain 2017 by I.B. Tauris & Co. Ltd
Reprinted by Bloomsbury Academic in 2020, 2022

Copyright © Veena R.Howard, 2017

Veena R.Howard has asserted her right under the Copyright, Designs and
Patents Act, 1988, to be identified as Editor of this work.

Cover image: Indian Lotus flower or Nelumbo Nucifera.
GOPAN G NAIR/Getty Images.
Cover design: Sandra Friesen

All rights reserved. No part of this publication may be reproduced or
transmitted in any form or by any means, electronic or mechanical,
including photocopying, recording, or any information storage or retrieval
system, without prior permission in writing from the publishers.

Bloomsbury Publishing Plc does not have any control over, or
responsibility for, any third-party websites referred to or in this book. All
internet addresses given in this book were correct at the time of going
to press. The author and publisher regret any inconvenience caused if
addresses have changed or sites have ceased to exist, but can accept no
responsibility for any such changes.

A catalogue record for this book is available from the British Library.

A catalog record for this book is available from the Library of Congress.

ISBN: HB: 978-1-7845-3263-5
PB: 978-1-3502-2474-2
ePDF: 978-1-7867-3212-5
eBook: 978-1-7867-2212-6

Typeset in Stone Serif by OKS Prepress Services, Chennai, India

To find out more about our authors and books visit www.bloomsbury.com
and sign up for our newsletters.

We dedicate this volume to Rita M. Gross,
who continues to teach us many meanings of dharma
through her body of work.

* * * * *

[T]here cannot be a universal definition of religion, not only because its constituent elements and relationships are historically specific, but because that definition is itself the historical product of discursive processes.
Talal Asad (Distinguished Professor, CUNY Graduate Center)

For much of their history, people in the Indian subcontinent went on with their rituals, pilgrimages and acts of religious piety without objectifying religion into an exclusive entity. As a consequence, there are indeed words for faith, rites, piety, beliefs and gods, but not for an overarching community of believers.
Harjot Oberoi (Professor, University of British Columbia)

In the Sanskrit language, religion goes by the name dharma, which in the derivative meaning implies the principle of the relationship that holds us firm, and in its technical sense means the virtue of a thing, the essential quality of it.
Rabindranath Tagore (Indian poet and writer)

Contents

Preface

This term [Dharma] and the notions underlying it clearly constitute the most central feature of Indian civilization down the centuries, irrespective of linguistic, sectarian, or regional differences.
    – Patrick Olivelle (Professor, University of Texas, Austin)

Teaching comparative religion in the classroom can be exciting, but it can also pose problems of overgeneralization, oversimplification, or, at times, over-differentiation of religious ideas. This is often due to compartmentalization of religious concepts into tidy categories. Many textbooks neatly follow a structure that gives the impression that all religious traditions follow parallel, and even intersecting, systems of thought. But scholars point out challenges to this way of thinking: is the category of Christian salvation equivalent to liberation in Hindu and Jain traditions? Is the Buddhist tradition's notion of *nibbana*, or liberation, similar to the Hindu notion of *moksha*? Can the Abrahamic concept of monotheism be compared to the Sikh tradition's one God (known as *Sat Nam* and *Wahe Guru*)? In his acclaimed book, *God is Not One: The Eight Rival Religions That Run the World*, Stephen Prothero draws attention to the problem of relying on the mantra "all religions are one" and confronts the common misconception that all religions are fundamentally the same.

This book furthers the discussion of this issue by asking the following rudimentary questions: is the term "religion" even applicable for all religions? Can the idea of "God," arising out of Western theological assumptions, be universally applied to all religious traditions? Scholars of South Asia wrestle with these questions, as well as the category of religion itself. For instance, some use the Indic category of *dharma* in order to underscore presuppositions that are distinctive of the Indian traditions. Here, we employ the term *dharma* (Sanskrit: *dharma*; Pali: *dhamma*; Punjabi: *dharam*; these spellings throughout the book emphasize each tradition's unique interpretations) to add yet another layer of complexity to this issue, not to settle any debates, with the hope that such nuanced exploration will lead to a better understanding of Indian traditions. Indic traditions are often foreign to Western students despite (or perhaps because of) their representation in popular culture. Furthermore, this book challenges the premise that all religious traditions categorized as Dharma traditions are essentially similar, because they share historical and cultural contexts and certain common beliefs. This assumption has been implied in the Constitution of India, where the term "Hindu" is used *culturally* for traditions that originated in India because of their common origins and overlapping religious philosophies and practices. But the constitution also privileges Indic traditions' distinct religious practices and holidays, thus acknowledging their unique identities.

These inquiries, as well as students' questions in courses on the religions of India, have inspired this book. Students wonder whether these traditions should be better understood as "spiritualties," or more simply as "ways of life," because they lack some of the basic characteristics that correspond to their understanding of religion. In other words, students discover some fundamental, structural idiosyncrasies in traditions that originated in India and find it difficult to put them in the normative category of "religion" with which they are more familiar. For example, the issues of identity (based on exclusive dogmas), fluidity (shared religious spaces), and plurality (multiple dissenting and complementing voices) specifically generate comparative discussions. My own experience growing up in India in a family that participated in rituals and studied religious texts of different Dharma traditions has provided me with phenomenological insights into the religious landscapes within the Indic milieu. In praxis, the image that is so vivid in my mind is of my father reading both Sikh and Hindu holy books, *Guru Granth Sahib* and the *Bhagavad Gita* daily, with equal reverence. In my academic study of religion, I have grappled with the issues of identity and plurality in the milieu of Dharma traditions; my conversations with other scholars of Indian traditions have revealed similar experiences. Therefore, the idea for this volume is to use the paradigm of *dharma*, while actively resisting it as a uniform category, to study the following religious traditions that originated in India: Hindu, Jain, Buddhist, and Sikh.

Some scholars have begun to use the category of Dharmic traditions as a framework to compare Indic traditions and Abrahamic religions. The intentional use of this term is meant not only to underscore the shared elements of these traditions, but to confront the problem of overgeneralization—within the Indic context—which is important for a serious study of any tradition. Moreover, we are including a chapter on Indian Sufism, because even though the Sufi tradition is associated with Islam it has been an important part of India's religious and social culture over millennia. Not only are the writings of Sufi poets included in the Sikh scripture, but Sufism also represents a long history of interfaith interactions and cross-fertilization of ideas among Sufi traditions, Hindu Sants, and Sikh Gurus.

The chapters in this book have been authored by experts in each of the traditions. This volume does not follow a conventional textbook structure; instead, we have allowed for one that is more organic so each author can create a framework that best explores the concepts of each tradition. The book is meant to provide a comprehensive survey of each of the Dharma traditions that originated in India and to give a broad overview of the category of *dharma* itself. Furthermore, it should lead to an understanding that *dharma* (or *dhamma, dharam*)— a term often contested by some scholars as too indicative of homogenization and a strong association with "Hindu" traditions— is, by definition, heterogeneous. Indeed, there are certain shared principles among these traditions, but there are also distinct patterns that define the unique identity of each.

It is hoped that this volume will prove helpful to teachers, students, and all who are interested in the study of Indic traditions. In order to make this book accessible to undergraduates and a wide range of readers, we have avoided the use of diacritic marks on foreign terms; instead we have used italics to draw attention to their original meanings (even though some of them have been naturalized into English). This book can be used in religion and cultural studies courses. The chapters of this book can be read separately or it can be read in its entirety for a class. Even though the order of the chapters is chronological, each essay could be treated as a stand-alone work.

Editor's Note

This project was supported by Fresno State's 2015–16 Provost's Research, Scholarship, and Creative Activities Award and a grant from the Uberoi Foundation for Religious Studies, dedicated to the study and development of traditions that originated in India. I am grateful for their support, which helped me in editing and preparing the manuscript for publication. I deeply appreciate the patient and consistent support of Alex Wright, my editor at I.B.Tauris, during the publication process. I also want to extend my thanks to many colleagues, students, and friends for their help in various ways. Above all, I am thankful to the authors of this volume for their conversations, time, and effort: Jeffery Long ("Hindu Dharma"), Christopher Chapple ("Jain Dharma"), Rita Gross ("Buddha Dharma (*Dhamma*)"), Jagbir Jhutti-Johal ("Sikh Dharam"), and Arthur Buehler ("Sufism in India"). Sadly, Rita Gross, a dear friend and colleague to all of us, unexpectedly passed away before the publication of this book. She was an avid proponent of bringing the category of *dharma* into the broader conversation of religious studies, and was enthusiastically waiting to see our finished product in print. To her loving memory, we dedicate this volume.

List of Contributors

Arthur F. Buehler is Professor Emeritus at Victoria University of Wellington in New Zealand. He has published many scholarly books and articles on Sufism and its relationship with both Islam and other Indian religious traditions. Dr. Buehler's academic contributions include *Recognizing Sufism: Contemplation in the Islamic Tradition* (I.B.Tauris, 2016) and *Sufi Heirs of the Prophet: The Indian Naqshbandiyya and the Rise of the Mediating Sufi Shaykh* (2008).

Christopher Key Chapple is the Navin and Pratima Doshi Professor of Indic and Comparative Theology and Director of the Master of Arts in Yoga Studies at Loyola Marymount University in Los Angeles. Professor Chapple's fields of expertise include Jainism, yoga, ecology, and various dimensions of ethics. He has published numerous works, including *Yoga in Jainism* (2015); *Yoga and the Luminous: Patanjali's Spiritual Path to Freedom* (2008); *Reconciling Yogas: Haribhadra's Collection of Views on Yoga* (2003); and *Nonviolence to Animals, Earth, and Self in Asian Traditions* (1993).

Rita M. Gross (1943–2015) was Professor of Philosophy and Religious Studies at the University of Wisconsin-Eau Claire until her retirement in 1998. She published many influential books and articles in what became her main fields of study: Buddhism and feminism. Professor Gross was also a Tibetan Buddhist practitioner and teacher (officially known as a *lopön*), a practically oriented aspect of her life that many of her publications reflect. Dr. Gross's various scholarly works include *Religious Diversity—What's the Problem? Buddhist Advice for Flourishing* *with Religious Diversity* (2014); *Feminism and Religion: An Introduction* (1996); *Religious Feminism and the Future of the Planet: A Buddhist– Christian Conversation* (with Rosemary Radford Ruether, 2001); and *Buddhism After Patriarchy: A Feminist History, Analysis, and Reconstruction of Buddhism* (1993).

Veena R. Howard is Assistant Professor in the Department of Philosophy at California State University, Fresno. She specializes in the field of South Asian religious traditions and philosophies, Gandhian philosophy, and peace and conflict studies. She is the author of *Gandhi's Ascetic Activism: Renunciation and Social Action* (2013), as well as numerous articles, including "Lessons from 'The Hawk and the Dove': Reflections on the Mahābhārata's Animal Parables and Ethical Predicaments," *Sophia Journal of Philosophy* (2016); and "Rethinking Gandhi's Celibacy: Ascetic Power and Women's Empowerment," *Journal of the American Academy of Religion* (2013).

Jagbir Jhutti-Johal is Senior Lecturer in Sikh Studies for the Department of Theology and Religion at the University of Birmingham, UK. She was a commissioner for the Commission on Religion and Belief in British Public Life, as well as a board member for the European Society for Intercultural Theology and Interreligious Studies. Dr. Jhutti-Johal has published articles and books in the field of Sikh tradition, including *Sikhism Today* (2011), with particular emphasis on gender issues, marriage practices, diversity, and healthcare issues within the Sikh faith.

Jeffery D. Long is Professor of Religion and Asian Studies at Elizabethtown College in Pennsylvania. Professor Long's field of expertise is Hindu religions and philosophies, with particular emphasis on the school of Jainism and its focus on perspectivalism and nonviolence. He has also authored several books, including *Historical Dictionary of Hinduism* (2011), *Jainism: An Introduction* (I.B.Tauris, 2009), and *A Vision for Hinduism: Beyond Hindu Nationalism* (I.B.Tauris, 2007).

1

Toward an Understanding of Dharma: The Questions of Identity, Hybridity, Fluidity, and Plurality

Veena R. Howard

If the term "religion" is problematic, it is also challenging to name the religion of the other ... The term dharma (law, teaching, way of life) is probably the closest to an equivalent in Indian language to the meaning of "religion" in the West.

— Carl Olson (Professor, Allegheny College, PA)

Introduction

This book is about the family of four major religious traditions that originated on the Indian subcontinent: Hindu, Jain, Buddhist, and Sikh. These Religious Traditions are generally studied under the categories of "religions of India" or "South Asian religions." If one were asked to identify one concept that is broadly shared by India's various religious texts, philosophical *pandits* (traditional Indian scholars), and popular practices, it would be *dharma*. It is a concept which has neither been confined to any one religion or philosophy nor defined in any singular way, as will be discussed later in the chapter. The term *dharma* is derived from its Sanskrit root verb *dhr*, which means "to hold," "to support," or "to sustain," and while it defies a single definition or interpretation, the term is used generally in Indic traditions to mean "ethics," "law," "duty," "teaching," and "religion." Thus, *dharma*—when indicating religion—encompasses moral principles that guide human conduct, laws that maintain order, and duties that lead to individual fulfillment and social harmony. In short, *dharma* is a harmonizing principle of the cosmos. Humans, through virtuous and religious disciplines and ritualistic actions, sustain this order. A contemporary scholar of comparative religion, Karen Armstrong, defines religion as such: "I say that religion isn't about believing things. It's about what you do. It's ethical alchemy. It's about behaving in a way that changes you, that gives you intimations of holiness and sacredness."[1] Armstrong's definition is mostly compatible with Indian traditions' self-understanding of religion, although India's traditions expand the effects of an individual's actions to the cosmic scale and thus refraining from confining these actions to the purview of the interpersonal. What one individual does affects everything else. Whether it is in the sense of the underlying unity of all beings (Hindu Dharma), understanding all life as imbued with a soul (Jain Dharma), the dependent origination of all life (Buddhist Dhamma), or the essential prerogative to serve all (Sikh Dharam), the emphasis is in all cases on *both* the individual *and* the collective. Thus, religion is not simply a relationship between God and humans; it is implicated in all aspects of life. The concept of *dharma* in each of the Indic traditions is intricately connected to the idea of performing duty, doing good deeds, religious practice, behaving in a certain way, and achieving fulfillment. Nevertheless, each tradition uniquely defines "duty" and "practice."

In the contemporary world, which is marred with religious tensions, the use of the term *dharma* in place of religion may generate ambiguity in the minds of some scholars. It may suggest an appropriation of all traditions originating in India into the broader Hindu system of *dharma*. Some Hindu followers confuse Indian religious systems with Indic civilization, notwithstanding each tradition's self-understanding, original taxonomies, and practices.[2] Or perhaps the use of the word *dharma* may instead invoke images of the New Age movement's usage of the term *dharma*, expressed in idioms such as Jack Kerouac's "Dharma Bums". But in this book, we use the Indic category of *dharma* in place of "religion" to depict a system of thought with its imbedded multivalent meanings of duty, righteousness, ethics, law, teachings, and justice.[3] The term is used neither to imply that all Dharma traditions are the same due to their common heritage, nor should it suggest they are completely different from religions that did not originate in India.[4] We use the term to bring attention to the problem of mapping the category of religion—conventionally defined as a structured, exclusive, theological system and social identity—on to India's traditions, whose social and religious identities historically have overlapped. In the Euro-American context, the separation of religion and society arises from the idea that faith and reason are two different things, and that religion is "a matter which lies solely between Man and his God," to use Thomas Jefferson's words. This thinking was introduced only recently to India by the colonial powers. Contemporary scholar of religion Harjot Oberoi draws attention to the historical fact, saying that religion as "a systematized sociological unit claiming unbridled loyalty from its adherents and opposing an amorphous religious imagination … [is] a recent development in the history of the Indian people."[5] Oberoi is referring to the basic world views of Western institutionalized religions, which, prior to the interface of Indian thought with Western notions of religion, had not defined Indian traditions.

Before the nineteenth century, the idea of enclosed spaces around specific religiosity was foreign to Indian systems of spirituality, just as exclusive allegiance to any one religion was alien to the Chinese systems of thought.[6] Furthermore, the use of the term *dharma* is meant to draw attention to the many shared presuppositions and principles of these traditions, while also emphasizing their unique approaches and their theological (or lack thereof) and ethical frameworks. We use this prismatic model of *dharma* in this book, insofar as it is a paradigm that best defines major religious traditions as they originated in India. "But," the student may inquire, "why not simply employ the more commonly used term 'religion?'"

Dharma vs. Religion: The Question of Category

An answer to the question posed above can be found in the words of a prominent scholar of Indology, Wilhelm Halbfass:

> Just as there is no traditional Indian word which precisely corresponds to "philosophy," there is also no exact equivalent for "religion." In modern Indian linguistic usage […] *dharma* appears as the designation of religion in general as well as in the titles of particular religions.[7]

As Halbfass points out, *dharma* and "religion" have become synonymous, but the fact remains that there is no Indian terminological equivalent of the term "religion" as a noun. The term *dharma* is always attached to its lexical verb root, and thus comprises many meanings. According to Oberoi,

> It is not without reason that Indian languages do not possess a noun for religion as signifying a single uniform and centralized community of believers. If the work carried out in linguistic cognition is correct, the absence of such a term is most revealing [...] From the time of the so-called Sapir-Whorf hypothesis, it has been widely acknowledged that language plays a pivotal role in our construction of reality and the way we act on that reality.[8]

The authors of this book elicit attention to the native Indian concept of *dharma* in order to draw attention to the ways in which it questions any "universal definition of religion." This volume invites the reader to consider the historical and cultural context of Indian traditions and to attempt to disrupt the type of thinking that is conditioned by Western cultural ideas "religion." Specifically, the term "religion" presumes a series of characteristics, including theological claims, religious institutionalization, dogma, authority, exclusive identity, ethical codes of conduct, ritual, and scripture. Comparative religion students might experience some confusion upon encountering the conspicuously non-theistic Buddhist and Jain traditions, or Hindu tradition's clearly pluralistic tendencies. Despite certain shared elements, religion cannot be defined universally across cultures and traditions. According to anthropologist Talal Asad, "[T]here cannot be a universal definition of religion, not only because its constituent elements and relationships are historically specific, but because that definition is itself the historical product of discursive processes."[9] Historically, the colonial regime in India introduced the concept of religion, which was a primary reason for the formation of each Indic religion's distinct identity. Thus, the concepts of religion and spirituality—with their specific lexis and underlying meanings—must be reckoned with. It is not simply an issue of whether to use the term *dharma* or "religion," but also one of how to convey the self-understanding of a tradition, which is inextricably embedded in the language and the myths of the tradition. In other words, the goal is not simply to use the terms religion and *dharma* interchangeably, but to bring attention to how religiosity is constructed and viewed within these traditions.

The field of religious studies draws on approaches of prominent thinkers who define religion in terms of, for example, sociology (Emile Durkheim), economics (Karl Marx), anthropology (Claude Lévi-Strauss), and psychology (Sigmund Freud). The field is also founded on a thorough examination of theology, mythology, and ritual. Sthaneshwar Timalsina points out,

> The problem in the aforementioned definitions is that these have brought to light various existential issues to the fore while silencing the contemplative domains. This lacuna has encouraged some scholars from within the Dharma tradition to drop the overall identity of religion, suggesting that "religion" fails to address the scope of Dharma.[10]

The "contemplative" aspect he refers to includes the individualistic pursuit of truth, which makes the practice of "religion" a personal path that is independent of a religious authority, rather than a communal or institutional affair, as has been the implied interpretation by most academic interpretations of religion. This individualistic pursuit of truth has been termed in our contemporary times as spirituality—a personal, non-institutionalized path. Such individualistic pursuit arises out of reliance on the existential individualism and aversion for institutionalized religion. However, Dharma traditions accommodate the aspect of individualistic spirituality within their fold, but it is always connected to a higher purpose and the *telos* of collective well-being. Many Indian thinkers have grappled with the issue of communality versus individuality. Mahatma Gandhi, who used various elements of *dharma* (both in terms of ethics and duty) for his political activism, has commented on this idea: "One's *dharma* is a personal possession. One is oneself responsible for preserving it." He categorically adds that, "What can be defended in and through a group is not *dharma*, it is a dogma."[11] Thus, according to Gandhi, following one's *dharma* is not conforming to a group ideology, although he defined his *dharma* as the service of others.

As mentioned earlier, *dharma* is a concept that is both similar and yet distinct from the term "religion," as per its normative usages, but it does not adequately correspond to the Western construct of the term. *Dharma* is a multivalent Indic term that has been interpreted variously within Indian schools of philosophy and tradition. The philosophical systems and theological and ethical points of view expressed within the Dharma traditions share common characteristics. However, there are also significant differences in patterns among traditions. With respect to religion, shared patterns have led scholars to create groupings such as "Abrahamic religions" (Judaism, Christianity, and Islam) and "East Asian Traditions" (Taoism, Confucianism, and Buddhism). But such categorization by no means suggests these traditions are essentially identical. This is evidenced by each of the three traditions' distinct theologies, exclusive truth claims, and soteriological goals, along with the inevitable tensions that arise from these distinctions.

Because of the shared patterns of the Hindu, Jain, Buddhist, and Sikh traditions, some scholars have begun to characterize them as "Dharmic religions." A prominent UK Sikh scholar, Jagbir Jhutti-Johal, argues that despite "deep similarities, overlaps and commonalities" it is important to pay attention to the differences among "Abrahamic" and "Dharmic" religions in order to have a true interfaith understanding.[12] The 2015 "Report of the Commission on Religion and Belief in Public Life" in the UK states:

> The broad distinction between Abrahamic faiths (Christianity, Islam and Judaism) and Dharmic faiths (generally considered to include Buddhism, Hinduism, Jainism, and Sikhism) is widespread throughout the world in both academic and popular usage.[13]

Jhutti-Johal's intent is to make students of religion and public authorities consider the shared and unique teachings of Indic traditions, while also not overlooking their similarities with Abrahamic traditions.

In this book our use of the term *dharma* is motivated by two objectives. The first, to confront the common tendency to subsume various Indic traditions under the concept of a universalized notion of "dharma," as well as the tendency to confine all systems of religious thought under the Western construct of "religion." Second, to alert students to these traditions' distinctive nature in the context of comparative religion courses, so that they are prepared to encounter those unconventional characteristics not commonly associated under the rubric of "religion."

Comparative Study of Religion and the Issue of Categorization

Since the development of the religious studies field in the Western academy, the use of the term "religion" across cultures has become a convention. However, some scholars of comparative religion point out how problematic it is to apply the term "religion" to non-Western traditions, stating that "Hinduism," "Buddhism," and "Confucianism," for example, were "coined for the convenience of Western scholars."[14] A scholar of comparative religion, Willard G. Oxtoby, identifies the issue:

> [W]hen the Christian world of the West viewed other traditions, it sought to define them in terms parallel to the way it understood its own Christianity. The Christian historical self-understanding imposed three of its own predilections on what is described.[15]

Oxtoby specifies the following: "emphasis on creeds," "sacred-secular dichotomy," and the belief that "one can only follow one religion at a time."[16] Pedagogically, these three presuppositions are not helpful in the study of Indic traditions, which have historically focused on practice instead of belief, given how *dharma's* various lexical connotations emphasize integration of religious principles in both the sacred and secular aspects of life, and consist of fluid boundaries among traditions.

The following points warrant attention when using the term "dharma" in the study of Indic traditions:

1. *Dharma* as religion is not circumscribed by the theological concerns that have generally been considered motivating for humanity's quest for truth, finding meaning in existence, and as motivators of good actions. Scholars have defined theological concerns variously, including Rudolf Otto's "Holy" (*Mysterium Tremendum*), William James' "Unseen Order," and Mircea Eliade's "Sacred," which form the basis of what is known as "religion." However, when one looks for the "holy" in Dharma traditions, it cannot be found in any neatly defined category. Hindu Dharma has multiple understandings of the Divine and what is holy, including the idea that the entire universe is one reality. Thus, the sacred is neither exclusively "other" nor "beyond." Buddhist and Jain systems of thought do not even acknowledge a personal or

creator god. The entire teaching, or *dhamma*, of the Buddha
is oriented toward the end of existential suffering. Jain Dharma
also focuses on liberation from karmic bondage, rather than an
experience of the sacred "Other." Thus, the focus is on the
realization or the "seeing" of the truth in this life. Sikh Dharam
holds the belief in a Divine Being, but its emphasis is on "truthful
living" and good deeds.

2. *Dharma* as a category is not solely demarcated by exclusive
doctrines or dogmas, which generally mandate commitment to
one religion at a time. According to Arvind Sharma: "This concept
of religion, as involving adherence to only one religion, was
institutionalized in India through the agency of the British census
and subsequently in separate electorates for the Muslims and the
Sikhs".[17] According to the census introduced by the British in the
early twentieth century, there were communities that identified
themselves as "Hindu-Sikhs" and "Hindu-Mohammadans
[Muslims]."[18] In this case, the religion was a "localized affair"
and not broadly structured. Traditionally, the focus is on praxis
and teachings rather than belief and preaching (in terms of
proselytizing). Texts and traditions continue to be reinterpreted
to confront contemporary challenges and address new issues.
Although each tradition has its soteriological "belief system," it
does not exclusively define them. Instead, these systems are
defined by the ways in they can be used to resolve life's
all-encompassing problems. In fact, the four Indic traditions were
not habitually classified as four different faiths—contrary to how
they are being studied in classrooms today—but instead as
innumerable sub-sects, which were structured according to
individual preferences for deities, saints, religious rituals, and
one's own philosophical outlook. It is this dialectical mentality
that allowed some in the Indic traditions to identify with more
than one faith. For example, in the early twentieth century, there
were enough people in the Punjab area who identified themselves
as Hindu-Sikhs that the British authorities were impelled to create
a new "Hindu-Sikh" category for the census of religious groups.
Many scholars, including Oberoi, W.C. Smith, and Mark
Juergensmeyer note the effects of introducing the category of
religion into Indian religious culture. According to Oberoi, Smith
has shown,

with ample historical evidence how the concept of religions as contraposed ideological communities is a western invention that, over a period of two centuries, soaked the rest of the world, prompting people globally to conceive of themselves as members of an exclusive religion.[19]

Yet, even today some communities in the Punjab area practice both Hindu and Sikh traditions simultaneously, which will be further explored later in the chapter.

3. *Dharma* is by definition inherently dialogical and dialectical. India's traditions use dialogue as a means by which different viewpoints and differences of perspectives can be configured. Brian Black notes how Amartya Sen, a respected contemporary thinker,

> has brought attention to India's long tradition of accommodating diversity through public discourse and debate. This toleration of diversity through public discourse, according to Sen, has been "explicitly defended by strong arguments in favour of the richness of variation, including fulsome praise of the need to interact with each other in mutual respect, through dialogue."[20]

This salient feature is reflected throughout the history of Dharma traditions, namely, dialogue helps to promote respectful inter-action with the Other. This fact is evidenced by the incorporation of both pluralistic and dissenting voices within a single scriptural text or religious community. Many crucial ideas of philosophy—and ethical issues such as caste and rebirth, peace and nonviolence, and god and liberation—are considered through inter-religious dialectic and dialogue. Since the early part of the first millennium, Hindu philosophers debated with Buddhist and Jain thinkers about the nuances of theology, metaphysics, and epistemology. Guru Nanak, the founder of the Sikh tradition, had many dialogues with Hindu *yogis* and philosophers as well as with Sufi *shaykhs*, or teachers. The Sikh scripture *Guru Granth Sahib* even contains poetry from Hindu and Muslim Sants. It is true that the dominating castes, or groups, tended to assert authority, but the inclusion of such voices is a testament to the category of *dharma*, which is by its very nature multivalent. Such dialogue led to the emergence of alternative approaches to theology, questioning the status quo regarding gender and social hierarchy, and even rejecting the systems that were then hegemonic. For example, the medieval Sant tradition of India emerged as a syncretistic Hindu–Muslim tradition, but simultaneously expanded Hindu themes in innovative ways. In modern times, Gandhi was in constant dialogue with his contemporary Christian, Muslim, and Hindu interlocutors. Furthermore, the truths promulgated in scriptures are also open to interpretation. Gandhi's views are worth noting: "I decline to be bound by any interpretation (of the scriptures) however learned it might be if it is repugnant to reason and moral sense."[21] Even though *shraddha*, or trusting the words of the teacher and the teaching, is important, the emphasis on reason is a common motif throughout the Dharma traditions. The Buddha emphasized that one should only believe in his teachings after putting them to the test.

4. *Dharma*, with its multitude of meanings, is inherently pluralistic. The ancient *Rig Veda*'s famous saying, "Truth is One; the Wise speak of it various ways," has been used by various modern Hindu thinkers and sages to assert the underlying unity of different traditions and paths. (Notably, there are have been various elaborations on this text that draw attention to its meaning in the context of the *Rig Veda*.) However, it is important to note that this axiom emphasizes the plurality of approaches and limitations of human conceptions involved in constructing the nature of reality and acknowledges variant epistemological systems. Thus, it is not surprising that diverse and even conflicting arguments can be found in the same scripture on the same topic. Even more importantly, each opinion is considered with full attention by philosophers of Dharma traditions. For example, Indic religious philosophers traditionally debated with both atheists and materialists (who did not believe in either God or life after death). Plurality is deeply engrained in the Hindu tradition with regard to the deities and social stratification according to distinct capacities and age groups, as well as different paths to liberation. There is a Jain principle asserting that reality is ascertainable through many ways, each of which demands full consideration. Buddhists embrace plurality through the notion of distinct *yanas* (vehicles), by means of which one can reach *nirvana*. Lastly, Sikh Dharam includes a plurality of voices in the scripture, including those of Hindus and Sufis. The pluralistic nature of *dharma* is

further evidenced from the many uses of the term and its elements. *Dharma* is defined variously, and these definitions add ever-new dimensions by not confining it to sectarian categories or undermining other definitions. As Sen observes, tolerating religious diversity is "implicitly reflected in India's having served as a shared religious space—in the chronology of history—for Hindus, Buddhists, Jains, Jews, Christians, Muslims, Parsees, Sikhs, Baha'is and others."[22]

5. The idea of *dharma* frustrates the bifurcation between secular and sacred, which is obvious in the articulation of rights and prohibitions regarding religion in India's constitution, for example, Sikhs' right to bear a Kripan (one of the "Five Ks"); and the establishment of Holi (Hindu), Eid (Muslim), Christmas (Christian), and Guru Nanak's Birthday (Sikhism) as religious holidays. The Indian Constitution goes on to describe secularism as the impartial attitude toward all religions. The concepts of religion and secularism have been debated by scholars and politicians alike. As Klaus Klostermaier persuasively argues:

> Since *dharma* was supposed to be the overarching rule of life, everything came under its purview and great care had to be taken to find expressions of *dharma* in particular circumstances. The universal nature of *dharma* also explains the absence of the division between a "religious" and "secular" sphere, so fundamental to the modern West.[23]

By its very nature, *dharma* cannot be confined within the boundaries of private and public or secular and sacred, since it encompasses moral disciplines, many of which fall into the realm of civic virtues. Gandhi, for example, transformed the virtues of nonviolence (*ahimsa*) and truth (*satya*)—two moral principles essential to all Dharma traditions—into methods used to fight against the British Empire. Nevertheless, he was not propagating Hinduism or Dharma traditions. The division between religion and the state in the West arose because of the historical reality that the Church wielded too much power in Europe. However, the Indian constitution designates India as a secular state, because India is a nation of many religions, sects, and groups with many interpretations of *dharma* (or no religious beliefs at all). The Indian term *dharm-nirpekshta* is used to describe this system, which is hastily translated as "secular," but in Indian terms it implies non-preference to any one religion and respect for various religions. This attitude exhibits a resemblance to the third-century King Ashoka's proclamation of acceptance of different religious sects.

India's second president, Sarvepalli Radhakrishnan, was also a prominent philosopher and defined secularism in the Indian context as follows: "secularism is not defined as 'irreligion' or 'atheism' or even stress on material comforts [... but rather] lays stress on the universality of the spiritual values which may be attained by a variety of ways."[24] Radhakrishnan further clarified:

> The religious impartiality of the Indian State is not to be confused with secularism or atheism. Secularism as here defined is in accordance with the ancient religious traditions of India. It tries to build up a fellowship of the believers, not by subordinating individual qualities to the group mind but by bringing them into harmony with each other. The fellowship is based on the principle of diversity in unity which alone has the quality of creativeness.[25]

The fellowship among the various traditions imbued the culture of the Indian subcontinent, which was most obvious in shared religious and cultural spaces.

6. Since a general emphasis has been placed on the plurality of Dharmic traditions, and not on exclusive doctrines, religious ritual spaces and symbols are organically shared by multiple traditions. According to Oberoi: "For much of their history, people in the subcontinent went on with their rituals, pilgrimages and acts of religious piety without objectifying religion into an exclusive entity."[26] Historically, it has not been uncommon to participate in the rituals of traditions other than one's own, and ritual spaces can likewise have symbols and statues of deities from other traditions. Ethnographers like Nicola Mooney note the prevalence of shared Hindu and Sikh symbols and customs in rural communities.[27] Some Hindu families consecrate symbols and photos of gods and Gurus on their home altars. Similarly, some Buddhist monasteries in India consecrate Hindu gods' photos on their altars. Ravinder Kumar notes that rituals, myths, and folk deities are shared among Hindus and Muslims in

rural communities. Muslims not only participate in the Hindu festival of Diwali, but also Janmashtami, the festival commemorating Lord Krishna's birth.[28]

Even today, Sufi shrines are frequented by Hindus, Sikhs, and Muslims alike. In the United States, the raised platform of the Portland Hindu Temple in Portland, Oregon, exhibits the statues and photos of Hindu gods, the Buddha, Lord Mahavira, Guru Nanak, and Mother Mary with baby Jesus. As one can see, though academics and staunch orthodox believers may seek to debate and demarcate the boundaries of religions, it is important to avoid dismissing the reality that a hallmark of these Indic traditions is their shared religious and ritual spaces. This is most visible in praxis. Most ritual spaces are open to all people, and adherents of one tradition may freely attend the religious and cultural events of other faiths. In short, the nature of the boundaries among the four Indic traditions historically has been permeable. In the words of Ron Geaves:

> The late twentieth century saw a polarization and increasingly rigid compartmentalisation of both (Hindu and Sikh) communities but there remain tens of thousands of Sikhs, especially in rural Punjab, who are indistinguishable from Hindus except for their claim to be Sikhs. Their homes contain Hindu images, they acknowledge caste distinctions and observe purity and pollution rules.[29]

The permeable boundaries within religions continue today, despite religious leaders' and scholars' efforts to compartmentalize them. The above-described characteristics of *dharma* lead us to consider some of the common philosophical principles, which have been uniquely interpreted by each of the traditions.

Shared Patterns, Distinct Expressions

Although Indian traditions do share certain principles, it is important to note that they have been uniquely interpreted by each tradition. A broad overview of each tradition's nuanced approach to these philosophical concepts—all essential to their religiosity—provides a glimpse into the plurality of viewpoints that characterize the Indic traditions. A select few of these many shared features are *karma*, reincarnation and *samsara*, and *moksha*.

Karma

Karma, the principle of cause and effect, is a pan-Indic concept found in the Hindu, Jain, Buddhist, and Sikh traditions and is intrinsically tied to each tradition's ethical framework. However, *karma* is not a uniform idea, which can be reduced to such simple slogans as "what goes around comes around." *Karma* literally means "action"—as in, actions performed through body, speech, and mind—and these actions are naturally associated with their effects, which may appear not only in the present life but may also extend to future lives. Thus, *karma* becomes the principle of "cause and effect" that can stretch across many lifetimes. This becomes an essential element in Indian ethics to explain the present existential conditions in which humans find themselves, as well as a tool to discourage bad actions and encourage good ones. Many Indian texts deal with issues related to *karma* through elaborately ornamented narratives and rigorous philosophical argumentation. A preeminent example of how these texts and literary outputs addressed the intricacies of karmic reciprocity is found in discussions concerning the ways in which current *karma* will shape one's future rebirths in the wheel of *samsara*. Depending upon an individual's karmic situation, humans can be reborn as animals, in heaven or hell, or in the empirical world of suffering and sickness, or they could finally attain liberation through the transcendence of *karma*. Therefore, *karma*'s intimate relationship with birth, death, and rebirth is a basic shared assumption throughout all Indian traditions. However, each tradition configures the concept uniquely within their ethical framework.

Dharma traditions' texts and philosophies commonly demonstrate how one's present birth and circumstances are the result of previous actions. The *Upanishads*, the ancient Hindu philosophical texts, contain one of the earliest accounts of the idea of *karma*:

> As [one] does and acts, so [one] becomes; by doing good [one] becomes good, and by doing evil [one] becomes evil—[one] becomes virtuous through good acts and vicious through evil acts.[30]

The teachings pertaining to *karma* are conveyed through sacred stories that narrate the deeds of characters stretching across countless lifetimes. Many of the narratives found in the *Mahabharata*—perhaps the most popular Hindu text due to its richly engaging stories—seek to explain life's complex situations by revealing a character's previous lives. For instance, Draupadi, the central female character in the *Mahabharata*, is married to five husbands, so the text narrates how certain decisions she has made in past lives resulted in her marriage with five husbands. In popular culture, the notion of karmic actions is often likened to a bank, in which *karma* is deposited and one withdraws the sum according to the balance available. The idea of *karma* is also linked to fate and destiny—not in the sense of chance, but in terms of previous actions coming to fruition. Even though *karma* may seem fatalistic, one's present actions and choices nevertheless determine future actions, and those actions and choices are in many ways conditioned by the influences of past deeds. However, this conditioning should not be equated with determinism. Although all present actions and decisions are irrevocably influenced by prior deeds, one is still free to choose how to respond to each and every situation that arises. A prominent text of Hindu tradition the *Bhagavad Gita* offers a unique methodology to escape the bondage of *karmas* by becoming detached with respect to the fruits of one's actions and offering them to the Divine.

The Jain and Buddhist traditions similarly explain present existential conditions by appealing to actions committed in past lives, although they do not subscribe to a belief in a personal god as Hindus do. The following quote, taken from the *Dhammapada*—a compendium of the Buddha's sayings—offers a good example of the Buddhist view of *karma*:

> The doer of good rejoices here and hereafter; he rejoices in both the worlds. He rejoices and exults, recollecting his own pure deeds. The evil-doer suffers here and hereafter; he suffers in both the worlds. The thought, "Evil have I done," torments him, and he suffers even more when gone to realms of woe.[31]

Thus, good and evil actions determine the conditions of rebirth in future lives. The Buddhist texts also emphasize the notion of "skillful" and "unskillful" actions. Skillful or correct action includes the practice of the five essential precepts, including abstaining from violence, untruth, and sexual misconduct. Unskillful actions are motivated by selfish desires and lead to rebirth in hell and lower life forms.

Jain Dharma, although conforming in some ways to the above-described conceptualizations of *karma*, developed its own detailed theories. For Jains, *karma* is not only responsible for one's present birth, family, health, countenance, and wealth, but is also likened to a form of subtle matter that obscures the purity of the soul. Since Jain Dharma, like Buddha Dhamma, does not conform to the belief in the existence of a personal god, the law of *karma* becomes the principal determinant of one's birth and present condition. The second century Jain text *Bhagavati Aradhana* underscores the importance of one's choices and actions: "There is nothing mightier in the world than karma; karma tramples down all powers, as an elephant a clump of lotuses."[32]

Another important early Jain scripture, the *Uttaradhyayana Sutra*, describes the connection between actions, *karma*, and reincarnation as follows:

> The universe is peopled by manifold creatures, who are, in this *Samsara*, born in different families and castes for having done various actions. Sometimes they go to the world of the gods, sometimes to the hells, sometimes they become Asuras in accordance with their actions. Sometimes they become *Kshatriyas*, or *Kandalas* and *Bukkasas*, or worms and moths, or (insects called) Kunthu and ants.[33]

Thus, the Jain teachings on *karma* exhort spiritual aspirants to examine their own actions for the answers to their suffering and joy, not an external source.

Although Sikh Dharam is an Indian tradition that rose to prominence rather late compared with the Buddhist, Hindu, and Jain traditions, it too placed great emphasis on the proper understanding of *karma*. Like the Buddhists, Jains, and Hindus, the Sikhs saw action as the main culprit behind present conditions, and *karma* as the grand perpetuator of innumerable births and rebirths in the cyclical world-system. Until one can discriminate accurately between proper and improper forms of action, one is condemned to further reincarnations in the world, with all its attendant suffering, which can be seen in the Sikh scripture, the *Guru Granth Sahib*: "Burnt by desire, and bound by the karma of their past actions, they go round and round, like the ox at the mill press."[34] Ego consequently propels one to act in a selfish way. To curtail such selfishness and avoid the accumulation of injurious *karma*, Sikh Dharam advocates the avoidance or control of the five vices—*kam, krodh, lobh, moh,* and *ahankar* (lust, anger, greed, covetousness, and ego, respectively)—all of which lead an individual to perform unwholesome actions that then lead to the perpetuation of samsaric existence.

Reincarnation and *Samsara*

Despite theological differences, all the Indian traditions of this book uphold the doctrine of rebirth, or reincarnation. Briefly, what this doctrine amounts to is that the essence of what is seemingly one's present life—whether in the case of humans, animals, or even insects—in fact stretches across many lifetimes. In that case, one's current existence represents merely a momentary snapshot of the much greater cosmic journey that the individual is undergoing. In other words, the nature of one's current existence is always preconditioned or shaped by how one acted in previous incarnations. Individuals who perform evil actions will likely face a future existence within one of various hells or, more generally, an environment hostile to spiritual growth. Individuals who perform upright actions will likely be reborn in surroundings that encourage spiritual progress. Such is the essentially karmic nature of all existence and the karmic law that underlies the trajectories of all sentient beings, including animals, plants, humans, gods, and goddesses. The *Guru Granth Sahib* epitomizes the Sikh belief in rebirth:

> In so many incarnations, you were a worm and an insect; in so many incarnations, you were an elephant, a fish and a deer. In so many incarnations, you were a bird and a snake. In so many incarnations, you were yoked as an ox and a horse. Meet the Lord of the Universe—now is the time to meet Him. After so very long, this human body was fashioned for you.[35]

This "philosophy of life" leads to a unique understanding of animals and other forms of sentient life around us. In our previous lives, we might have been animals or other living beings. Thus, it is not surprising that nonviolence and compassion to all sentient beings are considered great virtues in these traditions. All the traditions consider human life to be a privilege and admonish the practitioner to follow the path of morality.

Thus, reincarnation, rebirth, or transmigration (all terms are nearly synonymous) are inextricably attached to *karma*. Actions performed in the past determine one's present existential situation through the medium of *karma*. Likewise, actions performed in the present—in thought, word, and deed—will shape one's future rebirths. Therefore, the performance of actions, *karma*, and reincarnation is interdependent, each element exerting an influence on the other. A common term used by all Indian schools to describe this intricate cosmic web of birth, death, and rebirth is *samsara*.

Samsara is often brought up in discussions that concern the nature of time and, more specifically, time's cyclical nature. What this means is that for many Indian traditions—given their belief in *re*-birth, and *re*-incarnation—time is cyclical rather than linear, recurrent rather than restrictively teleological. In Buddhist tradition, *samsara* is symbolized by a wheel in constant motion. In the Dharma traditions, there are many evolutions and dissolutions of the universe. The quintessential part of all living beings (i.e., the soul or self) transmigrates across countless lifetimes, taking on innumerable forms that are determined by the actions being performed. The totality of these various cycles of birth, death, and rebirth are often referred to as the "wheel of *samsara*."

If there is one thing all the Indic traditions can agree upon, it is that samsaric existence is ultimately marked by suffering, dissatisfaction, and ignorance. Even though suffering is intermixed with joy, the suffering of death and rebirth are the hallmarks of *samsara*. All sentient life is born, endures for a time, grows old, and inevitably dies—only to begin the cycle once again. This cycle is described in various ways in the different traditions. Nevertheless, a salient theme is that the ultimate goal is liberation from the dizzying and incessant ride of *samsara*. This goal is known as *moksha* in Hindu Dharma, *nibbana* in Buddha Dharma, *kevalam* in Jain Dharma, and *mukti* in Sikh Dharam. All Indic traditions elaborate a methodology that any human being can employ in order to transcend the wheel of *samsara* with its various forms of suffering.

Moksha

Although *moksha* is defined as many different things according to its various articulations across Indian systems of thought, most of these systems do agree that liberation is tantamount to a release from *samsara*. In other words, most Indian schools of thought see *moksha* as the transcendence of suffering, rebirth, and karmic influence, all of which are constituent threads in the greater tapestry of samsaric existence. The ultimate goal of life is not to attain heaven, but to attain final release from the cycle of death and rebirth leading to the state of ultimate peace.

Generally, in Jain and Buddha traditions, the concept of God, or grace, is not included, so liberation is described as a state beyond suffering and, therefore, the ultimate joy. For some Indian traditions—particularly the devotional schools of Hinduism and Sikhism—grace (*prasad*) is a central factor in effecting one's release from the perpetual rounds of reincarnation. As proclaimed in the *Guru Granth Sahib*:

> A million good deeds and virtues,
> A million acts of approved philanthropy,
> A million austerities at shrines of pilgrimage,
> Practising Sahaj yoga in an out-of-way place,
> A million heroic deeds fighting and attaining Nirvana,
> A million acts of absorption, learning and recitation of the Puranas,
> With the Lord who has brought this about the world and ordained transmigration,
> Says Nanak, of little avail are arguments, His grace alone gains true liberation.[36]

Here it is made evident that righteous actions, philanthropic character, and even the sustained practice of spiritual exercises are insufficient to achieve *moksha*. Rather, it is believed that these endeavors, effective as they may be, can bring about *moksha* for the seeker *only* when coupled with God's grace.

For the Jains, *kevalam* (liberation) and the means of attaining it are understood quite differently. The Jain teachings emphasize that *all* action—irrespective of either its righteous or evil nature—produces karmic traces that bind the individual to the wheel of *samsara*. This means that any action inevitably produces *karma*, and *karma*—no matter whether it is essentially pure or impure in form—is ultimately responsible for rebirth in *samsara*. It is only when all *karma* has been summarily erased that the aspirant achieves liberation. To bring about the cessation of all *karma*, the only logical approach would be the discontinuation of any activity that produces *karma* (in other words, *all* activity). According to one of Jainism's most celebrated texts, the *Tattvartha Sutra*:

> Absence of the causes of bondage and annihilation of all karmas due to total dissociation (*nirjara*) achieved as a result of self-restraint and austerities is called liberation/ emancipation of the soul.[37]

It is clear in this passage that, for the Jain, the way to achieve *moksha* is to dissociate oneself from all action. Practically speaking, this means that in many cases monks are to fast and remain entirely motionless.[38] After the gradual annihilation of all karmic material stuck to the soul, the Jain practitioner is believed to reach a state of omniscience and "aloneness" that is called *kevalam*. According to Jain philosophical cosmology, one who has purged all karmic traces literally ascends to a realm at the top of the universe, where one dwells with other beings who also have transcended the bondage of samsaric existence. Again, according to the *Tattvartha Sutra*:

> Immediately after liberation the soul darts up to the end of the cosmos (loka). Where does the soul go after annihilation of all the karmas? The emancipated soul, i.e. free from all the bonded karmas, goes to the summit of the cosmos.[39]

This state is the highest achievement of freedom and beyond the cycle of *samsara*.

In Buddhist discussions of liberation, the term *nirvana* (Pali: *nibbana*) is used more often than *moksha*. According to the Buddha's teachings, human beings have been circulating throughout the wheel of *samsara* from the beginningless time. *Tanha* (literally "thirst") propels the selfish desires that are the main factors perpetuating samsaric existence. The *Samyutta Nikaya*, a collection of discourses attributed to the Buddha, gives a succinct expression of this: "Craving is what produces a person; His mind is what runs around; A being enters upon samsara; Kamma [*karma*] determines his destiny."[40] However, the Buddhist teachings ultimately say that in ignorance (*avijja*) lies the root of suffering caused by the wheel of *samsara*. The Buddha focused on the root of suffering and the path of its eradication, and was silent about the concepts of an enduring self, a soul, and a personal god, which are found in the Hindu tradition. In Buddhist teachings, selfish attachments to the idea of an enduring self or soul principally lead one into further rebirths. Hence, it is only when all phenomena (including one's own self) are seen correctly as impermanent (*anicca*), marked by suffering (*dukkha*) and with no permanent self (*anatta*), that one finds *nibbana*. *Nibanna* is the state where suffering caused by selfish desires and attachment to individuality ends. It is described as a state of peace and happiness (*sukha*).

As in the Buddhist formulation, *moksha* in Hindu traditions is often analyzed in terms of ignorance (*avidya*), although Hindu thinkers describe the concept in different ways. Hindu Dharma describes *moksha* broadly in three ways, depending on the theological or philosophical framework of a sect: self-realization, God-realization, and the freedom from the cycle of *samsara*. Furthermore, there are several paths described to attain liberation. Some philosophical traditions within Hindu Dharma emphasize the reality of the self (*atman*) and its essential unity with the Supreme Being—what is called *Brahman*. For example, the monistic Hindu school of Advaita Vedanta believes that the *atman* and *Brahman* are in fact identical, and it is only through error (*avidya*) that this identity is not realized. Generally, in Hindu tradition *moksha* is understood either as the realization of the ultimate unity of the self and the Divine, or the realization that the inner self is identical with the Supreme Divine, as achieved through deep introspection and contemplation. In the words of a renowned Vedanta philosopher, Shankaracharya: "The realisation of one's identity with the Brahman is the cause of liberation from the bonds of Samsara, by means of which the wise man attains Brahman, the One without a second, the Bliss Absolute."[41] However, Hindu tradition is not monolithic and there exist systems that do not describe *moksha* in terms of an absolute unity between the *atman* and *Brahman*, and instead describe it as unity (but not identity) with personal God (*Ishvara*) achieved through the path of devotion. The worshippers revel in the love of God. These are only a few examples of the broad scope that the path to liberation can take in Hindu Dharma.

In addition, Dharma traditions provide distinctive systematic meditation regimens and/or devotional practices to achieve the state of liberation. All traditions use the concept of yoga in some way, not in terms of physical exercises, but physical and mental disciplines that enable humans to transcend the cycle of death and rebirth. The patterns articulated above provide a brief glimpse into the many shared elements of different Dharma traditions, and the multiplicity of these elements' interpretations will become even clearer in later chapters of the book. Indeed, the term *dharma* itself has gone through many interpretations, which will be discussed in the following section.

Dharma: Not a Monolithic Category

As we have seen, the Dharma traditions share certain paradigms and principles, but they also have significant differences with regard to philosophy, theology, and practice. Heterogeneity is embedded in the fabric of the *dharma* paradigm. As Peter Flügel notes, "Heterogeneity and processes of bricolage, mixture, syncretism or hybridization are merely the consequences of external cultural interaction, migration and travel ... but situated at the very heart of religious and cultural life."[42] *Dharma* and its derivative, "Dharmic traditions," are used for heuristic purposes, but they represent more than mere group identification, as does the term "Abrahamic." At times, "Dharmic" and "Abrahamic" have been be used to convey these traditions' shared patterns, cultural spaces, and linguistic structures of the groups of the traditions. Each Dharma tradition is unique in its approach to the questions of life. Furthermore, *dharma* is used to underscore the idiosyncratic presuppositions that characterize the Indic traditions and to highlight their unique taxonomies.

Dharma, linguistically and conceptually, allows for a diversity of meanings, including morality, duty, and teaching, which is evidenced by its multifaceted usages throughout India's philosophical and religious history. Therefore, the term *dharma* has been philosophically and ethically defined in various ways since the times of its earliest formulations. A brief overview of the many meanings and interpretations ascribed to *dharma* in Indic texts and by various Dharma traditions will help to dispel the notion that *dharma* is a monolithic, rather than an intricately varied, concept. However, nuanced meanings of terms can be easily overlooked and lead to inexact representations. For example, the constitution of India, which uses the somewhat inaccurate term "Hindu" to designate the Buddhist, Jain, and Sikh traditions, made the claim on the basis of shared cultural spaces, philosophical paradigms and ethical principles. Furthermore, "Hindu" is a derived from the Indus River and refers to the native inhabitants of India. However, in using the term "Hindu," which has come to be specifically associated with Hindu religion, the language of the constitution seems to overlook the distinct self-understandings of these religions and their unique identities.

In general, *dharma* encompasses the entire gamut of possible meaning, all of which are connected to the root *dhr* with its various meanings that connote the principle of ethics and sustenance. Thus, *dharma* should not be considered a purely theoretical or speculative term. Rather, it should be understood through one's own empirical experiences. In the words of Paul Hacker: "[T]he Hindu concept of *dharma* is radically empirical. To learn what *dharma* is, one must go to India."[43] Hacker's statement means that *dharma* is a lived reality, complex and ever-shifting, that applies to all Dharma traditions and can only be discerned through the personal experiences of those who practice it, live it, and teach it. Gandhi held that, "[D]*harma* means morality. I do not know any *dharma* which is opposed to, or goes beyond morality. *Dharma* is morality practiced to its ultimate limits."[44] In this case, Gandhi provided a crystallized and simplified definition of *dharma*, making morality the yardstick of religion. However, *dharma* is not always defined so simplistically, and it is important to take a brief look at the different meanings attached to *dharma* in the eminent texts and traditions of India.

As has been discussed earlier, one common error in a preliminary discussion of *dharma* is the assumption that it corresponds to, or is identical to, the term "religion." Conflating these two terms—while not entirely inaccurate—inevitably results in many distortions, unwarranted generalizations, or oversimplifications. As Paul Hacker notes:

> [D]*harma* appears now as an equivalent for the European word religion. Now this translation is not so very different from that which was put forth by the Hellenistic Greeks. The Greek *eusebeia* is also, if stated simply, in many instances translatable by "religiosity" or "religion." While the modern habit of using *dharma* as a cipher for the concept "religion" is a point of entry into the meaning of *dharma*, we cannot simply equate them. What is true of the juxtaposition of *dharma* and *eusebeia* is also true of *dharma* and religion: both concepts overlap without coinciding, and the translation developed in living contact suggests an important element of its meaning.[45]

Although religion is not the most appropriate term for *dharma*, it can nevertheless be a helpful approximation, especially given the understanding of *dharma* in a contemporary context. To get a better idea of the myriad nuances contained in the term, we must investigate how the term has been positively defined in the various Indian traditions. The variety of connotations that such an analysis yields is summarized by K.T. Pandurangi:

Literally, *dharma* stands for that which is established or that which holds people steadfastly together. Its other meanings are law, rule, usage, practice, custom, ordinance and statute. Spiritual or moral merit, virtue, righteousness and good works are also denoted by it. Further, *dharma* stands for natural qualities like burning (of fire), liquidity (of water) and fragility (of glass). Thus one finds that meanings of *dharma* are of many types—legal, social, moral, religious or spiritual, and even ontological physical.[46]

While each Indian tradition has its own idiosyncratic understandings of *dharma*, the common set of presuppositions taken into account by these various systems of thought has led to a shared conceptualization of the religious philosophies and social structures. Just a small sampling of these shared conceptualizations of *dharma* can be specified as, for example, a cosmological or regulatory principle to maintain order,[47] a code of virtuous or upright conduct that individuals should follow, and a system or specific path (teaching) taken up by individuals to achieve liberation. Indian systems of philosophy have presented nuanced interpretations of *dharma*, and these have changed significantly as they percolated through different Indian traditions.

The development of *dharma* in classical Hindu texts is intimately intertwined with hierarchical social structures, such as the *varnashrama* system, which stratified the society by occupation and stages of life. Specific duties and obligations were prescribed for individuals according to their birth on the different rungs of the social order (*varna*, or caste) and the chronologically different periods in their lives (*ashrama*, or stages of life). These were prescribed duties known as *varnashrama-dharma*, or "duties of *varna* and *ashrama*," which regulated the personal, social, and political life of upper-caste Hindus. A warrior (*kshatriya*), for instance, engages in battle just as priests (*brahmins*) perform ritual sacrifices and disseminate knowledge of the sacred scriptures. But of both are asked to renounce the worldly duties when reaching the retirement stage (*vanaprastha ashrama*). In short, a specific *dharma*—a complex of duties, customs, and behavioral patterns—is associated with an individual in accordance with his or her particular social status, stage of life, and gender.

Hindu texts also include an interpretation of *dharma* which more specifically conveys a personalized form of duty, or what might be envisaged as one's own "destiny" or "calling." This personal vocation, known as *svadharma*, symbolizes the constant struggle to find one's own way in life.[48] For example, in the *Bhagavad Gita*, the warrior Arjuna is in a state of immense despondency because of his being beholden to two different sets of dharmic duties that are both binding and incompatible. On the one hand, Arjuna, as a member of the warrior *kshatriya* caste, must engage in battle if the situation calls for it. This is inescapably his duty as a *kshatriya*. On the other, Arjuna is committed to the protection of his family and loved ones and is thus revolted at the idea of having to go to war against his relatives and friends, who comprise the rival clan against whom he must battle. A more technical way of describing Arjuna's dilemma is to say that he is forced to deal with a situation that involves what Hindus call *apad dharma*, or performing a specific duty to confront a dire consequence which may require disregarding other important personal obligations.[49]

Apad dharma might be best described as "*dharma* in times of crisis." It attempts to answer questions that may arise when one is supposed to act virtuously but cannot. An illustration might help to clarify this. Suppose an individual has committed herself to the principle of *ahimsa* (nonviolence), like Gandhi, but encounters a violent person who is indiscriminately on a killing spree. Would Gandhi use a method of nonviolence? In Gandhi's own words: "Suppose a man runs amuck and goes furiously about, sword in hand, and killing anyone that comes in his way, and no one dares capture him alive. Anyone who dispatches this lunatic will earn the gratitude of the community and be regarded as a benevolent man."[50] For Gandhi, who was committed to the *dharma* of nonviolence, such violence was an exception during a crisis.

Similar instances are often evidenced in cases of warfare. Thus, *apad dharma* directly addresses these difficult "exceptions to the rule" and acquiesces to the fact that moral principles are not *a priori* and can therefore be re-evaluated in accordance with specific times and situations. While by no means implying moral relativism, it does attempt to underscore the complexity of life, which requires a thorough understanding of *dharma* to sustain order. It is important to note that the existence of *apad dharma* and its conceptual subordination to *dharma* at large is a clear example of the inadequacy of the term "religion" as a one-to-one translation.

In addition to these sociological determinations of *dharma*, Hindu texts often link this concept with the general moral tenor of any particular place or time—what is often called the "ethos" of an age. *Dharma* in these contexts is the signifier of the overall status of cosmic order. An often-cited explication is found in the *Bhagavad Gita*, in which the God Krishna declares to Arjuna: "Whenever *dharma* declines I incarnate in this world to establish *dharma*."[51] Here *dharma* is used in two senses: as righteousness and cosmic order, two of the meanings of *dharma* shared throughout many Indian traditions.

Apad dharma is one end of the spectrum, giving guidance to those in a time of crisis. On the other end of the spectrum, Hindu texts champion *sadharana dharma*, which might be best described as common ethical principles prescribed for all human beings irrespective of caste, status, and gender. Essentially, *sadharana dharmas* are moral virtues or right actions. These virtues include truth, nonviolence, charity, forgiveness, non-possessiveness, perseverance, and patience. These are civic virtues that are related to the idea of *karma* and not circumscribed by any religious mandate. After all, a virtuous life has the goal of accruing good *karma*. The Hindu epics of the *Mahabharata* and the *Ramayana*, which have guided the conduct of Hindus for centuries, cherish those who follow these virtues and elevate them to a godly status. Unlike *svadharma*, which is specific to each individual, *sadharana dharma* is to be observed and upheld by all, regardless of caste, creed, gender, or ethnicity.

Finally, *dharma* also approximates what could be translated as law (not in the sense of what one *must* do, but rather that which *should* be done). The *Dharma Shastras*, the laws on *dharma*, lay out prescriptive rules that should be followed for societal harmony. For example, the *Laws of Manu*, the prominent treatise on the Hindu laws, specifies the laws for both the men and women of various castes. The text also distinctly specifies laws regarding women, which circumscribed their roles in society.

Despite various interpretations, *dharma* has generally been described as "subtle" and "allusive." Due to the variety of individual capacities humans can hold and the situations they confront, *dharma* may differ from one person to another. Nevertheless, the underlying principle remains: actions oriented toward sustaining harmony, civility, order, righteousness, and justice are all within its purview. In other words, to know *dharma* is to know the universe as an ethically charged, karmic system of cause and effect. Every action that is undertaken, down to the most seemingly insignificant thought, has repercussions. To know *dharma* is to be aware of this characteristic quality of reality and one's place in the universe, in relation to other individuals and beings, and to comport oneself accordingly.

Thus, *dharma* in Hindu tradition is complex and multifarious. The other Indic traditions define *dharma* in unique ways, while sharing some of the connotations found in Hindu traditions. In Buddhist traditions, the concept of *dharma/dhamma* parallels many of the above-described meanings, although the sociological overtones found in the terms *svadharma* and *varnashrama-dharma*— which stratified society and privileged some members over others— are notably all but absent. Rather, as the author of the "Buddha Dharma" chapter in this volume points out, *dharma* is closely linked with "right" or "reliable" teachings,[52] and specifically those of the Buddha himself. Other common Buddhist translations of *dharma* include virtue, truth, and law (also common to most Indian schools of thought). The various terms meaning order, norm, virtue, truth, and Buddha's teaching collectively convey the meaning of the root verb of *dharma*, meaning "holding firm" and "sustaining."

Several illustrations of *dharma* as a basic, ethical principle are found in the *Dhammapada*, a collection of sayings ascribed to the Buddha. In these passages, *dharma* is often expanded into a series of simple teachings, which assist one's spiritual well-being and development. In the sense of law or the jurisdiction of ethical principles, the *Dhammapada* states: "For hatred does not cease by hatred at any time: hatred ceases by love, this is the eternal Dhamma."[53] It is the right state of mind that engenders the cognition of the right path: "If a man's thoughts are unsteady, if he does not know the true law, if his peace of mind is troubled, his knowledge will never be perfect."[54] The Buddha simultaneously emphasizes right conduct and right mindfulness as the principles of *dhamma*.

The Buddha often explained the *dhamma* by way of simple ethical axioms. For instance, he taught that negative thoughts are catalysts for further negative thoughts, which eventually generate spiritually unfruitful future incarnations. *Dhamma* is therefore generally classified into four broad, yet interrelated, domains of meaning: "Teaching," comprising the content of the Buddha's teachings and his instructions; "Good Conduct or Behavior," which includes practice of justice and righteousness; "Truth," with respect to both one's conduct and the essence of reality; and "Nature," or the basic constituents of reality and their characteristics (as impermanent, marked by suffering, and without an enduring or substantial nature).[55]

The early Pali texts describe the Buddha as "a wheel turning monarch of the law" (*dharmaraja*) who taught the *dhamma* that is "lovely in its beginning, lovely in its middle, and lovely in its ending."[56] Historically, Emperor Ashoka (third century BCE), who adopted Buddha Dhamma, became a catalyst of spreading Buddha's teaching throughout the Indian subcontinent, Sri Lanka, and East Asian regions. Various rock inscriptions that he used to "broadcast an imperial program" assist historians and scholars in understanding *dhamma* during his time. In one of the edicts, the term "dhamma" appears in three different languages: Prakrit (*dhamma*), Greek (*eusebeia*), and Aramaic (*qsyt*).[57] According to Ashoka, *dhamma* should be practiced by all people, and so he used his imperial resources to spread it:

> In the past, over many centuries, killing, violence done to creatures, discourtesy to relatives, and disrespect for Brahmins and Samanas have only increased. But now, thanks to the *dhamma* conduct ... of King Priyadassi, beloved of the gods, the sound of drums has become the call to *dhamma*.[58]

In this passage, *dhamma* has two meanings: first, the moral or virtuous conduct of the king, and second, the teachings of the Buddha. The Buddha's Dhamma has many parallels with Hindu renderings of *dharma*, but its unique interpretation construes *dhamma* as the nature of everything that arises and ceases to exist. *Dhamma* is the impermanent and dependently originated truth of all things. In other words, the ultimate *dhamma* is that all phenomena are transient and interdependent. Thus, many activists and practitioners define *dhamma* to mean "interdependence," in terms of understanding relationships among fellow beings. For example, the prominent twentieth-century Buddhist thinker and activist B.R. Ambedkar states "Dhamma is righteousness, which means right relations between man and man in all spheres of life," and thus connotes Buddhist teachings as the tool for sustaining righteous intrapersonal relationships.[59]

In the Jain tradition, the concept of *dharma* broadly came to have three meanings: (1) ethics related to the religious and social conduct of both a lay person and the ascetic; (2) a concept relating to the eternal *jiva*, or self; and (3) that by which *moksha* is brought about. An example of Jain Dharma can be found in the *Tattvartha Sutra* of Umasvati, which defines *dharma* as "the highest forbearance, modesty, uprightness, purity, truthfulness, restraint, austerity, renunciation, non-attachment and continence."[60] These activities envision the removal of accumulated *karma*, and especially accumulated deleterious *karma*. For the Jains, while all activity, virtuous or not, produces *karma* it is immoral action that nevertheless produces negative *karma*. The solidification of this negative *karma* literally weighs down the individual *jiva* and prolongs samsaric existence.

From this we see that *dharma* was also conceived as a thing along ontological lines. Indeed, in early Jain teachings *dharma* had a fundamental role as a basic element of the universe. Thus, in the *Uttaradhyayana Sutra*, an early text in the tradition,

> Dharma, Adharma, space, time, matter, and souls (are the six kinds of substances); they make up this world, as has been by the *Ginas* [sic] who possess the best knowledge [...] The characteristic of Dharma is motion [...].[61]

Importantly, *dharma* in this sense has very little connection with virtuous activity, and instead it is depicted as a primitive constituent of the universe. Nonetheless, aside from this role in early Jain teachings, *dharma* as righteous conduct remained connected with the ultimate, overarching goal of *moksha*. Like the Buddhist and Hindu schools of thought, the Jain tradition is ultimately concerned with spiritual liberation.

To this end, the Jain tradition advocates the ceasing of all action to the utmost extent that this is possible, and acquiring the correct knowledge of the essence of all phenomena. Vows such as *ahimsa*—the prominent Jain principle of nonviolence—are effective in this goal insofar as they limit the production of new *karma*: if one avoids violent action towards all things, one is unlikely to generate new, deleterious *karma*.

The end goal of these practices is to remove all karmic coverings so that the individual *jiva* becomes buoyant. Once karmic accretions have been cast aside, what remains is an all-knowing being that the tradition refers to as "Omniscient One," or *Kevala Jnanin*. Thus, it is through knowing *dharma*, in the sense of correctly seeing the reality of all things, and by acting accordingly to it (i.e., virtuously, honestly, non-covetously, and non-violently) that the individual soul achieves *moksha*, the pinnacle of Jain spiritual practice. Religious Studies scholar Jeffery Long articulates Jain Dharma's philosophy of doctrine as "the model of unity in diversity with respect to truth" and thus defining *dharma* as the paradigm of physical, emotional, and mental tolerance and nonviolence.[62]

In the Sikh tradition, *dharma* is intimately connected with the concepts of right living and ethical conduct, as in the other major Indic traditions. However, in the Sikh teachings these meanings are coupled with the notion of grace; specifically, they are linked to the grace of a Guru, who is a necessary condition for the attainment of *moksha*.

Unlike many Buddhist, Jain, and Hindu traditions, which elevate ascetic ideals to a high status, ethical conduct in Sikh Dharam is primarily concerned with upright communal living. In other words, the Sikh scripture does not espouse the mendicant lifestyle of the traditional Hindu ideal *sannyasa*, or worldly renunciation. Rather, it emphasizes making an honest living and maintaining a family environment. The realm of righteousness is protected by Dharamraj, the King of Dharam, who keeps account of good and bad deeds and judges accordingly. Righteous conduct is also not systematized as a list of abstentions (e.g., from violence or untruth), but is classified in terms of restraining and controlling psychological inclinations, such as lust, anger, attachment, greed, and ego, because these are the roots of unrighteous acts.

Nevertheless, aside from the Sikh tradition's socially engaged understanding of *dharam*, the Gurus make it clear that the Divine Name alone is sufficient: "The karma of actions, the Dharma of righteousness, social class and status, are contained within Your Name."[63] Ultimately, praising the name of the Lord is eternal *dharam*: "O Nanak, sing the Kirtan [chant] of the Lord's Praises; this alone is the eternal faith of Dharma."[64] Thus, the path of *dharam* was simplified by the Gurus and was made accessible to all, irrespective of caste, gender, and social status. *Dharam* is the path by means of which one could eventually attain a state beyond suffering and cyclical existence. However, contemporary movements are defining *dharma* in their unique way. For example, the Sikh Dharma International Organization has defined their version of tradition, which incorporates yoga practices, as 3HO (Happy, Healthy, and Holy) and is spreading the teaching of Sikh tradition in the United States and other countries. Simultaneously, *dharma* is also being articulated in the traditional terms as compassion (*daya*), which is one of the most important elements of Sikh teachings.[65]

Conclusion

This analysis is meant to underscore that *dharma* is not only multidimensional but also variegated. It is too simplistic to suggest that all Dharma traditions are expressions of one true *dharma*, or of one subtle *a priori* concept. Many books elucidate and critically analyze this concept in philosophy and practice. The purpose of this book is to bring "religion" and *dharma* into a broader conversation that underscores both the shared and unique elements of *dharma* found in these four Dharmic traditions. The one common theme emerging among all the traditions is the interpretation of *dharma* along moral lines. In practice, this emphasis is the axis around which these traditions revolve. This introductory chapter is meant not only to familiarize the reader with the concept of *dharma*, which can become controversial when used unequivocally across Indic traditions, but is also meant to provide a more comprehensive study of the underlying principles of Indic traditions. The authors of the chapters on each of the Dharma traditions are experts in their respective traditions. They provide in-depth surveys of the traditions, which reveal the parallel principles and distinct differences among them (and other religions of the world). The authors structure their chapters according to the importance of subject matter, which is meant to *sustain* and highlight the distinguishing characteristics with regard to each tradition's beliefs and practices.

Notes

1. Interview with David Weich. Accessible at http://www.powells.com/post/interviews/karen-armstrong-turn-turn-turn (accessed July 17, 2016).
2. I try to avoid the use of "ism" in the names of religions. Huston Smith's astute quote, "all –isms lead to schisms," demonstrates how distinct boundaries can lead to adversary relationships among religious philosophies and traditions.
3. Mittal and Thursby use the category of *dharma* (with its "near equivalents" *dhamma* and *dharam*) for the religious traditions originated in India. See Sushil Mittal and Gene Thursby, *Religions of South Asia* (London: Routledge, 2006), *passim*.

4. Rita Sherma states that in India "a variety of denominations, guru lineages, and schools of thought existed without the sharp demarcations that are present today. As a result, present day Hindus are particularly prone to conflate all the religious traditions of Indian origin as part of one whole. That 'whole' however, is called 'Hindu' [...], and is identified not with a 'religion' as we understand the word today (that is exclusive to all other religions) but with a civilization." Rita D. Sherma, "The Ecosystem of Religions: A Hindu Perspective," in Christopher Lewis and Dan Cohn-Sherbok, eds., *Sensible Religion* (Oxford: Ashgate Publishing, 2014), 101.

5. Harjot Oberoi, *The Construction of Religious Boundaries: Culture, Identity, and Diversity in the Sikh Tradition* (Chicago: University of Chicago Press, 1994), 17.

6. Many scholars are of the opinion that "religion," in the institutionalized sense that it is used in the West, was in fact superimposition of colonialists and Others, rather than a term that picks out any particular concept that indigenous Indian traditions would have used. For instance: "The Indian reaction to the psychosocial and politico-economic trauma of the long and complex process of colonial rule was paradoxical. On the one hand, it reproduced the myth that colonialism constructed: India is one unitary and homogenous entity held together by its essential religiosity, which can be captured under the label Hinduism. Thus, the colonized Other claimed for itself some integral features which the colonial Self ascribed to it." Sathianathan Clarke, "Hindutva, Religious and Ethnocultural Minorities, and Indian-Christian Theology," *Harvard Theological Review* 95(2) (2002): 200.

7. Wilhelm Halbfass, "*Dharma* in the Self-Understanding of Traditional Hinduism," in *India and Europe: An Essay in Understanding* (Delhi: Motilal Banarsidass Publishers Pvt. Ltd., 1990), 310.

8. Oberoi, *Construction*, 12–13.

9. Talal Asad, *Genealogies of Religion: Discipline and Reasons of Power in Christianity and Islam* (Baltimore: Johns Hopkins University Press, 1993), 15.

10. Professor S. Timalsina teaches at San Diego State University. This excerpt is from one of his unpublished articles that he shared with me.

11. Pushparaj Jain, "Mahatma Gandhi's Notion of Dharma: An Explication," in Ashok Vohra, Arvind Sharma, and Mrinal Miri, eds., *Dharma: The Categorical Imperative* (New Delhi: D.K. Printworld Ltd., 2005), 107.

12. Scholar Jagbir Jhutti-Johal is one of the contributors to the 2015 "Report of the Commission on Religion and Belief in British Public Life," *Living with Difference: Community, Diversity, and the Common Good* (Cambridge: The Woolf Institute), 2015. Available at https://corabliving-withdifference.files.wordpress.com/2015/12/living-with-difference-online.pdf, 25 (3.18) (accessed December 20, 2016).

13. It is stated in the report that the usage of the category of "Dharmic" religions "is open to a range of objections and criticisms, however, and is not universally accepted. Sikhism, for example, is considered a Dharmic religion by many Sikhs but not by all." *Ibid.*, 30 fn. 14.

14. Arvind Sharma and Rita D. Sherma, eds., *Hermeneutics and Hindu Thought: Toward a Fusion of Horizons* (Springer Science+Business Media B. V., 2008), 19.

15. *Ibid.*, 20.

16. *Ibid.*, 21–2.

17. *Ibid.*, 24.

18. *Ibid.*

19. Oberoi, *Construction*, 17–18.

20. Quoted in: Brian Black, "Dialogue and Difference: Encountering the Other in Indian Religious and Philosophical Sources," in Brian Black and Laurie Patton, eds., *Dialogue in Early South Asian Religions: Hindu, Buddhist, and Jain Traditions* (Farnham, UK: Ashgate, 2015), 243.

21. Anthony J. Parel, ed., *Gandhi, Freedom, and Self-Rule* (Lanham, Maryland: Lexington Books, 2000), 126.

22. Amartya Sen, *The Argumentative Indian: Writings on Indian History, Culture, and Identity* (New York: Farrar, Straus and Giroux, 2005), 16.

23. Klaus Klostermaier, "Hindu *Dharma*: Orthodoxy and Heresy in Hinduism," in *A Survey of Hinduism*, 3rd ed. (New York: State University of New York Press, 2007), 33.

24. Quoted in P.C. Chatterji, *Secular Values for Secular India* (New Delhi: Published by Lola Chatterji, 1984), 15.

25. *Ibid.*, 15.

26. Oberoi, *Construction*, 13.

27. Nicola Mooney, *Rural Nostalgias and Transnational Dreams: Identity and Modernity among Jat Sikhs* (Toronto: University of Toronto Press, 2011).

28. Ravinder Kumar, *The Making of a Nation: Essays in Indian History and Politics* (New Delhi: Manohar Publishers, 1989), 175.

29. Quoted in Darren Todd Duerksen, *Ecclesial Identities in a Multi-Faith Context: Jesus Truth-Gatherings (Yeshu-Satsangs) Among Hindus and Sikhs in Northwest India* (Eugene, Oregon: Pickwick Publications, 2015), 258.

30. Swami Madhvananda, trans., *Brihadaranyaka Upanishad* (Almora, India: Published by Swami Yogeshwarananda, Advaita Ashrama, Almora, 1950), 712.

31. Sarvepalli Radhakrishnan, ed., *The Dhammapada, With Introductory Essays* (Oxford: Oxford University Press, 1960), 62–3. An online version of the *Dhammapada*, with both the Pali and Chinese original text, is available at https://www2.hf.uio.no/polyglotta/index.php?page=fulltext&view=fulltext&vid=80&mid=0 (accessed December 14, 2016).

32. Paul Dundas, *The Jains* (London: Routledge, 1992), 97.

33. Hermann Jacobi, trans., *Gaina Sutras, Translated from the Prakrit, Part II* (Oxford: Clarendon Press, 1895), 3.1–4, 15.

34. *Guru Granth Sahib*, 800. All references to the *Guru Granth Sahib* (also known as *Sri Guru Granth Sahib*) for purposes of accessibility, will refer to a digitized version of the text. The entire *Guru Granth Sahib*, along with the original Gurmukhi script, is available at http://www.srigurugranth.org/ (accessed January 10, 2017).

35. *Guru Granth Sahib*, 176.

36. *Ibid.*, 476.

37. Vijay K. Jain, ed., *Acarya Umasvami's Tattvartha Sutra* (Calcutta: Vira Sasana Sanga, 1960), 146.

38. Canonical sources of "motionlessness" can be found in the Uttaradhyayana Sutra. See: Jacobi, *Gaina Sutras Vol. II*, 1.30, 5 and 30.6, 180. For secondary material, consult Dundas, *The Jains*, 170–2.

39. Jain, *Tattvartha Sutra*, 148.

40. Bhikkhu Bodhi, trans., The *Connected Discourses of the Buddha: A New Translation of the Samyutta Nikaya* (Somerville, Massachusetts: Wisdom Publications, 2000), 129.

41. Swami Madhavananda, trans., *Vivekachudamani of Shri Shankaracharya* (Almora, India: Advaita Ashrama Mayavati, 1921), 101.

42. Quoted in Jessica Frazier, *The Continuum Companion to Hindu Studies* (New York: Continuum International Publishing Group), 3.

43. In Paul Hacker, "Dharma in Hinduism," *Journal of Indian Philosophy* (2006), 486.

44. Jain Pushparaj, "Mahatma Gandhi's Notion of Dharma: An Explication," in Ashok Vohra, Arvind Sharma, and Mrinal Miri, eds., *Dharma: The Categorical Imperative* (New Delhi: D.K. Printworld Ltd., 2005), 109–10.

45. Hacker, "Dharma in Hinduism," 481.

46. D.P. Chattopadhyaya and K.T. Pandurangi, eds., *Purvamimamsa from an Interdisciplinary Point of View History of Science* (*History of Science, Philosophy and Culture in Indian Civilization*, Vol. II, Part 6) (Delhi: Munshiram Monoharlal Publishers, 2012), xvii.

47. It should be noted that several scholars have rejected the interpretation of *dharma* as a cosmological principle of the universe. For instance, Halbfass writes: "[T]he idea of a cosmic lawfulness present in the nature of things is far removed from the traditional Hindu understanding of the concept of *dharma*." Wilhelm Halbfass, "*Dharma* in the Self-Understanding of Traditional Hinduism," in Wilhelm Halbfass, *India and Europe: An Essay in Understanding* (Delhi: Motilal Banarsidass Publishers Pvt. Ltd., 1990), 315–16.

48. There are interesting parallels between the terms *svadharma* and *sadhana*. For more, see: Klaus Klostermaier, "Hindu *Dharma*: Orthodoxy and Heresy in Hinduism," in Klaus Klostermaier, *A Survey of Hinduism*, 3rd ed. (New York: State University of New York Press, 2007), 37.

49. Some scholars are of the opinion that *dharma* is in fact embodied or encoded in the characters of these epics. In other words, they maintain that an effective way of approaching the concept of *dharma*—and

eventually, of acquiring an appropriate knowledge of what *dharma* is—is through studying characters such as Rama, Sita, and Arjuna, and their varied responses to the imbroglios that are presented throughout the stories in which they figure. For more, see: Arti Dhand, "The Ethics of Dharma: Quizzing the Ideals of Hinduism," *Journal of Religious Ethics*, 30(3) (Fall, 2002), https://www.jstor.org/stable/40018090?seq=1#page_scan_tab_contents (accessed April 10, 2017), 347–72.

50. Quoted in, Bindu Puri, *The Tagore-Gandhi Debate on Matters of Truth and Untruth* (New Delhi, India: Springer, 2015), 91.
51. Winthrop Sargeant, trans., *The Bhagavad Gita* (New York: State University of New York Press, 2009), 207.
52. Rupert Gethin, "He Who Sees Dhamma Sees Dhammas: Dhamma in Early Buddhism," in Patrick Olivelle, ed., *Dharma: Studies in its Semantic and Cultural, and Religious History* (Delhi: Motilal Banarsidass Publishers, 2009), 92–6.
53. S. Radhakrishnan, *The Dhammapada* (Ch. 1.5), 60.
54. *Ibid.*, (Ch. 3.6), 71.
55. Rupert Gethin, "He Who Sees Dhamma Sees Dhammas: Dhamma in Early Buddhism," in Olivelle, *Dharma*, 92–6.
56. Alf Hiltebeitel, *Dharma* (*Dimensions of Asian Spirituality*) (Honolulu: University of Hawaii Press, 2010), 36.
57. Hiltebeitel, *Dimensions*, 12.
58. Alf Hiltebeitel, *Dharma: Its Early History in Law, Religion, and Narrative* (New York: Oxford University Press, 2011), 47.
59. http://www.columbia.edu/itc/mealac/pritchett/00ambedkar/ambedkar_buddha/04_01.html (accessed October 22, 2016).
60. Olle Qvarnstrom, "Dharma in Jainism: A Preliminary Survey," 601.
61. Jacobi, *Gina Sutras*, 153.
62. Jeffery Long, "Dharma Paradigm and Ethos: Some Insights from Jainism and Vedanta," 5. Available at https://internationaljournaldharmastudies.springeropen.com/articles/10.1186/2196-8802-1-2 (accessed October 22, 2016).
63. *Guru Granth Sahib*, 154.
64. *Ibid.*, 299.
65. http://www.sikhiwiki.org/index.php/Dharma_is_the_son_of_compassion (accessed October 22, 2016).

Selected Bibliography

Ashok, Vohra, Arvind Sharma and Mrinal Miri, eds. *Dharma: The Categorical Imperative*. New Delhi: D.K. Printworld Ltd., 2005.
Black, Brian and Patton, Laurie, eds. *Dialogue in Early South Asian Religions: Hindu, Buddhist and Jain Traditions*. Farnham, UK; Burlington, Vermont: Ashgate, 2015.

Bodhi, Bhikku, trans. *The Connected Discourses of the Buddha: A New Translation of the Samyutta Nikaya*. Somerville, Massachusetts: Wisdom Publications, 2000.

Chatterji, P.C. *Secular Values for Secular India*. New Delhi: Lola Chatterji, 1984.

Chattopadhyaya, D.P. and K.T. Pandurangi, eds. *Purvamimamsa from an Interdisciplinary Point of View* (*History of Science, Philosophy, and Culture in Indian Civilization*, Vol. II, Part 6). Delhi: Munshiram Monoharlal Publishers, 2012.

Clarke, Sathianathan. "Hindutva, Religious and Ethnocultural Minorities, and Indian-Christian Theology." *Harvard Theological Review*, 95(2) (2002): 197–226.

Dhand, Arti. "The Ethics of Dharma: Quizzing the Ideals of Hinduism." *Journal of Religious Ethics*, 30(3) (Fall, 2002): 347–72.

Duerksen, Darren Todd. *Ecclesial Identities in a Multi-Faith Context: Jesus Truth-Gatherings (Yeshu-Satsangs) Among Hindus and Sikhs in Northwest India*. Eugene, Oregon: Pickwick Publications, 2015.

Frazier, Jessica. *The Continuum Companion to Hindu Studies*. New York: Continuum International Publishing Group, 2011.

Gethin, Rupert. "He Who Sees Dhamma Sees Dhammas: Dhamma in Early Buddhism." In *Dharma: Studies in its Semantic, Cultural, and Religious History*. Edited by Patrick Olivelle. Delhi: Motilal Banarsidass, 2004.

Hacker, Paul. "Dharma in Hinduism." *Journal of Indian Philosophy*, 34(5) (2006): 479–96.

Halbfass, Wilhelm. *India and Europe: An Essay in Understanding*. Delhi: Motilal Banarsidass Publishers Pvt. Ltd., 1990.

Hiltebeitel, Alf. *Dharma: Dimensions of Asian Spirituality*. Honolulu: University of Hawaii Press, 2010.

Howard, Veena R. *Gandhi's Ascetic Activism: Renunciation and Social Action*. Albany, New York: State University of New York Press, 2013.

Jacobi, Hermann, trans. *Gaina Sutras, Translated from the Prakrit*, Part II. Oxford: Clarendon Press, 1895.

Jain, Pushparaj. "Mahatma Gandhi's Notion of Dharma: An Explication." In Ashok Vohra, Arvind Sharma, and Mrinal Mini, eds., *Dharma: The Categorical Imperative*. New Delhi: D.K. Printworld Ltd., 2005.

Lewis, Christopher and Dan Cohn-Sherbok, eds. *Sensible Religion*. Oxford: Ashgate Publishing, 2014.

Klostermaier, Klaus. *A Survey of Hinduism*, 3rd ed. New York: State University of New York Press, 2007.

Kumar, Ravinder. *The Making of a Nation: Essays in Indian History and Politics*. New Delhi: Manohar Publishers, 1989.

Mittal, Sushil and Gene Thursby, *Religions of South Asia*. London: Routledge, 2006.

Oberoi, Harjot. *The Construction of Religious Boundaries: Culture, Identity, and Diversity in the Sikh Tradition*. Chicago: University of Chicago Press, 1994.

Olivelle, Patrick. *Dharma: Studies in its Semantic, Cultural and Religious History*. Delhi: Motilal Banarsidass Publishers, 2009.

Parel, Anthony J. *Gandhi, Freedom, and Self-Rule*. Lanham, Maryland: Lexington Books, 2000.

Puri, Bindu. *The Tagore-Gandhi Debate on Matters of Truth and Untruth*. New Delhi, India: Springer, 2015.

Qvarnström, Olle. "Dharma in Jainism—A Preliminary Survey." *Journal of Indian Philosophy*, 32(5), 599–610.

"Report of the Commission on Religion and Belief in British Public Life." In *Living with Difference: Community, Diversity, and the Common Good*. Cambridge: Woolf Institute, 2015. Available at https://www.humanism. scot/wpcontent/uploads/2015/12/Living-with-Difference-CORAB-Report. pdf (accessed July 20, 2016).

Sen, Amartya. *The Argumentative Indian: Writings on Indian History, Culture, and Identity*. New York: Farrar, Straus and Giroux, 2005.

Sharma, Arvind and Rita D. Sherma, eds. *Hermeneutics and Hindu Thought: Toward a Fusion of Horizons*. Springer Science+Business Media B.V., 2008.

Singh, Nikky-Guninder Kaur. *Sikhism*. London: I.B.Tauris, 2011.

Talal, Asad. *Genealogies of Religion: Discipline and Reasons of Power in Christianity and Islam*. Baltimore: Johns Hopkins University Press, 1993.

2

Hindu Dharma: Unity in Diversity— A Pluralistic Tradition

Jeffery D. Long[1]

> *One who protects Dharma is protected by Dharma.*
>
> – Manusmriti[2]

What is Hindu Dharma? An Overview

Hindu Dharma—more widely known in the Western world as Hinduism—is an ancient set of beliefs and practices that encompasses a vast range of human values and experiences. Emerging from the diverse cultures of the Indian subcontinent, Hindu Dharma responds to some of the most profound questions raised by human beings: Who am I? What is the purpose of my life? What is happiness, and how can it be achieved?

Unlike religious traditions familiar to most Western readers, Hindu Dharma has no founder, no essential dogma, and no single, centralized institutional authority dictating the beliefs of Hindus. An enormous range of belief systems and conceptions of reality thrive under the capacious umbrella of Hindu Dharma. There are Hindu monotheists, polytheists, atheists, and other variations. There are Hindus whose main occupation is performing rituals aimed at upholding the welfare of the world, and ones whose spiritual lives are interwoven with the day-to-day work of providing for their families and fulfilling their social responsibilities. Some Hindus channel all their energy towards meditative practices aimed at the realization of a divine reality dwelling in the hearts of all beings. All of these ways of life, and more, are seen as being equally Hindu and are accepted as such. There is no single, correct way to be a Hindu. If one is trying to define Hindu Dharma, a good starting place might be to say that this tradition is defined by its pluralism, the rich variety of paths and viewpoints it accommodates and embraces. This pluralism is affirmed in the most ancient of Hindu sacred texts—the *Rig Veda*—which states: "Truth is one; the wise speak of it in many ways."[3]

Hindu Dharma is such an internally diverse tradition that it is likely that every statement made in this essay will be met with disagreement by groups of Hindus, who will find that a particular statement does not represent practice or worldview accurately. In the words of John Cort, describing Indian culture in general, "Anyone who has ever taught about India knows that for every true statement about India there is an opposite, contradictory, yet equally true statement."[4]

Even the claim that Hindu Dharma is highly diverse can be met with the objection that it is deceptive if taken to mean that there is no underlying unity or cohesion at all to Hindu thought or practice. Indeed, some scholars might say, "'Hinduism' does not exist." Many Hindus, of course, find this claim offensive, and with good reason. While Hindu Dharma is, indeed, internally highly diverse, there are also areas of agreement in this tradition. What might be called a "Hindu mainstream" has emerged over time, and elements of this mainstream Hinduism can be traced far into the past.[5] Intriguingly, other ancient and widespread traditions—such as Buddhism, Christianity, and Islam—are also internally diverse, yet one does not find the existence or integrity of these traditions widely questioned.[6] There *is* a unity underlying Hindu diversity, and Hindu pluralism should not be taken to mean that "anything goes" in Hinduism. One should pay attention to both sides of the *Rig Veda*'s ancient equation: "Truth is one" *and* "The wise speak of it in many ways."

This unity-in-diversity is reflected in the vast range of practices and beliefs observed by close to one billion people who follow Hindu Dharma in one form or another. Though it is a global community, it is concentrated heavily in one country: India. Hindus outside India are mostly persons of Indian origin or descent; but there is a growing number of Hindu adherents from many ethnic and national backgrounds: African Hindus, East Asian Hindus, European Hindus, Latino Hindus, and so on. Hindu Dharma has the third-largest following compared to other major world religions, with Christianity and Islam as first and second, respectively. It is the largest of the four Dharma traditions (Hindu, Jain, Buddhist, and Sikh), and its various elements—from the concepts of sacred duty (*dharma*) and action (*karma*) to the spiritual paths *(yoga)*—have been guiding principles for its diverse adherents.

Unifying Elements: *Dharma, Karma, Samsara, Moksha, Purushartha*, and Yoga

In this section, we will provide an overview of the essential elements of Hindu Dharma. Indeed, these elements are interpreted differently by scholars and followers, and they continue to evolve in their meaning with the changing times.

Karma, Dharma, Fate, and Free Will

One teaching that commands nearly universal acceptance among Hindus is that one's personal actions and intentions matter in a radical way. Specifically, many Hindus believe that for every thought, word, and deed there is a corresponding reaction. Good actions—actions performed out of compassion, a sense of responsibility, or duty ("duty" being the most commonly used translation of the term *dharma*)—produce good effects for the one who performs them. These effects could be seen as a reward, although in most cases it would be a mistake to think of them as gifts granted by God for good behavior. It is more like a law of nature, akin to gravity. Good attracts good. Similarly, bad actions—actions performed out of selfishness or cruelty, without concern for the happiness or well-being of others—produce bad effects. This, again, could be seen as punishment. But this is not punishment meted out arbitrarily by an angry or a whimsical deity. It is simply the way the cosmos works.[7] This is the idea of *karma*: a universal law of action and reaction. As we shall see, it is a concept with many profound implications.

One of these implications is that the cosmos is not a random, chaotic place. It is an orderly system. A universal law, like *karma*, implies a lawful cosmos where events do not occur by sheer accident. The deepest meaning of *dharma*—one of the many meanings of this term—is "cosmic order," or the lawful nature of existence. *Karma* can be seen as an effect or manifestation of *dharma*. It is the primary means by which the order of the cosmos becomes evident in our lives. Our duties (the choices that ensure the best karmic outcomes) make up our personal *dharma*: a way of living that ensures a maximum degree of harmony between human beings and the deepest order of existence.

Another implication of *karma* is that, though the cosmos is orderly, living beings do have free will. The cosmic reality is ordered, but it is not absolutely fixed. The idea of *karma*, at least in most formulations, presupposes an agent of action, who is able to choose one option over others. Our fate (*niyati*) is not entirely predetermined. This view is contrary to a popular understanding that deems *karma* as fatalistic. At the same time, *karma* does imply *some* measure of predetermination. At any given moment, the options from which we are free to choose make up a limited, finite set. Our freedom is not infinite—it is limited by our own past choices. Actions have inevitable effects, and logically our current set of limited options is an effect of choices we have made in the past. We have created our own limitations and conditions that circumscribe our freedom.

Conversely, the limited, but nevertheless real, freedom we exercise in the present will shape the set of choices available in the future. The future is created with the choices made in the present, as the present situation was created by past choices. If, for example, I have walked into my house, the next choice I make must be made from inside it. I cannot climb Mount Everest from inside my house, at least not literally. I must choose to leave my house to make that option available. Freely choosing means navigating the effects of past choices. Infinite freedom would thus mean freedom from the past— freedom from *karma*. The idea of *karma* is thus a kind of middle way between the ideals of absolute freedom and absolute predetermination often debated by philosophers.

This idea of *karma* also plays a major role in Hindu understandings of personhood and moral responsibility. If we have played some part, through our past choices, in the creation of our present circumstances, we cannot blame any divine higher power for our sufferings in this world (though there is also a concept of fate (*niyati*) which plays a prominent role in some Hindu texts and can be seen as referring to the fixed nature of actions already performed in the past). *Karma* is an empowering concept, for if our choices have led to our current situation, this means we have the power to shape our future with the choices that we make here and now. In the words of a prominent Hindu leader, Swami Vivekananda: "If I set the wheel in motion, I am responsible for the result. And if I can bring misery, I can also stop it."[8]

Karma and Rebirth: Expanding the Field of Moral Responsibility

Is this idea that we are ultimately responsible for all that happens to us a realistic assessment of human existence? What about those circumstances which are beyond our power to change? People suffer debilitating injuries, incurable diseases, and congenital disorders. There are unjust social, political, and familial structures in which one might be trapped, that lie beyond one's immediate ability to change or escape. The idea of *karma* is challenged by the magnitude of unalterable human suffering, and by the even greater magnitude of the sufferings of all living beings, human and non-human. In the face of the sufferings of living beings, many of which are clearly undeserved, one could simply give up trying to make sense of the conditions of this world and assume that it is simply a random—and often cruel—place that bears no relation to our moral intentions or actions. How does one affirm the idea of *karma* in the world that we actually experience? Perhaps we should give up the idea of *karma*.

This may be a tempting thought. However, the temptation to give up the idea of *karma* can itself be countered thusly: if life really has no meaning other than to try to survive and avoid or alleviate suffering, then, in the words of scholar John Hick, this is "bad news for the many" who have not succeeded in this quest, but have instead suffered greatly.[9] Most human beings have led very difficult lives. Also, the amount of suffering in the world is magnified exponentially if we include the sufferings of all living beings, and do not consider only humans. The hope that sustains most human beings and helps us cope with our suffering is that there is some larger purpose that underlies and makes sense of our current experiences—a better possibility waiting beyond this life that will retroactively justify the agonies of the present. Hick calls this hope, which seems to underlie many of the world's religions, "cosmic optimism."[10] It is the hope that all our suffering has not been in vain.

In keeping with this hope, the traditional Hindu response to the magnitude of suffering is to resist giving up the idea of *karma*— and thus not to see the world simply as a cruel and random place.

Although there were skeptics in ancient India (just as there are in India today) who rejected the idea of *karma*, this rejection does not reflect the mainstream of Hinduism.[11] The Hindu mainstream affirms that every moment of suffering and joy can be explained by the actions of those who suffer and enjoy them.

The mainstream Hindu response to the problem of suffering is to expand the concept of the reality of life itself. The entirety of existence is not limited to this life. The present life is only one link in the continuous life cycle. If *karma* does not appear to work in the lifetime of a given person, and if the idea of *karma* is itself not to be rejected, but rather is necessary to our ability to see suffering as meaningful, then the lifetime of a given person must not present us with the whole picture of that person's existence. Another central Hindu concept—which is also one of the chief implications of the idea of *karma*—is *samsara*, the cycle of death and rebirth. All living beings—from minuscule creatures to intelligent human beings—are continually born and, after death, are reborn. This is representative of a holistic view of life in the universe.

If the current lifetime of a being does not make up the span of that being's entire existence, then the physical body cannot be one's whole being. Instead, the body is the vehicle through which the living being (*jiva*) experiences the effects of its past actions and makes the choices that will create its future circumstances (This idea is also expressed in other Dharma traditions in various ways.) The living being itself has no beginning and no end. It was not created at any particular point in time—has always existed and will always exist, inhabiting a series of bodies. Each body is determined by the *karma* of the living being at a given time, based on its own actions and choices. According to the *Bhagavad Gita*, one of the most revered and celebrated of Hindu sacred texts:

> There never was a time when I did not exist, nor you [...] And there never will be a time when we do not exist. Just as the embodied one [the *jiva*] experiences childhood, and youth, and old age, in this body, in the same way he enters other bodies. The wise are not disturbed by this [...] Just as a man discards worn-out clothes and gets others that are new, so the embodied one discards worn-out bodies and enters others that are new.[12]

It is important to note that the living being need not inhabit only a human body. This tradition is not focused only on human suffering, as living beings inhabit bodies of all species. This is why many Hindus are vegetarian. Animals possess a *jiva*, a soul or a life force, just as human beings do, and each *jiva* has the same nature. We have all inhabited many types of body—human, animal, plant,[13] and celestial—and will likely do so again. To paraphrase Arvind Sharma: We are not human beings having a spiritual experience; we are spiritual beings having a human experience.[14]

Karma and Compassion

When one bears in mind the ideas of *karma* and rebirth, what may appear to be needless, undeserved, or insurmountable suffering in the life of any given being may actually be serving a larger purpose in the spiritual growth of that being. Assuming that rebirth is a real phenomenon, and that the *jiva* truly has no beginning and no end, then the circumstances of a given lifetime are simply a snapshot of the whole existence of the being in question. A particular experience of suffering may be a necessary challenge that a living being must overcome to make progress on its spiritual journey. This is true of one's own suffering, which may be teaching us lessons such as patience, or that the body does not make up our whole being and is to be transcended. It is also true of the sufferings of others, which may teach us lessons—such as compassion—and give us an opportunity to serve our fellow beings.

The idea of *karma* can be misconstrued to imply that one has no moral obligation to alleviate the suffering of others because that suffering is deserved due to the past choices of those who suffer it. This understanding of *karma* arguably does not take into account that the choices exerting karmic effects on oneself include choices that involve one's response to the sufferings of others. As elucidated by a contemporary nun in the Vedanta tradition of Hinduism, Pravrajika Vrajaprana:

> Doesn't the law of karma [...] imply that we can be indifferent to our fellow beings because, after all, they're only getting what they deserve? Absolutely not. If a person's karma is such that he or she is suffering, we have an opportunity to alleviate that suffering in whatever way we can: doing so would be good karma [...] If we choose *not* to do whatever is in our limited power to alleviate the pain of those around us, we're chalking up bad karma for ourselves. In fact, we're really hurting ourselves.[15]

Similarly, feelings of excessive self-pity or guilt—the thought that I am suffering because "I did something wrong in a past life"—are unproductive. Morbid thoughts such as these ignore the fact that even if our present suffering is our own creation (or the creation of one of our past incarnations), we have the freedom in the present to make new decisions. The current choices lead to different future circumstances, perhaps even in our present life.

Why *Karma* Exists

The idea of *karma* raises further questions that draw our attention to deeper implications of this concept. Why is there *karma* at all? Who or what determines what is good *karma* and what is bad? In other words, why do actions motivated by compassion produce good results—in this life or a future life—and why do actions motivated by selfishness or cruelty produce bad results for the one who commits them? Finally, what precisely do we mean by spiritual progress in the journey of the living being from lifetime to lifetime?

One Hindu explanation for the existence of *karma* is the deep interconnection and unity of all that exists. What happens to one being, in a sense, happens to all. This is why, if we inflict suffering, we suffer, and if we are compassionate, we experience compassion and joy, either in this life or another. So, good *karma* is an effect of action that reflects and reinforces the insight that the other is, in a sense, myself—that I should treat others as I wish to be treated, for we are in fact essentially one. Bad *karma* is an effect of action that reflects and reinforces a sense of distance between self and other, a kind of blindness to the deeper unity that connects all beings. *Karma* is thus a device by which one learns, through trial and error, the essential nature of existence.

Hindu Morality

The idea of good and bad *karma* is not merely theoretical—it makes a real difference in the lives of Hindus. A great deal of Hindu activity, both in the ritual sphere and in the sphere of social relations, is focused on the cultivation of good *karma* (*punya karma*) and the avoidance or expiation of bad *karma* (*papa karma*). A higher, transcendental goal of going beyond the cycle of rebirth (*moksha*, the ultimate spiritual freedom) is strongly affirmed. The trial and error process of *karma* and rebirth is an essential part of the journey toward this goal. However, many Hindus see this goal as remote. The immediate goals are to live well in the present and to ensure that one lives well again in the next life. The attainment of these goals is ensured by an adherence to *dharma*, or duty— that is, by behaving morally. Hindu morality, or *dharma*, is fundamentally rooted in the ordered nature of existence itself (also called *dharma*). The order of the cosmos finds its reflection in the ordered nature of society and one's personal existence at any given moment.

Hindu morality is divided into two basic categories: *sadharana dharma* (universal duties) and *svadharma* (personal duties).

First, *sadharana dharma* consists of duties that apply to all beings. These duties are divided into two subcategories: *yama* and *niyama*. *Yama* refers to an ethical code of restraint and the avoidance of certain actions regarded as unethical, or adharmic. *Niyama* injunctions refer to certain actions or virtues that ought to be performed or cultivated. *Yama*, in other words, tells one *what not to do*, and *niyama* tells one *what to do*.

There are five ethical principles listed under each of these categories. The *yamas* are the following:

1. *Ahimsa*: non-injury; freedom from even the desire to harm any living being.
2. *Satya*: truth; refraining from lying, breaking promises, or any form of dishonesty.
3. *Asteya*: non-stealing.
4. *Brahmacharya*: self-control in the area of sexuality; celibacy outside of marriage and fidelity within marriage.
5. *Aparigraha*: non-attachment; freedom from materialistic or covetous feelings.

The *niyama*s are the following:

1. *Shauca*: purity; inner and outer.
2. *Santosha*: contentment; material and spiritual.
3. *Tapas*: ascetic practice; disciplines that help control the body and mind.

4. *Svadhyaya*: self-study; this includes both the examination of one's conscience and the study of sacred texts and spiritual philosophies.
5. *Ishvara-pranidhana*: contemplation of God; loving reflection on the divine reality.

The second form of Hindu code of morality, *svadharma*, is particular to certain persons at certain times. Traditionally, it consists of the specific obligations attached to one's caste (*varna*) and the stage of life that one currently occupies (*ashrama*). There are four primary *varnas*, each of which is further subdivided according to specific duties (*dharmas*) attached to each. The *Brahmana*—or *brahmin varna*—consists of duties connected primarily with intellectual, parochial, and religious life. The *kshatriya varna* consists of duties involved with maintaining social order: military service, law enforcement, and administration. The *vaishya varna* consists of work connected with economic production. Finally, the *shudra varna* consists of duties that involve service and physical labor, also including areas such as medicine, that ensure physical health. The tendency of *varna* to be passed on in families, as a matter of heredity, has been a source of controversy among Hindus. It is particularly problematic when coupled with the tendency to rank these duties hierarchically based on principles of purity. The system of *varna* has evolved (or devolved, according to Gandhi) considerably from the early Vedic period to the present context of Indian society. Earlier textual sources depict fluidity as well as a more egalitarian view in the *varna* system than what we see in more recent times. It is also important to note that each *varna* is further divided into *jatis*, whose focus is more specific than the *varnas* of which they are part. Among the *kshatriya varna*, for example—traditionally made up of warriors— there are *jatis* that specialize in particular skills, such as archery, swordsmanship, wrestling, and so on. In a contemporary Indian context, when people refer to caste, it is typically to these many *jatis*, and not to the basic four *varnas*, to which they are referring. Additionally, the ranking of particular *jatis* in the larger systems varies from region to region. What is often depicted as a very simple caste system of four basic categories is, therefore, in lived reality highly complex and has changed over time.

Less controversial than the castes are the *ashramas*, or stages of life. The first of these, *brahmacharya* (notice that we have already encountered this term as one of the *yamas*), is the student stage. Its name signifies an emphasis on sexual discipline during this stage. It usually occurs over the course of adolescence and beginning—at least for members of the "higher" *varnas*—with a ritual rebirth (*upanayana*). Through a ritual ceremony a young person is invested with a sacred thread and is thus initiated into adulthood. The second stage is *grihastha*, the stage of the householder, which begins with marriage and continues until one's children are married and other household duties have been fulfilled. The third stage is *vanaprastha* (literally, "forest dweller") and implies retirement, in which one begins to withdraw from one's responsibilities. At this stage, one is traditionally cared for by their children, often sharing a home with an adult child, that child's spouse, and with the grandchildren. The fourth stage is *sannyasa*, or renunciation, where one completely renounces worldly ties in order to pursue the spiritual goals of life. Nevertheless, the ascetic life, focused wholly on spiritual pursuits, can be chosen at any time in life.

Traditionally, each *varna* and *ashrama* had particular responsibilities associated with it that account for the diversity among people. There is an understanding in the Hindu tradition that not all people are the same, and that each person may have different ethical duties at various stages in life. At the same time, *sadharana dharma* provides an underlying ethos to which all people are expected to adhere, although there are occasions when the principles of universal duty and those pertaining to a particular time and place must be negotiated. For example, the universal duty of nonviolence (*ahimsa*) and the particular duty of the warrior (*kshatriya*) charged with protecting society from physical attack may create conflict in the agent and require sagacious discernment, as in the case of Arjuna in the *Bhagavad Gita*.

Purusharthas: The Aims of Human Existence

These universal and particular duties are enumerated in the legal literature, or *Dharma Shastras*. These texts also outline principles for negotiating difficult (*apad*) situations. The *Dharma Shastras* conceive of human life as having four different goals, or *purusharthas*:

1. *Dharma*: duty, obligation, and moral virtue. It encompasses principles of how one ought to behave in society. These duties

also define how one acquires good *karma* and avoids bad *karma*. Duty and morality are not the arbitrarily defined norms of a given society, but are instead intimately interwoven with the nature of existence. Again, our personal actions and choices matter radically. Through *karma*, they shape both our present and our future. The *Dharma Shastras* provide a guide to navigating life in the light of this understanding.

2. *Artha*: wealth or power, the means by which one can enjoy life and do good actions in the world. It would be wrong to see Hindu Dharma as a purely otherworldly tradition, focused solely on transcendence (only one of the four goals of life). Material wealth and its enjoyment are fitting goals for human beings to pursue, so long as these are undertaken within the constraints of right behavior (*dharma*).

3. *Kama*: desire, including satisfaction of sexual desires. The enjoyment of the senses is also a perfectly legitimate human pursuit, so long as it is conducted in ways consistent with *dharma*.

4. *Moksha*: freedom from all attachments, and ultimately from the cycle of death and rebirth. It points beyond the cycle of death and rebirth, and even beyond *dharma*, to a reality beyond the senses, time, and space. This transcendental goal—unlike sensory enjoyment, wealth, or even moral goodness (the result of which is experienced as good *karma*)—is lasting and permanent. *Moksha* is eternal. Enjoyment of the senses and wealth are goals which require constant activity, or work (another meaning of the word *karma*), to achieve and continue experiencing them. Even *dharma* requires activity to be maintained. The good *karma* that one receives from performing *dharma* is, at a certain point, experienced and "used up" and must be replenished. Even good activity involves karmic effects. And karmic effects entail re-entry into the cycle of death and rebirth (*samsara*) so that these effects can be experienced. The ongoing pursuit of enjoyment and its means, as well as the responsible maintenance of the universal order, inevitably keeps us in the cycle of rebirth. One could say that these activities *constitute* this cycle.

Moksha: What is it? How is it Attained?

At a certain point—in its journey through many lifetimes—the living being begins to tire of the seemingly aimless pursuit of happiness and the avoidance of suffering. One begins to ask, "Is there an end to this constant pursuit?" This inquiry leads to the desire for liberation from the cycle of action and reaction (*karma*). This freedom (*moksha*) is the ultimate, transcendental goal of Hindu practice (though, again, not the immediate goal of all practice, or a goal that all Hindus choose to pursue in this life). According to Hindu tradition, *moksha* is that toward which all beings are finally progressing—a state of absolute freedom and infinite bliss, without limitation.

There is an enormous variety and internal diversity within the Hindu tradition with regard to the question of what happens after *moksha* and how it is achieved. There is an obvious distinction between the views of those Hindus who pursue *moksha* and those who do not (including some, such as the ancient materialist thinkers, called Lokayatas or Charvakas, who did not believe in any spiritual reality). The varied schools of thought will be explored in greater depth later in this chapter. But for now, we may simply observe that some Hindu schools of thought see *moksha* as a blissful awakening to the true nature of existence, where one's true identity or self (*atman*) is ultimately identical with the infinite ground of all being (*Brahman*). Some see *moksha* as eternal life in joyful, loving union with a personal deity, not unlike Christian visions of salvation (though with important differences). And some see it as both, or as altogether beyond description (*acintya*) and, thus, hesitate to speculate on it in any tangible terms.

The ways to achieve *moksha* may also vary among Hindus. A path or spiritual discipline aimed at liberation is called *yoga* (literally "union"). The concept of yoga in the contemporary Western world is one that has been, for complex reasons, largely detached from its roots in Dharma traditions, especially Hinduism. It is primarily associated with a set of stretching exercises and postures (*asanas*) whose practitioners may or may not see themselves as pursuing a path to *moksha*. Modern postural yoga, however, is only one segment of the system of yoga.[16]

In the modern period, Swami Vivekananda codified four basic types of paths to *moksha* by drawing upon ancient Hindu sources and practices. Each path may be suited to people of different mindsets. They include: Karma yoga, Jnana yoga, Bhakti yoga, and Dhyana/Raja yoga.

1. Karma yoga—the yoga of action, or work—is the performance of one's duties in a spirit of detached, selfless service. The idea, as it is

elaborated in the *Bhagavad Gita*, is that if a good action is performed with no attachment to its karmic fruits or results (*karma-phala-vairagya*), then such action does not lead to rebirth. One is able to offer up the results of one's good works as a sacrifice for the good of the world. Indeed, in its earliest formulations the concept of Karma yoga referred to ritual actions—acts of sacrifice—offered to deities as a means of upholding the world (*loka-samgraha*). It later comes to refer to an action, as long as it is a good (dharmic) action, performed selflessly with no thought of benefit for oneself.

2. Jnana yoga—the yoga of wisdom or knowledge—employs the intellect for the discernment of the nature of the reality. One immerses oneself in spiritual teaching and applies it to one's own life, identifying with the divine self within, which is ever-free and unbound by the constraints of *karma*. Once the practitioner realizes that he or she has never been the doer of action, but is actually identical with the divine self, one becomes free from the cycle of rebirth.

3. Bhakti yoga—the yoga of devotion—is the most popular of the yogas. It consists of the cultivation of a relationship of intense love and absolute dependence upon the divine self, revealed to be the supreme personality behind the cosmic process. Since Bhakti yoga relates to the realization of the divine, it is important to understand the nature of divine reality, or God, in Hinduism. This is therefore a central focus of Hindu theology.

4. Dhyana yoga—the yoga of meditation—also known as Raja yoga, the "royal yoga," consists of the systematic practice of withdrawing attention from the senses and focusing the mind inward, on its own dynamic process (*citta-vrtti*), and then on the cessation or calming of this process (*nirodha*). This ultimately leads to direct absorption (*samadhi*) into the divine self within the inmost core of one's being, and thus to liberation.

Even though these four yogas focus on different aspects of human life, they are not mutually exclusive. For example, Jnana yoga and Bhakti yoga both lead to the same goal—*moksha*. But the emphasis in schools of thought focused upon Jnana yoga is on the impersonal (attribute-less) character of *Brahman* as a reality, which pervades all existence, including oneself. On the contrary, the emphasis in *bhakti*-based systems is placed more upon divinity as a Supreme Being that is distinct from oneself (though usually still residing within all). This divinity is a personal being with whom one shares a loving relationship. How this Supreme Being is conceptualized varies among the Hindu devotional traditions, with each tradition centered on a specific deity identified with the Supreme Reality. Nevertheless, the basic philosophy these traditions share is that devotion and its cultivation make up the pre-eminent path to freedom from the cycle of rebirth. This *moksha* is seen as a gift from the freely given, loving grace of God, whereas in traditions more focused upon Jnana yoga it is seen as awakening to the reality that was always already there in the depths of one's being. Karma yoga neither excludes nor is excluded by other yogas. It can be seen as a means of purifying oneself of egotism through humbly taking up the service of all. Dhyana, too, can be practiced in tandem with the other yogas and is in fact a practice shared by a variety of Dharma traditions.[17]

Hindu Theology

The divine or supreme self (*paramatman*) is one. In this sense, Hindu Dharma can be seen as monotheistic, affirming the reality of a supreme divinity who is known variously as *Ishvara* (Lord), *Bhagavan* (Blessed One), or—as English has become a more prominent Hindu medium of communication—God. At the same time, there are numerous Hindu deities. These two facts, the simultaneous unity and diversity of divinity in Hinduism, can be confusing to those raised in a context in which monotheism and polytheism are seen as mutually exclusive. However, Hindu Dharma is, in different senses, both monotheistic and polytheistic. Many Hindus believe the one God, or Supreme self, dwells within all beings and manifests in many diverse forms. These forms include the major deities of Hindu Dharma as well as, for some Hindus, the deities of all the world's major religions (though this last one is a somewhat controversial topic). A better term than either monotheism or polytheism for characterizing main-stream Hindu conceptions of divinity is *panentheism*, meaning that divinity is present within and pervades all things and all beings, and that all that exists subsists within the being of the godhead.

This idea of omnipresent divinity has profound implications for the issue of how many Hindus view other religions. If divinity is present in all beings, might this truth also have been discovered by insightful persons from all cultures and periods of history, and not only within Hinduism? Indeed, prominent Hindu teachers, such as Sri Ramakrishna and Mahatma Gandhi, have asserted that all true religions are paths to the same ultimate goal, and that all conceptions of ultimate reality refer to a particular aspect of a shared infinite ultimate reality.

This teaching of religious pluralism is controversial for many reasons. It can be argued that Hinduism's charitable embrace of the various forms of the divine lacks sensitivity toward theological distinctions in various religions. It can also be as argued that it dilutes distinctive Hindu understandings of divinity. However, it can also be argued that such a pluralistic approach is an improvement upon visions of divinity that involve claims that one religion alone has access to the highest reality.

Topics such as these (i.e., the nature of divinity and religious pluralism) are the focus of Hindu theology, an activity in which Hindu thinkers have engaged since the Vedic period. What is divinity, and how can human beings have access to the divine?

Much Hindu theological reflection focused on particular forms of divinity has occurred in the Bhakti traditions. As we have already learned, devotion to any form of the divine may be termed as Bhakti yoga. Bhakti traditions are focused upon the various Hindu deities, and devotional activity constitutes much of mainstream Hindu practice. The Vaishnava traditions focus on Lord Vishnu—the all-pervasive preserver of *dharma*—as the supreme deity. Shaiva traditions focus upon Lord Shiva, the Lord of yoga and dancer of the cosmic dance of creation and destruction. The Shakta traditions focus upon *Shakti*, the divine energy of the universe, wife of Shiva, mother goddess, and embodiment of the power of creation. Other popular Bhakti traditions include the Ganapatyas, who see Lord Ganesha—the elephant-headed son of Shiva—and Shakti as supreme. The Sauras see Surya, the sun god, as supreme. Each of these traditions is monotheistic, in the sense that it is focused on one deity as the supreme embodiment of the infinite, universal self. But they are also polytheistic inasmuch as each sees its particular deity as manifesting in a variety of forms (including, in some cases, the other major deities). And of course, Hindu Dharma more broadly is polytheistic in the sense that it includes each of these traditions as part of itself and as a valid path to liberation. The *smriti* literature (including the epics of Hindu Dharma) in fact specifically claims that each of these deities is a form of the infinite *Brahman*, or the ground of all being.

In addition to the idea of one Supreme Reality with a variety of forms, Hinduism also affirms the existence of a whole host of local deities and spiritual beings that act as aides or assistants to the Supreme deity. This host of spiritual beings, or *devas*, are not unlike the angels of the Abrahamic traditions. In Hinduism, these beings are worthy of worship in their own right, as bestowers of specific benefits and blessings. Again, Hindu theology does not neatly fit into the categories of polytheism and monotheism. Rather, these categories are fluid.

Hindu Dharma, or Just *Dharma*?

Many of the specifics of Hindu Dharma as described thus far are not unique to Hindu traditions. The enumeration of the aims of life and of specific duties—particularly in the area of *svadharma* (one's individual *dharma*) and the duties of the various *varnas* and *ashramas*—are rejected by the other Dharma traditions. This is especially true of the hereditary system of passing on *varna*, which is widely known today as the "caste system." But this is a blurry line of demarcation, for there are also Hindus who reject the idea of a hereditary caste. And there are likewise adherents of the other Dharma traditions, including those of Sikh Dharma and even of Abrahamic religions in India (such as Indian Christians and Muslims) who participate in and uphold this system. Caste is thus better seen as an Indian social system shared across religious and dharmic boundaries than as a specifically Hindu institution, although the Hindu *Dharma Shastras* have played a considerable role in codifying and affirming it. It is also the case that the philosophy of *bhakti*, with its idea of a supreme divine personal reality is not a central focus of the Buddhist or Jain traditions, which typically deny or at minimum do not engage with the idea of a Supreme God. However, the Sikh tradition is strongly oriented toward the idea of a supreme personal deity, and even Buddhists and Jains have practices of *bhakti*, or devotion, oriented around the enlightened beings of their respective traditions. The conceptual systems rationalizing these practices, though, are distinct from Hindu devotional theologies. Many Buddhists and Jains also affirm the reality and worship of the deities seen by many Hindus as the *devas* (aides or helpers to the Supreme Being). In Buddhism and Jainism, as well as in Hinduism, the *devas* are not the Supreme Reality, but rather are advanced souls who have reached a highly elevated state due to their good *karma*. All of these ideas discussed above are rooted in the *Vedas*, the sacred teachings of Hinduism.

Vedic Authority

Hindu Dharma shares its principles of *karma*, *dharma*, *samsara* and *moksha*, as well as practices associated with the yogas and the pursuit of the *purusharthas*, with the other Dharma traditions. However, Hindu Dharma is defined as distinct from other Dharma traditions by its affirmation of the spiritual authority of a set of texts known collectively as the *Veda*. The *Veda* (also known as the *Vedas*, indicating its multiple volumes) is the oldest extant set of Hindu writings. Indeed, the earliest Vedic text, the *Rig Veda*, is the oldest religious text in the world that is still in use by a living tradition. The term *veda* itself means "wisdom." It refers to a timeless knowledge, transcendent of both time and space, as well as to the texts that comprise this knowledge.

The *Vedas* are composed in Vedic Sanskrit and have been transmitted orally for many centuries. The most ancient parts of the *Veda* describe a complex set of rituals. Although performed only infrequently or in an attenuated manner, Vedic rituals and Vedic philosophy have formed the foundation of Hindu thought and practice for thousands of years. Reflections on the implications and deeper meanings of these rituals are the earliest examples of Hindu philosophy, some of which can be found in the Vedic texts themselves. The last Vedic texts to be composed—known as the *Upanishads*—present the earliest utterances of a system of thought known as Vedanta, which is the central philosophy of contemporary Hindu Dharma.

The section of the Hindu community traditionally tasked with preserving the *Veda*—both the knowledge of the texts themselves, as well as the proper performance of the rituals it enjoins—is known as the Brahmins. For much of history the Brahmins have been a hereditary group who are the custodians of Vedic knowledge. This knowledge has been passed from father to son over three millennia, although there are important exceptions to this as well.[18] Acknowledgment of the

Brahmins' religious authority, along with affirmation of the *Veda* as an authoritative text, can be said to define Hindu Dharma as distinct from the other Dharma traditions, because the Jain, Buddhist, and Sikh traditions do not see any special authority in the *Veda* or the Brahmins. (In practice this is not always a sharp line of division; for example, Vedic deities play positive roles in some Buddhist and Jain texts, and some Hindu groups are also critical of Brahmins.[19])

This fact seemingly contradicts our earlier statement that there is no single institutional authority that dictates to Hindus what to believe and do. At first glance it might appear that Brahmins and the *Veda* make up just such an authority, but the situation is actually far more complex. First, the Brahmins themselves are not a unified group. Since the ancient period, there have been many varying Vedic schools of thought. The *Veda* is a vast set of texts that give expression to a variety of perspectives, including monism (the idea that reality is singular), monotheism, polytheism, and even skepticism. All these points of view claim Vedic authority. Second, although the *Veda* is seen by mainstream Hindus as being the ultimate authority in spiritual matters, there are many other sources of authority to which Hindus adhere. These sources may include local and family traditions, post-Vedic religious writings, as well as teachers who are regarded as enlightened beings or even *avataras* (divine incarnations). Furthermore, many Hindu traditions think highly of the authority of one's individual reason and experience, and so, according to the *Dharma Shastras*, it is the final court of appeal when duties are in conflict. So, even though the authority of the *Veda* and the Brahmins can be seen as a defining feature of Hindu Dharma, the Hindu tradition nevertheless remains remarkably decentralized, allowing for considerable internal variety, complexity, and individual freedom in areas of religious and philosophical belief. In order to make sense of the complex web of the above-discussed philosophical and religious ideas of Hindu Dharma, it is essential to understand its origins.

Historical Development

Sanatana Dharma: A Hindu Perspective

Before delving into the history of Hindu Dharma as reconstructed by academic scholarship, it is important to note that from a Hindu perspective the term "Hindu" is a recent construct and does not appear in the *Vedas* or any early texts. The term "Hinduism" limits this tradition to the specific geographic location—the region of the Sindhu or Indus River, located in what is today Pakistan. The inhabitants of this region were called "Hindu" (a permutation of "Sindhu") by medieval Persian merchants, and so the practices of the people of this region came to be known as "Hinduism."

The term that is generally used in the Vedic texts is *Sanatana Dharma*, meaning eternal order of the cosmos. Thus, the term *sanatana*—which implies the eternal and ever-evolving nature of *dharma*—is preferred by Hindus. From a Hindu point of view, *Sanatana Dharma* is not a religion primarily concerned with believing something on faith that can never be demonstrated or directly experienced. Certainly, faith (*shraddha*) is an important and central Hindu virtue. However, the ideal of many Hindu traditions is that a practitioner—as a result of serious, dedicated practice—will gain personal insight and direct experience of the religious truth. In other words, a dedicated practice leads one from a state of faith—a belief that something is true because authoritative persons or texts have said so—to a state of knowledge and a direct realization of truth. From this perspective, Hindu Dharma is less like a religion than it is a spiritual science in that it is a collection of techniques and methods aimed at achieving a transforming insight into the nature of reality (which is yet another meaning of the term *dharma*). As renowned philosopher Sarvepalli Radhakrishnan explicates, Hindu Dharma is "not a religion, but religion itself in its most universal and deepest significance."[20]

The *Veda* is thus seen, from this perspective, not as a collection of texts composed merely by human authors, nor even as a divine revelation, as in the Abrahamic tradition's sense of the scripture.[21] Rather, the *Veda* is *apaurusheya*, or "not-man-made." It is a set of eternal truths perceived by the ancient *rishis*, or seers, who communicated these truths in Sanskrit poetry. The *Veda*, like *Sanatana Dharma* itself, has no beginning or end in time because Hindu Dharma associates divine knowledge with the eternal divine.

Bearing this Hindu perspective in mind, however, we must explore the specific historical processes by which the eternal *dharma* has unfolded into the realm of human consciousness in time and space. And for this exploration, we might turn to such fields as history, archaeology, linguistics, and anthropology.

The Controversial Question of Hindu Origins: From Prehistory to 1000 BCE

As mentioned earlier, Hindu Dharma today has a global following. However, by far the vast majority of Hindus are persons of Indian descent and live in India or adjacent countries in the wider geographic region known as South Asia: Nepal, Sri Lanka, Pakistan, and Bangladesh. The history of Hindu Dharma is inseparable from the history of India, and from Indian civilization. Human beings have been present in the Indian subcontinent almost as long as there have been human beings. It is believed that the first waves of migration out of Africa carried a group of early humans to southern Asia about seventy thousand years ago, and various groups of migrants have passed in and out of the subcontinent ever since.[22] The following sections highlight the various stages of the development of the tradition, known as Hindu Dharma, along with the existing debates.

Indus Valley Civilization

The first settled, non-nomadic cultures began to appear in southern Asia in the region of Mehrgarh (a town in, what is now, Pakistan) around 7000 BCE. On the basis of excavated art and pottery, a close continuity has been claimed between this early community and the Indus Valley Civilization (one of the four great ancient, river-based civilizations, along with those of the Sumerians, Egyptians, and Chinese). This civilization was at its technological height from roughly 2600 to 1900 BCE. With planned cities and very advanced knowledge of sanitation and irrigation, the people of the Indus Valley achieved one of the highest standards of living in the ancient world.[23]

Unfortunately, the writing system of this civilization has not been deciphered. This makes all claims about its religious beliefs and practices a matter of conjecture, based, as they are, on interpretation of artifacts rather than on the direct statements of the Indus people. Nevertheless, some evidence may indicate possible continuities between beliefs and practices in the Indus Valley and those of, what is now known as, Hindu Dharma. Examples include figures in postures resembling the practice of some form of yoga and terracotta figurines resembling the Indian Classical-age Hindu deities Shiva and Shakti. For some contemporary Hindu scholars, the presence of large public baths resonates with the contemporary Hindu practices of ritual bathing. There are also figurines that make the traditional Hindu gesture of respect (*anjali*), which consists of placing the palms of the hands together, that resemble the contemporary gesture of reverence (*namaste*). Again, because only very small samples of the writing system of this civilization have been discovered and they cannot yet be deciphered, it is difficult to be certain about any continuity between this ancient civilization and what we now know as Hindu Dharma. That being said, this early civilization does seem to indicate some relationship with contemporary Hinduism.

The Indus Valley Civilization entered a rather drastic period of decline around 1900 BCE primarily due to geological factors. A series of devastating earthquakes resulted not only in the destruction of many Indus cities, but also in changing the course of the Indus River. Consequently, some cities were flooded, and others that had been prosperous trading ports were left high and dry. It has also been recently discovered that the monsoon winds on which the subcontinent depends for rain failed from about 2200 to 2000 BCE, leading to a two-century-long drought.[24] This drought was devastating to a civilization that was dependent upon agriculture for food supplies and riverboats for the transportation of goods.

Recent studies have also revealed that the Indus had a companion river that—judging by the number of settlements found along its former banks—was more central to the life of the civilization than the Indus itself. Some scholars identify this river with the Sarasvati, an ancient river mentioned prominently in the *Veda* and other Hindu literature. This river is described as having dried up or gone underground.

Aryan Migrations and the *Vedas*

Many scholars debate the question of any relationship between the Indus Civilization and the *Vedas*. According to mainstream scholarship, the next phase of early Indian history begins with the arrival of migrants from Central Asia. Filtering gradually into the northwestern part of the subcontinent starting around 1900 BCE (just as the Indus Valley Civilization was declining), these migrants are believed to be the Aryans—an Indo-European language-speaking people (a language related to both European and northern Indian languages) who used small chariots of a kind developed in southern Russia between 2300 and 2000 BCE. They gradually blended into the indigenous population, and the language and cultural practices of this community are preserved in the *Veda*. According to this view, the early Vedic texts date from roughly 1700 to 1000 BCE. This migration theory may explain why Sanskrit, the language of the *Veda*, is related to European languages such as ancient Greek, Latin, Gaelic, and German, and also why Vedic religion and culture bear strong similarities to the religions and cultures of pre-Christian Europe.

Alternative Viewpoints and Contemporary Debates

Geographic points of reference in the *Veda* suggest that these texts were composed in the northwestern region of the Indian subcontinent, showing the greatest familiarity with the area now known as Punjab. They also suggest that the community that composed them did not see themselves as newcomers to the region, there being no overt references to another homeland or to migration from such a homeland to India. Vedic Sanskrit also shows evidence of a non-Indo-European substrate. This suggests that the community was multilingual, having had a good deal of interaction with people of another language group, adopting words and ways of speaking that differed from those of their migrant ancestors by the time the *Veda* was composed.

It was long believed by many scholars that Indo-European culture was brought to India in a sudden and violent invasion, and that this "invasion" was the cause of the fall of the Indus Valley Civilization. But scholars now believe that this was not the case. The evidence points instead to the geological changes and drought mentioned earlier as the chief factors in the decline of the Indus culture. According to the current theory, Indo-European immigrants did not cause the destruction of the Indus Valley Civilization, but rather filled the vacuum created by the already declining civilization.

It is also likely that the descendants of the Indo-European migrants helped to preserve the Indus culture. For example, Vedic references to the Sarasvati River in the linguistically present tense as a wide, flowing river with many settlements on its banks suggest that the Vedic texts are a repository not only of Indo-European culture brought from outside of India, but of elements of the culture of the Indus Valley Civilization and other indigenous features. This is consistent with the idea that the Vedic texts are the products of centuries of cultural intermixture and hybridization: a blend of elements shared with Proto-Indo-European or Indo-Iranian culture and elements native to the subcontinent.

According to an alternate view of select Hindu scholars, the *Veda* pre-dates the Indus Valley Civilization, and was written at the time of the mixed pastoral and agricultural society of the Mehrgarh region that existed between 7000 BCE and the advanced urban phase of the Indus Valley that began around 2600 BCE. This view is more consistent with traditional Hindu accounts of ancient Indian history, including astrological references to the locations of stars at the times when certain events described in Hindu texts are said to have occurred. It seeks to explain the resemblances between Indian and European languages and cultures by arguing that India—not Central Asia—is the location of the original Indo-European culture.[25]

Mainstream scholarship tends to reject this view, based on such factors as the non-Indo-European substrate elements in Vedic Sanskrit—the most ancient Indo-European language found in India— and discontinuities between the culture of the Indus Valley and that of the *Veda*.

The debate between those scholars who argue that Vedic culture is the result of a mixture of an Indo-European culture brought to India from Central Asia and indigenous elements, and those who claim India to be the Indo-European homeland, is a highly contentious and politicized one. Early versions of the Indo-European migration hypothesis posited a violent invasion of "Aryan" peoples into India. This idea played a prominent role in the mythologies of racialist and racist movements in the nineteenth and twentieth centuries— including that of the Nazis, who appropriated the ancient dharmic symbol of the *swastika* (symbol of auspiciousness and good luck used by Hindus, Jains, and Buddhists) as their emblem. It also fits into a way of writing Indian history that downplays India's contributions to the global culture and knowledge, and instead portrays many important features of Indian culture as constructs of outside influence.[26] Many Hindu scholars reject the notion of Indo-European migration as part of an ideology that seeks to denigrate and dominate India and Indian culture in the name of upholding Western political, economic, and cultural supremacy.

At the same time, the "out of India" theory has also been attacked as part of an ideology of Hindu supremacy. The idea behind this criticism is that if the earlier "Aryan Invasion Theory" erred by assuming that all that is great in Indian culture must have come from outside India, then the "out of India" theory similarly operates from the fallacy that *nothing* great in Indian culture could have come about due to outside influence. Furthermore, it overlooks the rich, multicultural past of India.

Setting political controversy aside, what does the evidence suggest? It is probably fair to say that there remain too many unknown factors (particularly deciphering the language and meaning of the small pieces of text available in the Indus Valley script) to reach a definitive conclusion. A full, comprehensive, and uncontested picture of the origins of Hindu Dharma thus remains elusive, yet there is enough evidence that points to early native strands of this multifaceted tradition.[27]

The Late Vedic Period: From 1000 BCE to the Start of the Common Era

Our picture of Hindu history becomes much clearer, and also less contested, as we move beyond the Indus Valley and the early Vedic period and enter into the later Vedic period of the first millennium BCE. It was during this period that the second great urbanization took place in South Asia. The decline of the Indus Valley Civilization (roughly 2600 to 1900 BCE) was followed by a period in which the cultural center gradually shifted eastward from the Indus and the now dried-up Sarasvati region to that of the Ganga (Ganges) River.

In the Ganges region, Indian civilization was reborn, as many large cities and trade centers along the banks of this river and its tributaries emerged. These include the ancient and holy city of Kashi (Banaras) which continues to be a popular pilgrimage site for Hindus to the present day. The Ganges is as sacred to Hindus as the Sarasvati and the Indus seemed to have been for the people of the Indus Valley Civilization, and many of the holiest pilgrimage sites of the Hindu tradition can be found along its banks.

As material standards of living improved with the advancement of trade and technology made possible by a more settled lifestyle, the attention of people became directed towards cultural and spiritual development, at least for those whose position in the stratified society (*varnas* and *ashramas*, as discussed above) allowed for such pursuits. The centuries from 1000 BCE to the beginning of the Common Era thus saw the rise of several major Hindu systems of thought and of two other Dharma traditions—Jain and Buddhist. Although all these paths of practice and belief were built upon more ancient foundations, during this period these systems began to take something closer to the forms in which we know them today.

In terms of Hindu intellectual history, this period marks a transition from a Vedic culture based primarily on sacrificial rituals (*yajna*) to a culture with two streams: (1) ritualistic focus and (2) inward focus upon knowledge and personal transformation. However, it would be incorrect to see these as absolutely opposed or separate. Both are rooted in the *Veda* and form the basis of what we now call Hinduism. One could see these as distinct approaches to the meaning and purpose of the Vedic revelation as well as forming the foundation of the Karma, Jnana, and Dhyana/Raja yogas as these are known today. Devotional sensibilities and Bhakti yoga became more prevalent later in the formation of Hindu thought.

The Sacred Compositions: Structure of the *Veda*

The *Veda* as a totality is also known as *shruti*. The term *shruti* means "that which is heard." It refers to the Vedic literature, from the *samhitas* to the *Upanishads*. The concept of *shruti* is somewhat analogous to the concept of revelation in the Abrahamic religions. The metaphor at play in the word *revelation* is a visual one: one *reveals* or *shows* something to others by bringing it into their field of vision. *Shruti* is an auditory revelation. It refers to the sacred sound (*mantras*) heard by the ancient rishis, or sages, who perceived the *Veda* in the depths of their meditations. They recited these sacred *mantras* in a tradition that continues to this day.

From a very early period, the *Veda* was divided into four main collections. The first and the oldest of these is the *Rig Veda* (the *Veda* of "adoration"). The *Rig Veda* consists of 1,028 hymns or songs, divided among ten *mandalas* (books or chapters). These hymns evoke and praise deities known as devas, or "shining ones." The devas embody or preside over the various forces of nature. Indra is the lord of the devas and god of thunder; Agni is the sacred fire that is at the heart of Vedic ritual (*yajna*); and Surya is the god of the sun. Soma is the god of the moon and a sacred plant, the juice of which was consumed by Brahmin priests in ancient times (although the secret of which plant is involved in this process was lost long ago); Vayu is the god of the wind; Yama is the god of death; Ushas is goddess of the dawn; and Sarasvati is the goddess of wisdom and of the ancient river bearing her name. There are many others as well. Many of the hymns of the *Rig Veda* are philosophical, inquiring into the nature of reality and the process of the ongoing creation, destruction, and recreation of the cosmos. Vedic ritual plays an important role in maintaining the cosmic process and order.

The second collection, the *Yajur Veda* (the *Veda* of "sacrificial prayer"), describes how to perform the Vedic rituals. The third collection, the *Sama Veda* (the *Veda* of "melody"), explains the proper way to chant and sing Vedic verses in a ritual context. The fourth collection, the *Atharva Veda* (the *Veda* of magical formulas) was compiled later than the other three, and it is less directly connected with the primary Vedic rituals. Its first half contains verses for protection and its second half is more philosophical, pertaining to the questions of nature of reality, the purpose and the ultimate goal of life, the methods to achieve this goal, and so on.

The four *Vedas* are further subdivided into sections, each of which can be traced to a different historical period. By exploring each section of a particular text, one can trace the development of Hindu thought from the ancient period of the *Samhitas* to the end of the first millennium BCE, when the last of these sections, the *Upanishads*, was composed. The Vedic *Samhitas* are consecutively followed by the *Brahmanas*, the *Aranyakas*, and finally by the philosophical treatises, known as the *Upanishads*. Together, these four Vedic collections span a time period of over one thousand years of intellectual, cultural, and spiritual development.

The texts making up the second section of the *Veda*, the *Brahmanas* ("Priestly Texts") date from roughly 800 to 600 BCE. Together, the *Samhitas* and the *Brahmanas* make up what is called the *karma kanda* or "action portion" of the *Veda* because it is focused on ritual performance.

In the *Aranyakas*, "Forest Texts" (composed from around 600 to 500 BCE), and even more fully in the *Upanishads* (secret or esoteric doctrine, composed from around 500 BCE to the first century of the Common Era), the emphasis of the Vedic literature shifts from the correct performance of ritual to the transforming power of the knowledge that enables the ritual to work. This does not mean the ritual ceases to occur, but rather implies that a subset of the Brahmins chose to focus more upon inner knowledge than upon external action.

In the *Upanishads*, "Philosophy Texts" (the fourth and final Vedic collection), it is revealed that the highest aim of existence is achieving the realization that *Brahman* (the ground of being) and *atman* (one's innermost self) are one and the same. This realization leads to freedom from the cycle of death and rebirth. The *Upanishads* are known as the *jnana kanda*, or "wisdom portion" of the *Veda*, and also as Vedanta, the "end of the *Veda*." The "end" both in the literal sense of being chronologically the last part of the *Veda*, but also in the sense of comprising the wisdom of the ultimate end or aim of the Vedic path. Vedanta is also the name by which the philosophy of the *Upanishads* has come to be known.

Two Vedic Strands: Sacraments and Esoteric Wisdom

The oldest portions of this collection are known as *samhita*, which contain sacred hymns. Traditionally, the correct performance of sacred rituals has been emphasized. Many rituals described in the Vedic *samhitas* are performed only rarely, if at all, in the contemporary Hindu tradition. Others are performed frequently, even daily, by Hindus in the present day. All of the major life sacraments of Hindu Dharma (*samskaras*), such as the Hindu wedding, the naming of a child, the formal transition to adulthood, and the Hindu funeral, are derived from the *Veda*. All rituals are performed around the sacred fire and begin with the invocation of, and offerings to, Agni *deva*, the deity of the fire and the messenger of the devas. Other rituals, though not directly drawn from the *Veda*, are focused not around the sacred fire, but on a carved image (*murti*) of a deity. These are performed according to Vedic principles and regulations in Sanskrit. This centrality of the Vedic ritual to major life events and the pervasiveness of Vedic principles—even in Hindu rituals that are not found in the *Veda* itself—is a testament to their importance in Hindu life.[28]

According to early Vedic thought, the correct performance of the Vedic ritual is essential to upholding and maintaining cosmic order.[29] Most important is the ritual of sacrifice (*yajna*). The oldest Vedic sacrifices are modeled on, and conceived as, repetitions of the original sacrifice through which the devas create the world from the body of a primordial being (the Cosmic Man, or *Purusha*) as recounted in the *Purusha Sukta* of the *Rig Veda*. This being offers himself in sacrifice in order to enable the creation of the cosmos. In terms of later Hindu thought, this sacrifice can be perceived as an image for the oneness of existence—the idea that the cosmos has emerged from a single divine being that is its foundation. In later philosophical systems such as Vishishtadvaita Vedanta (Qualified monism) and Tantra, this understanding expressed the idea that the physical cosmos is quite literally the body of God, as a divine incarnation.

Vedic sacrificial rituals tap into the power of creation—an energy field, or Supreme Reality—known as *Brahman* (literally "that which is expansive," which later came to be known as the Supreme Being). The Vedic priests, or Brahmins, both know how to perform the sacrifice correctly and comprehend the esoteric connections (*bandhus*) between the elements of the sacrifice and corresponding aspects of the cosmos. Brahmins are believed to have the ability to tap into the divine creative power through precise rituals for the purpose of ensuring the health and prosperity of the community. The Sanskrit language of the *Veda* is notoriously difficult to learn and has not been a vernacular for thousands of years. Most Hindus encounter the *Veda* as a set of sacred sounds recited by a priest in the course of a ceremony. It is the precise chanting of the sacred *mantras* that renders it potent for sacraments. The ritual is a kind of code through which the deepest mysteries of existence may be unraveled. These mysteries are made gradually more explicit and philosophical (i.e., analysis of nature of the ultimate reality and self, ethics, and methods for achieving liberation) in each successive collection of Vedic literature. The crystallization of wisdom can be seen in the *Upanishads*.

The *Upanishads* are not only the repository of conversations among sages and students about the nature of self and reality, they also interpret early Vedic rituals as symbolic. These texts set up guidelines for the highest realization. In the first millennium BCE, the path to the highest realization was seen as difficult, for it traditionally required one to separate from the various day-to-day activities and ritual responsibilities of *dharma*. Even if *dharma* was performed well and guaranteed good *karma*, it nevertheless pulled one back into the cycle of rebirth. A life of renunciation (*sannyasa*) is therefore the way of life followed by the Upanishadic sage. It involves withdrawing from society to seek spiritual wisdom and ultimate freedom. This way of life makes up the fourth stage of life (*ashrama*), according to the *Dharma Shastras*, and is still pursued by Hindu ascetics today.

An analogous path is followed by ascetics of the Jain and Buddhist traditions that became prominent during the Upanishadic period.

A central feature of the renouncer's quest for wisdom and direct realization of *Brahman* involves the practice of *dhyana*, or meditation. This ancient practice could be an inheritance of the Indus Valley Civilization as evidenced by the meditating figurines found during archeological excavations. *Dhyana* finds its classic textual expression in a late text, the *Yoga Sutra* of Patanjali (composed between 100 BCE and 500 CE). The goal of *dhyana* in Vedanta is the direct realization of *Brahman* through the absorption of consciousness to such a degree that the distinction between subject and object—which is a feature of most experience—disappears. This state is known as *samadhi* (union), the eighth and final step of the eightfold path of Patanjali's system. Even though the path of meditation is common to these texts, there are significant philosophical differences between the Vedanta and the Yoga systems. Adherents of many philosophical viewpoints have been able to adopt the practice laid out in Patanjali's *Yoga Sutra*, and adapt it to their own aims.

Movement from Meditation to Devotion

The path of Bhakti yoga emerges in the later *Upanishads* such as the *Shvetashvatara Upanishad* but even more so in the post-Vedic *smriti* literature of the first millennium CE. *Bhakti* makes the goal of liberation from rebirth available to a wider cross-section of society. This way of devotion does not rely on complex Vedic rituals or the wisdom of ascetic renouncers. The basic premise is that the Supreme *Brahman*, the ultimate object of all spiritual aspiration, is not only an impersonal energy or pure state of consciousness, but is also, and indeed is primarily, a loving personal deity who desires to liberate all beings.

The precise forms that devotion takes, as we have seen earlier in this chapter, vary across the Hindu traditions. In the late first millennium BCE, a set of traditions emerge which orient themselves to specific deities, seen by their devotees as the supreme personal embodiment of *Brahman*—God with a capital "G," as someone with a Western religious background might say—or as *Bhagavan* or *Ishvara*. Some of these deities, chiefly Vishnu and Shiva, play relatively minor roles in the *Veda*, where the main focus is the prominent Vedic *devas* such as Indra and Agni.

The primary means of both cultivating and expressing devotion to one's preferred form of the Supreme Being—one's *ishtadevata*, or "chosen deity"—is a ritual performance of worship (*puja*). In keeping with the *bhakti* philosophy that seeks to make *moksha* available to all—without the need for complex rituals, mastery of difficult texts, or advanced meditative states—*puja* is relatively simple. Most Hindus perform this ritual daily in their homes, though a devotee many also perform more complex pujas on special occasions with the aid of a priest, either in a temple or in one's home. Again, the specifics of *puja* may vary within different traditions (*sampradayas*) but the basic model of *puja* is akin to the act of welcoming an honored guest into one's home. The devotee invites the deity into the sacred space, often into a carved image of the deity, but one can also use everyday objects for this purpose, such as a pot or a food item like a coconut or betel nut. In this ritual performance, the praises of the deity are sung, the ceremony may include reciting a story (*katha*) concerning the deeds of that deity, and offering a bath, fresh clothing, and food to the deity. The deity returns the devotional offerings in the form of divine grace or blessings. The most common representation of this exchange in *puja* is the offering of food items, which are then consumed by the worshipper after the ritual has ended. This ritual food, which now represents the divine grace, is called *prasada* ("grace"). It is often distributed by the worshipper to their friends and family. *Puja* can be very simple or very complex. The simple offerings of devotees and their devotional submission over rigid or precise ritualistic performance satisfies the deity. Objects such as fruit and flowers offered to the deity and reverential gestures representing profound metaphysical relations and the philosophy behind the worship emphasize the attitude of devotion over correct or precise ritualistic performance. This simplicity is what enables *puja* to be done so easily. In the words of Lord Krishna in the *Bhagavad Gita*, "A leaf, or a flower, a fruit, or water, whatever one offers to me with devotion—I accept it, because it is a gift of devotion, because it is offered from the self."[30] This path of devotion is easily accessible to all and represents the heart of Hindu life.

The Hindu Renaissance: From the Beginning of the Common Era to 1000 CE

The end of the first millennium BCE and the beginning of the first millennium CE marks a period of transition, and the beginning of what is sometimes characterized as a Hindu renaissance. Simultaneously with the composition of the later *Upanishads* and the emergence of the philosophy of *bhakti*, two Dharma traditions, distinct from Hinduism, became prominent in India: Jainism and Buddhism. For a few centuries, these traditions in fact eclipsed Hinduism in popularity among the ruling classes. In the early Common Era, though, Hindu traditions were re-asserted. How did this process unfold?

The fifth century BCE brought the emergence of great religious figures: Lord Mahavira, the twenty-fourth great enlightened being (Tirthankara) of the Jain tradition, and Siddhartha Gautama, the Buddha, founder of Buddhism. The teachings of both of these figures have much in common with the ideas found in the *Upanishads*, which were of course being composed at this time as well. Both Jainism and Buddhism share with Hinduism a strong emphasis on *karma* and rebirth, the aim of liberation from this cycle, as well as a focus on cultivating insight by following an ascetic way of life. They also share the practices of meditation and moral virtues such as *ahimsa*.

However, Jainism and Buddhism also presented critiques of certain Vedic traditions. Specifically, Lord Mahavira and the Buddha both rejected the practice of animal sacrifice included in some Vedic rituals (and that are still practiced by some Hindus today, though quite rarely). They were also critical of the idea that members of the Brahmin community were endowed with spiritual authority solely on the basis of birth into that community. The Buddha, for example, redefines a Brahmin: "[N]ot by lineage, not by caste does one become a brahmin. He is a brahmin in whom there are truth and righteousness."[31]

The fourth century BCE saw the rise of the Maurya Empire. Emperors of this era were more favorably inclined toward non-Vedic traditions such as Jainism, Buddhism, and the now-extinct Ajivika tradition (a heterodox school of philosophy that emphasized determinism), than toward the Brahmanical tradition. The third Maurya ruler, Ashoka, reigned from 268 to 233 BCE and is particularly well known for his patronage of Buddhism. Under Maurya patronage, Buddhist and Jain monks were endowed with monastic centers, resources for committing their sacred texts to writing, and support from wealthy merchant communities. Even in the present, Jain monks continue to draw much of their material support from these lay communities for their ascetic way of life.

Various philosophical viewpoints—theistic and nontheistic—and various interpretations of *dharma* flourished and co-existed during this era. Not only Buddhist and Jain systems of thought, but also Hindu philosophies, such as Samkhya (a highly psychological form of cosmology), Yoga (a system of psychophysical disciplines), Nyaya (logic), Vaisheshika (an atomistic cosmology), Mimamsa (the study of Vedic ritual), and Vedanta (the philosophy of the *Upanishads*), were freely pursued at this time. The root texts of all of these systems of thought were composed during this period and formed the basis for centuries of later commentary and philosophical speculation.

After the fall of the Maurya Empire in 184 BCE, Hindu rulers— rulers whose main religious allegiance was to Vedic traditions— became far more prominent. The rise of the Gupta Empire, which reigned over northern India from 320 to 550 CE, led to a corresponding increase in the fortunes of the Brahmins. Under their patronage, Hindu art, architecture, and literature flourished along-side Buddhist and Jain institutions, often under the very same patrons. This demonstrates a cultural and spiritual respect of different Dharma traditions of the time, despite a higher preference to promote Hindu Dharma, just as Ashoka respected Jain and Hindu traditions while primarily promoting Buddhism. It was during this period—beginning from roughly 200 BCE and extending up to approximately 1000 CE—that much of the literature that defines contemporary Hindu thought and practice was composed.

It is important to note that in premodern India, the patronage of rulers and other laypersons was rarely exclusive to only one tradition. With rare exceptions—and apart from specialists in particular traditions such as Brahmins, and Buddhist and Jain monks—a popular pluralism has historically tended to characterize religiosity in India. As evidenced by Chinese pilgrims' records, Hindus, Buddhists, and Jains frequently took part in the same celebrations and worship of deities. Rulers and wealthy patrons gave gifts not exclusively to one religious community, but to many. King Ashoka, although identified primarily with Buddhism, proclaimed in his edicts that all religions should be respected, "for all of them desire self-control and purity of heart," and that, "One should listen to and respect the doctrines professed by others [...] All should be well-learned in the good doctrines of other religions."[32] This attitude is echoed in select Hindu, Buddhist, and Jain texts, which see other traditions not as wholly false or evil, but as stages on the way to truth. It is not that there was never any violence or persecution by one tradition against another. But such events were remarkably rare, especially in comparison with the religious warfare that has characterized much of human history in other parts of the world.

An Overview of the Hindu Canon: Epics, *Puranas*, and the Law Books

As mentioned previously, affirmation of the authority of the *Veda* is a definitive feature of Hindu Dharma. Most contemporary Hindus, however, are not intimately familiar with this literature. There is a large compendium of post-Vedic writings that guide the conduct of the followers of Hindu Dharma.

Hindu literature is broadly divided into two major portions, known as *shruti* and *smriti*. We discussed *shruti*, or the *Vedas*, in the earlier section. *Smriti* means "that which is remembered," and it refers to sacred tradition not considered as authoritative or *as* sacred as the *Veda*, which is the original, direct words of revelation. It has authority because it is based on the essence of the *Veda*'s teaching. The difference between *shruti* and *smriti* could be compared to the difference between seeing an incident for oneself and hearing about it later from an eyewitness. The eyewitness' testimony, even if authoritative and reliable, is not the same as actually being there and seeing the incident for oneself. The *smriti* refers to a vast collection of literature more vast than the *Veda* itself and is more familiar and accessible to the average Hindu than the *Veda*. It conveys the wisdom of the *Veda* in accessible narratives to larger masses of Hindu society, while retaining the more ancient, sacred, and technical knowledge of the *Veda* in the specialized domain of the Brahmins.

The *smriti* literature contains voluminous texts that span many genres. The oldest texts in this category are the *vedangas*, or "limbs of the *Veda*." These include the skills that a Brahmin needs to master to fulfill his traditional duties, such as grammar, mathematics, and astrology. These texts were composed in their current form around the same time as the *Upanishads*, between 500 BCE and the start of the Common Era.

The most popular among the masses are the two *itihasas*, or historical epics: the *Ramayana* and *Mahabharata*. Indeed, these are the sources of conveying moral wisdom to children and adults alike. Many Hindu children know the main storylines of these texts by heart.

The *Ramayana* tells the life story of Lord Rama (or Ram, as he is better known in modern languages such as Hindi, Bengali, and Gujarati) an incarnation or *avatara* of Vishnu, the supreme deity, though he is not himself aware of this for most of the story. Rama's wife, Sita, is an incarnation of the goddess Lakshmi, goddess of prosperity and wife of Vishnu, the sustainer god. This epic is a moral tale of familial bond and fulfilling one's obligations. Sita is abducted by an evil monster (*rakshasa*) named Ravana, lord of Lanka. It is then necessary for Rama to rescue her, with the help of his younger brother Lakshmana. Many non-human animals assist them in this task, including an army of intelligent apes led by Hanuman, a devotee of Rama. Hanuman is an ape and holds the status of a deity among many others in the Hindu pantheon. So great is Hanuman's devotion to Rama that he has become a model of the courage and self-sacrifice that is possible for the sincere practitioner of Bhakti yoga. This epic continues to be popular in India and has many adaptations of the story in India as well as in many south-east Asian countries, including Cambodia, Thailand, and Indonesia.

The identification of Rama with Lord Vishnu shows the centrality of Vaishnava tradition and devotionalism in the era of this text's composition. This Vaishnava orientation is also evident in the other great Hindu epic, the *Mahabharata*.

The *Mahabharata* is a more ethically nuanced and narratively complex tale when compared to the *Ramayana*. It involves a great war between the two sets of cousins of a royal family. The 100 brothers, the Kauravas, deprive their cousins, the Pandavas, of their birthright to the kingdom. The Pandavas are the heroes of the text and must then fight a war to preserve their honor and to win control of the kingdom. Their friend and relative—Lord Krishna, who, like Rama, is an incarnation of Vishnu—aids them. The sacred lore about Krishna is vast and in some interpretations, he is the supreme deity himself. The *Mahabharata* is a voluminous text of eighteen books—about three times the length of the Bible and about four times the length of the *Ramayana*.

A small portion of the *Mahabharata*, the *Bhagavad Gita*, or "Song of the Blessed One," independently holds the status of a sacred book, and is highly revered. It has been the object of theological commentary by numerous Hindu philosophers, intellectuals, and activists over the centuries. For many modern Hindus, it has a status almost equivalent to that of the Bible for Christians—a holy text summarizing the main teachings of the tradition. In it, Krishna summarizes for the Pandava hero Arjuna many of the major currents of Hindu thought present at the time of its composition. Its presentation of Vedic philosophy is held by some to be on par with that of the *Veda* itself. It is sometimes referred to as the *Gitopanishad*—an *Upanishad* (mystical teaching) in the form of a *gita* or song.

The *Ramayana* and the *Mahabharata* are both extremely popular works. In addition to the Sanskrit versions composed early in the Common Era, there are many versions in the more popular spoken languages of India, such as Hindi, Bengali, Gujarati, Marathi, and Tamil. In fact, it is through these popular versions that the stories of both texts are best known. They have also formed the basis of popular plays and songs and, in the modern period, comic book adaptations, television series, and video games. Stories from these epics are often used to teach moral lessons or impart spiritual teachings in Hindu families. These texts thus form the basis for much of contemporary Hindu thought and practice.

In addition to the historical epics, this period also saw the composition of the *puranas*, or "ancient lore." There are eighteen major *puranas* and numerous minor ones. The major *puranas* are divided into three collections of six texts each. Each of these collections is dedicated to the Hindu deity who is the major focus of the stories found within them. The three deities are the most popular objects of devotion: Vishnu, Shiva, and Shakti.

The historical epics and *puranas*—primarily dating in their current form from the period 200 BCE to 200 CE—likely contain much older material. The dating of Hindu texts is a subject of debate among scholars. The historical war on which the *Mahabharata* is based is believed to have occurred around the tenth century BCE, although traditional Hindu chronology places it around 3100 BCE. Krishna (the son of Devaki) and a king named Dhritarashtra, both major characters in the *Mahabharata*, are mentioned in the *Chandogya Upanishad*, one of the oldest of the *Upanishads*, probably dating to

500 BCE, if not earlier. And although Vishnu and Shiva are not mentioned prominently in the *Veda*, it is likely that their status as objects of popular religious devotion is quite ancient.

The *Dharma Shastras*, or Hindu legal texts, are also products of this renaissance period, at least in their current form. These texts present a comprehensive vision of society and the life of the individual. The ordering of the society was delineated by the *varna* system (popularly known as the "caste system") while the life of an individual was systematized by the series of four *ashramas* (stages of life). As we have already seen, the *varna* system was an object of Jain and Buddhist criticism that rejected the idea that Brahmins, who rank foremost in this system, were gifted with any special spiritual authority based on their birth into this station in life. There are also references in Hindu texts where a Brahmin is identified not by hereditary birth but by holy deeds.

Schools of Philosophy

Hindu *darshana* ("worldview") is a Sanskrit term for Indian philosophy found in the *sutra* literature of the six systems of philosophy. This literature was also largely composed and codified starting in the last two to three centuries BCE and continuing into the period of the Hindu renaissance. *Bhashya*, or commentarial literature, continues to be written on these sutras in the contemporary times. Philosophy is an area where the internal diversity of Hindu Dharma is especially evident, as there is not one single orthodox system of thought, but many.

By the early modern period, a system of organization and order among the Indian philosophical schools had emerged. These systems were primarily divided according to whether they acknowledged Vedic authority. Those which did not—the *nastika*, non-theistic systems—were the materialist Carvaka or Lokayata system as well as Jainism and Buddhism. Those which did acknowledge Vedic authority—the *astika*, or "orthodox" systems—were six in number. They are often depicted as three pairs, which reflects the fact that the members of each pair share certain basic affinities.

Samkhya and Yoga systems teach a basic dualism of the living being—spirit (*purusha*) and matter or material nature (*prakriti*). Karmic bondage occurs because spirit has confused itself with matter and needs to awaken to its true nature. Samkhya (literally "enumeration") essentially describes or enumerates the various elements making up the cosmos. The Yoga system (the system of Patanjali's *Yoga Sutras* mentioned earlier) systematizes the practice by which the liberation of spirit from nature can be achieved. Some forms of Samkhya are theistic, whereas others appear quite similar to Jainism as they perceive qualities of divinity within each individual spirit, and do not focus upon a central supreme being or *Bhagavan*. The Yoga system is theistic and recommends the *yamas* and *niyamas* (moral disciplines), including *Isvara-pranidhana* (contemplation of God), as preliminary practices leading up to meditation and final separation from *prakriti* (material nature).

Nyaya and Vaisheshika are realist systems of logic and cosmology. "Realist" philosophers take the perceived physical world, and what can be deduced through the intellect, to be real (as opposed to being simply a mental construct). Phenomena are not considered to be merely mind-created illusions or appearances. Vaisheshika is essentially a system of ancient Indian science, describing a world made up of atomic particles and the various properties that the elements possess. Nyaya defines traditional Indian logic: the rules by which argumentation should proceed. Both these systems are theistic and give arguments for the existence of *Ishvara* (God) and for Vedic authority.

The Mimamsa system is devoted to the interpretation of the *Veda*. It is divided into two sections: Purva Mimamsa (sometimes simply called Mimamsa) is focused on the ritual portion of the *Veda*, and Uttara Mimamsa (Vedanta) on the wisdom teachings of the *Upanishads*. Mimamsa continues the ancient tradition of Vedic ritualism and develops, on its basis, philosophies of language and knowledge. Vedanta develops the idea of *moksha* and the techniques for its realization. It eventually becomes the predominant system of Hindu thought, assimilating elements of the other systems of philosophy along the way.

In addition to the epics, ancient legends and myths of Hindu deities (*Puranas*), legal texts, and the philosophical literature of the six *darshanas*, the *smriti* literature includes a vast range of treatises on topics such as medicine (Ayurveda), architecture and art (*Vastu Shastra*), singing, dancing, and acting (*Natya Shastra*); politics and economics (*Artha Shastra*); the enjoyment of sexuality (the *Kama Sutra*), and many other topics as well. The basic goal of all of this literature is to apply Vedic principles to the entire range of human experience.

Cultural Shifts and Unorthodox Movements

The production of this vast literature during the Hindu renaissance was the work of those who were in a position to carry it out: the highly literate Brahmin community maintained by the support of the rulers and wealthy classes of Hindu society. A wider cultural shift, however, was occurring in India as a whole, which is reflected not only in this literature, but also in the similarly vast body of vernacular devotional poetry produced during this period by devotees from all sections of society. This shift was due to a religious sensibility infused with the idea of loving devotion to a personal deity as a path to *moksha.* The philosophy of this Bhakti movement offered liberation to all sincere devotees, regardless of caste or gender. This movement was so popular that it had a significant impact upon the formal Vedic religion of the Brahmins, which itself came to emphasize theistic devotion, while at the same time maintaining its earlier emphasis on ritual purity. The vernacular Tamil poetry of the Alvars in South India—devotees of Vishnu comprised of men, women, and also members of the humblest strata of society—came to be revered by many as the "fifth *Veda.*"

Even more radical than the Bhakti movement that also emerged during this period is Tantra: A system of yoga, or spiritual practice, that inverts the traditional yogic emphasis on turning away from the senses and bodily impulses, such as sexuality. On the contrary, it uses the senses as instruments for spiritual liberation. Tantra, like *bhakti*, is in its origins a popular movement that makes advanced spiritual attainment available to anyone regardless of caste, gender, or social status. Tantric practice is based on the idea that the senses can be utilized for the purpose of transcending the senses.

At its most extreme (and well outside the Hindu mainstream), "left-handed" or *vamacara* Tantric practice deliberately transgresses traditional Vedic norms of purity, with the aim of demonstrating the non-dualistic realization of divinity in all beings. If all is *Brahman*, then purity and impurity are effects of a false consciousness that seeks to divide the basic unity of existence. Practitioners meditate in cremation grounds—traditionally regarded as impure, not to mention frightening, spaces—and utilize human skulls as begging bowls. Other rituals are of an overtly sexual nature. Such practices are highly esoteric and are performed under the strict guidance of a *guru*.

Far less extreme, but also based on the same fundamental philosophy of using the senses to transcend the senses, are practices such as the chanting of *mantras* (sacred verses) and visualization of sacred images such as *murtis* (statues of deities), *yantras* (abstract geometric depictions of a deity), and *mandalas* (diagrams of the cosmic reality), as objects of contemplation. Tantric practices of this kind, which do not violate Vedic norms, are very central to contemporary Hindu practice.

The popularity of both *bhakti* and tantric practices (of the mainstream variety) is likely due to the fact that, rather than requiring practitioners to adhere to the very difficult ascetic principle of overcoming the senses and turning attention completely inward, they enable the practitioner to tap into the power of inner emotions and aesthetic sensibility. Such practices help channel these important and powerful human energies toward a spiritual end. Thus, they make advanced spiritual goals possible for householders—persons involved in social duties and family life—rather than being the exclusive prerogative of monastics or wandering renouncers. It is fair to say that *bhakti* is *the* central Hindu practice in modern Hindu Dharma, even more than the practices of study and contemplation.

A similar development took place in this period among Jain and Buddhist communities. Mahayana and Vajrayana Buddhist traditions incorporated *bhakti* and Tantra into their methods. Jainism, because of its emphasis on the ascetic ideal, was quite wary of Tantric developments. However, Tantric influence is evident in Jain temple art and in the incorporation of mantras into Jain worship during this period. But *bhakti* is no less important to Jains than it is to Hindus.

Hindu Dharma and Islam: Interreligious Interactions

As the first millennium of the Common Era ended and the second began, India started to experience incursions from outside powers, such as Arabs, Afghans, Turks, and Mughals. With the coming of

Islam—a religious tradition at first brought peacefully, through trade, then through successive waves of military invasion—Hindus entered a phase characterized by great insecurity and equally great creativity.

Historically, this was a period of great confusion. Due to these foreign invasions, many temples and monastic institutions were destroyed, and major blows were dealt to the Dharma traditions. Buddhism almost died out completely in India, surviving only in pockets of South Asia, such as Nepal, Bhutan, and Sri Lanka. But it continued to thrive in other parts of Asia to which it had been transmitted by Buddhist monks. It had effectively almost ceased to exist in India as a separate tradition by the year 1300. Hindu traditions survived this period because the practices, stories, and beliefs that make up the Hindu civilizational ethos pervaded the lives of the common people. These Hindu elements were not dependent on vulnerable monastic institutions, making them difficult to uproot. The decentralized nature of Hinduism essentially spared it the fate of Buddhism, as did the peripatetic nature of most of Hindu monasticism. Powerful Hindu dynasties, such as the extensive empire of Vijayanagara, thrived in the southern half of the subcontinent until the sixteenth century but it also eventually succumbed to repeated invasion and attack.

However, as the initial shock of invasion subsided, and Islam became a part of the Indic religious landscape, Hindus and Muslims began interacting with one another in far more constructive and creative ways. Adherents of Hindu Bhakti movements and the Sufis of Islam, especially, began to see one another's traditions as potential repositories of deep spiritual wisdom and practices that each could appropriate for attaining nearness to the divine. Hindus began to adopt Sufi spiritual guides (*pirs*) and Muslims were similarly drawn toward Hindu spiritual figures. For example, Sant Kabir, who lived from 1440 to 1518, is claimed even today by both Hindus and Muslims as a revered teacher of sacred wisdom.

This inter-religious cooperation and cross-fertilization is remarkable given the fact that it is hard to conceive of two religions more different from one another than Hindu Dharma and Islam. Islam is emphatically monotheistic, regarding even the Christian trinity as a pagan remnant and a corruption of the original monotheism taught by the prophet Jesus (as he is seen by Muslims). It is equally aniconic. Images of the divine are often associated with the corrupt social order of pre-Islamic Arabia, in which a wealthy priesthood determined who was able to see the gods, and who was not. The diversity of the forms of divinity in Hinduism and its celebration of imagery are seen even today by many Muslims as a blasphemous holdover from a pagan era.

Similarly, the Islamic tradition—although there are important exceptions to this tendency—is generally insistent that there is one way to salvation: through obeying the injunctions of Allah as conveyed by His messenger, the Prophet Muhammad. This is in stark contrast with the pluralism of the yogas and forms of the divine available as objects of devotion in Hindu Dharma. However, there are some Hindu traditions that are equally insistent upon the unique efficacy of particular practices and the unique divinity of specific figures. For example, the Dvaita Vedanta of Madhvacharya believes that devotion to Lord Krishna alone leads to *moksha*. But such exclusivism is more the exception than the rule for Hindu traditions. Islam, consequently, is an actively proselytizing tradition, while most Hindu traditions are not. Nevertheless, a movement for facilitating "reconversion" of Muslims and Christians in India, whose ancestors were Hindu, has emerged in the contemporary period.

In the popular piety of medieval India, however, one sees members of both communities, Hindus and Muslims, shaking off the formal distinctions that their respective religious leaders would prefer to maintain. Rather than focusing upon their differences, Hindu and Muslim saints and Sufi *shaykhs* (masters) of this time emphasized a shared sense of the all-pervasive divine presence and its availability to all who approach it with true devotion and a sincere, humble heart. Sufi saints began to incorporate the names of Hindu deities into their litanies of the many names of Allah, and Hindu devotees integrated into their practices of chanting verses from the Qur'an and about making pilgrimages to the tombs of Sufi saints. The sharing of holy days and places remains a characteristic of Hindu and Islamic practice in South Asia even today. This is a continuation of the Indian popular pluralism reflected in a much earlier period in the edicts of the Emperor Ashoka.[33]

This mutual accommodation was made possible by the strong presence in both traditions of movements that were generally uncomfortable with—and often rejected in the strongest terms—any emphasis on rigid formality, which was seen as interfering with the sincere and spontaneous quest for divine presence. These were the Sufi movement of Islam and the Bhakti movement of Hinduism.

This process of popular mutual assimilation was eventually facilitated at the level of the state. The Mughal emperor, Akbar, who reigned from 1556 to 1605, formally adopted a policy of toleration toward all religions. It included a charitable attitude toward the Christianity taught by the European missionaries arriving on Portuguese merchant ships along the southwest coast of India in the fifteenth century. Furthermore, in a rare gesture, he allowed for the building of a temple for his Hindu wife's deity, Krishna, in his palace and developed his own version of a syncretic religion known as Din-i-Illahi—"Religion of God." Not surprisingly, Akbar consistently ran afoul of the exponents of Islamic orthodoxy in his imperial court. His policy of toleration both mirrored and accelerated what was already happening at the popular, village level between Hindus and Muslims in his realm.

The Sant (Saint) movement of this period consisted of figures of Hindu and Islamic origins, such as the aforementioned Kabir. He rejected the sectarianism of both Hinduism and Islam and was revered by the followers in both religions. He taught that sincere devotion has far greater importance than formal sectarian affiliation or religious identity. This movement culminated in the figure of Guru Nanak, who lived from 1469 to 1539. In his famous teaching that "there is no Hindu, there is no Muslim," Nanak captured the spirit of this era. Rather than leading to a unification of the two traditions, however, Nanak's teachings eventually led to the emergence of a new tradition, Sikhism, which is a spiritual path distinct from both Hinduism and Islam, yet contains affinities to both in its practices and its doctrines.

At the same time, however, there were reactions against this widespread spirit of mutual synthesis and accommodation. The Mughal emperor Aurangzeb, who reigned from 1658 to 1707, aggressively sought the forcible conversion of both Hindus and Sikhs to Islam, returning to the earlier policy of destroying temples and torturing and slaughtering any intransigent religious leaders who refused to convert. The memory of the wounds of this period still runs deep and have led to situations in which later leaders, including the British and the political parties of independent India and

Pakistan, have been able to exploit the fears of both communities for the sake of political gain. And yet such division and mutual suspicion occurs against a wider backdrop of the toleration, mutual respect, and assimilation established in the period of the more enlightened inter-religious relations that characterized the Sant movement and the rise of Sikhism. However, this greater environment of tolerance and pluralism is, at times, endangered by militant tendencies and a hardening of negative attitudes among these religious groups co-existing in India. There continue to exist voices that fuel intolerance toward the other. However, such voices are balanced by those that seek to revert back to the ethos of pluralism and unity.

Hindu Dharma and the West: Modern Movements

The European, and especially the British, colonization of India began in earnest in the eighteenth century and marks another occasion for great insecurity, but also creativity, for the Hindu traditions. The twin challenges of Western science and Christianity led to a crisis for many Hindus, especially in Bengal in eastern India. During the late eighteenth and early nineteenth centuries, Bengal was the first region to experience a large-scale British presence— Calcutta being the main administrative center of the British East India Company. Hindu responses to British culture were vast, ranging from complete indifference, particularly from those orthodox Brahmins who saw the foreigners as mere barbarians with little religious or philosophical interest, to a total capitulation on the part of those Hindus who found European civilization superior to their own. The most creative response, however, came from those Hindus who found much to admire in British culture. Many social and religious leaders accepted the validity of many criticisms of Hinduism launched by Christian missionaries, but they were also critical of what they perceived as Western materialism and a lack of spiritual depth that they found in their ancient texts and systems of thought.

The first of the Hindu reformers was Ram Mohan Roy (1772– 1833), often called the "father of modern Hinduism." He founded a reform organization called the Brahmo Samaj, or "Community of Brahman." He translated the *Upanishads* into vernacular languages and successfully lobbied the British administration to ban the practice of *sati*, or widow immolation. Roy also interpreted Hinduism in monotheistic and unitarian terms, as a wisdom tradition centered on the worship of a formless divinity. He was critical of all aspects of both Hinduism and Christianity that he regarded as non-rational.

Similarly, another prominent leader Swami Dayananda Saraswati (1824–83) was critical of the puranic, mythology-based Hinduism of this period. He established the Arya Samaj organization. Rather than focusing on the esoteric wisdom of the *Upanishads*, as Brahmo Samaj had done, Dayananda focused upon the early Vedic *samhitas* as the wellspring of authentic Hindu practice. He both revived and popularized the practice of worship centered on the sacred fire, as opposed to the use of images, which he viewed as a later accretion upon "pure" Vedic worship.

These movements, however, failed to capture the imagination of the Hindu community as a whole, primarily due to their rejection of the use of images in worship, or *murtipuja*, a practice that had been central to Hindu religious expression for centuries. Greater success in the area of Hindu reform came with the Vedanta movement inspired by Sri Ramakrishna (1836–86) and led by his chief disciple, Swami Vivekananda (1863–1902).

Ramakrishna himself was not a Hindu reformer, but a highly traditional Hindu spiritual figure in the mold of the great *bhakti* saints of the classical and medieval periods. Known for his powerful ecstatic visions, he claimed to have experienced *samadhi*, or the highest spiritual state of absorption in the divine. He incorporated practices of all of the major Hindu spiritual paths, as well as those of Christianity and Islam. He concluded, on this basis, that all religions are paths to the divine. Though barely literate, he could discuss the finer points of Hindu philosophy with highly learned scholars on the basis of his direct experience of spiritual realities. The Western-educated elites of Bengali society, including many members of the Brahmo Samaj, were captivated by his teaching and personality. Because he based his teaching on direct experience and not on the interpretation of scripture, Ramakrishna's path was seen as open to scientific verification, and therefore more in keeping with a modern sensibility than traditions based upon ancient texts alone. And yet his path involved a wholehearted embrace of many practices and a sensibility that the reformers had rejected, such as the use of images and a very emotionally charged spirituality of devotion. His path was a heady mix for those Hindus who wanted to embrace the social reforms and rationalistic approach of the reformers, but who also felt nostalgic for the traditions of their upbringing. Under the leadership of Swami Vivekananda, the Ramakrishna Mission and the wider movement it inspired had a broader impact on Hindu culture when compared to Brahmo and Arya Samaj.

Vivekananda, who lived only a short life of thirty-nine years, had a great effect on transforming Hinduism from a family of traditions confined largely to the Indian subcontinent, and almost exclusively to persons of South Asian ethnic origin, to a world religion. His teachings allowed the religion to be open to non-Indians as well. It was already the case in Vivekananda's time that many Westerners were drawn to Hindu traditions, such as the Transcendentalists of New England and the Theosophists, who had come to South Asia as "reverse missionaries" to instill pride among both Hindus in India and Buddhists in Sri Lanka in their religious heritage. But Vivekananda took the step of initiating Westerners into a Hindu monastic order for the very first time, beginning with Margaret E. Noble (better known to Hindus by her monastic name, Sister Nivedita). Many Hindus consider his celebrated speech to the Parliament of the World's Religions in Chicago in 1893 as the most important event representing the arrival of Hinduism onto the world stage.

By initiating Westerners into Vedanta, Vivekananda opened the floodgates to a range of Hindu spiritual masters who visited the West. Many of them settled permanently. They taught their paths and practices to audiences eager for an alternative to what many saw, and continue to see, as the narrow, dogmatic provincialism of Christianity and the equally narrow, spiritually stultifying worldview of scientific materialism. The first master to follow in Vivekananda's footsteps was another Bengali, Paramahamsa Yogananda (1893–1952), who in 1920 established the Self-Realization Fellowship in California. This was designed to promote the practice of Kriya yoga, the form of meditation that was taught to Yogananda by his *guru*, Sri Yukteshwar Giri. The acceptance of Yogananda's teachings by Westerners was facilitated by his emphasis on Jesus as an enlightened master and an exemplar of yogic wisdom. Another prominent teacher, Jiddu Krishnamurti (1895–1986), emerged from the shadow of the Theosophical movement, which had groomed and hailed him as the next "World Teacher." He broke away from the Theosophists and taught a path of radical self-inquiry, finding a ready audience in the counterculture of the 1960s. Maharishi Mahesh Yogi (1918–2008) similarly appealed to the counterculture via its heroes, The Beatles, who aided him in his promotion of Transcendental Meditation by very publicly attending his seminars in England and Wales. The Transcendental Meditation movement created a world-wide sensation when The Beatles followed him to India in the summer of 1968 for a retreat at his Rishikesh ashram in India, in the foothills of the Himalayas.

A.C. Bhaktivedanta Swami Prabhupada (1896–1977) established the Hare Krishna movement in 1966 when he brought a very traditional form of Vaishnava devotionalism to North America. This was a dramatic contrast with his contemporaries, who carefully tailored their traditions to the tastes and concerns of their Western audiences. Like the Maharishi, Bhaktivedanta Swami also found endorsement from the royalty of the counterculture. The *mahamantra* of Gaudiya Vaishnavism was even included as the refrain of George Harrison's 1970 hit song, "My Sweet Lord."

In addition to the Jnana, Dhyana, and Bhakti yogas taught by Swami Vivekananda, Jiddu Krishnamurti, Maharishi Mahesh Yogi, Para-mhamsa Yogananda, and Bhaktivedanta Swami, the Tantric traditions of Hinduism also found representatives among the Hindu teachers who came to the West in the twentieth century. Swami Muktananda (1908–82) brought the Siddha yoga tradition of his master, Swami Nityananda. He was succeeded by a prominent female *guru*, Swami Chidvilasananda, famously known as Gurumayi, who presides over this tradition to the present day. And most controversial of all was Bhagwan Rajneesh, later known as Osho (1931–90). He endorsed left-handed Tantric practices involving controversial sexual methods. His teach-ings, with its accompanying emphasis on sexual freedom, dovetailed better with the sexual revolution of this period than with the traditionally conservative sexual morality of Indian Hindus.

Meanwhile, as these and other Hindu teachers brought their varied teachings and forms of practice to the West, Vivekananda's original Vedanta Society continued to be active. A steady stream of monks of the Ramakrishna Order came to North America, establishing and nurturing Vedanta centers in cities such as New York, Boston, Washington, DC, Los Angeles, and San Francisco. California, especially—both prior to and during the period of the counterculture—was a major center for Hindu activities that appealed primarily to a Western audience. Swami Prabhavananda (1893–1976), a long-lived, highly active monk of the Ramakrishna Order and founder of the Vedanta Society of Southern California in 1930, initiated such literary luminaries as Aldous Huxley and Christopher Isherwood. In turn, they did much to promote the Vedanta tradition among their readers.

A skeptic could of course question the extent to which any of the movements based on the teachings of spiritual teachers from India have become, or will become, deep-rooted and authentically "Western" forms of religiosity. Like Western Buddhism, the Western Hindu traditions have begun to produce their own leaders, raised with a Western cultural ethos. These new leaders are not simply depending upon Indian teachers for their spiritual and organizational sustenance. Satguru Shivaya Subramuniyaswami (1927–2001) was born Robert Hansen. He inherited the mantle of a Shaiva Siddhanta Sampradaya, or teaching lineage, from his Master Yogaswami. Thus, Western Hinduism produced a spiritual master who was acknowledged as such not only by his devotees, but by Hindus globally, including quite conservative Hindus such as the founders of the Hindu Acharya Sabha. Subramuniyaswami founded the prominent journal *Hinduism Today* that presents itself as "the voice of the global Hindu community"—a claim that the Hindu community largely endorses. The phenomenon of high-profile, celebrity adherents endorsing Hinduism or specific Hindu practices—such as The Beatles' endorsement of Transcendental Meditation and George Harrison's close and lifelong affiliation with the Hare Krishna movement—continues. The most recent example is the actress Julia Roberts, whose film version of Elizabeth Gilbert's auto-biographical memoir, *Eat, Pray, Love* includes a representation of life in the Siddha yoga ashram in Ganeshpuri, India. Though it is far from being a mass movement, Hinduism does seem to have found a home in the West.[34]

Contemporary Issues

The contemporary global Hindu community is a vibrant one, so much so that *Hinduism Today* describes itself as "an international journal affirming the *Sanatana Dharma* and recording the history of a billion strong global religion in renaissance."[35] Hindus have a strong and increasingly assertive presence on the Internet and in the social and political realms, not only in India, but also across the globe. In the contemporary era, many recent factors have made a significant impact upon Hindu consciousness. These factors include Hindu migration to numerous countries, emergence of non-Indian converts and Hindu-based groups, and the wider social and cultural changes due to the emerging factors of globalization. Hindu Dharma has also been influenced by revolutions in communication technology, religious terrorism and extremism, the ecological and economic crises, and the spread of democracy, and global movements for human rights. We shall now look briefly at the variety of issues currently faced by the Hindu community, and the kinds of responses the tradition has put forward.

Caste and Gender Issues

Debates surrounding caste and gender issues in the Indian context overwhelm the social media and academic circles. According to Vedanta philosophy—certainly as interpreted by modern Hindu thinkers like Vivekananda, but even tracing back to ancient sources—there is a fundamental equality among living beings. Non-discriminatory attitudes toward various beings based on an underlying unity are basic to the path to liberation. The *Bhagavad Gita*, for example, famously states that, "Wise persons look upon an educated and cultured Brahmin just as they look upon a cow or an elephant or a dog, or even a low-caste dog-eater."[36] It also states that:

> Whoever sees me [Krishna] everywhere and sees everything in me will never be separated from me, nor will I be separated from him. The *yogin* who is aware of the oneness of life is devoted to me, the one who dwells in all beings. Wherever he happens to find himself, he remains within me.[37]

This is the basis of the radical, spiritual egalitarianism evident in the Bhakti movement, and also the deliberate inversion of traditional concepts of purity and impurity found in *Tantra* and other orthodox Hindu traditions.

The Hindu community, both in India and globally, has embraced, adapted to, and also contributed to the emergence of an egalitarian, democratic social and political order. This spiritual ideal has been marshaled in support of these developments, particularly by such figures as Vivekananda and Gandhi. Traditionally, however, this egalitarian ideal on the spiritual level has co-existed with hierarchical arrangements in the social realm. Even the Buddha and Lord Mahavira did not advocate for an overturning of the ancient Indian socio-political order, or for doing away with the system of hereditary occupations that has come to be called "caste," as it is rationalized in the Hindu *Dharma Shastras* in terms of *varna* and *ashrama*. The argument of reformers within the Dharma traditions has been based primarily on the assumption that the hierarchical division of society is part of the natural order of things, and therefore of *dharma*. But a person's placement in this hierarchy should not be seen as a reflection of their spiritual capacities or inherent worth. Rather, all beings should be looked on as potentially divine. Patriarchy—when social privilege is accorded to men over women purely on the basis of gender—has been similarly rationalized as part of the natural order of things, but not as impugning the inherent dignity or divinity of all beings as deserving of love and respect.

Unsurprisingly, given human propensities toward greed and power seeking, the caste and gender-based social hierarchies of India have frequently been, as Hindu reformers have argued, abused. And more radical reformers have argued that hierarchy is itself intrinsically violent and incompatible with the highest ideals of Hindu Dharma, and that its introduction into Hindu society is entirely pernicious and destructive. A classic example of the divergence between the views of mainstream Hindu thinkers and more radical Hindu reformers in this regard is the clash between the views of Mohandas K. Gandhi and B.R. Ambedkar on the issue of caste.

Mohandas K. Gandhi (1869–1948), popularly known to his admirers as Mahatma or "Great Soul," upheld the view, also articulated by prior reformers like Dayananda Sarasvati and Vivekananda, that the original ideal of *varna* was oriented toward social good. As different people have different talents to offer society, it has been argued that the caste was not originally the hereditary phenomenon that it later became. There is certainly some evidence for the view that occupation was not always hereditary in Hindu society. For example, in the *Rig Veda* (9:112.3),[38] the speaker identifies himself as a bard, his father as a physician, and his mother as a grinder of corn. These are all distinct occupations, but are here presented as being pursued by members of the same family. This would be impossible if occupations were always hereditary in Vedic society. Determination of occupation by heredity must have therefore arisen during a later period. Late Vedic and post-Vedic Hindu literature also includes prominent characters that pursue careers different from those of the castes in which they were ostensibly born. Gandhi thus believed that the hereditary "caste" system and the prejudices to which the members of "lower" castes have been subjected were deviations from the original Vedic ideal. He campaigned against caste-based prejudices, and he hoped (like prior reformers) to reform the system. He referred to members of the most marginalized castes (known as the "untouchables") as harijans, or "children of God," whose lowly station in life had made them more spiritual than the proud high-caste Hindus. He also advocated for their admittance into temples from which they had been barred as "impure" persons. He famously referred to the practice of untouchability as a cancer on the body of Hinduism.

B.R. Ambedkar (1891–1956) was another leader in the Indian independence movement. Unlike Gandhi, Ambedkar came from a low-caste background. He rejected Gandhi's views as paternalistic. He coined the term *dalit*, or "the oppressed," as the preferred term for members of marginalized communities. Ambedkar played an important role in independent India in that he was also the author of the constitution. He famously converted to Buddhism, leading thousands of his fellow Dalits in the process. His rationale was that since he was fundamentally committed to an Indic and dharmic worldview and way of life, he could not convert to Christianity or to Islam, but he saw Hindu Dharma as being so thoroughly implicated in the phenomenon of prejudice based on birth (*jati*) that he could no longer identify with it in good conscience.[39]

Regarding patriarchy, the roles of women in Hindu Dharma—not unlike the roles of the various caste communities—have been far too complex throughout the centuries for any generalization to be adequate. Prior to the modern period, many Hindu sources consist of prescriptive texts such as the *Dharma Shastras* that reflect what their Brahmin authors regarded as ideal gender roles. In these texts, laws for women often relegate them to a lower status, although there are also references that elevate women to the status of goddesses. In the epics, women are depicted as both strong and submissive, which provides a complex picture regarding gender. However, because of a lack of other ample textual resources it is nearly impossible to deduce from these sources what the lived experiences of women were at any given time.

Did most people follow the injunctions of the Brahmins closely? Or was the entire point of these injunctions to change a ground reality that was radically different from what their authors felt should be the case? It is likely that both situations—as well as a mix of both—occurred at different times and in different locations. When alternative voices are available, such as in the folk tales and vernacular literatures of local non-Sanskrit traditions or in the inscriptions left by kings or wealthy patrons of religious institutions, they suggest a more diverse picture than do the Brahmanical texts. Such voices intrude into the texts of the Brahmins from time to time, just as with regard to the issue of caste, one can find the voices of Satyakama, Valmiki, and Ekalavya who were from "lower castes."[40] A broad set of generalizations based on the sources that are available in abundance (Brahmanical texts) sometimes reflect, and sometimes are in radical discontinuity with, the social realities of actual Hindu women.

The overall orientation of the Brahmanical tradition is decidedly patriarchal. The system of *varnas* and *ashramas* defines the ideal life trajectory of a male. It is males who receive the sacred thread (*upanayana*) and who take up an occupation appropriate to their caste after marriage and entering the stage of the householder. They then retire, entering the *vanaprastha* stage. Alternatively, they may at any point renounce the life of a layperson and undertake *sannyasa*.

In the *Dharma Shastras* a woman's social role is entirely defined in terms of her relationships with men—her father in childhood, her husband as a married woman, and her sons, first as their caretaker, and then, perhaps, as the recipient of their care in her old age. A woman may enter retirement *with* her husband, or have it forced upon her by widowhood. Her daughters will join the families of their husbands where their first duty lies in taking care of their husbands and their husbands' parents.

Again, the degree to which this Brahmanical ideal has been observed in practice is open to question. In the modern period, it has been observed quite rigorously, particularly in rural settings. But it is also set aside quite decisively, often among the wealthy and well educated. Pre-modern exceptions did exist. For example, some independently wealthy women were patrons of particular religious communities, and others were courtesans by trade.

In the classical model, a good deal of evidence exists that the religious life was the only route for a woman to live independently from male domination. Here, women could even rise to a considerable level of social authority, wielding power—even over men—as gurus and as highly revered saints. Indian Medieval-era female figures, such as Andal, Mahadeviyakka, and Mira Bai could transgress their traditional social roles because they did so out of love for God, eschewing traditional married life and establishing themselves as major spiritual teachers.

This model continues into the modern period, with such figures as Anandamayi Ma, Mata Amritanandamayi, and Gurumayi Ma, who are highly revered and independent religious leaders. It may be argued that the price of such independence is the total religious commitment that these women's lives display. But it would also be wrong to presume that the sole motive of these women has been personal freedom from societal constraints and precludes a spiritual aspiration as an absolutely central element—as in, a desire for *moksha* or to be nearer to God.

Feminist discourse has made inroads into modern Hinduism along with discourses on democracy and human rights. Though Hindu Dharma is in many ways a conservative tradition, it has also proven to be adaptable through the centuries. In recent years, women's freedom movements have defied what were formerly bastions of orthodoxy on the basis of the same doctrine used to undercut the caste system: the unity of all beings. Women have engaged in the public reading of the *Veda* and also have received the sacred thread (traditionally only a Hindu male privilege). As more women in urban areas have taken up jobs outside the home—either out of desire or economic necessity—they are being seen as co-householders with their husbands.

At the same time, patriarchy still lurks in contemporary Hinduism, as it does in various other religious traditions. A preference for sons over daughters has led to a heinous practice of aborting female fetuses. And the ongoing practice of dowry—in which the family of a bride is expected to pay a considerable fee to the family of her husband—fuels the preference for sons who bring money into the family when they marry, whereas daughters cost money. Dowry death has been viewed as the result of this practice, where families conspire to marry their sons to women, extract a dowry from the woman's family, and then murder the woman, sometimes doing this serially. These customs are illegal and perpetrators face tough sentences. But they continue due to socio-economic reasons implicated with old traditional mindset, despite the fact that many Hindu leaders condemn such customs.

The practice of *sati*, or widow immolation, is nearly unheard of, contrary to what many people may believe. The last such event, at least to receive publicity, occurred in 1987, under widespread condemnation from the wider Hindu community. The practice was never widely prevalent and was legally banned in 1829, due largely to the activism of the Hindu reformer, Ram Mohan Roy.

The presence of a vigorous Goddess tradition with its wide range of assertive and powerful goddesses might suggest a broader feminist streak in Hinduism than is actually the case. The worship of goddesses and the roles of actual women have largely been independent variables, yet the female divine model is available for those who chose to exercise their inner power. Gandhi referenced this trope when he asked women to awaken their feminine power.

The range of options available for traditional Hindu women is often discussed in terms of the contrast between the heroines Sita and Draupadi of the *Ramayana* and *Mahabharata* respectively. Sita is obedient to every wish of her husband. She suffers through his troubles, the humiliation society imposes on her, and even the indignity of the fire test. Draupadi, on the other hand, is also a faithful wife who suffers with her five husbands. But when her rights are violated and she is humiliated—her heroic husband does not protect her honor and he gambles her away—she speaks up for her rights. She questions her husband's choices, simultaneously displaying a considerable knowledge of *dharma* and the proper conduct prescribed for men in the law books. Of the two, Sita has generally been upheld as the model of the devoted Hindu woman. The case of Draupadi has been construed as an alternative model, put forth from within the Hindu tradition, that can serve as a guide for a woman to live (i.e., with dignity and a voice in her own destiny).[41]

Within the Hindu community, a variety of groups and movements have emerged seeking to overcome the phenomena of caste prejudice and patriarchy. One such organization called Navya Shastra ("New Scripture") has argued that the ancient *Dharma Shastras* have only provisional authority that is limited to a particular period of history that has passed. The organization insists that a new conception of *dharma* needs to emerge, based on Vedic ideals but more appropriate to the contemporary era. They assert that the understanding of the presence of universal *Brahman* dwelling in all should be reflected in the laws of democratic institutions, thus leading to the creation of an egalitarian society. Most recently, Navya Shastra has argued for LGBT equality on a Vedantic basis. The website "Queers United" writes:

> The organization [Navya Shastra] notes that Hinduism has never classified homosexuality as a sin against God. While some ancient law codes have spoken out against homosexual acts, the tradition has never called for the persecution of homosexuals. In fact, there is ample evidence that alternative lifestyles have been accepted throughout Hindu history. Several modern Hindu leaders have also spoken positively of gay rights, though disappointingly, a significant percentage of American Hindus remain uncomfortable with homosexuality. "According to the Hindu contemplative tradition, we are all manifestations of the one universal spirit, straight or gay, and worthy of the same respect and rights," said Jaishree Gopal, Navya Shastra Chairman.[42]

It is evident that a plurality of viewpoints exists in Hindu Dharma. Followers of Hinduism continue to adapt to new norms and address new challenges using ancient wisdom.

Hindu Nationalism

The best-known and most celebrated of the leaders of India's movement for independence from British rule was Mahatma Gandhi. Gandhi tapped into ancient ideals—not only of Hindu Dharma, but also of Jainism and Christianity—to develop a method of non-violent resistance to oppression. Gandhi championed an ideal nation in which people of all spiritual communities would live together to form a harmonious and mutually supportive society. True to this vision, the Republic of India adopted a secular constitution after independence, in which the rights of religious minorities are protected.

The independence movement, however, was not unanimous in its vision. There were both Hindu and Muslim leaders who were deeply suspicious of each other due to deep fears about the inter-communal violence that might transpire after independence. On the Muslim side, this was reflected in a push for the partition of India and Pakistan. On the Hindu side, it was reflected in Hindu nationalism. Known as Hindutva ("Hindu-ness"), this political ideology is loosely united around the concept of India as a Hindu state. It was defined by

Vinayak Damodar Savarkar (1883–1966) in an essay of the same name. Hindutva is a concept of Hindu identity that conflates it with Indian identity. According to Savarkar, a Hindu is one who is of Indian descent, who claims India as his or her homeland, and who adheres to a religion of Indian origin—that is, one of the Dharma traditions described in this volume. Those Indians who do not practice a religion of Indian origin are often seen by Hindu nationalists as "less Indian" than self-identified Hindus. Hindu nationalism is characterized by a general sense of Hindu Dharma as a tradition endangered by the adherents of other ideologies (primarily Islam, Christianity, and secularism).

Hindu nationalism has been widely criticized by political opponents within India and by scholars globally. The Indian constitution is based on the ideal of secularism, according to which all religions are welcome in India and all Indians are free to practice whichever religion they choose. As an ideology that advocates an identification of "Indian-ness" with "Hindu-ness," Hindu nationalism conflicts with this secular idea. Despite this, some Hindu nationalists openly advocate a Hindu state, arguing that the inherent openness to diversity that is part of Hindu Dharma is sufficient to guarantee the rights of religious minorities, and that a secular constitution is therefore unnecessary in a Hindu state. Hindu nationalists are critical of what some call the "pseudo-secularism" of the Indian government, whose protection of minority communities the Hindu nationalists regard as appeasement carried out at the expense of the Hindu majority.

The primary source of discomfort among many critics of Hindutva is the association of militant Hindu nationalist rhetoric with violence against religious minority communities in India, especially Muslims. In fact, Gandhi was assassinated by a Hindu nationalist, Nathuram Godse, who felt that Gandhi had betrayed the Hindu community by not doing enough to prevent the partition of India and Pakistan.

The Hindu nationalist organizations form a loose coalition known as the Sangh Parivar that includes such groups as the Rashtriya Svayamsevak Sangh (RSS), the Vishva Hindu Parishad (VHP), and the Bharatiya Janata Party (BJP). In 2014, the BJP won a considerable majority in the Indian parliament, propelling an outspoken Hindu nationalist, Narendra Modi, to the office of Prime Minister. Contrary to fears expressed by many scholars and media

figures that a Modi victory would lead to a state of oppression for
religious minorities in India, the focus of the BJP government—as of
this writing in 2017—has been upon improving the economy of
India. Prime Minister Modi has tended not to invoke the more
radical figures of the Hindu nationalist movement, such as Savarkar,
and instead focuses on more mainstream figures such as Swami
Vivekananda and Gandhi.

Hindu nationalism has been characterized by many scholars as a
Hindu analogue to the fundamentalist movements found in other
religious traditions in that it has more of the features of a majoritarian
political movement than a strictly religious one. It appears to
represent a reaction to modernity and the pressures upon a
traditional religious belief system and way of life. Although Hindu
Dharma, as a spiritual and theological worldview, is accepting of an
enormous array of diverse beliefs and ways of living and practicing,
Hindu nationalism reflects the fear within the Hindu community of
being overwhelmed by other traditions, two of which—Christianity
and Islam—have been used in the past as ideologies to justify the
conquest of India.[43]

Environmental Issues

The ecological crisis is felt especially in India because the rapid
industrialization since independence has resulted in a heavily polluted
environment. The quality of both the air and water in much of India is
quite poor, and the decimation of the Indian economy in the wake of
European colonization has created a situation in which a massive
number of Indians—Hindu and non-Hindu alike—exist in material
conditions that many in the West would find unlivable.

Like activists in the independence movement, activists in the Indian
Environmental movement have looked upon Hindu traditions as
sources of inspiration. The Earth itself is a living organism, according to
traditional Hindu thought, and is worshipped as a goddess (*Bhu Devi*).
The sanctity of rivers and of water generally is a motive for cleaning the
heavily polluted rivers of India such as the Ganges. The Chipko
movement emerged in 1973 in opposition to logging in the Himalayan
foothills of Uttarakhand. Inspired by the Hindu ideal of sacred forests
and the nonviolent methods of Gandhi, activists protected their sacred
forest from being cut down by loggers by forming a human chain
encircling the trees and by hugging the trees. This practice led to the

name "Chipko" and, beyond India, to the term "tree hugger" for anyone concerned about the protection of the environment.

As in many other parts of the world, the conflicting needs of developing an economy in which all human beings can have at least a minimal standard of decent living while at the same time protecting the environment, presents a challenge for India. Hindu Dharma, like the other Dharma traditions, has teachings that lend themselves to an ecological ethos, such as the presence of divinity in all living beings, and a non-anthropocentric emphasis on the soul (*jiva*) as an entity capable of rebirth in both human and non-human forms. This will no doubt continue to be a source of creative inspiration for Hindu ecological activists.[44]

Engaged Ethics

Perhaps Swami Vivekananda's most revolutionary teaching was that Karma yoga is a form of selfless service, including the provision of education, food, and medical care to the poor, and is a path to *moksha* worthy not only for householders, but also for the monks of the Ramakrishna Order. For most of history, the main tasks of the renouncer were taken to be study and meditation (*jnana* and *dhyana*). Karma yoga, or serving society, was considered to be the work of householders. Though having a precedent in older texts, such as the *Bhagavad Gita*, the ideal of the active life, and of *seva* (service) as a spiritual path was given renewed prominence by Vivekananda and his followers. Vivekananda inspired many Hindus, especially Gandhi, to serve the poor and destitute of India. *Seva*, as social service, is today seen as a central Hindu virtue.

It is important to understand this engaged Hindu ethic, particularly in light of stereotypes of Hindu Dharma as a wholly otherworldly tradition, unconcerned with the material well-being of its adherents. *Karma* is sometimes misunderstood by interpreters of Hinduism as a kind of fatalism, according to which one is simply resigned to the circumstances of one's current life as the inevitable result of past deeds. All one can do, according to this view, to improve one's current lot is one's immediate duty (usually taken to be the hereditary occupation associated with the community of one's birth) and hope for a better rebirth. When linked to the massive poverty of contemporary India, this is a view that essentially blames Hindu Dharma for the suffering of most Hindus, who are represented as a passive mass of humanity bound by their religion to do nothing to better their situation. This judgment is based on an interpretation of the idea of *karma* which, as discussed earlier, teaches that our current situation is certainly our own doing, and we have the power to make choices that will lead to a different outcome. It also shows a blinkered understanding of history. For the poverty of India, a land of fabulous wealth for most of human history, is a relatively recent phenomenon, attributable not to Hindu Dharma, but to colonial exploitation prior to Indian independence and a mismanagement of resources in the following decades. Hindu relief organizations such as the Ramakrishna Mission—perhaps the largest organization of this kind—have played a major role in poverty relief. Their existence belies the notion that Hinduism teaches merely passive acceptance of human suffering, especially the suffering of others, without any effort to provide relief or assistance.

Notes

1. Portions of this essay are drawn, although in a revised form, from the introduction to my *Historical Dictionary of Hinduism* (Lanham, Maryland: Scarecrow Press, 2011), 1–22.
2. *Dharmo rakshati rakshitaha, Manusmriti,* Chapter 8, Verse 15. The most literal translation of this famous expression would be, "Dharma [when] protected protects."
3. *Rig Veda* 1.164: 46c; translation mine. In some recensions of the *Rig Veda,* this verse appears as 1.164: 94.
4. John Cort, *Jains in the World: Religious Values and Ideology in India* (Oxford: Oxford University Press, 2001), 15.
5. A good edited volume that summarizes the debate among scholars over the coherence of the Hindu tradition and the use of the term Hinduism is J.E. Llewellyn, ed., *Defining Hinduism: A Reader* (New York: Routledge, 2005). Other important works on this topic include Hermann Kulke and Gunther-Dietz Sontheimer. *Hinduism Reconsidered* (New Delhi: Manohar Publishers and Distributors, 2001); Brian K. Pennington, *Was Hinduism Invented? Britons, Indians, and the Colonial Construction of Religion* (Oxford: Oxford University Press, 2007); Andrew Nicholson, *Unifying Hinduism: Philosophy and Identity in Indian Intellectual History* (New York: Columbia University Press, 2010); and D.N. Jha, *Rethinking Hindu Identity* (New York: Routledge, 2014).
6. Though scholars do tend to acknowledge that all attempts to describe the world's major religions involve some amount of oversimplification that

fails to do justice to the highly complex realities of the lived practices of millions of adherents. Thus, Paul J. Griffiths, for example, refers to the world's major religions as "semifictional entities." Paul J. Griffiths, *An Apology for Apologetics: A Study in the Logic of Interreligious Dialogue* (Eugene, Oregon: Wipf and Stock, 1991), 5.

7. In some forms of Hinduism, though, a divine being does play a role in ensuring that all karmic rewards and punishments are experienced, as they ought to be. But this is not seen as a whimsical or accidental activity on the part of God. It is, rather, a part of the work God performs in order to ensure the smooth and orderly, dharmic working of the cosmos. *Dharma* itself is not arbitrary. It is, rather, impersonal, absolute justice. Surendranath Dasgupta, *A History of Indian Philosophy*, *Volume Five* (Delhi: Motilal Banarsidass, 1922), 4, explains the divine role in karmic reward and punishment in one of the major theistic traditions of Hinduism, the Shaiva tradition:

> Ordinarily the idea of grace or *karuna* would simply imply the extension of kindness or favour to one in distress. But in the *shaivagamas* [a collection of Hindu scriptures] there is a distinct line of thought where *karuna* or grace is interpreted as a divine creative movement for supplying all souls with fields of experience in which they may enjoy pleasures and suffer painful experiences. The *karuna* of God reveals the world to us in just the manner as we ought to experience it. Grace, therefore, is not a work of favour in a general sense [that is, an arbitrary gift], but it is a movement in favour of our getting the right desires in accordance with our *karma*. Creative action of the world takes place in consonance with our good and bad deeds, in accordance with which the various types of experience unfold themselves to us. In this sense, grace may be compared to the Yoga philosophy, which admits a permanent will of God operating in the orderliness of the evolutionary creation [...] for the protection of the world, and supplying it as the basis of human experience in accordance with their individual *karmas*.

8. Swami Vivekananda, *Complete Works*, *Volume One* (Mayavati: Advaita Ashrama, 1979), 320. Or in the words of George Harrison, "Since our problems have been our own creation, they also can be overcome." (From "This Is Love," *Cloud Nine*, Dark Horse Records: 1987).

9. John Hick, *The Fifth Dimension: An Exploration of the Spiritual Realm* (Oxford: Oneworld Publications, 1999), 19–24.

10. *Ibid.*, 57.

11. These skeptics were known as the Lokayatas or Charvakas. They taught a materialist and atheist worldview not unlike that of contemporary skeptics. For more information on this topic, see: Debiprasad

Chattopadhyaya, *Lokayata: A Study in Ancient Indian Materialism* (New Delhi: People's Publishing House, 1973).

12. *Bhagavad Gita* 2:12–13. George Thompson, *The Bhagavad Gita: A New Translation* (New York: North Point Press, 2008), 9. The original Sanskrit word translated as "the embodied one" in this verse is not *jiva* but *dehin*—literally, "one who possesses a body." The referent, though, is the living being, or *jiva*. And *Ibid.*, 2:22.

13. A range of views exists within Hindu Dharma, as well as among the Dharma traditions more broadly, regarding whether a plant possesses *jiva* in the same sense in which other life forms do. The Jain tradition, for example, affirms that plants contain many *jivas*. In the Buddhist tradition, on the other hand, the focus is not so much on all living beings as on all *sentient* beings (generally regarded as excluding plants, though there are exceptions to this in Buddhism in East Asia). Some Hindus would deny that a human being could be reborn as a plant, or part of a plant, whereas other Hindus would accept this possibility. There are also Hindus who deny that a human being could be reborn as an animal, seeing the series of rebirths as progressing through an evolutionary scale. This is one example of the internal diversity of the tradition—many views on the possible kinds of rebirth—that is combined with an underlying unity—acceptance of the concept of rebirth itself. See Ellison Banks Findly, *Plant Lives: Borderline Beings in Indian Traditions* (Delhi: Motilal Banarsidass, 2010).

14. Arvind Sharma, *Gandhi: A Spiritual Biography* (New Haven & London: Yale University Press, 2013), 3–4.

15. Pravrajika Vrajaprana, *Vedanta: A Simple Introduction* (Hollywood, California: Vedanta Press, 1999), 13–14.

16. The term "modern postural yoga" was coined by religion scholar Mark Singleton. See: Mark Singleton, Mark, *Yoga Body: The Origins of Modern Posture Practice* (Oxford: Oxford University Press, 2010).

17. The most prominent of these is probably Buddhism. In fact, in an interesting historical side note, it is worth pointing out that the term *dhyana*, or meditation, pronounced *dhyan* in vernacular Indic languages such as Hindi, was taken, along with the practice, to China by Buddhist monks, where it came to be pronounced as *ch'an*. Subsequently, *ch'an* was transmitted to Japan, where it was pronounced *zen*. *Zen* is the Japanese pronunciation of the Chinese pronunciation of the Sanskrit term for meditation.

18. Several very important sages of the Vedic tradition were not Brahmins by birth. These include the sage Satyakama (*Chandogya Upanishad* 4.4:1–5), who was the illegitimate son of a servant woman, Vyasa, the compiler of the *Veda* and author of the *Mahabharata*, and Valmiki, author of the *Ramayana*.

19. The Vedic deities Indra and Brahma play a pivotal role in the life story of the Buddha, helping the young Siddhartha to escape from his father's palace and later persuading him to preach, after attaining *nirvana*, thus leading to the emergence of Buddhism. Vedic deities are depicted as

guardians in Buddhist temples in places as distant from India as Japan, such as at the temple of the thousand-and-one forms of Avalokiteshvara in Kyoto (a temple known as Sanjusangendo). And Sarasvati and Lakshmi— goddesses of wisdom and wealth, respectively, in Hinduism—are commonly depicted and worshipped in Jain temples. Jains celebrate the Hindu festival of Divali as Mahavir Nirvan Divas, commemorating the final passing away of the twenty-fourth Jain Tirthankara, Mahavira. See: Jeffery D. Long, *Jainism: An Introduction* (London: I.B.Tauris, 2009), 26.

As an example of the reverse case, there are groups that are widely regarded as Hindu though they reject Vedic authority. For example, the lingayats or virashaivas, a community mainly from southern India with a devotional focus on the deity Shiva, are so sharply critical of the Brahmins and of the *Veda* that many argue that their tradition is not a part of Hindu Dharma at all, but rather is a distinct, separate religion. Lingayats, though, are widely seen as Hindu by other communities largely due to their very strong devotion to a popular Hindu deity, and the centrality of this devotion to their spiritual path.

20. Sarvepalli Radhakrishnan, *The Hindu View of Life* (New York: Macmillan, 1973), 18.

21. Though there are Hindu schools of thought which do see it in this way, such as the ancient Naiyayikas, who affirm that the *Veda* is authoritative due to the fact that it was spoken by *Ishvara*, or God.

22. See B.S. Ahloowalia, *Invasion of the Genes: Genetic Heritage of India* (Houston, Texas: Eloquent Books, 2013), 28–30.

23. See Jonathan Mark Kenoyer, *Ancient Cities of the Indus Valley Civilization* (Oxford: Oxford University Press, 1998); Dilip K. Chakrabarti, *India: An Archaeological History* (New Delhi: Oxford University Press, 1999); Gregory L. Possehl, *The Indus Civilization: A Contemporary Perspective* (Walnut Creek, California: Altamira Press, 2002); and Jane R. McIntosh, *A Peaceful Realm: The Rise and Fall of the Indus Civilization* (Boulder, Colorado: Westview Press, 2002).

24. http://www.deccanherald.com/content/389730/200-year-long-drought-wiped.html.

25. This view has been advanced by Klaus K. Klostermaier. In: Klaus K. Klostermaier, *A Survey of Hinduism*, 3rd ed. (Albany, New York: State University of New York Press, 2007), pp. 17–29 as well as: Georg Feuerstein, Subhash Kak and David Frawley, *In Search of the Cradle of Civilization* (Wheaton, Illinois: Quest Books, 2001).

26. An especially powerful critique of this way of writing about India, which sees Indians as passive "patients" rather than as active agents in their own historical development, in: Ronald Inden, *Imagining India* (Bloomington, Indiana: Indiana University Press, 2001).

27. The most comprehensive and evenhanded account currently available of this topic is: Edwin Bryant, *The Quest for the Origins of Vedic Culture:*

The Indo-Aryan Migration Debate (New York: Oxford University Press, 2004). The interesting and noteworthy fact that Jain scholars make claims regarding the Jain nature of the Indus Valley Civilization is explored briefly in Long, *Jainism*, 45–56.

28. Though, as noted earlier, this is not always a hard and fast division, as Buddhist and Jain rituals also share some of the formulas and structures of Vedic ritual, and all four of the Dharma traditions, for example, make use of the sacred syllable *Om*. Buddhist monks of the Tantric Shingon sect in Japan perform a fire ritual known as *goma* that is basically the same as the Vedic *homa* ritual. Kevin Trainor, ed., *Buddhism: The Illustrated Guide* (Oxford: Oxford University Press, 2001).

29. In Vedic literature, especially early Vedic literature, the term for cosmic order is *rta*. Over time, this term gradually came to be replaced by the term *dharma*.

30. Thompson, *Bhagavad Gita*, 9:26.

31. *Dhammapada* 26:11. Sarvepalli Radhakrishnan, trans., *The Dhammapada* (New Delhi: Oxford University Press, 1950), 180.

32. Ashoka's Rock Edicts Numbers 7 and 12. Ven. S. Dhammika, *The Edicts of King Ashoka*, available at http://www.accesstoinsight.org/lib/authors/dhammika/wheel386.html, 1994 (accessed January 15, 2017).

33. See Peter Gottschalk, *Beyond Hindu and Muslim: Multiple Identity in Narratives from Village India* (New York: Oxford University Press, 2005).

34. See Philip Goldberg, *American Veda: From Emerson and The Beatles to Yoga and Meditation – How Indian Spirituality Changed the West* (Bourgon, Indiana: Harmony, 2010); Lola Williamson, *Transcendent in America: Hindu-Inspired Meditation Movements as New Religion* (New York: New York University Press, 2010); Ann Gleig and Lola Williamson, eds., *Homegrown Gurus: From Hinduism in America to American Hinduism* (Albany, New York: State University of New York Press, 2013); Paul Oliver, *Hinduism and the 1960s: The Rise of a Counter-culture* (London: Bloomsbury, 2015); and the forthcoming Jeffery D. Long, *Hinduism in America: A Convergence of Worlds* (London: Bloomsbury, publication anticipated in 2017).

35. https://twitter.com/hinduismtoday.

36. *Bhagavad Gita* 5:18, translation is mine, adapted from Thompson.

37. Thompson, *Bhagavad Gita* 6:30–31.

38. Alternatively, *Rig Veda* 9:113.3.

39. Regarding the issue of caste, see Nicholas Dirks, *Castes of Mind: Colonialism and the Making of Modern India* (Princeton, New Jersey: Princeton University Press, 2001); and Bernard S. Cohn, *India: The Social Anthropology of a Civilization* (Englewood Cliffs, New York: Prentice Hall, 1971).

40. Satyakama and Valmiki are both figures who, despite having very humble backgrounds in terms of caste, came to be viewed as important sages of the Vedic tradition. Ekalavya, on the other hand, also from a "low" caste, is a character from the *Mahabharata* who sought to elevate his status to that of

a warrior, and was quite brutally punished for doing so, being forced to cut off his own thumb by a Brhamin Guru. He has thus become a symbol of the Dalit experience.

41. Excellent sources for further information on this topic are the essays in the volume, co-edited by Tracy Pintchman and Rita D. Sherma, *Woman and Goddess in Hinduism: Reinterpretations and Re-envisionings* (New York: Palgrave Macmillan, 2011).

42. "Queers United," available at http://queersunited.blogspot.com/2008/10/navya-shastra-urges-california-voters.html (accessed December 15, 2016).

43. For a good overview of Hindu nationalism, see: Christophe Jaffrelot, *The Hindu Nationalist Movement in India* (New York: Columbia University Press, 1996), and for a Hindu critique of and alternative to this movement, see: Jeffery D. Long, *A Vision for Hinduism: Beyond Hindu Nationalism* (London: I.B.Tauris, 2007).

44. See Pankaj Jain, *Dharma and Ecology of Hindu Communities* (London: Ashgate, 2011); and Christopher Key Chapple and Mary Evelyn Tucker, eds., *Hinduism and Ecology: The Intersection of Earth, Sky, and Water* (Cambridge, Massachusetts: Center for the Study of World Religions, 2000).

Selected Bibliography

Ahloowalia, S. *Invasion of the Genes: Genetic Heritage of India.* Houston, Texas: Eloquent Books, 2013.

Bryant, Edwin. *The Quest for the Origins of Vedic Culture: The Indo-Aryan Migration Debate.* New York: Oxford University Press, 2004.

Chakrabarti, Dilip K. *India: An Archaeological History.* New Delhi: Oxford University Press, 1999.

Chapple, Christopher Key and Mary Evelyn Tucker, eds. *Hinduism and Ecology: The Intersection of Earth, Sky, and Water.* Cambridge, Massachusetts: Center for the Study of World Religions, 2000.

Cort, John. *Jains in the World: Religious Values and Ideology in India.* Oxford: Oxford University Press, 2001.

Dasgupta, Surendranath. *A History of Indian Philosophy.* Delhi: Motilal Banarsidass, 1922.

Dirks, Nicholas. *Castes of Mind: Colonialism and the Making of Modern India.* Princeton, New Jersey: Princeton University Press, 2001.

Frawley, David, Subhash Kak, and Georg Feuerstein. *In Search of the Cradle of Civilization.* Wheaton, Illinois: Quest Books, 2001.

Gleig, Ann and Lola Williamson, eds. *Homegrown Gurus: From Hinduism in America to American Hinduism.* Albany, New York: State University of New York Press, 2013.

Goldberg, Philip. *American Veda: From Emerson and The Beatles to Yoga and Meditation – How Indian Spirituality Changed the West.* Bourgon, Indiana: Harmony, 2010.

Gottschalk, Peter. *Beyond Hindu and Muslim: Multiple Identity in Narratives from Village India*. New York: Oxford University Press, 2005.

Griffiths, Paul J. *An Apology for Apologetics: A Study in the Logic of Interreligious Dialogue*. Eugene, Oregon: Wipf and Stock, 1991.

Hick, John. *The Fifth Dimension: An Exploration of the Spiritual Realm*. Oxford: Oneworld Publications, 1999.

Inden, Ronald. *Imagining India*. Bloomington, Indiana: Indiana University Press, 2001.

Jaffrelot, Christophe. *The Hindu Nationalist Movement in India*. New York: Columbia University Press, 1996.

Jain, Pankaj. *Dharma and Ecology of Hindu Communities*. London: Ashgate, 2011.

Jha, D.N. *Rethinking Hindu Identity*. New York: Routledge, 2014.

Kenoyer, Jonathan Mark. *Ancient Cities of the Indus Valley Civilization*. Oxford: Oxford University Press, 1998.

Klostermaier, Klaus K. *A Survey of Hinduism*, 3rd ed. Albany, New York: State University of New York Press, 2007.

Llewellyn, J.E., ed. *Defining Hinduism: A Reader*. New York: Routledge, 2005.

Long, Jeffery D. *Historical Dictionary of Hinduism*. Lanham, Maryland: Scarecrow Press, 2011.

——— *Jainism: An Introduction*. London: I.B.Tauris, 2009.

——— *A Vision for Hinduism: Beyond Hindu Nationalism*. London: I.B.Tauris, 2007.

McIntosh, Jane R., *A Peaceful Realm: The Rise and Fall of the Indus Civilization*. Boulder, Colorado: Westview Press, 2002.

Nicholson, Andrew. *Unifying Hinduism: Philosophy and Identity in Indian Intellectual History*. New York: Columbia University Press, 2010.

Oliver, Paul. *Hinduism and the 1960s: The Rise of a Counter-culture*. London: Bloomsbury, 2015.

Pennington, Brian K. *Was Hinduism Invented? Britons, Indians, and the Colonial Construction of Religion*. Oxford: Oxford University Press, 2007.

Pintchman, Tracy and Rita D. Sherma. *Woman and Goddess in Hinduism: Reinterpretations and Re-envisionings*. New York: Palgrave Macmillan, 2011.

Radhakrishnan, Sarvepalli. *The Hindu View of Life*. New York: Macmillan, 1973.

Sharma, Arvind. *Gandhi: A Spiritual Biography*. New Haven, Connecticut & London: Yale University Press, 2013.

Singleton, Mark. *Yoga Body: The Origins of Modern Posture Practice*. Oxford: Oxford University Press, 2010.

Trainor, Kevin, ed. *Buddhism: The Illustrated Guide*. Oxford: Oxford University Press, 2001.

Vivekananda, Swami. *Complete Works*. Mayavati: Advaita Ashrama, 1979.

Vrajaprana, Pravrajika. *Vedanta: A Simple Introduction*. Hollywood, California: Vedanta Press, 1999.

Williamson, Lola. *Transcendent in America: Hindu-Inspired Meditation Movements as New Religion*. New York: New York University Press, 2010.

3

Jain Dharma: The Eternal Law of *Ahimsa*

Christopher Key Chapple

*All things breathing, all things existing, all things living, all beings whatever,
should not be slain or treated with violence, or insulted, or tortured, or driven
away. This is the pure, unchanging, eternal law [dharma], which the wise
ones who know the world have proclaimed.*

– Acaranga Sutra

Introduction and Early History

The terms "Jain/Jaina" and "Jainism" refer to an ancient religious and
philosophical system that remains vital in India and throughout the
modern world. Over the course of India's history, Jains have been
known for their adherence to vegetarianism and philanthropic
endeavors, and even Mahatma Gandhi utilized many Jain practices
such as nonviolence (*ahimsa*) and commitment to truth (*satyagraha*) in
his quest for social justice in India. The first verse of the prominent text
Tattvartha Sutra (*c.*450 CE) encapsulates Jain teaching, highlighting
three jewels: "Right insight, right knowledge, and right action comprise
the path to liberation."[1] These three jewels (*ratna-traya*) are different
from the three "gems" of Buddhism (refuge in the Buddha, *dhamma*,
and *sangha*) and encompass the essence of Jain religiosity. *Samyak
Darshana* comprises right insight into reality; *Samyak Gyana* indicates
right knowledge developed through comprehensive apprehension
of reality; and *Samyak Charita* signifies right conduct (including

abstaining from lying, violence, etc.) for the individual to remove the layers of *karma* from the soul. These three components are intricately linked and guide the conduct of Jains.

Philosophically, Jainism posits two features of human existence that exist in dynamic tension: the soul (*jiva*), which is innately pure and blissful, and *karma*, which takes a distinctly physical form in Jainism. Every time one commits an action, there is a sticky, colorful karmic residue that remains and obscures the pure and blissful nature of the soul. Jain Dharma, or religious teaching, states that the influx of *karmas* causes present and future difficulty. The Jain spiritual path entails the progressive neutralization and eventual elimination of *karmas* so that one may achieve freedom from its influences—a state known as *moksha* or *kevala*.

Many metaphors and parables have been used to describe the ascent to freedom. One metaphor likens the spiritual path to climbing a mountain, leaving below the difficulties of birth, life, death, and rebirth (*samsara*). Another example describes personality types according to the density of their *karmas*. People with the most intransigent *karmas* will exert violence to obtain their desires. People who have purified their *karmas* exhibit the qualities of patience and calmness, taking only what is freely given without the generation of harm. Individuals are urged to become adept at adhering to the Jain vows of nonviolence, truthfulness, non-stealing, sexual propriety, and non-possession. As the troubling *karmas* fall away through this process of spiritual achievement, one gains a radiant transparency.

Jainism can be traced to a very early period in Indian history. The Greek geographers who described Alexander the Great's exploits in India referred to the Jains as "gymnosophists," marveled at their austerity, and commented on the fact that they included women among their accomplished scholars. Megasthenes (*c*.350–290 BCE) noted that the Jains were part of a group known as the *Garmanes* (*Shramanas*), literally "Strivers," who emphasized meditation in distinction from the Brahmins who practiced ritual and textual recitation in Vedic rituals, as has been discussed in the earlier chapter.[2] However, not all Jains renounced the world. Jain laity has been known for its business skills since the early history of Jainism. Early in the history, Jains gained notice as accomplished traders and merchants (known as Banias, though not all Banias are Jains) and even today Jains hold prominence in the business world as publishers, textile manufacturers, jewelers, and producers of pharmaceuticals. They have often played supportive roles in government, contributing particularly to the areas of law and finance. For a short period (*c.*900–1200 CE) in southern and western India, they provided political leadership. Kumarapala, who reigned in Gujarat from 1143 to 1172, converted from Shaivism to Jainism and provided significant support to Jain scholarship at his court.

Establishing accurate dates for major events in Indian history remains difficult. Though we know that the period from 1500 to 300 BCE saw great creativity and the birth of what we refer to today as Hinduism, Jainism, and Buddhism, we have little material evidence of their origins. The obvious reason is that cities and monuments were crafted in wood. Early philosophical and religious compositions were written on palm leaves, all of which have crumbled and turned to dust in the intervening years. The advance of first Greek and then Roman traders into India seems to have introduced stone-based monument sculpture to India. Though the Buddha had forbidden the crafting of images of his personage, Hellenistic traditions eventually prevailed, and the Gandharan civilization—in what is today Afghanistan—produced some of the most spectacular art in world history, including the remarkable *bodhisattva* images and the now-destroyed Bamiyan Buddhas. The Jains, perhaps because of their prominence in the world of trade, were the first to sanction the creation of stone images of their revered religious leaders. The earliest trove of Indian sculptural art—dating from around 300 BCE—can be found in the city of Mathura, south of Delhi, and includes images of the Jinas, the heroic spiritual teachers of the Jain tradition. This tradition of carving and revering stone images continues today among many Jain communities. An examination of the images (*murtis*) found in Jain temples helps to understand the legends and attendant theology of this tradition, particularly when matched with the earliest surviving Jain texts.

Twenty-Four Tirthankaras and the Development of the Tradition

Twenty-Four Tirthankaras

In Jain temples, twenty-four images of nearly identical meditating figures can be found. Known as the Tirthankaras, or "forders of the stream," these individuals embody the pinnacle of Jain spiritual attainment: freedom from all *karma*. Each statue carries a signifier at its base to indicate the particular narrative associated with each religious leader. The twenty-four Tirthankaras are exemplary and represent the bridge to attaining the ultimate freedom.

The first Tirthankara is known as Rishabha (The Bull), or Adinath (The First Teacher). The stories associated with him have been told most elaborately in the ninth-century text, *Adipurana*. This narrative credits Adinath with the following accomplishments: the discovery and implementation of agriculture, government, marriage and other social customs, law, and, eventually, religion. In order to realize the religion that he created, Adinath renounced his kingdom, dividing it into two domains with each ruled by one of his two sons—Bahubali and Bharata. Adinath took up the life of a wandering ascetic, eventually abandoning all possessions, including his clothes, and subsisted on food freely offered. One day, his mother, who had both lamented and celebrated her son's departure, randomly encountered Adinath. Seeing her son caused such an upwelling of joy that she departed her body, ascended to the limits of the universe, and attained the perfect freedom known as *kevala* (a state of eternal consciousness). She became the first liberated human being, or the first *siddha*, which was especially remarkable because this was her first human birth, having dwelt as a microbe in her immediately prior incarnation. (The Jain tradition, like other Dharma traditions, adheres to the belief in the concepts of rebirth, but it has its unique views about *karma*, rebirth, and reincarnation.)

The second *siddha* was Adinath's second son, Bahubali, who fell into a horrible boundary dispute with his brother Bharata. On the verge of total warfare, Bahubali felt immense remorse just before the battle, anticipating the destruction that would inevitably result from assaulting his brother. He stood in the classic meditative pose known as *kayotsarga* ("renouncing the body"), a standing position with elbows slightly akimbo. Bahubali stood there for so long that birds nested in his hair and vines grew up his legs. The world's largest monolithic stone sculpture—crafted from a single block of rock—commemorates this moment. Located in the South Indian pilgrimage city of Shravanabelagola, the Bahubali statue stands 57 feet high on the top of a hill. Every twelve years, a magnificent ritual takes place with the anointing of this statue with vats of red, golden, white, and clear liquids.

Within the Jain tradition, many other influential teachers arose. Jain temples tend to depict the lives of the first and the last three of the twenty-four Tirthankaras because of the available legends of these three teachers. The twenty-second Tirthankara, Neminath, reportedly was a noble cousin of the Hindu god Krishna, and it is believed that Krishna arranged the marriage between Neminath and the princess Rajamati/Rajul. However, on the way to the marriage ceremony Neminath caught a glimpse of the cooking tent. Hundreds of animals were being prepared for slaughter—including goats, chicken, and fish—for the wedding feast. Neminath heard their piteous cries. He quickly associated the wedding with all the agonies of worldly life and immediately stepped away from the nuptial festivities, embarking on the path of nonviolence and meditation. He renounced everything, became a great teacher, and eventually attained final freedom or *kevala*. No historical artifacts or textual records affirm the life and teachings of Neminath or his predecessors. However, historians have established the existence of the twenty-third Tirthankara, Parshvanath, and he has been dated to the eighth century BCE. His narrative will be told later in this chapter.

Lord Mahavira and the Revival of Jain Philosophy

The twenty-fourth and most recent Tirthankara, Mahavira Vardhamana, lived at the same time as the Buddha in approximately 500 BCE. He was known by his followers as a great spiritual warrior, or Jina. The word *Jina* comes from the Sanskrit root *ji*, "to conquer." The goal is to perfect the conquest of *karma* and bring oneself to a state of luminous transparency. Thus, the word Jain derives from the word Jina, the ones who have "conquered" the troubles of *karma* that result in repeated rebirth. The ideal which the Jain monk and nun—and indeed, as far as may be possible for the Jain layperson—strives for is complete imperturbability. But in this dedicated striving a Jain should feel a calm, patient cheerfulness in the knowledge that, whatever the hardship, he or she is wearing away *karma* and preparing for the bliss of full salvation. Thus, the goal of the *jina* requires complete self-control:

If another insults him, a monk should not lose his temper,
For that is mere childishness a monk should never be angry.
If he hears words harsh and cruel, vulgar and painful,
He should silently disregard them, and not take them to heart.
Even if beaten he should not be angry, or even think sinfully,

But should know that patience is best, and follow the Law.
If someone should strike a monk, restrained and subdued,
He should think, "[It might be worse] I haven't lost my life![3]

The Jinas' difficult journey culminates in the achievement of the state of perfection. According to the tradition, all the Tirthankaras, as well as other perfect beings, dwell in the *Siddha Loka*, and are said to exist at the heights of the universe in an eternal state of energy, consciousness, and bliss.

The birth of Mahavira, traditionally dated at 599 BCE, was heralded by a sequence of dreams experienced by his mother Queen Trishala, a woman of the *kshatriya*, or warrior caste. According to some stories, the future Jina lay quietly in his mother's womb to avoid causing her pain, only stirring slightly to assure her that he was alive. As a child in a royal family, he received a good education. According to the Svetambara sect (whose monks wear white robes), he married the princess Yashoda, fathered a daughter named Priyadarshana and then waited until his parents died before renouncing the world. But according to the Digambara sect (whose senior monks go naked), he never married and left home before his parents died. Thus, a difference of renunciation narratives is found in the two sects.

Despite some disagreements, both traditions agree that Mahavira renounced the world at age thirty. According to the Digambaras, he renounced clothing immediately, choosing the life of a naked ascetic, while the Svetambaras say this happened thirteen months into his ascetic practices. He wandered and meditated for twelve years, enduring great hardship, including extended periods of fasting and physical attacks from detractors. After twelve years, he achieved perfect freedom (*kevala*), said to be "infinite, supreme, unobstructed, unimpeded, complete, and full."[4] He lived until the age of seventy, attracting thousands of monastic followers and lay disciples.

Later Developments: The Two Sects

A few generations after Mahavira, Chandragupta, the grandfather of the emperor Ashoka (who adopted the practice of Buddhism and was the catalyst for its dissemination across India and beyond), converted to Jainism. According to the legend, a drought plagued northern India around 350 BCE, and King Chandragupta wandered south to the city Shravanabelagola in the Indian state of Karnataka. Another group of Jains wandered to the west. The two groups lost touch with one another and developed separate literary and ritual traditions. This apparently marks the forming of the two sects in Jainism. The southern group took the name Digambara, sky (*dig*) clad (*ambara*), requiring total nudity of male monastics. Both sects have different versions of the story of Mahavira's renunciation. According to the Digambara sect, Mahavira undertook the life of renunciation while his parents were alive and that his renouncement of clothing was an intentional act, demonstrating control of the senses and abandonment of all shame.

According to the Svetambara sect, Mahavira waited until the death of his parents before renouncing the world to spare them the sorrow of his departure and his nudity was more accidental than intentional in that it was the result of his intense austerities that caused him to lose attention even to his clothes. The monks and nuns of the Svetambara religious orders are white (*sveta*) clad (*ambara*), possessing only a single change of white clothing. The two sects developed different textual and philosophical traditions, though both Digambaras and Svetambaras emphasize the importance of adhering to the five vows. An important difference can be found in their respective teachings on gender. The Svetambaras consider the nineteenth Tirthankara to have been a woman, Mallinath. Digambaras, however, assert that women must be reborn in a male body in order to achieve final liberation. Nonetheless, many women enter Digambara religious orders. Despite having different sacred books and producing distinct teachers and lineages, women have increasingly assumed positions of leadership in both the Digambara and Svetambara communities, which will be discussed later.

Jain Teachings

Nonviolence and Essential Vows

Approximately one or two generations after Mahavira (*c.*400–500 BCE), the earliest texts of the Svetambara sect of Jainism arose: the *Acharanga Sutra* and the *Sutrakritanga*.[5] In this early material, we find statements of fundamental Jain teaching regarding compassion and nonviolence. The Jain scriptural canon was orally passed down for centuries before being written down around the fifth century CE. In this early material, we find statements of fundamental Jain teaching regarding compassion and nonviolence. Lord Mahavira's philosophy, summarized in the

Acharanga Sutra, sets forth an unprecedented biocosmic vision. The text provides the details of how Mahavira carefully observed life as found in animals, plants, and microbes and exhorted his followers to spare life wherever possible in all its myriad forms. He proclaimed, "All beings want to live!" Nonviolence (*ahimsa*) becomes the foundational teaching of Jainism. Furthermore, he set forth careful instructions for the practice of the spiritual life through one's adherence to five vows:

1. The first of the five vows—nonviolence (*ahimsa*)—is said to contain the key to advancement along the spiritual path. Observance of this vow requires abstaining from harming any being that possesses more than one sense-organ and requires a strict vegetarian diet.
2. The second vow—truthfulness (*satya*)—mandates honesty in speech and action.
3. The third vow—non-stealing (*asteya*)—urges Jains not only to avoid taking more than is offered but also to avoid taking more than is needed.
4. The fourth vow—sexual restraint (*brahmacharya*)—allows one to avoid harming other human beings who might be hurt physically or emotionally by a sexual encounter, and also precludes harming the micro-organisms that congregate in the private regions of the body.
5. Lastly, the fifth vow—non-possession (*aparigraha*)—requires that one own only the bare necessities of life.

The *Acharanga Sutra* represents the earliest systematic discussion of nonviolence in India (perhaps throughout the world) and advocates a variety of practices to ensure its observance. These rules, which number into the hundreds, delineate a way of life for Jain monks and nuns that set them apart from virtually all other religious orders.[6] Monks and nuns refrain from killing animals or eating any forms of animal flesh. Additionally, they are urged not to injure the earth or water, kindle or extinguish fires, or "act sinfully to plants."[7] The ascetic, who takes up the life of complete renunciation, is even charged with avoiding harm to bodies borne by wind, which presumably include insects and microorganisms (*nigoda*).[8] Furthermore, monks and nuns are instructed to follow disciplines, including constant wandering except in the rainy season, getting rid of all possessions, and not taking up a permanent abode.[9] Often their possessions are limited to the clothes on their backs and the bowl from which they eat. The most advanced Digambara monks renounce even their clothing and bowl. Jain monastics are restricted in the types of food they may accept, and must carefully inspect all food to make certain that it harbors no obvious additional life forms. In a certain sense, the detailed attention to life, and a fervent avoidance of causing death to any living being, places the Jain practitioner in a state of intimacy with death. Even in the contemporary practice of Jainism, a list of rules promulgated by Acharya Tulsi on January 18, 1991, includes instructions that demonstrate the seriousness with which the Jain community regards practices designed to wear away and disperse one's *karma*.[10]

Purgation of *Karmas*: The Way to Attain Liberation

The *Tattvartha Sutra*, written by Umasvati in approximately 450 CE, succinctly posits the nine core principles of Jain philosophy of *karma*, summarized as follows:

1. Multiple forms of life or souls (*jiva*) have existed since beginningless time. These souls can never be created nor destroyed and will live forever, in birth-after-birth.
2. These souls interact with four non-living forces (*ajiva*): matter/ *karma*, time, space, and movement (*dharma*, which in Jain technical usage refers to the capacity of the soul to vibrate and move).
3. Purposeful actions committed by the soul cause an influx of *karma* (*asrava*) that adheres to the soul, obscuring its innate energy, consciousness, and bliss.
4. These adhesions of *karma* result in the bondage (*bandha*) of the soul.
5. *Karma* may take virtuous or auspicious (*punya*) forms.
6. Karmic particles can be evil or inauspicious (*papa*).
7. The "stoppage" (*samvara*) of the influx of *karma* occurs through adherence to the vows.
8. This results in the sloughing off of *karma* (*nirjara*).
9. Once freed from all *karma*, one enters liberation/freedom (*moksha/ nirvana/kevala*).

In addition to these philosophical principles, the *Tattvartha Sutra* provides geographical and biological views of reality, delineating specific continents, multiple parallel universes, and historical epochs and eons.

Human Life and the Complexity of *Karma*

Umasvati lists 148 different varieties of *karma* that determine the quality, location, and duration of each life. The karmic material shrouds the soul, alters its state of being, and prevents the soul from attaining final liberation. The spiritual quest entails a systematic expulsion (*nirjara*) of all *karma*. Jainism provides minute details regarding the various categories of *karma*. Thirty types of *karma* (with additional subcategories) obstruct the soul in four destructive ways and must be expelled willfully. The negative *karmas* are detrimental to achieving liberation.[11] One's actions determine future birth: in the hellish, earthly, or heavenly realms, or—in the case of freedom from all *karma*—in the realm of transcendence beyond the material world of bondage to *karma*. In the earthly realm, life may be elemental, microbial, vegetative, or locomotive. Life dwells in rocks, clods of earth, drops of water, flowing streams, radiant sunbeams, flickering flames, and gusts of wind. There are also viruses and bacteria, fungi and plants, as well as all manner of insects, fish, reptiles, birds, and mammals, including humans. The *Tattvartha Sutra* places these souls into a hierarchy according to the number of senses of various species. Elemental, microbial, and vegetative souls possess only the sensation of touch. Worms add the sense of taste. Crawling insects also possess smell. Flying insects add the ability to see. Higher-level organisms—including human beings, cows, lions, and birds—can also hear and think.

At the human level, one finds complex descriptions of eight forms of *karma*, classified as knowledge obscuring, insight obscuring, productive of feelings, deluding, age determining, body determining, heredity determining, and power hindering. The categories are further expanded to outline from 148 to 168 sub-varieties of *karma*, said to be colorful, particulate, and sticky. The deeper the hue, the more troublesome the *karma*.

Due to the density of past *karmas*, all individuals, including human beings, arrive in the world cloaked in ignorance, which is the first of the rungs (*gunasthana*) of a fourteen-step ladder. The spiritual path begins at the fourth stage, the awakening of insight (*samyak-drishti*). The fourteen steps are as following:

1. Ignorance (*mithyadrishti*)
2. Forgetfulness of awakening, tending toward descent (*sasvadana-samyagdrishti*)

3. Indifference to awakening (*samyag-mithyadrishti*)
4. Insight or the enlightened moment (may last forty-eight minutes) (*avirati-samyagdrishti*)
5. Partial self-control through adherence to vows (*deshavirata-samyagdrishti*)
6. Self-control with negligence (*pramatta-samyata*)
7. Self-control without negligence (*apramatta-samyata*)
8. Gross passions remain (*anivrtti-badara-samparaya*)
9. Subtle passions remain (*sukshma-samparaya*)
10. No passion, temporary delusion (*upashanta-kasaya-vitaraga*)
11. Action uninfluenced by prior *karma* (*apurvakarana*).
12. No passion, diminished delusion (*kshina kashaya vitaraga*)
13. Remnants of life span, name, feeling, family (*sayoga kevala*)
14. Total freedom (*ayoga kevala*)[12]

At the fourteenth and final stage one attains total freedom, whereby one's soul separates eternally from all remnants of *karma*, exhausting one's life span, and abandoning name, feeling, and family identity. Death for the liberated soul does not result in extinguishment. Rather, one enters into a state of perpetual knowledge, bliss, and energy, unrestrained by the taints of *karma*. Thus, Jain philosophy provides a systematic way to eliminate the layers of *karma* and for attaining total freedom.[13]

The status of the liberated soul remains the object of speculation. Umasvati states that the soul soars to the limits of the universe (*Tattvartha Sutra*, 10.1–7).[14] Padmanabh Jaini notes that "it must be borne in mind that any description of the perfected being, or of the infinite cognition and bliss which characterize him, is purely conventional. In reality such things, lying as they do beyond the space-time limitations of ordinary human consciousness, cannot be described at all."[15] However, scholar Paul Dundas, referring to the early Jain text *Aupapatika*, is careful to point out that Jainism does specify that the soul "rises [...] to the realm of the *siddhas*, the liberated *jivas* at the top of the universe where it will exist perpetually without any further rebirth in a disembodied and genderless state of perfect joy, energy, consciousness and knowledge."[16] He also notes that the Jains are scrupulous in specifying that the individuality of the enlightened soul will continue. Jainism does not entail any merging into a universal soul or state of oneness, which is different from, for instance, the Advaita Vedanta Hindu idea of *moksha*, in which the soul merges into the divine *Brahman*. In Jainism, this ascent results in an eternal state of freedom—an inconceivable yet compelling image.

Jain Philosophy: Multiple Views (*Anekantavada*)

The Jain idea of *Anekantavada* refers to the principle of multiplicity of viewpoints. *Syadvada* (conditioned viewpoints expressed through "perhaps") and *Nayavada* (perspectivalism) are two essential Jain concepts that frame the philosophy of *Anekantavada* (non-absolutism) in Jainism. These two concepts not only hold epistemic value in understanding reality, but are also bound to the ideal of religious tolerance and acceptance of diverse philosophical notions. The concept of *Anekantavada* can be traced back to the teachings of Mahavira. However, this concept is not mere relativism, but rather comprises a way to affirm the multiplicity of points of view. The early Digambara philosopher Kundakunda (*c*.200 CE) posited that reality might be assessed in two ways: a provisional realm of conventional transactions and a sublime realm of higher truth. This approach finds parallels in both Hindu and Buddhist philosophies that share a common concern about how to account for the many ambiguities and seeming contradictions that arise in religious life. For example: Is it better to cultivate societal involvement through observance of teachings on *dharma*? Or is it better to heed the inclination toward worldly renunciation when considering the path of spiritual liberation? Kundakunda sees benefits to both approaches.

Both Svetambara and Digambara Jains assent to the principles of provisional truths and a sevenfold assessment of reality. Most things can be declared possible but retain an indeterminate quality. The following adage captures the spirit of this provisionality: "in a certain way, this particular aspect of an experience or object or feeling may be described, but not all possible aspects can be taken into account through conventional language."[17] In the *Upanishads*, one finds a fourfold analysis of reality: waking, dream, deep sleep, and "the fourth" unspeakable realm of pure consciousness. Nagarjuna's Madhyamaka Buddhism posits a fourfold truth, negating any abiding essence in existence, non-existence, both, and neither. Jain philosophers added two additional components: provisionality of all four descriptions of possible aspects of experience, and the inclusion of three additional caveats recognizing the limitations of language.

For the past 1,500 years, Jains have been careful to take all perspectives into account when engaging in declaratory language. Their philosophy of perspectival provisionality may be summarized as follows:

1. In a certain way, a thing exists (*syad asti eva*)
2. In a certain way, a thing does not exist (*syad nasti eva*)
3. In a certain way, a thing both exists and does not exist (*syad astyeva syannastyeveti*)
4. In a certain way, if existence and nonexistence are taken simultaneously, things are inexpressible (*syad avaktavyam*)
5. Hence, existent and inexpressible
6. Nonexistent and inexpressible
7. Existent, nonexistent, and inexpressible

The first view acknowledges the existence of things within the world and speaks of the waking reality upon which we all presumably agree. The second view, familiar to students of Indian thought but not generally considered in Western analyses, reminds us that the very existence of a thing reminds us of its nonexistence. This book was neither here before it was written, nor will it endure eternally. The third view combines the first two, pointing out that things exist as moments within time but are subject to arising and decay. To speak of a thing purely in its existent phase as if it were eternal would be incorrect; to speak of things disparagingly because they are bound for destruction would represent an equally incorrect, nihilistic view. The fourth view points out that the true nature of a thing can never be expressed adequately; no matter how much I might want to say in order to describe someone dear to me, words fail to do more than denote particular, fragmentary aspects. Even to describe an apple becomes an impossibility. How can one speak of an apple without taking into the account the tree from which it came, the person who planted the tree, the surface of the front of the apple, the surface (unseen) of the back of the apple, the nature of its interior, including its flesh, core, and seeds? The saying, "A rose by any other name is still a rose," becomes in the Jain rendering, "A rose has so many names it is in fact unspeakable." Consequently, once the paradox of ineffability is admitted, each of the earlier views is further qualified: existence is also unspeakable, nonexistence is unspeakable, and the joining of both is also unspeakable.[18]

A beloved version of this philosophy can be found in the story of the six blind men and the elephant, a story that is also found both in Hindu and Buddhist texts. According to this parable, six blind men approach an elephant. One blind man feels the sturdy leg and declares the elephant to be a tree. Another butts up against its side and states it is a wall. Another feels its tail and takes it to be a snake. Another grabs the elephant's ear and uses it as a fan. Each is convinced of his opinion, and yet none of the blind men is completely correct. Similarly, humans may think they have understood a situation, but the complexity of truth always defies simple explanations.

The concern for inflicting no harm can also be seen in an elaborate philosophical system in which claims of unequivocal truth—that can become a harbinger for entrenched presuppositions and prejudices—are called into question. According to Jainism, every occurrence can and must be seen from multiple points of view (naya). A thing exhibits seven qualities that distinguish it from other things.[19] Using the example of a book, the first category would refer to our perception of a book. The second category places the book within a genre of other similar objects. The third sees its function, perhaps as a cookbook. The fourth requires opening it and seeing recipes inside. The fifth proclaims, "this is a cookbook." The sixth looks into the motivations of the author, who presumably wanted to share some techniques and ingredients. The seventh acknowledges that this book was published at a particular time and in a particular place. Jainism emphasizes complexity and a need to regard objects or things in all their depth and implications. H.R. Kapadia referred to the subtlety of Jain philosophy as "intellectual ahimsa."[20] He and others have proclaimed that this thought system makes Jains open to multiple perspectives and innately predisposed to have an attitude of tolerance towards non-Jain views.[21] John Cort has argued against this assertion, pointing out that both the teachings of perspectivalism (naya) and of the many-sided (anekanta), sevenfold analysis advance a specific Jain argument that supports the existence of the soul, the reality of binding karma, and the belief in the possibility of liberation from bondage. This may be viewed as a form of flexible fundamentalism, recognizing that Jains hold firmly to their worldview and its resulting ethic while simultaneously honoring the existence of other systems of thought and practice.[22]

Jain Yoga

The term "yoga" was originally employed in Jain literature to describe the process through which *karmas* adhere to and obscure the soul. In the early centuries of the first millennium, the sense of the word "spiritual practice," as employed in the *Bhagavad Gita* and Patanjali's *Yoga Sutra* gained popularity. Jain authors followed suit, generating analytical and descriptive literature that described Jain forms of spiritual practice as yoga. Haribhadra Virahanka (sixth century) describes a fivefold yoga system in his 527-verse Sanskrit text, the *Yogabindu*. The author explains Jain yoga in a systematic fashion, most notably as a path of purification through which the spiritual aspirant traverses the five steps of self-reflection, cultivation, meditation, equanimity, and the quieting of fluctuations.

The later Jain scholar Hemacandra (1088–1173 CE), who worked under the patronage of the Gujarat Jain king Kumarapala, also employed the frame of Eightfold yoga (similar to that of Patanjali's *Yoga Sutra*, which is discussed in the chapter on Hindu Dharma). Hemacandra's *Yogashastra*—one of the earliest handbooks to include information later popularized in the Hatha yoga texts—starts with an exposition of correct behavior. It correlates Patanjali's *yama* and *niyama* ("ethics" and "observances," above) with Jain ethical practice. It then provides a description of yoga postures and various forms of breath control in great detail. Like Patanjali's system, it describes the accomplishments of inwardness and concentration before itemizing stages of meditation and the final state of release. This attainment of freedom corresponds to Patanjali's eighth and final stage, *samadhi*.

In Jainism, the four yogas of Karma, Raja, Jnana, and Bhakti—which are described in the *Bhagavad Gita*—are also present in their distinctive forms. Jain teachings emphasize the concepts of performing actions with detachment, called Karma yoga. An understanding of the truth of reality and cultivating a state of ongoing equipoise are necessary in this practice. Karma yoga takes the performance of actions in the world very seriously, suggesting that the Jain *yogi* must seek to transform his or her place in the world away from attached action to detached action. Karma yoga requires effort and mindful purification through acts of personal sacrifice (*tapas, yajna*). In a sense, because of their strong adherence to vows, all Jains may be viewed as engaging in Karma yoga.

Meditation, or Raja yoga, finds modern Jain expression in the practice of *Preksha* Meditation, focusing on pure and impartial perception. Generally practiced for forty-eight minutes each morning, it entails a sequence of breathing exercises and visualizations. Breathing is diaphragmatic, and one performs alternate nostril breathing as outlined in the small book *Preksha Dhyana: Perception of Breathing*. Acharya Mahaprajna (1920–2010), who introduced this system in modern times, sets forth these two primary techniques as "perception of slow and deep breathing or *dirgha-shvasa-preksa*" and "perception of breathing through alternate nostrils or *samavrtti-shvasa-preksa*."[23] The *preksha* meditation system blends contemporary physiology with color theory, aura assessment, *chakras* (energy centers), *kundalini* (coiled energy) *asanas* (yogic postures), and *pranayama* (breathing exercises). These practices fall under the general instructions given for meditation in Hindu texts, such as the *Yoga Sutra* and the sixth chapter of the *Bhagavad Gita*, referred to collectively as Raja yoga. *Preksha* meditation provides an avenue to accomplish the central goal of the Jain tradition: the expulsion of deleterious *karmas* from the mind-body continuum.

The practice of Jnana yoga can be found in another branch of contemporary Svetambara Jainism. Acharya Shiv Muni and his assistant, Shri Shirish Muniji Maharaj, teach a form of meditation on the mantra *so 'ham* (that I am), the very same "great saying" (*mahavakya*) found in the *Upanishads*. The term *So* here refers to the perfected beings in the *Siddha Loka*. The emphasis on the inviolability of the soul bears a strong resemblance to the Jnana yoga, which focuses on the indestructible and divine nature of the soul.

Bhakti yoga, in the Jain context, is regarded as being closely related to the pan-Indian cultural practice of taking *darshan*. This process has been defined as such by Diana Eck: "to stand in the presence of the deity and to behold the image with one's own eyes, to see and be seen by the deity."[24] Taking *darshan* in Jain temples in North America or India entails standing, sitting, and bowing before images of the Tirthankaras and deities—such as the goddess Padmavati—but also to be present in the company of a great teacher, or *guru*. The central devotional prayer of the Jains, the *Namaskara Mantra*, celebrates veneration of the Tirthankaras and *siddhas* who have left the body but can be represented in sculpture, as well as the living teachers (*acharyas*), preceptors (*upadhyayas*), monks (*sadhus/munis*) and nuns (*sadhvis*).[25] Lawrence Alan Babb has written eloquently about the non-expectation in worship that characterizes Jain religiosity in his book *Absent Lord: Ascetics and Kings in a Jain Ritual Culture*. Because of the thoroughgoing voluntarist philosophy of Jainism—meaning Jains are supposed to be self-reliant seekers who ask no assistance from God or teacher—all spiritual advancement must be generated from the will of one's own soul.[26] Unlike other Hindu schools of Bhakti yoga, for the Jains, inspiration may be found in the example of others, but no material help can be expected from liberated beings or even living monks or nuns. In this respect, Jain practice is different from the Hindu practice of devotion or supplication for favors and grace. Whitney Kelting states that Jain devotion may be seen as an act of mimesis, in that Jain women—by creating and singing hymns (*stavan*) to the saints of the tradition—hope to take on their qualities.[27]

Women and Gender

The role and status of women may be viewed from two perspectives, human and divine. Two lifestyles are available for women: married life and the life of a nun. Overwhelmingly, Jain women choose to become wives, generally entering into marriage by the age of twenty, most often arranged by the parents. The ideal wife is said to be a "partner, lover, confidant, and soul-mate" to her husband.[28] As Kelting states:

> It is considered most important that a *pativrata* (wife) be completely faithful to her husband and produce sons by her husband for the benefit of her husband's lineage. The expectation spans the entire life span of a woman; a woman should have no other romantic involvement before, during, or after her marriage [...] [T]here is also an expectation of complete emotional fidelity, which includes not being emotionally intimate with other men, not being seen with men outside the family, and not speaking badly about one's husband. This fidelity is extended beyond a husband's death, for widows.[29]

Wives and mothers are responsible for the spiritual atmosphere within the home as well as being the prime communicators of Jain teachings and values. Women frequently visit temples, where they meet with other women to sing and share with one another their devotional compositions known as *stavan*.[30] Women also engage in complex fasts to ensure auspiciousness within the home, including taking only bland foods (*Ayambil Oli*)[31] and completing a "full fast with no food at all (*Upvas*)"[32] for up to seven days or even a month.

Some young women and some widows decide to enter monastic life, a process that normally requires years of discernment. As with monks, Jain nuns dedicate themselves to a life of great rigor, no longer preparing food for themselves or others. They renounce all ornamentation, wearing only a simple white garment. They wear no shoes and forego any artificial means of conveyance, by not accepting rides and always moving about on foot. Many nuns will carry a kerchief to cover their mouths while speaking to avoid harm to the many life forms found in the air, and a broom to sweep insects safely out of harm's way. Twice each year they will pluck out their hair. It is customary for nuns to travel in twos, staying only three days at a time in one locale except during the rainy season when they will take shelter at a safe, friendly place provided by the lay Jain community, perhaps adjacent to a temple or in a purpose-built shelter. Each day Jain nuns commit themselves to six observances:

1. *Samayika* (equanimity)
2. *Chaturvimshatistava* (praise of the twenty-four Tirthankaras)
3. *Vandana* (homage to the teacher)
4. *Pratikramana* (repentance of faults and negligence)
5. *Kayotsarga* (abandonment of comforts of body)
6. *Prayakhyan* (renunciation)

By committing themselves to a life of monasticism, Jain nuns seek to purge their karmic involvement with worldly life, connecting with the realm of divinity. One novice nun, when asked about her decision, told Professor Anne Vallely, "I don't want to marry—it would be impossible. I don't want to be in worldly life. I want to study and practice *sadhana* (spirituality)."[33]

Both laywomen and nuns look to narratives of spiritual women—either as humans or as goddesses—for inspiration. As noted earlier, the first person to achieve the goal of freedom from all *karma* was Marudevi, the mother of Rishabha, the first Tirthankara. Rishabha is said to have fathered one hundred sons and two daughters. One daughter, Buddhi, invented reading and writing. The other, Sundari, created the science of mathematics. Contemporary Jains point to this story to explain the high degree of educational attainment found among Jain women in the present time. According to Svetambara tradition, the nineteenth Tirthankara, Mallinath, was a woman.

Many Svetambara narratives, after explaining complex exploits including successive births and rebirth, state that husband and wife take vows of renunciation in their old age and then achieve liberation. The story of Neminath, the twenty-second Tirthankara and the cousin of Krishna who renounced the world on the way to his wedding, includes such a narrative. His wife-to-be, Rajamati/Rajul, was left,

> standing at the threshold of her house. Rajul lamented her fate, but after fifty-one days, when Nemi obtained omniscience and it was clear that he was not returning, Rajul resolved to follow Nemi to Girnar and renounce with him. Finally, Rajul and Nemi achieved liberation at their deaths on the same day and were, in a sense, reunited.[34]

This story demonstrates Jain certainty that women are spiritual co-equals with men.

Jain material culture also attests to the worship of goddesses. The caves of Khandagiri near Bhubhaneshwara (c.800 CE) link seven goddesses with seven of the twenty-four Tirthankaras. The contemporary cosmological temples constructed in Hastinapur by the Digambara nun Pujya Ganini Shri Gyanmati Mataji include a female companion for each of the Tirthankaras, evoking a semblance of the liberated soul (jiva/purusha) still in proximity of material creation (prakriti). At the entrance to many Jain temples, one will find altars in honor of Sarasvati and Sri/Lakshmi, the pan-Indian goddesses of knowledge and wealth, as well as Jain-only goddesses such as Padmavati (explained below) and Cakreshwari (Goddess of the Wheel). Within the worship space of some temples, including the Jain Center of Southern California, one can find the images of sixteen Vidya-dharas, the goddesses or Yakshis of protection and inspiration.

The goddess Padmavati brings an element of the feminine into the abiding temple iconography associated with the twenty-third Tirthankara, Parshvanath. Over the course of many lifetimes, the king Dharanendra and his wife Padmavati assisted Parshvanath as he progressed toward the final goal of perfect freedom. Parshvanath as a young prince encountered a nemesis from a past life, Kamath, a yogi, who was engaging in a five-fire ceremony. Kamath placed himself in the midst of four sacrificial fires and was himself generating heat (*tapas*). Parshvanath criticized this practice, saying that the fires were causing harm to living beings. He urged the removal of a log from one of the fires, and when it was split open, two snakes emerged and died. Kamath was reborn as Meghamali, the king of clouds, and the snakes were reborn as Dharanendra and Padmavati, King and Queen of Cobras. At the age of thirty, Parshvanath renounced the world, therefore angering Meghamali, who then sent wild animals to disturb the former prince's meditations. Parshvanath remained steadfast. In a rage, Meghamali sent a powerful monsoon downpour in an attempt to drown Parshvanath. The King of the Cobras lifted him from below, and his wife rose up from the water's bottom to shield Parshvanath with her many hoods. This miraculous collaboration spared Parshvanath and won the Cobra Queen a special place in the Jain narrative. She inspired the construction of many temples dedicated solely to her, which are found throughout India.

The status of women in the Jain Dharma is complex. In the realm of total freedom, the *Siddha Loka*, all sexual differentiations disappear. In the transactional realm of the heavens, gods and goddesses alike can be found. In the human realm, some women find spiritual fulfillment as wives, some as nuns. From the beginning, as indicated in the *Kalpa Sutra*, nuns outnumbered monks by at least two to one; at the time of Mahavira's death, 36,000 women and 14,000 men had taken monastic vows.[35] Women continue to hold leadership roles in monastic communities, and laywomen remain primarily responsible for the key marker of Jain religiosity: the preparation of vegetarian food.

The Ethical Challenge of Jainism: End of Life (*Sallekhana*) and the Ultimate Freedom

The Jain attitude toward death holds that the soul can never be killed and that the falling away of the body is inevitable. Some Jains prepare for death by gradually fasting up to the end of their lives. The Digambara community refers to the practice as *Sallekhana*, which literally means the "thinning out of existence," while the Svetambara community refers to the practice as *Santhara*, or "passing over" or "crossing." Each community has developed particular rules for gaining permission to start this final fast. The vow of *Sallekhana* is a rare

practice, observed only by some devout Jain ascetics or householders at
the end of life that entails gradually reducing intake of food and
liquids. It is considered that *Sallekhana* leads to the highest practice of
ahimsa as the practitioner seeks to detach from all passions and desires.
It cannot be undertaken unless approved by the community and, in
the case of some Digambara renouncers, one must leave one's own
monastic group and conduct the fast with the assistance of some other
monastic community that agrees to facilitate the process. The Jains do
not consider this practice to be a form of suicide.

The most frequently quoted text regarding the Jain practice of
fasting to death is the *Ratnakarandaka Shravakacara*, written by
Samantabhadra in the second century CE. It provides details for this
practice:

> One should give up gradually all solid foods, increase the taking of
> liquids like milk, then give up even liquids gradually and take warm
> water. Thereafter, one should give up warm water also, observe the fast
> to the best of one's ability with determination and depart from the body
> repeating the *namaskara mantra* continuously until the last.[36]

One thousand years later, the *Purushartha Siddhyupaya* of Acharya
Amritchandra also instructs the reader in the practice. Acharya
Amritchandra makes clear to the reader that this is not a form of
suicide, but rather a deep expression of religious faith.[37] In Jain
cosmology, the practitioner aspires to expel all of one's *karma* to
eventually reach the state of eternal liberation from the cycle of birth,
death, and rebirth (*samsara*). The path of Jainism includes many
disciplines to reduce one's *karma*, such as vegetarianism, fasting, and
adherence to the five vows including nonviolence and truthfulness.
During the final phases of one's life, the Jain tradition urges more
rigorous practice to ensure the most auspicious course for one's death.

In the late fall of 1989, I found myself amidst a crowd of a
hundred-or-so Jain monks and nuns, gathered around an octo-
genarian, a white-clad female monastic who was physically propped
up by her sixty-year-old daughter—also a nun—to receive blessings
from their *guru*, Acharya Tulsi (1914–97). The emotion in the room
was palpable. Through the words carefully chosen by S.L. Gandhi
to translate the *acharya*'s message from Hindi into English, the
following details were revealed: this woman, Sadhvi Kesharji, had
entered the Jain monastic life more than fifty years prior, raising
her young daughter within the monastic community. As with all

members of the Svetambara Terapanthi (a sub-sect of Svetambara Jainism) nuns, she abided by all the great rules of her faith, taking care not to commit harm to any living beings, to be truthful and honest, to remain celibate, and to refuse all possessions beyond a simple change of clothes, a bowl for food, and a few books. For decades, she had wandered the length and breadth of India, without shoes, speaking only from behind a mouth covering (a tradition of covering one's mouth with a white cloth to avoid any violence to microbes), and accepting food only freely given by lay Jains. With no home, no kitchen, no husband, and as a single mother, she transcended the many identities associated with being a woman living in the physical world to choose instead a life that focused on the care of her soul.

According to the teachings of Acharya Tulsi, as communicated to me that day, the soul can never die. This worthy nun had purified her *karma* and had reached a state of great happiness, sufficient to prepare her for this last ordeal in this life. Although the *sadhvi* (female ascetic) had been diagnosed with a terminal form of kidney disease, her life force would never perish: it would assume a new form when this particular body ceased living. Four weeks before my arrival in the desert town of Ladnun, Rajasthan India, she had undertaken the religiously sanctioned vow of fasting unto death. Acharya Tulsi praised her resolve, noted her cheeriness, and affirmed that this final act would hasten the process of karmic purification. Eating—even while observing the careful vegetarian diet practiced by Jains worldwide— always entails some violence: to vegetables, to grains, to cows, to the microbes that fester in yogurt, and even the violence committed by cooking fires kindled by the laywomen who prepare the food. By setting aside all nutrition and hydration, this nun welcomed death with bravery. In the words of Acharya Tulsi, she affirmed the greatest of Jain teachings: nonviolence is the greatest vow and the soul (*jiva*) can never be destroyed. Through Sallekhana, the soul of the practitioner is liberated from the bondage of negative *karma*.

For Jains, a good death entails entering into one's next birth fully conscious. According to the Jain tradition, one's state of mind at the point of death, as well as the quality of life lived in the last quarter of one's existence, predetermines the next birth. Acharya Tulsi explained in a subsequent conversation that Sadhvi Kesharhji would move instantly to her next life—a good life buoyed by years of monastic practice. The human body is a vehicle for the life-force (the soul or spirit). The life force passes from one form to another, and the body is to be cherished as a worthy home for the soul: all spiritual work takes place within the body. Ultimately, however, the body must be left behind, either to find a new host or to ascend to the *Siddha Loka*, a place of perfect freedom.

This aspect of Jain spirituality continues to set the Jain tradition apart from all others in Indian traditions. Voluntary death through fasting is an option in the Jain tradition when death is imminent due to disease, or when one is unable to function self-sufficiently. In the case of Jain monks, the fast might commence when one is no longer able to abide by monastic rules governing nonviolent behavior due to debilitating old age or infirmity. The fast unto death generally takes place at the close of an average lifespan. It would be unacceptable for a young, healthy person to enter the final fast. Due to the Jain teaching on the eternal nature of the soul, the final fast can be seen both as a rite of transition into a new life as well as a rite of incorporation that affirms the strength of the surviving family members' religious commitment.

The observance of this vow underscores the radical nature of the Jain theory of the human person. According to Jainism, the pure essence of a person resides in the *jiva*, or soul, which possesses infinite consciousness, energy, and bliss. This soul is eternal and uncreated but becomes trapped and defined by obscurations of *karma*. The purpose of Jain asceticism is to struggle with this *karma* that fences in and restricts the soul and causes the soul to be reborn repeatedly. By battling against *karma* through the adherence to the vows of nonviolence and the other ethical disciplines, past *karma* is gradually released.

The fast unto death dramatically illustrates the unique perspective held by adherents to the Jain faith: utter aloneness (*kevala*) and self-determinism. Each individual soul is autonomous, and its perspective can never be shared by any other soul. The soul owes no debt to any creator, as Jainism does not postulate a belief in a creator god. The soul, therefore, can only blame itself for pain, and can credit only itself for pleasure. For the Jain community, fasting to death celebrates a life well lived and emphasizes key aspects of Jain philosophy. First, it demonstrates a willingness to devote oneself in a final and lasting way to the observance of nonviolence because by not eating, no harm is done to any living being. Second, it functions to burn off residues of *karma* that otherwise would impede the soul and cause further bondage. It purifies the soul by releasing the fetters of past attachment (*nirjara*).

According to the *Bhagavati Aradhana* of Shivakotiacharya, the right situation must exist for one to enter into the process of ritual death. One of three occasions are deemed suitable: (1) suffering from an incurable disease, (2) encountering severe famine, or (3) facing impossible conditions to sustain the spiritual life. Acarya Samantabhadra's *Ratnakarandaka Shravakacara* lists similar requirements: calamity, famine, senility, incurable or unbearable disease, and inability to follow spiritual precepts.[38] When S. Settar typologizes the historical deaths documented in the inscriptions at Shravanabelagola (a historic Jain pilgrimage site) in South India, he lists four categories:

1. Sensed the imminence of death
2. Suffered an accident, more or less fatal in nature
3. Realized the impossibility of sustaining the spiritual life
4. Experienced emotional hurt or disillusionment in life

This last category goes beyond the strict reading of the textual sources and might be categorized as a foolish death in some circumstances. Nonetheless, some persons have entered the final fast for this reason and have been lauded by the tradition. Settar notes that "when Queen Shantala died her mother Macikabbe sustained a deep emotional hurt, and this led her to decide not to 'remain behind' in the world ...."[39] Her final fast took place in the early twelfth century, resulting from the realization of the ephemeral nature of the world. Saint Nandisena (seventh century) "realized the illusive character of this world," and declared: "Fleeting are the treasures of beauty, pleasure, wealth and power, like the rainbow, like the streaks of lightning or like the dew. I do not like to prolong my existence on this earth".[40] According to the inscription, he then fasted to death.

The process of entering the final fast is not random: it requires years of physical and mental preparation. Years of study (*svadhyaya*), humility brought through discipline (*vinaya*), control of mind (*samadhi*), and increasing competence in meditation (*bhavana*) all take a significant length of time to cultivate. As Settar notes, "All these involve a long period of intense meditation on the self [...] This slow process, involving gradual and guarded subjugation of the mind, may extend over as long a period as twelve years."[41] For the final phase of this process, one gains permission to leave one's home cluster of monks and join another order (*gana*). A supervisor, known as a *niryapak acharya*, is appointed to be the overseer and counselor for the candidate, known as a *kshapaka* (translated by Settar to mean "aspirant for the destruction of the *karmas*").[42] A place for the final fast is chosen carefully—often a cave or a hut—which, after the tenth or eleventh century, was often a location with "specially erected pavilions or mandaps [a tent or stage]."[43] The supervisor slowly weans the candidate away from food. The ritual begins with the abandonment of solid foods, taking only liquid foods and eventually resorting to complete fasting. The supervisor encourages and strengthens the will of the fasting person by providing spiritual support.[44]

Some have regarded this entry into a final fast as a form of religious extremism. The High Court of Rajasthan forbade its practice in 2015, though the decision has been set aside and the case has been taken to the Supreme Court on appeal. However, some practical wisdom may also be found in this tradition. In the developed world, medical procedures often prolong the inevitable process of dying, sometimes causing great discomfort to the patient and the patient's family. The modern world's path to death has become a dance of avoidance. Some data suggests that in the United States, the last six months of life take away approximately half of the nation's total medical expenditures. The Jain art of conscious dying, which requires an acceptance of the inescapability of the decline and decay of the body, might help inform and further inspire the hospice movement and point toward acceptance rather than denial of death.

Jainism and Social Issues: Animal Protection and Ecology

The unique cosmology of Jainism predisposes its adherents to see the soul as making a pilgrimage toward freedom through various life forms including animals. Jain cosmology consists of a storied universe in the shape of a female figure. In the lower domains of the pelvis, legs, and feet can be found seven hells wherein souls suffer due to their self-inflicted negative *karmas*. In the region of the solar plexus, one finds the earthly realm, or middle world (*manushya-loka*), consisting of three continents and two oceans. Animals and humans can be found here. Through good actions, well-meaning humans can ascend to numerous heavenly realms. Those with remarkable resolve may even escape the wheel of life and death and enter the state of perfect freedom.

The treatment of animals receives close attention. Harming animals densifies one's *karma*. The benevolent treatment of animals advances one along the spiritual path. The first part of the *Acharanga Sutra*—representing the earliest stratum of Jain literature (fourth or fifth century BCE)—offers an eloquent and detailed appeal for the benevolent treatment of animals:

> Some slay animals for sacrificial purposes, some slay animals for the sake of their skin, some kill them for the sake of their flesh, some kill them for the sake of their blood; others for the sake of their heart, their bile, the feathers of their tail, their tail, their big or small horns, their teeth, their tusks, their nails, their sinews, their bones; with a purpose and without a purpose. Some kill animals because they have been wounded by them, or are wounded, or will be wounded. He who injures these animals does not comprehend and renounce the sinful acts; he who does not injure these, comprehends and renounces the sinful acts. Knowing them, a wise man should not act sinfully towards animals, nor cause others to act so, nor allow others to act so.[45]

This respect for animals pervades Jain literature and philosophy, and the Jain tradition even came to associate most of its twenty-four Tirthankaras with a particular animal.[46] Although stories of each of these are not readily available in English translation, a listing of the names and their attendant animals conveys a sense of the centrality of these animals in the tradition. For example, the first Tirthankara is associated with a bull, the second with an elephant, the twenty-third with a snake, and the last, Lord Mahavira, with a lion. It is similar to those Hindu deities who are associated with various animals and creates a sense of connection with the animal kingdom. The Jain tradition, due to its emphasis on personal asceticism, seems a somewhat unlikely candidate for social activism. However, individual Jains, both lay and monastic, have been strong advocates for changing the status quo throughout its history, particularly regarding the treatment of animals and in defense of religious pluralism.

In order to enhance one's spiritual advancement and avoid negative karmic consequences, the Jain religion advocates benevolent treatment of animals. According to the Jain Sutra, monks and nuns are not allowed even to lift their arms or point their fingers while wandering from village to village. It has been said, "This is the reason: the deer, cattle, birds, snakes, animals living in water, on land, in the air might be disturbed or frightened."[47] In Jain texts, passage after passage has Jain teachers exhorting their students, particularly monks and nuns, to avoid causing harm to all living creatures. The speaking, walking, eating, and eliminatory habits of the Jain monks and nuns all revolve around a pervasive concern not to harm life in any form. Ultimately, the ideal death for a Jain, lay or monastic, is the fast unto death, which allows for a conscious transition to the next birth without creating any harm to living beings.

Manifestations of this concern for nonviolence can be found in the institutions of the *pinjrapole* (animal hospital) and the *goshala* (cow shelter). Perhaps the most visible of such institutions can be found in the commercial district of Old Delhi, India. Rescued birds are brought there for rehabilitation, given food, water, splints for broken wings, and medicine as needed. More than three thousand other animal shelters operated by Jains can be found throughout India. Some specialize in cows, others in insects. Many of the *pinjrapoles*—particularly in the state of Gujarat—include insect rooms. These rooms serve as receptacles for dust sweepings brought by Jains. Knowing that these sweepings will include small insects, they will bring them to the *pinjrapole* where they are placed in a closed room and sometimes given grain for sustenance. When the room is full, it is shuttered and locked for up to fifteen years. At the end of this waiting period it is assumed that "all life will have come to its natural end," and the contents are then sold as fertilizer.[48] This reflects the depth of concern that Jains feel for preserving life forms. The origins of the Jain *pinjrapole* are somewhat difficult to trace. It could have developed in the early phases of Jainism (Ashoka's inscriptions from the third century BCE show similar concerns for animal welfare) or during the apex of Jainism, which lasted from the fifth to the thirteenth centuries. In the state of Gujarat, a succession of kings gave state patronage to Jainism, such as Mandalika of

Saurashtra in the eleventh century and Siddharaj Jaisinh, King of
Gujarat, and his son and successor, Kumarapala, in the twelfth
century. Kumarapala (1125–59) declared Jainism the state religion of
Gujarat and passed extensive animal welfare legislation.

To give both an historical perspective and a modern view of the Jain
pinjrapole, the Gazetteer of the Bombay Presidency lists the following
animals in the Ahmedabad Pinjrapole at the beginning of 1875: "265
cows and bullocks, 130 buffalo, 5 blind cattle, 894 goats, 20 horses,
7 cats, 2 monkeys, 274 fowl, 290 ducks, 2,000 pigeons, 50 parrots,
25 sparrows, 5 kites (hawks), and 33 miscellaneous birds."[49] Exactly
one century later, one finds the situation little changed, with similar
lists of animals and a board of directors (exclusively Jain) continuing to
employ the services of a bookkeeper to keep track of the accounts and
seeking financial support from various prominent businesspeople and
trade organizations. Vegetarianism has long been the primary
distinguishing practice of the Jain community. As advocates against
animal sacrifice for centuries, Jains have campaigned tirelessly for
animal welfare and, more recently, broader ecological causes. With the
advent of industrialized agriculture, they have called into question the
usage of food produced from milk.

A revision of the traditional Jain practice of dietary nonviolence
has been championed by Pravin K. Shah, an influential educator
within the American Jain community. Shah, visiting a dairy farm
in Vermont, became appalled at the poor treatment of cattle in
contemporary agricultural practice. He also personally struggled with
an elevated cholesterol count. In seeking to remedy both ills, he
posted an influential essay on the Internet urging the Jain community
to adopt a vegan diet. He notes that in order to maximize milk
production cows are kept continually pregnant and that many
hormones and drugs are used. Additionally, mother cows are killed
after producing milk for four years, and approximately three-quarters
of their calves are killed within six months to produce veal and to
reduce the overall number of cattle.[50] Shah also criticizes the harmful
effects of dairy farming. Negative aspects include the waste generated
by the slaughter process (230,000 pounds per second), the green-
house gases produced by the world's cattle herds (100 million tons of
methane per year), the excessive amount of water required for
livestock (2500 gallons per pound of meat compared with 60 gallons
for a pound of potatoes), and the vast amount of land given over to

grazing. Shah proclaims that "Jainism in Action is an eco-friendly religion which preserves and protects the Earth and Environment, respects the lives of animals, birds, fish and other beings, and promotes the welfare of society through the application of its primary tenets of Ahimsa and Non-possessiveness."[51] This modernization of the tradition combines good citizenship with a romantic view of nature, neither of which originates from the tradition itself, but can be seen as presenting a good rationale for becoming vegan.

Jainism and Its Broad Appeal

Even though Jain Dharma has a strong tradition of asceticism, historically its teachings have inspired social change. During periods of Mughal rule in India, Jain financiers and advisors helped protect the status of the Jain community, avoiding the degree of persecution suffered by the Sikhs and many Hindus in the hands of the Mughals. The Jain monk Hiravijaya Suri (1527–95) even persuaded Emperor Akbar to declare the observance of Paryushan— the annual seven-day Jain observance of repentance—to be an imperial holiday of sorts and ordered the closure of slaughterhouses for its duration. In modern times, Mahatma Gandhi—a global symbol of nonviolent resistance for social justice because of his role in liberating India from British colonialism through the enactment of nonviolent principles—was profoundly influenced by the Jain tradition. He sought to eschew all forms of violence in his personal life and used the methods of nonviolence and truth (*ahimsa* and *satyagraha*) for fighting against political and social injustices. He even titled his lengthy autobiography *The Story of My Experiments with Truth*. He learned of Jainism during his childhood in Gujarat (an Indian state with a large Jain presence) and from Raichandra, a prominent Jain lay teacher. In his writings, Gandhi gives high praise to Raichandra for his lessons in combining spiritual life with worldly engagement.

Another modern example of social engagement, Acharya Tulsi (1914–97), promulgated a campaign known as the Anuvrat movement in 1949. He saw that newly independent India needed a moral compass, and he distilled and reinterpreted the standard Jain precepts for contemporary times. Though carrying no legislative weight, they remain a talking point for the process of making moral decisions and have influenced monastic and lay leaders within the Terapanthi Svetambara community (a Jain sect, which is aniconic and emphasizes vows and rules of moral conduct). The vows are eleven in number, with explanatory subdivisions:

1. I will not deliberately kill any innocent creature (includes suicide and feticide).
2. I will not attack anyone (non-support of aggression; advocacy of disarmament).
3. I will not take part in violent agitation or any destructive activity.
4. I believe in human unity (no discrimination allowed based on color, race, gender, or caste).
5. I will practice religious tolerance (no sectarian violence).
6. I will be honest in business and general behavior (commit no harm or deception).
7. I will practice continence and limit material possessions.
8. I will not apply unethical means in elections.
9. I will not encourage or practice evil social customs.
10. I will lead a life free from addiction (no alcohol, drugs, or tobacco).
11. I will strive to minimize environmental pollution (no cutting of trees; no wasting water).

The final vow, "not to pollute," indicated that Acharya Tulsi was ahead of his time. During a private interview in 1989, he stated that his lifestyle and that of his monks and nuns presented the best alternative to resource-intensive consumerism. With just one change of clothes, miniature books that could only be viewed with a magnifying glass, and minimal eating utensils, he claimed that the abstemious practices of his community rendered negligible harm to the environment.[52] Simplified versions of these vows were prepared over a number of years for students, teachers, business people, officers, employees, voters, and for those interested in spiritual practice. These vows function similarly to the Quaker queries and the Jesuit Examen in that they prompt a reckoning with one's conscience in a systematic fashion. Though perhaps originally intended as a social movement with broad impact, they have served to sharpen attention within the worldwide Terapanthi community to the wider implications of Jain moral teachings.

With the liberalization of India's economy and the consequent advent of globalization in 1991, pollution rose to alarming levels by the end of the 1990s. Dr. L.M. Singhvi, a member of a blended Hindu-Jain family, used his prominence in the fields of law and government to draw attention to this issue. He served as High Commissioner (Ambassador) from India to the United Kingdom in the 1990s and was a member of India's Parliament for many years. He was tireless in his advocacy of Jain causes. He presented the "Jain Declaration on Nature"[53] to Prince Philip in 1990 on the occasion of Jainism's participation in the World Wildlife Fund Network on Conservation and Religion. It was reprinted in 2002 as the appendix to the book *Jainism and Ecology*. The Declaration outlines the core principles of Jainism, reframing them as dialogue partners in the emerging discourse on religion and ecology. The Declaration states that Jainism presents an ecological philosophy and consequently summarizes various aspects of the faith in light of its particular attention to nature. The first part discusses Jain teachings on nonviolence, interdependence, recognition of multiple perspectives, emphasis on equanimity, and commitment to compassion, empathy, and charity. The second section provides a synopsis of Jain biological categories as delineated earlier in this chapter. The third and final part highlights the Jain Code of Conduct as an exemplary method for bringing about environmental justice. Key aspects include the restatement of the five Jain vows (described earlier in this chapter), the history of Jain kindness to animals, the Jain advocacy of vegetarianism, the teachings on restraint and avoidance of waste, and finally, the value of charity in the tradition.

A prominent contemporary Jain-influenced environmentalist is Satish Kumar. Kumar became a Jain monk at the age of nine. He remained within his order until the age of eighteen when he left the Terapanth Svetambara monks to pursue a life dedicated to social change. He worked with the land distribution movement of Vinoba Bhave (a social activist who was a close follower of Gandhi) and then became an anti-nuclear activist, walking from Delhi through Pakistan and Afghanistan to the heart of the Soviet Union, pleading with officials in Moscow to end the production of nuclear weapons. He then walked to Paris and from there spoke with government officials in London and Washington, DC, canvassing the four extant nuclear powers in the 1960s, in an attempt to bring conscience to bear upon the blind building of horrific stockpiles of weapons.[54] Eventually, Satish Kumar settled in the UK, and in 1991 he established Schumacher College. For more than a dozen years, this Gandhian-inspired center for graduate studies has conducted programs focusing on environmental sustainability. In an essay titled "Jain Ecology," Satish Kumar interprets the five traditional vows (*vratas*) in light of an ecological application. He writes that *ahimsa* "means avoiding contact with scenes of cruelty and refraining from activities that cause pain and disharmony."[55] He states: "Living in truth (*satya*) means that we avoid manipulating people or nature."[56] Not stealing (*asteya*) "means refraining from acquiring goods or services beyond our essential needs [...] If you take more from nature than meets your essential need, you are stealing from nature."[57] He states that sexual restraint (*brahmacharya*) "not only recognizes the dignity of the human body but also the body of nature" and that non-possession (*aparigraha*) allows one to become free "from nonessential acquisitions and from materialism."[58]

This interpretation of Jain religious principles in light of environmental concerns reveals what appears to be a natural extension of the tradition. However, the actual application of these principles requires a complex process of decision making. For instance, Mahatma Gandhi, an advocate for the mercy killing of animals in cases of extreme pain, came under severe criticism from the Jain community who claimed that the violence required to end the life of an animal far outweighed the *karma* of allowing nature to take its course. In his work at Schumacher College, Satish Kumar has foregrounded the contemporary rhetoric of environmentalism, though his inspiration draws deeply (if quietly) from his Jain roots. The College's mission statement expresses a need to bring about social change through a deeper connection with oneself and one's relationship with the Earth:

> Schumacher College was founded in 1991 on the conviction that a new vision is needed for human society and its relationship with the earth [...] The College offers rigorous inquiry to uncover the roots of the prevailing world view; it explores ecological approaches that value holistic rather than reductionistic perspectives and spiritual rather than consumerists values [...] A unified residential education offering physical work, mediation, aesthetic experience and intellectual inquiry creates a sense of the wholeness of life.[59]

Another example of social activism can be found in the Jain involvement in the free distribution of prostheses. The Jain community has been at the forefront of the crafting of high quality prosthetics. Jaipur Foot was established in 1975.[60] Its founder, D.R. Mehta, was given the Magsaysay Award and the Padma Bhushan Award in 1981—the highest civilian honors bestowed in Asia and India, respectively. Jaipur Foot has provided, free of charge, 1.3 million artificial legs and feet to those in need, primarily in India but also in other parts of Asia, Africa, and Latin America. To the extent that life has been enhanced through the use of free distribution of these prosthetic limbs, the Jain community has embraced one of the key tenets of modern humanism, namely to use technology in a quest to improve the quality of life.

Global Jainism

The Jain tradition has spread far from its original home in India, which began when Jains moved to East Africa for business opportunities during the time of the British Raj. Jainism first came to America when Virchand Raghavji Gandhi (Mahatma Gandhi's contemporary and the earliest emissary of Jainism to the US) spoke at the 1893 World Parliament of Religions in Chicago. In 1933, Champat Rai Jain presented his talk *"Ahimsa* as the Key to World Peace" at a meeting of the World Fellowship of Faiths. Migrations to the UK and Canada continued as allowed by Commonwealth Law after India's independence in 1947. A handful of Jains came to the United States from India and East Africa in the 1950s on student visas, and some settled in the US. Several factors contributed to a sharp rise in the number of Jains in the US during the 1960s. First of all, in 1965 the Asian Exclusion Acts of the 1880s and 1920s were overturned by federal legislation that allowed greater numbers of non-whites to become permanent residents and citizens. Jains began to arrive into the United States after the changes to immigration policy went into effect in 1965 as part of the Civil Rights movement. Mass exoduses of the Jain community from Africa also contributed to this trend. Kenya and Tanzania expelled large numbers of South Asians in 1967 and 1968, many of whom were Jain merchants. In 1971, all Indians were required to leave Uganda during the repressive regime of Idi Amin. Many Jains left for

England, and several then proceeded to the United States. The flow to the US was made possible just a few years earlier when proponents of the Civil Rights movement successfully lobbied in 1965 to allow persons to enter the United States in greater numbers from Asia and Africa.

The Jain community in North America has evolved from a small cluster of families struggling to adjust to the American ways of life into a self-assured network of well-established business families and professionals. Throughout the 1960s and 1970s, Jains often teamed with Hindus to create worship spaces to serve both religions. There are now more than seventy Jain centers in North America. These include the Jain Center of New York established in 1966; the first Jain-only temple, opened by the Jain Centre of Boston in 1973; the Jain Meditation International Centre in New York, established in 1975; Siddhachalam, a Jain Ashram in the Poconos, was instituted in 1983; the Jain Center of Southern California, founded in 1979; and the Jain Society of Chicago, which dedicated its temple in 1993. Other temples can be found in Washington, DC, New Jersey, Texas (Richardson), and many other states. Every two years, the Jain community convenes a major convention sponsored by the Federation of Jain Associations in North America. Surveying event attendance and temple rosters, Bhuvanendra Kumar estimated in 1996 that between sixty to one hundred thousand Jains live in North America.[61] Twenty years later, that number certainly exceeds one hundred thousand.

Most Jain temples in North America attempt to accommodate both Svetambara and Digambara forms of worship. The nurturing of Jain identity through the building of cultural centers and temples, and the ways in which the educational aspects are emphasized, reflects a centuries-old US practice for maintaining minority identity. For instance, both Jews and Catholics built institutions to serve as gathering places and to educate the young, often along ethnic lines. It would seem that with the proliferation of temple-building, the success of various newsletters and journals within the Jain community, and the huge attendance at the semi-annual JAINA (Jain Associations in North America) Conventions, that the Jains are well established in North America. They would like to claim that they have taken all the necessary steps to guarantee the continuation of their faith for future generations.

Conclusion

The Jain religious tradition, even with its comparatively small numbers of approximately four-to-six million followers, remains a vital tradition in India and beyond. For decades, Jains have set up new homes in East Africa, the United Kingdom, North America, and elsewhere, thus creating a global network of study groups and temples. The Internet has bolstered communication, by making entire libraries and study guides available worldwide. More than seventy Jain community centers and temples have been built in North America since the late 1980s, and the Jain community now actively supports many scholarly activities, including twice-monthly schools at nearly every Jain center, and outreach institutes, particularly at the University of London, Florida International University, and at the California State Polytechnic University in Pomona, California. The International School for Jain Studies invites dozens of international students to visit India each year to learn about Jain faith and practices. Academic scholarship about Jainism has blossomed since 1995, with numerous doctoral dissertations investigating such topics as Jain history and society, the role of monasticism, and the place of women in the tradition.

Jainism holds a prominent place in religious history. Its ethical system—related to its biocosmic view of reality—inspired Mahatma Gandhi and continues to inspire vegetarians, environmentalists, and animal advocates worldwide. The Jain ethic of vegetarianism is uniquely linked with an ideology of spiritual liberation through ethical vows such as nonviolence. Having always been a minority religion within Buddhist, Hindu, Muslim, and now Christian societies (in the case of Europe and North America), Jain thinkers have long grappled with how to maintain identity markers such as vegetarianism in often hostile contexts. By adhering to the gentle approach of nonviolence, expressed in the adage "live and let live," Jains have been able not only to survive but also to thrive as a minority voice of conscience, setting an example of how to be mindful and respectful of others, even beings such as animals who seemingly have no voice.

Notes

1. Horace Leonard Jones, trans., *The Geography of Strabo* (New York: G.P. Putnam, 1930), 103–5.

2. (Samyagdarshanajnanacharitrani) "Samyag-darshana, samyagjnana aura samyak-charitra," tinom milaka moksha ka marga hai, arthat moksha ki prapti ka upaya hai (Right perception, Right knowledge, and Right conduct, three together form the path to liberation.) In Vijay K. Jain, ed., *Acharya Umaswami's Tattvartha Sutra* (Calcutta: Vira Sasana Sangha, 1960), 2.

3. Quoted in: Ainslie E. Embree, ed., *Sources of Indian Tradition Second Edition Volume One: From the Beginning to 1800* (New York: Columbia University Press, 1988), 6.

4. Hermann Jacobi, trans., *Kalpa Sutra* (Reprint: Dover, 1968), 120.

5. Paul L. Dundas, *The Jains* (London: Routledge, 2002), 23.

6. For example: "All beings are fond of life; they like pleasure and hate pain, shun destruction and like to live, they long to live. To all, life is dear. Living beings should not be slain, nor treated with violence, nor abused, nor tormented, nor driven away." Hermann Jacobi, trans., *Jain Sutras* (Reprint: Dover, 1968), 39. A digital copy of the book is available at http://www. sacred-texts.com/jai/sbe22/sbe2234.htm (accessed January 15, 2017).

   "A great sage, neither injuring nor injured, becomes a shelter for all sorts of afflicted creatures, even as an island, which is never covered with water," *Ibid.*, 61; "I renounce all killing of living beings, whether subtle or gross, whether movable or immovable. Nor shall I myself kill living beings nor cause others to do it, nor consent to it." *Ibid.*, 202; "All beings, those with two, three, four senses, plants, those with five senses, and the rest of creation, experience individually pleasure or displeasure, pain, great terror, and unhappiness. Beings are filled with alarm from all directions and in all directions." *Ibid.*, 11. "He who injures does not comprehend and renounce the sinful acts; he who does not injure comprehends and renounces the sinful acts. Knowing them, a wise man should not act sinfully towards animals, nor cause others to act so, nor allow others to do so." *Ibid.*, 12.

7. *Ibid.*, 11.

8. *Ibid.*, 14.

9. *Ibid.*, 138–9.

10. Peter Flügel, "The Codes of Conduct of the Terapanth Saman Order," *South Asia Research* 23(1) (2003), 19–22. For example, generally, one should not use a lift for up to three stories. One should not keep more than the prescribed limit of bedding and covering cloths. The prescribed limit is of the following types: 5 overclothes, 2 underclothes, 3 bodices, 2 uniforms, 1 shawl, 1 woolen shawl, 2 blankets, 1 wrapping cloth, 3 small bodices, 2 handkerchiefs, 2 mouthmasks, 1 towel, 2 glasses, 2 ballpoint pens, 2 pencils, 2 toothbrushes. One should not keep more than three bowls. One should not eat from bowls made of metal. A bowl must be made of plastic, wood or clay (metal is considered too valuable and requires violence for its production). One should not watch TV. If some householder shows a community program merely for information, this is

another matter. One should not keep clothes, books, and so on, in a closed box for a long time. One should not use more than one plastic bag at the time of begging.

11. Summary reinterpreted from Padmanabh S. Jaini, *The Jain Path of Purification* (Berkeley: University of California Press, 1979), 131–3. Jaini lists the negative *karmas* as follows: (1) Delusional: engendering false views and incorrect conduct, leading to anger, pride, deceit, and four types of greed: unrelenting, inciting greed in lay-people, inciting greed in monks, and smoldering lethargy. Delusional *karmas* also result in vicious laughter, pleasure, displeasure, sorrow, fear, disgust, and the three types of sexual craving (a man for a woman, a woman for a man, and man for a man/woman for a woman) (2) Ignorant: incorrect function of senses and the mind; faulty reasoning; lack of intuition; lack of empathy; inability to adopt a universal view (3) Obscured: malfunctioning of the eyes, malfunctioning of the other senses, mistaken notions, and failure to perceive universal wisdom (4) Lack of energy.

12. For a more comprehensive discussion of this topic, see the chapters by Sogani and Chapple in Christopher Key Chapple, ed., *Yoga in Jainism* (London: Routledge, 2016).

13. "Omniscience arises when deluding karma is eliminated and as a result, knowledge-covering, intuition-covering and obstructed karma are eliminated. There is no fresh bondage because the causes of bondage have been eliminated and all destructive karma have worn off. The elimination of all types of karma is liberation. When all karmic bondage is eliminated, the soul soars upward to the border of cosmic space ... like castor seeds released from the pod and like the flame of fire." See Christopher Key Chapple and John Thomas Casey, *Reconciling Yogas: Haribhadra's Collections of Views on Yoga with a new Translation of the Yogadrstisamuccaya* (New York: SUNY Press, 2003), 26–38.

14. Umasvati, *Tattvartha Sutra* (*That Which* Is), trans. Nathmal Tatia (San Francisco: HarperCollins, 1994), 253–5.

15. Jaini, *Path of Purification*, 271.

16. Dundas, *The Jains*, 104–5. The *Acharanga Sutra* describes the liberated soul as follows (Jacobi, *Jain Sutras*, 52):

> Not long nor small or round nor triangular
> nor quadrangular or circular;
> not black nor blue nor red nor green nor white;
> neither of good nor bad smell;
> not bitter nor pungent nor astringent nor sweet;
> neither rough nor soft; neither heavy nor light;
> neither cold nor hot; neither harsh nor smooth.
> The soul is without body, without rebirth,
> without contact (with karma),
> not feminine nor masculine nor neuter.

The soul perceives and knows but there is no analogy
(to describe the liberated soul).
Its essence is without form.
There is no condition of the unconditioned.

17. See Chapters V and VI on Jain Doctrines of Relativity, in Jeffery D. Long, *Jainism: An Introduction* (London: I.B.Tauris, 2009).

18. Christopher Key Chapple, ed., *Jainism and Ecology: Nonviolence in the Web of Life* (Cambridge: Harvard University Press, 2002), 87–8.

19. John Koller, "Jain Ecological Perspectives," in Chapple, *Nonviolence*, 25. Philosopher John Koller summarizes this analysis as follows: *naigama* (the ordinary or undifferentiated), *samgraha* (the general), *vyavahara* (the practical), rju-sutra (the clearly manifest), *shabda* (the verbal), *samabhirudha* (the subtle), and *evambhuta* (the thus-happened).

20. Koller, "Jain Ecological Perspectives," 12.

21. H.R. Kapadia, *Introduction to Haribhadra Suri's Anekantajayapataka* (Baroda, India: Oriental Institute, 1947), cxviii.

22. Chapple, *Nonviolence*, 85–97.

23. Yuvacharya Mahaprajna, *Preksha Dhyana: Perception of Psychic Colours*, trans. Muni Mahendra Kumar and Jethalal S. Zaveri (Ladnun, India: Tulsi Adhyatma Nidam, 1986), 22.

24. Diana Eck, *Darshan: Seeing the Divine Image in India* (New York: Columbia University Press, 1998), 4.

25. *Namo Arihantanam*: I bow down to Arihanta; *Namo Siddhanam*: I bow down to Siddha; *Namo Ayariyanam*: I bow down to Acharya; *Namo Uvajjhayanam*: I bow down to Upadhyaya; *Namo Loe Savva-sahunam:* I bow down to Sadhu and Sadhvi. *Eso Panch Namokaro*: These five bowings down, *Savva-pavappanasano*: Destroy all the sins; *Manglananch Savvesim*: Amongst all that is auspicious; *Padhamam Havei Mangalam*: This Navkar Mantra is the foremost. "Jainworld.com: Jainism Global Resource Center," available at http://www.jainworld.com/education/j'uniors/junles01.html (accessed July 18, 2016).

26. Chapple, "Free Will and Voluntarism in Jainism," in Matthew R. Dasti and Edwin F. Bryant, eds., *Free Will, Agency, and Selfhood in Indian Philosophy* (New York: Oxford University Press, 2014), 68–84.

27. Mary Whitney Kelting, *Heroic Wives: Rituals, Stories, and the Virtues of Jain Wifehood* (New York: Oxford University Press, 2009), 107.

28. *Ibid.*, 98.

29. *Ibid.*, 16.

30. *Ibid.*, 14.

31. *Ibid.*, 224.

32. *Ibid.*, 232.

33. Anne Vallely, *Guardians of the Transcendent: An Ethnology of the Jain Ascetic Community* (Toronto: University of Toronto Press, 2002), 168.

34. Kelting, *Heroic Wives*, 112.

35. Dundas, *The Jains*, 49.
36. In T.K. Tukol, *Sallekhana Is Not Suicide* (Ahmedabad: L.D. Institute of Indology, 1976), 8.
37. Ajit Prasad, trans., *Purusarthasiddhyupaya of Amrtacandra* (Lucknow: Central Jaina Publishing House, 1933), 71–3, 44.

> On account of the absence of any emotion,
> there is no suicide by one acting in this manner
> On the certain approach of death,
> because of the observance of Sallekhana,
> the passions are attenuated.
>
> He who, actuated by passion,
> puts an end to life by stopping breath,
> or by water, fire, poison, or weapons,
> is certainly guilty of suicide.
>
> In the practice of Sallekhana,
> all passions, which cause Himsa, are subdued,
> and hence Sallekhana is said to lead to Ahimsa.

38. In Shadakshari Settar, *Pursuing Death: Philosophy and Practice of Voluntary Termination of Life* (Dharward: Karnatak University, 1990), 26.
39. *Ibid.*, 27.
40. *Ibid.*
41. *Ibid.*, 32.
42. *Ibid.*, 43.
43. *Ibid.*, 54.
44. *Ibid.*, 47–8, 63.
45. Jacobi, *Jain Sutras*, 12.
46. Jaini, *Path of Purification*, 165, lists: (1) Rishabha (bull), Ajita (elephant), Sambhava (horse), Abhinanda (ape), Sumati (partridge), Padmaprabha (lotus [flower, not animal]), Suparshva (nandyavatara figure), Candraprabha (moon), Suvidhi/Pushpadanta (crocodile), Shitala (swastika), Shreyamsa (rhinoceros), Vasupujya (water buffalo), Vimala (boar), Ananta (hawk or bear), Dharma (thunderbolt), Shanti (deer), Kunthu (goat), Ara (fish), Malli (water jar), Munisuvrata (tortoise), Nami (blue lotus), Nemi (conch shell), Parshva (snake), and Mahavira (lion).
47. Jacobi, *Jain Sutras*, 145.
48. Deryck O. Lodrick, *Sacred Cows, Sacred Places: Origins and Survivals of Animal Homes in India* (Berkeley: University of California Press, 1981), 22.
49. *Ibid.*, 80.
50. Shah, "Jainism and Environment," 30.
51. *Ibid.*, 31.
52. Chapple, *Jainism and Ecology*, 63.
53. L.M. Singhvi, "Jain Declaration of Nature," available at http://www.jainworld.com/jainbooks/Books/Jaindecl.htm (accessed July 18, 2016).

54. See: Kumar, *No Destination* (1992).
55. Chapple, *Jainism and Ecology*, 188.
56. *Ibid.*
57. *Ibid.*
58. *Ibid.*, 189.
59. Schumacher College September 2005–July 2006 Course Programme.
60. Visit: Jaipurfoot: www.jaipurfoot.org.
61. Bhuvanendra Kumar, *Jainism in America* (Ontario: Jain Humanities Press, 1996), 103–10.

Selected Bibliography

Babb, Lawrence A. *Absent Lord: Ascetics and Kings in a Jain Ritual Culture.* Berkeley, California: University of California Press, 1996.

Chapple, Christopher Key. "Free Will and Voluntarism in Jainism." In Matthew R. Dasti and Edwin F. Bryant, eds., *Free Will, Agency, and Selfhood in Indian Philosophy*, 68–84. New York: Oxford University Press, 2014.

———. "Dying and Death: Jain Dharma Traditions." In Adarsh Deepak and Rita DasGupta Sherma, eds., *Dying, Death, and Afterlife in Dharma Traditions and Western Traditions*, 45–6. Hampton, Virginia: DeepakBooks, 2006.

———. "Jainism and Nonviolence." In Daniel L. Smith-Christopher, ed., *Subverting Hatred: The Challenge of Nonviolence in Religious Traditions.* Cambridge, Massachusetts: Orbis Books, 1998.

———. *Nonviolence to Animals, Earth, and Self in Asian Traditions.* Albany, New York: SUNY Press, 1993.

———, ed. *Yoga in Jainism.* London: Routledge, 2016.

———, ed. *Jainism and Ecology: Nonviolence in the Web of Life.* Cambridge: Harvard University Press, 2002.

Cort, John E. *Jains in the World: Religious Values and Ideology in India.* New York: Oxford University Press, 2001.

Dundas, Paul L. *The Jains.* London: Routledge, 1992, 2002.

Eck, Diana. *Darshan: Seeing the Divine Image in India.* New York: Columbia University Press, 1998.

Embree, Ainslie E., ed. *Sources of Indian Tradition 2nd edition, Volume One: From the Beginning to 1800.* New York: Columbia University Press, 1988.

Fluegel, Peter. "The Codes of Conduct of the Terapanth Saman Order." *South Asia Research*, 23(1) (2003).

Folkert, Kendall W. and John Cort. *Scripture and Community: Collected Essays on the Jains.* Atlanta: Scholars Press, 1993.

Granoff, Phyllis, ed. *The Clever Adulteress and Other Stories: A Treasury of Jain Literature.* Oakville, Ontario: Mosaic Press, 1990.

Jain, Andrea R. *Selling Yoga: From Counterculture to Pop Culture.* New York: Oxford University Press, 2015.

Jaini, Padmanabh S. "Fear of Food: Jain Attitudes on Eating." In Padmanabh Jaini, ed., *Collected Papers on Jain Studies*, 281–96. Delhi: Motilal Banarsidass, 2000.

———. *Gender and Salvation.* Berkeley: University of California Press, 1993.

———. *The Jain Path of Purification.* Berkeley, California: University of California Press, 1979.

Kelting, Mary Whitney, *Heroic Wives: Rituals, Stories, and the Virtues of Jain Wifehood.* New York: Oxford University Press, 2009.

Koller, John. "Jain Ecological Perspectives." In Christopher Key Chapple, ed., *Jainism and Ecology: Nonviolence in the Web of Life*, 19–34. Cambridge, Massachusetts: Harvard University Press, 2002.

Kueperferle, Paul L., and Barry Lynch, dirs. *The Frontiers of Peace: Jainism in India* (BBC TV, 1986), available at http://southasia.wisc.edu/the-frontiers-of-peace-jainism-in-india/.

Kumar, Bhuvanendra. *Jainism in America.* Ontario: Jain Humanities Press, 1996.

Kumar, Satish. *No Destination.* Totnes: Green Books, 1992.

Lodrick, Deryck O. *Sacred Cows, Sacred Places: Origins and Survivals of Animal Homes in India.* Berkeley, California: University of California Press, 1981.

Long, Jeffery D. *Jainism: An Introduction.* London: I.B.Tauris, 2009.

Muni, Acharya Shiv. *The Doctrine of Karma & Transmigration in Jainism*, 2nd ed. Chennai, India: Sanskar Jain Patrika, 2007.

Tobias, Michael, dir. Ahimsa. JMT Productions. Public Broadcasting Corporation, 1989.

Tukol, T.K. and N. Shah. *Sallekhana Is Not Suicide.* Ahmedabad, India: L.D. Institute of Indology, 1976.

Vallely, Anne. *Guardians of the Transcendent: An Ethnology of a Jain Ascetic Community.* Toronto: University of Toronto Press, 2002.

Waldau, Paul and Kimberley Patton, eds. *A Communion of Subjects: Animals in Religion, Science, and Ethics.* New York: Columbia University Press, 2006.

Wiley, Kristi L. *Historical Dictionary of Jainism.* Lanham, Maryland: Scarecrow Press, 2004.

4

Buddha Dharma (*Dhamma*): "Reliable Teachings"—According to the Buddha and Buddhism

Rita M. Gross[1]

There is no term in Buddhist terminology wider than dhamma. It includes not only the conditioned things and states, but also the non-conditioned, the Absolute Nirvana. There is nothing in the universe or outside, good or bad, conditioned or non-conditioned, relative or absolute, which is not included in this term.

– Walpola Rahula

Introduction

No term in Buddhism is more important than the Indic key term *dhamma*,[2] which can be translated as "reliable teachings."[3] When I explain the term to an audience for the first time, I often tell a story about myself as a graduate student studying Sanskrit and memorizing my flash cards of Sanskrit verb roots. One of them was the root *dhr* meaning, amongst other things, "to be reliable." How could that be a verb? I wondered. But from that verb root, we get the noun *dhamma* (Sanskrit: *dharma*), which can mean many different things in different contexts. In the Buddhist context, one of its primary meanings is "teachings." Therefore, *dhamma* is one of the Three Refuges or Three Jewels (*Triratna*) of Buddhism. *Dhamma*—taken in the sense of the Buddha's teachings—was often proclaimed to be available to and accessible by all. Indeed, the Buddha encouraged disciples to rationally test and scrutinize all that he had said for themselves. For instance, in the Buddhist canonical text *Anguttara Nikaya*, one finds a description of the "six qualities of *dhamma*." Vishakha, a female disciple of the Buddha, recollects the Dhamma thus: "The Dhamma is well expounded by the Blessed One, directly visible, immediate, inviting one to come and see, applicable, to be personally experienced by the wise."[4] Thus, there is a marked emphasis on the *dhamma* (the Buddhist teachings) that can be accessible by all and is radically empirical. "Buddhism" is a Western term and is traditionally not used by followers of the *dhamma* taught by the Buddha, the Enlightened One, or more colloquially, the human being named Siddhartha Gautama, who woke up. The epithet "Buddha" literally means "the Awakened One." Buddha Dhamma (The Teachings of the Buddha) could be a more traditional translation for this set of teachings that many claim reliably leads from confusion and suffering to contentment and peace.

One could organize a presentation of Buddhism in many ways, but I choose to use one of the oldest and most basic of all formulae: the Three Refuges, which are Buddha (the Teacher), *dhamma* (his Teachings), and *sangha* (the Community that follows his teachings). According to older Buddhist primary sources, it is quite common for someone newly convinced of the cogency of the Buddha's teachings to declare that henceforth they will always go for refuge to the Buddha, the *dhamma*, and the *sangha*. From that usage, the formula became the most basic way to define the difference between Buddhists and non-Buddhists.

One formally becomes a Buddhist by "going for refuge" to the Buddha, *dhamma*, and *sangha* in a ceremony where one takes basic Buddhist vows in the presence of a living teacher and the community. The Three Refuges also serve as a mantra for the initiate: *Buddham sarnam gaccami/Dhammam sarnam gaccami/Sangham sarnam gaccami* (I take refuge in the Buddha/I take refuge in the *dhamma*/ I take refuge in the *sangha*). This vow involves a commitment to live one's life according to Buddhist principles. It can be, and often is, renewed daily during meditation practices. Thus, these Three Refuges constitute a basic Buddhist bottom-line and are shared by all forms of Buddhism— from early to current renditions of Buddhist teachings— although there can be found variations of interpretations in different schools of Buddhism.

Nevertheless, understandings of these Three Jewels have changed and developed throughout Buddhist history, allowing us to trace the history of Buddhist thought and institutions in a way that reveals core Buddhist values in a variety of historical and cultural contexts. Since Buddhism's scope is comprehensive, this chapter will focus on the most basic Buddhist teachings, while also discussing some historical developments regarding each of the Three Refuges. In each case, we will begin with the teachings of the historical Buddha as recorded in texts preserved in the Buddhist canon written in the Pali language, generally termed the Pali canon or *Nikayas*. (It is important to note that the Buddha taught not in Sanskrit, the language of Brahmanical texts, but rather in the regional dialects of Eastern India, including Magadhi. The earlier Buddhist texts were written down in Pali vernacular.) In many cases, we will also discuss the teachings of Mahayana (the "Great Vehicle," one of the three branches of Buddhism), which developed later and is preserved in other languages such as Sanskrit, Chinese, and Tibetan. Developments outside India will be discussed briefly, but will not be a major focus of this chapter.

"I Go to the Buddha for Refuge:" Buddha as the Untaught Teacher

Today, most people who study Asian religions or cultures have some idea about who or what the Buddha is. People may imagine a visual image of someone sitting cross-legged in meditation. They may also confuse him with the ever-smiling Dalai Lama, currently the most popular living Buddhist teacher. They may have some idea that Buddhism advocates peace and serenity. They usually also know that Buddhists talk a lot about "enlightenment," even though they may not know that "Buddha" is a title which means "The One Who Woke Up," or that the goal of Buddhists is to similarly wake up from confusion and ignorance to a deep understanding of wisdom and compassion. They may have some clue that he lived in India over two millennia ago, and they may know snippets of the most popular stories about his life. But they may also confuse Buddhism with Hinduism. Due to a prevalence of worship of the Buddha's images, some may not be aware that the Buddha himself did not deliberate on the idea of a "personal god," and that Buddhism is considered to be one of the world's few non-theistic religions and has been interpreted variously across many cultures.

But not many know of the fundamental principles of Buddhism. What do Buddhists mean when they "go for refuge to the Buddha?" Depending on what form of Buddhism people follow, this phrase can mean different things. Nevertheless, most Buddhists do share some common images and ideas about who or what the Buddha is. Recognizably similar visual images are found in many of the culturally diverse forms of Buddhism. Whether in Sri Lanka, Southeast Asia, Japan, China, Tibet, or in ancient Buddhist sites in India, one finds similar images of a person sitting cross-legged, meditating. This pose is so popular because often Buddhists assume—on account of the popular legends of the Buddha's "great enlightenment"—that Siddhartha Gautama, the human who became the Buddha, was sitting in that pose during his enlightenment experience under a tree in Bodhgaya, India. That site, popularly believed to be the location of the Buddha's enlightenment, was purportedly lost to Buddhist culture after 1200 CE, when Buddhism as a distinct religion almost disappeared from India. But it was re-discovered by Buddhist practitioners in the nineteenth century (it was made into a Hindu temple in the meanwhile, just as the Buddha himself was remembered in India as a saint and an incarnation of the Hindu deity Vishnu).[5] Today, hundreds of thousands of pilgrims and tourists flock to that site every year to meditate and chant liturgies under a descendant of what is believed to be the same tree under which the Buddha sat. Buddhists themselves also assume that same posture very frequently, even though there are variations of mediation postures among Buddhists. One of the primary meanings of "going to the Buddha for refuge" is taking him as one's role model. Just as the Buddha woke up and became enlightened through the practice of meditation, so Buddhists aspire to achieve the same.

In accordance with how Buddhism is often discussed in university classes today, and as many Western Buddhists believe, the Siddhartha Gautama was a human being who became a Buddha (he was not a *deva* or a supernatural deity). However, this should not be taken as the only view of all Buddhists. During his lifetime, the Buddha was endowed with a status of divinity by his close followers, and was revered as the "Lord" Buddha. In a conversation with a monk, the Buddha is reported to have told that monk to remember him as "Buddha."[6] In the *Vaikkali*

Sutta, the Buddha is reported to have told one follower, who lamented how he was not able to see the Buddha in person, that it was far more relevant to understand and follow his teachings than to see his physical form, and that "to see the Dharma is, in fact, to have seen him."[7] Thus, the Buddha emphasized the value of the practice of his teachings, instead of his physical presence. Nevertheless, very early in the Buddhist history, probably during his earthly lifetime, people began to regard him as someone with supernatural powers who could perform miracles, and even as a being who came into the world from some other realm. In other words, they saw him as someone who was not simply a mere human being.[8] This is consistent with Indic religious beliefs that deify spiritually awakened individuals. Nonetheless, to many Buddhists a key teaching has been that just as Siddhartha Gautama was born a human and became a Buddha, all humans have the potential to become awakened. Various Buddhist schools debate and cite the Buddha's words about the issues in understanding the historical Buddha as an ordinary human being or a supernatural being, but they are consistent in their reverence for him.

However, for most Buddhists, throughout history such questions were not of central importance with respect to their appreciation of the Buddha. For many Buddhists, he was a marvelous being and their familiar stories about him became a part of the culture. Because most people could not read or write in ancient times, oral stories and visual arts frequently took on the role of books in more literate cultures, and likewise informed people about their spiritual heroes and role models.

Due to the many ways that Buddhists circulated the stories and teachings of the Buddha, one sees representations of the Buddha and his life story in thousands of temples all over Asia. According to the Pali sources, he was conceived when his mother, the queen Maya, wife of King Sudhodhana of the Shakya Clan, dreamed of a white elephant (an auspicious sign in ancient India) entering her womb. He was born ten months later as his mother held on to the branch of a tree in Lumbini, just inside the Nepali border, on the Indian subcontinent. Immediately, he stood up, took seven steps and proclaimed that this would be his last birth. He was given the name Siddhartha Gautama. In his youth, he was confined to his palatial residence by his father, the king of the Shakya clan. Therefore, Siddhartha Gautama came to be known as Shakyamuni, "the sage of the Shakya clan." The King did not want him to see the world's miseries and feared such exposure would motivate the prince to renounce the world and seek enlightenment. Siddhartha was provided an education suitable to a prince and was married at sixteen. Despite his father's constraints, he did eventually see the world's miseries in the form of three sights: an extremely decrepit old person, an ill person, and a corpse. However, he also saw a fourth sight: a serene monk who had renounced the world and had found peace and, thus, release from misery.

After witnessing the reality of suffering, he was initially disturbed and ultimately resolved to renounce the world in order to seek the end of suffering. At the age of twenty-nine, he left his palace, wife, and newborn son to seek liberation from *samsara*, the unending cyclic existence of "birth, old age, sickness and death."[9] This cycle of death and rebirth is believed to be the fate of all who do not awaken from ignorance and confusion. For six years, he struggled to find the way to end suffering, first studying with ascetics and traditional teachers, and then practicing severe austerities, such as fasting almost to death. His first hint of release came with the realization that the extremes of both luxury and asceticism were dead-ends that could not lead to peace and freedom. He realized that he should instead seek a "middle-path" of avoiding all extremes.

According to various Buddhist accounts, with this newfound understanding he ate food, and then sat down under the Bodhi Tree at Bodhgaya. After forty-nine days of sitting, he would break through to enlightenment when the morning star arose the next morning, but first he had to fight an epic, cosmic battle with Mara, a Buddhist personification of evil and temptation. In the metaphorical sense, Mara represents the inward psychological causes of bondage, such as craving, greed, and lust, which were later elaborated upon in the Indian philosophical texts and popular portrayals in Tibetan sacred art. According to the legend, the "awakened" Gautama sat under the Bodhi tree and was inspired by Brahma (the Hindu creator god) to teach the way to others. Seven weeks after his awakening, he left Bodhgaya, walked to Sarnath, near the holy city of Varanasi, found his former companions engaged in ascetic practices, and delivered his first sermon to them. This sermon, which has been recorded in the Pali canon, contains the Four Noble Truths and the Eightfold Path. It was also later termed as the "First Turning of the *Dhamma* Wheel," signifying that the Buddha Dhamma had been officially proclaimed by a realized sage.[10] This was the beginning of the Buddhist religion. For forty-five more years, he and his disciples wandered throughout northern India, mainly in the contemporary state of Bihar, and taught the path to end suffering. Finally, at the age of eighty, he left his mortal body between two trees at Kushinagar. Irrespective of what various Buddhists schools may believe concerning who the Buddha was, most are familiar with, believe in, and revere this story of his life.

However, this familiar story of the life of the Buddha is not the only story about Siddhartha Gautama. Over the years, this story has changed a great deal and reflects the dreams and aspirations of followers who regard him as their personal refuge—the first of the Three Refuges. New elements are constantly woven into these stories, which eventually take the Buddha's story far back into cosmic history (with the *Jataka* stories about his previous lives recorded in the Pali canon) and into cosmic space outside our own universe (with stories about various Buddha-fields or cosmological realms associated with various Buddhas).[11] There are canonical sources and biographies of the Buddha, including one of the most cited, which is delineated in Ashvagosha's *Buddhacarita* (written around the second century CE). Furthermore, other biographies are sometimes conflicting in their content.[12] To tell the entire story of the Buddha—or even to recount various legends that have developed over the years and across cultures—would require a whole book. This storytelling continues even into the present day with a long series of Japanese comic books devoted to the life of the Buddha and a lavishly produced Indian "Bollywood"-style TV series of his life. The other recent biographies include Thich Nhat Hahn's long novel-like "biography" of the Buddha or the delightful "children's book" version of his life, *The Cat Who Went to Heaven*, written by Elizabeth Coatsworth.[13]

Throughout time, as often happens with great religious leaders, the Buddha's life became a template on which to superimpose contemporary values and views. But no *video* documentary of that life has survived, which makes it difficult, if not impossible, to locate the historical person behind the varied stories that have been told about him. For the historians and scholars who distinguish between legend and history—and value historical accuracy—this lacuna presents difficulties, especially when we analyze the earlier records about the Buddha.

Early Buddhist Records about the Buddha and What He Taught

Few would doubt there is an historical person behind the various legends of the Buddha, or that this person had a definitive religious experience that became the basis for his teachings. It is apparent that he became a successful religious teacher and one of the most influential individuals in history. The path he taught in the sixth through fifth century BCE eventually held sway over most of Asia, and in modern times it is rapidly becoming an important religious force in the rest of the world, including the United States.

However, few facts about the Buddha can be determined, including his birth and death dates. Scholars used to routinely cite the dates 563–483 BCE, taken from Sri Lankan historical chronicles that postdate the Buddha by many centuries. But recently, scholars have argued that those dates are too early, based on agreement in several disparate sources that there were five generations of teachers who succeeded the Buddha and about one hundred years between the death of the Buddha and the reign of emperor Ashoka, which is usually given as 268–233 BCE.[14] Emperor Ashoka, known as "Ashoka the Great" for his acts in the areas of politics, peace and religious pluralism, is said to have adopted Buddha Dhamma after witnessing the carnage caused by the war and violence.[15] He was also a catalyst for spreading the Buddha's message through various means, including advocating religious tolerance, building monuments, and issuing edicts. Because of the reliable sources of Ashoka's edicts and monuments, it seems that the Buddha Dhamma was widespread in India by the middle of the third century. Most Buddhists would concur that even if this could not be definitively proved with respect to the historicity of the Buddha, the *dhamma* attributed to him is nevertheless a reliable guide for human beings. Thus, it is not the historicity of the Buddha, but the truth of his teaching that is the foundation of Buddha Dhamma.

This idea can be found in the earliest layer of Buddhist records known as the Pali canon, especially in its *Vinaya* (Rules of Monastic Discipline) and *Suttas* (Discourses Attributed to the Buddha), that the Buddha's contemporaries were far more interested in the *dhamma* he taught than in his biography. The widely known, popular biographies of the Buddha—including his most common life story briefly narrated above—were all written many centuries after the Buddha's death, including Ashvaghosha's *Buddhacarita*.[16] There is no thoroughly composed narrative of his life within the massive Pali canon. Instead, we find brief snippets of biographical details contained in stories of how various *dhamma* teachings or disciplinary rules were promulgated. The emphasis is clearly on teachings and disciplinary rules, but stories of the Buddha developed around his personhood form the *dhamma* structure itself, as has been argued by various Buddhist sources.

In terms of Buddha Dhamma as a religion or way of life, this emphasis makes sense insofar as some early versions of Buddhism do not emphasize that the Buddha was a savior, but only that he discovered the way by which individuals can lead themselves to liberation. The Buddha's famous admonition—uttered just a few months prior to his death—proclaims, "You should live as islands onto yourselves, being your own refuge, with no one else as your refuge, with the *Dhamma* as an island, with the *Dhamma* as your refuge, with no other refuge."[17] He tells his disciples to take his *teachings*, not his *person* as their refuge.

However, some scholars point to the earlier texts as sources in which the Buddha emerges as a savior. Many concepts concerning the elevation of the Buddha to a divine status, merit transference, and the salvific power of *bodhisattvas* ("beings of wisdom") who dedicate themselves to save their fellow beings, became central to the Mahayana school of Buddhism ("the Great Vehicle"). As expressed in the early Pali literature, the Buddha's enlightenment was a solution to his own problems but did not involve solving those of others. That is up to us. "Be a lamp to thyself" (*Digha Nikaya*, 16.2: 26) was the teaching of the Buddha. (The term for lamp is "dipa," but it can mean both "island" and "lamp," which has led scholars and practitioners to define the Buddha's teaching variously.) Here, the Buddha is one's refuge because he pointed out the way that leads to awakening. If waking up from confusion is our basic problem, no one can do that for us, although others can serve as useful guideposts for our own journey because they have already walked the path that we are on. This is how the early literature portrayed this process. However, in the later Buddhist literature, the Buddha is portrayed as a compassionate being who descended to this earthly existence to aid the suffering masses. The Buddha's efforts to teach his followers can certainly be interpreted as his compassion for others.

A modern author, Bhikkhu Nanamoli (a Theravada monk), has painstakingly assembled a narrative account of the Buddha's life from the various incidents scattered throughout the Pali canon.[18] This "biography" is stunningly different from the more familiar biographies that go into great detail about the Buddha's conception, birth, early life, the renunciation of his family and the comforts of life, his austerities, the cosmic battle with Mara, and the enlightenment experience. In this account, the entirety of the Buddha's life, up until his enlightenment experience, is covered in the first 29 pages of the 346-page book and most of the significant events—presented so elaborately in other biographies—are entirely absent. For example, there is no grand battle with Mara at all and only a very simple, short account of his decision to abandon his family and luxurious life. Clearly, the emphasis in this biography is on his life as a teacher and founder of the *sangha*, the Buddhist community. In contrast, the *Lalitavistara*, a 345-page Mahayana Buddhist biography favored by Vajrayana and Tibetan Buddhists, composed about 600 years after the Buddha's death, ends with Buddha preaching his first sermon.[19] In the *Lalitavistara*, the entire teaching career, the point and purpose of the Buddha's life in earlier texts, is omitted. Though the earlier Pali texts are not without marvels and supernatural events, every episode in this text (*Lalitavistara*) of Siddhartha's life prior to enlightenment is replete with supernatural events. As we trace the historical development of what Buddhists mean when they take the Buddha as the first of the Three Refuges, some of the reasons for this drastic change in emphasis on the Buddha's personhood will become evident.

In the earliest stories about the Buddha, found in the Pali canon, he is first among equals, the untaught teacher who discovered the liberating *dhamma* on his own. However, this was the only major distinction between him and his disciples, at least those who were called *arahant*s (literally the "most deserving ones," who break free from the shackles of Mara and enter *nirvana*). Both Buddha and the *arahants* had realized the same liberating truth that freed them from *samsara* or the ceaseless round of rebirth. In that respect, they were equals. For early Buddhism, as well as for most contemporary followers of the early school of Buddhism called Theravada

("The Way of the Elders"), there is no higher goal or purpose in life than to reach freedom from *samsara*. Thus, taking the *bodhisattva* vow (compassionate dedication to helping fellow beings), which was a central element in later Mahayana Buddhism,[20] has been considered by some Theravadins to be contrary to the words of the historical Buddha and his contemporaries as portrayed in the Pali literature.

In the records of early Buddhism, becoming an *arahant* was not at all rare. Many followers of the Buddha Dharma were "awakened" very quickly, needing only to hear a brief teaching. By the end of the Buddha's life, there were many hundreds of *arahants*, and becoming an *arahant* remained the only, or at least the major, goal of Buddhist practice for many centuries. Thus, at that point in Buddhist history and for various forms of Buddhism that remain oriented towards the Pali texts, "to go for refuge to the Buddha" is literally to regard him as one's role model and a great Teacher who was moved by compassion to teach his wisdom to others. A practitioner strives to re-duplicate his wisdom and compassion to attain pace and freedom as the Awakened Teacher had done. This understanding of the Buddha as role model remains alive, even in forms of Buddhism that portray the Buddha in a more supernatural light. More than once I have witnessed a contemporary Vajrayana teacher giving refuge vows to students, urging them to literally take the human, historical Buddha as their role model. In one case, she suggested that the students be diligent and not delay for six long years to attain enlightenment just because that was how long it took Siddhartha.

Speculations and Divisions Over Who the Buddha Truly Was

Despite his being first-among-equals according to the Pali literature, it is hard to deny that there must have been something special about the Buddha. All the stories about the Buddha as a miracle worker develop out of this conundrum, even the conclusion that he must have been a being from another realm who temporarily inhabited a human body out of compassion for those of us still in *samsara*. He came to teach in terms comprehensible to all humans that meant he had to seem to be equally human. Similar to the case of Jesus of Nazareth, the thought that this wondrous teacher was as human as we are was difficult to sustain. In the case of Buddhism, that difficulty led to a great deal of mythologizing about Buddhahood, which in turn led to the eclipsing of the historical Buddha by the non-historical, cosmic Buddha (and *bodhisattvas* in some Buddhist sects), even though images of his human, earthly life remained ever popular.

However, unlike Jesus, Buddha is usually not depicted by Buddhists as a unique figure. In early Buddhism, it was thought that only a Buddha could become an untaught teacher who discovered the *dhamma* on his own. But how was this person, Siddhartha Gautama, and not anyone else, able to discover the *dhamma* unaided? There must have been something unique, or at least rare, about him. The answer to this, according to Buddhist accounts, is found in a vow Siddhartha had taken in a previous life. Impressed by an example of a different Buddha who appeared in a previous eon, Siddhartha (now the Buddha of our present age) took a vow to become just like him in the future.[21] The force of this vow kept him "on track" through countless lifetimes until causes and conditions came together in such a way that he was able to become the Buddha for our time, after taking birth as Siddhartha Gautama.

In the same way, according to the Buddhist sources, the Buddha of the future, the *bodhisattva* Maitreya, is now awaiting his turn for such causes and conditions to arise. Not surprising, in Indian culture there soon arose a vast literature detailing the Buddha's previous lives, other past Buddhas, and Buddhas in other universes. The *Jataka tales* of the Buddha's previous lives have been popularly used to demonstrate both the Buddha's journey across various lifetimes and his unique nature. It is important to recognize, however, that some Buddhists might construe the teaching of the *bodhisattva* vow as primarily pertaining to the Buddha *himself*, not to the Buddha's teachings. At least according to the Pali texts, he did not teach his students to take a *bodhisattva vow* to become Buddhas in the future lives. This might indicate that he did not think of himself as someone who had taken such a vow and that such ideas about him may date from a few generations after his death.

Even though the Pali texts portray the Buddha as having a *rupakaya*—a human, material body that became sick and old, had enemies, and eventually died—within a few generations after the Buddha's death, he was not as pervasively thought of or portrayed as a regular human being who had awakened to the truth. As Buddhist scholars explain the process from surviving literature, it seems that by the dawn of the first century CE most Buddhists found it difficult, even offensive, to think of the Buddha as a normal human being. In particular, as the growing literature (later identified as the Mahayana *sutras*) clearly demonstrates, the idea that the Buddha was mortal and died after eighty years was especially difficult for most Buddhists to accept. Even in the Pali *Mahaparinibbana Sutta*, a long section (that is probably a later interpolation into the text) presents a claim that the Buddha could have lived on for the rest of the century if only Ananda, the Buddha's closest disciple, had taken the hint the Buddha so obviously gave him to beg the Buddha to stay in this world (referring to the Buddha's last conversation). But unfortunately, Ananda's mind was "possessed by Mara," and so he did not take this hint.[22]

About a hundred years after the Buddha's death, Buddhism split into two divisions, Sthavira Nikaya (Theravada School descended from Sthaviravadins) and the Mahasamghikas (a school which later led to the formation of Mahayana Buddhism).[23] One of the disagreements between these schools concerned the status of the Buddha as either human or supernatural (though neither of them took seriously the claim that the Buddha was merely a human being), which led to the concept of different bodies of the Buddha. According to some accounts, Sthavira Nikaya split again, and one of its branches, the Sarvastivadin sect,[24] continued believing in the older tradition of two levels of Buddhahood, namely *rupakaya* ("form body," or the physical body of the Buddha) and *dharmakaya* ("truth body," or the embodiment of the awakening).[25] This branch did take the humanity of the *rupakaya* seriously, claiming that the Buddha's *rupakaya* had the same limitations as other bodies, but to them it was the Buddha's *dharmakaya* that made him (or other Buddhas) unique in ways that could not be duplicated by even his most astute disciples. For these Buddhists, he was no longer a realistic role model with respect to anything they could accomplish in this lifetime. For the Sarvastivadin, the phrase "going for refuge to the Buddha" referred only to his *dharmakaya*, not the impure, human-like *rupakaya*.[26]

Buddhists of the other main sect in the initial split, the Mahasamghikas, are often considered forerunners of Mahayana Buddhism. In contrast to the Sthavira Nikaya School, they developed a completely transcendent concept of the Buddha.[27] According to them, Siddhartha was an incarnated Buddha from another world taking form in our world out of compassion because the Buddha had attained enlightenment countless eons ago.[28] They held that his body was neither sullied by the world in any way nor subject to decay, old age, death, hunger, or the need for sleep. When it is reported in the discourses (*suttas*) that the Buddha ate and slept, the Mahasamghikas interpreted this to be a mere display for the benefit of the people in this world.[29] Their Buddha is omniscient and omnipotent and his lifespan is actually limitless. As such, he can take form in any of the worlds of the ten directions[30] to save beings, and there is no reason that multiple Buddhas could not exist at the same time in different universes.[31] According to Buddhist Mahasamghikas, "to go for refuge" meant relying on the Buddha, who is hard to distinguish from a deity, even though, as stated earlier, the Buddha himself was said to be silent about the idea of a personal god.

Three Forms of Buddha: Fully Developed *Mahayana Trikaya* Theory

Neither the Sarvastivadin nor Mahasamghika forms of Buddhism survive into the present. But both schools influenced the emerging Mahayana Buddhism, which developed a unique and multifaceted concept of Buddhahood that has also been expressed in various ways in contemporary times. These forms of Buddhism primarily prevail in East Asia and Tibet. Mahayana ideas about Buddhahood are not obvious in the teachings of the Pali canon and are not followed by Theravada Buddhists, who primarily prevail in Southeast Asia. To sum up this development, one could say that the historical Buddha receded in importance, to the point that he became almost inconsequential. At the same time, what had formerly been called the *rupakaya* level of Buddhahood split into two different levels: the *nirmanakaya* ("body of apparent manifestation") and the *sambhogakaya* (often translated as "enjoyment body").[32] Additionally, what had been called the *dharmakaya* came to be understood as a state of true or complete Buddhahood—an abstract, impersonal, and ever-present Buddha as Buddha truly is. These developments are coterminous with other emerging Mahayana ideas and practices and cannot be understood apart from them.

The *trikaya* ("three bodies") is one of the most difficult concepts of Buddhism.[33] Even many long-term Buddhists practitioners do not feel that they fully understand it. The theory of the "three bodies" explains that a Buddha manifests in three ways: *nirmanakaya* (the "manifest body," for example the body of Shakyamuni); *Sambhogakaya* (the "bliss body," the enlightened state); and *dharmakaya* ("truth body," the absolute). In this system, the historical Buddha, now typically called Shakyamuni, is considered to have appeared in the form of a *nirmanakaya*. So, ideally one should try to understand the *trikaya* theory by first clarifying *nirmanakaya*, which would be appropriate for discussions of the history of ideas about Buddhahood. However, in *trikaya* theory, it can be reasonably argued that the *dharmakaya* is the most fundamental form and generally equated with other foundational concepts in Mahayana thought such as *shunyata* ("emptiness") and *tathata* ("suchness"), all of which point to reality as it is. It must be remembered that when we speak of Buddha as *dharmakaya* it is always understood as the impersonal, abstract, formless Buddhahood, which is never to be anthropomorphized or personified. According to the *trikaya* theory, it is only on account of historical Buddhas, or beings that perfect their own indwelling, that Buddhahood can exist. That indwelling Buddhahood, always available but formless, takes form in two ways: as *sambhogakaya* and as *nirmanakaya*.

The term *sambhogakaya* first occurs in the writings of Asanga[34] (fourth century CE) and completes the Buddhist soteriological framework (now often studied under the rubric of "Buddhist Theology"), which pertains to the Buddha to whom practitioners go for refuge.[35] This means that about seven hundred years intervened between the life of the historical Buddha and the full development of concepts of Buddhahood, though precedents to *trikaya* theory are found in Mahayana *sutras* that pre-date Asanga and from which he drew.[36]

Sambhogakaya Buddhas are anthropomorphic in form, although they could not be mistaken for portraits of actual human beings. Portrayed in vivid primary colors, they often have multiple heads and limbs. They come in both female and male forms, either individually or in poses of sexual union. For most people, *sambhogakaya* Buddhas are not visible to the naked eye, but they appear to visionaries in certain meditative states, accounts of which have been narrated in various Buddhist texts and stories. They are also employed in visual representations that are routinely used in meditation practices common to Mahayana and Vajrayana Buddhist schools. (*Vajrayana*, literally, the "Diamond Vehicle," developed as an element of later North Indian Buddhism and is prevalent in Tibet.) To summarize these dimensions of Buddhism, the *sambhogakaya* can be understood as divine and eternal, yet still personal and anthropomorphic; the *dharmakaya* is abstract and impersonal; and the *nirmanakaya* is personal but not divine or eternal. If the term "myth" is properly understood (i.e., as it is used by scholars of religion as symbolic sacred tales, rather than the sense in which it is employed by the popular media, namely, as "untrue") these *sambhogakaya* beings could also be understood as mythical Buddhas and *bodhisattvas*. As such, they are extremely important in the everyday religious lives of East Asian and Tibetan Buddhists.

Finally, to return to *nirmanakayas*, which are the physical bodies of the Buddhas that anyone with normal human senses can appreciate and relate to, the most obvious example of *nirmanakaya* Buddhahood is the historical Buddha. Teachings on *nirmanakaya* bring the practice of taking refuge in the Buddha around full-circle, without losing the early understanding of the Buddha as a role model for the potential of awakening. Buddhahood is still exemplified by Shakyamuni, but is not limited to him. Instead, a *nirmanakaya* Buddha can also take "the form of an ordinary human being, an animal, or even a ghost, for liberating different forms of sentient beings."[37]

Thus, for a Buddhist who adheres to *trikaya* theory, taking refuge in the Buddha is multivalent. First, one is taking refuge in the historical Buddha as a teacher, role model, and exemplar of human potential. Furthermore, one is also taking refuge in the help and inspiration provided by the innumerable *sambhogakaya* Buddhas, who can be the object of daily meditation. Lastly, and fundamentally, one is taking refuge in *dharmakaya*, the omnipresent and unlimited principle of Buddhahood. Therefore, when such a person cites "the Buddha" as the source of their claims, it is always relevant to ask to which aspect of Buddhahood they are referring.

Stand-ins for Buddhas: Teachers in Buddhism

Except in some Vajrayana Buddhist practices, one does not normally "go for refuge" to one's own teacher, even though it is the teacher who bestows the knowledge. That being so, the student–teacher relationship in Buddhist tradition is sacred, as it is in the case of other Dharma traditions as well. Nevertheless, despite the myriad *sambhogakaya* Buddhas and *bodhisattvas*, teachers are the most important and revered exemplars one can meet. It has frequently been said that in some senses, the teacher is even more important than the Buddha because the teacher is alive and available for consultation, whereas the Buddha is not. One might not even know about the Buddha and Buddhist teachings without the teacher. This is consistent with Hindu Dharma and other Indic traditions' emphasis on the reverence of a *guru* who leads the individual to liberation.

Thus, in many forms of Buddhism, teaching authorization and lineage are taken very seriously as well as the responsibilities concerning the accurate and authentic transmission of *dhamma*. In many forms of Buddhism, such authorization does not require merely passing an examination, but is instead based on a personal relationship between teacher and student and on the teacher's knowledge of and trust in the student. Only those authorized as teachers themselves can give permission to others to teach the *dhamma*. Many forms of Buddhism claim to have unbroken lines of transmission reaching back to the original teachings of the Buddha, although these claims are often scrutinized by historical scholars.[38] This caution regarding the authorization of teachers points in two directions: on the one hand, such practices attempt to retain authentic traditions and teachings; but, on the other hand such practices also allow for relevant innovations that a trusted teacher will be able to introduce. Ideally, the *dhamma* both retains trustworthy authenticity and is kept up to date.

"I Go for Refuge to the Dharma:" *Dharma* as Reliable Teachings

Dhamma comprises the essential teachings of the Buddha, and "taking refuge in the *Dhamma*" implies the practitioner is committed to the truth of the Buddha's path. Though many forms of Buddhism affirm teachings that developed later, other Buddhists regard the teachings given by the historical Buddha and recorded in the Pali texts as foundational. The most important of those teachings are: The Four Noble Truths, interdependence, the four foundations of mindfulness, and the four immeasurables.[39] Volumes have been written about each set of these profound teachings, but they all, in a nutshell, tend to tell the follower to seek out an understanding and alleviation of human suffering. Almost as a slogan, Buddhists affirm that all beings treasure their own lives and seek happiness. Nevertheless, ignorance and self-centeredness cause us to go about seeking happiness in ways that do not yield desired results. If our ways of seeking happiness do not accord with reality as it is, they will result in suffering, not happiness; therefore, the first task is to identify ignorance and overcome it by replacing it with wisdom.

The Four Noble Truths

Given that the Buddha's first teaching after his enlightenment experience concerned the four truths, it is appropriate to begin our discussion of the reliable *dharma* with those truths.[40] These truths begin with the concern that there is suffering. This suffering is not inevitable, but it results from wishing things to be different than they are, wanting something impossible to obtain, and clinging to things that are fleeting. The first Buddhist truth, *dukkha*, is often interpreted as the claim that "all life is suffering." But that is not an accurate interpretation of the concept. Most experience various forms of unease and dissatisfaction, and the first truth only claims that conventional, everyday ways of seeking material happiness result in suffering, because these ways are misguided. How they are misguided is the content of the second truth, *samudaya* (source), which states that suffering results from a grasping or craving (*tanha*) that is rooted in ignorance with respect to how our world truly is. With a clear understanding of our world, we would realize it is foolhardy to long for things that cannot bring permanent joy and would desist from such grasping and clinging (*upadana*), because the longing itself intensifies our suffering. These two truths focus on the all-pervasive impermanence where nothing whatsoever—including what we mistake to be something permanent about or within ourselves—lasts. But the fact of impermanence is routinely ignored in our daily lives, and so we suffer even more.

The third truth is about cessation (*nirodha*) of suffering. When the causes of suffering cease, suffering also ends. At this point, the Pali/Sanskrit terms *nibbana/nirvana* come into play since *nibbana* literally means "blowing out," as in the case of a flame. It is this state, the cessation of suffering by overcoming selfish cravings, that is considered the highest goal of the Buddha's path. Some schools of Buddhism have posited that the cessation of suffering would entail bliss, while others have thought it must entail annihilation of the self. But other schools point out that dualistic thought and language, which are conceptual, are left behind when one attains *nibbana*, or the realm of the non-conceptual. Buddhists tend to be very aware of the limitations of language and concepts regarding their ability to comprehend ultimate reality (see DN, 15:32) and therefore often prefer to describe the *nibbana* state in negative, rather than positive, terms. For example, when grasping and ignorance cease, suffering ceases. We still experience birth, old age, sickness, and death, but they no longer bring us suffering because we have ceased grasping for or clinging to things that are impossible to obtain or keep. The positive terms that try to describe this state of mind include terms such as contentment, peace, and freedom—freedom form all attachments that bind an individual to *samsara*.

The fourth truth is *magga*, or the Eightfold Path as it is often understood, helps us to give up our quixotic quest for the permanence and security that is simply not possible to achieve in this worldly existence. Regarding this truth, it is important to consider the subtle fact that the Buddhist path *helps* us to go beyond suffering, but it does not *cause* the transcendence of suffering. This is because, according to some subtle Buddhist teachings later developed by Mahayana Buddhists, the enlightened mind is our birthright, and is therefore already present, but our grasping and confusion prevents us from realizing it. In some Buddhist teachings, the enlightened mind is compared to the sun and ignorance to clouds that may temporarily obscure the sun. Walking the path blows away the clouds, but it does not create the sun. This is similar to some Hindu teachings that postulate the self as eternal and self-luminous, although this may not be the understanding of early Buddhist schools that emphasized the movement (journey as implied by the path) from ignorance to awakening (Buddhahood). In any case, the fourth truth, the truth about the path that works, is very practical. The Buddha likened his path to the process of removing a poisoned arrow from a pierced person, who is suffering the agony of clinging and craving. Known as the Eightfold Path, because the Buddha listed eight aspects to the path in his first sermon, it is often condensed into three basic disciplines:

ethics consisting of correct conduct (including five precepts to abstain from violence, false speech, theft, sexual misconduct, and use of intoxicating substances), correct speech, correct action, and correct livelihood; meditation, consisting of correct effort, correct mindfulness, and correct concentration; and wisdom, consisting of correct view and correct intention.[41]

The Concepts of Interdependence, Impermanence, and No-Self

The Buddha also frequently taught about interdependence, or *paticcasamuppada* (Sanskrit: *pratityasamutpada*), in the form of teachings on the twelve interdependent links (Ignorance, Karma formations, Consciousness, Name and Form, Six Base-Sense Organs, Contact, Sensation, Craving, Clinging, Rebirth, Aging and Death). In their full form, these teachings are helpful to develop "correct view" but are complex and difficult to understand. Their main point is that when we look closely at how the world works we cannot help but see that nothing exists independently. Nothing exists permanently, in either an isolated or unrelated manner, apart from its matrix of causes and conditions. If we want to say that something exists, we must also immediately recognize that, in so far as it exists, it is only due to a dependence on its causes and conditions. Take away its causes and conditions and whatever we are looking at also disappears. This insight, which seems too obvious when viewed dispassionately, is usually difficult to fully realize and integrate into our daily lives. Conventionally, many things convince us that there is something permanent that we should strive for, and so we suffer because of how we attribute independent existence and permanence to things we experience, both internally and externally, when in fact all things and all states of mind are dependently arisen and are not lasting. Thus, the principle of dependent origination helps a practitioner to understand the nature of existence: that nothing is permanent (*anicca*), and the true nature of the self is interdependent—or, to put it another way, it is without an independent essence (*anatta*). *Anatta*, the concept of no-self, is closely linked with core Buddhist belief called the five aggregates (*skhandas*, which literally means "heaps, aggregates").[42] According to this concept, the purported individual self is actually a stream, or continuum, of five momentary psychophysical aggregates, which together are mistaken for an enduring and substantial human individual. These five aggregates are: form (*rupa*), sensation or feeling (*vedana*), perception (*sanna*), mental formations (*sankhara*), and consciousness (*vinnana*).[43]

One common way of explaining the difficult concept of *anatta* (no permanent, enduring self) is by means of an example, the well-known "parable of the chariot." In a famous dialogue, a monk named Nagasena convinces a king that what is ordinarily called a "chariot" could only be three things: the parts of the chariot taken individually (spokes, wheels, etc.), the sum total of the parts, or an entity different from those parts. The king Menander finally concedes that the chariot is neither of these three options, thus affirming Nagasena's doctrine of "no-self." This parable, a simile for the individual, is important because it is directly connected with the teachings of the five aggregates. According to the Buddhist, the five aggregates (analogous to the parts of the chariot) are mistaken for a substantial person (analogous to the chariot as a whole). Studying this example enables one to extrapolate that an individual person is, just like the chariot, actually a designation because it cannot be comprised of the aggregates taken either individually or collectively, or as an entity different from those five psychophysical elements. In other words, the word "person," just as the word "chariot," is merely a label for matters of convenience, with no real ontological status.[44] Notably, the issue of selfhood has not been elaborated in the Pali canon, except on a few occasions.

Buddhist Meditation: Four Foundations of Mindfulness and Four Immeasurables

The other two sets of fundamental early Buddhism teachings are the four foundations of mindfulness and the four immeasurables (*Brahma-viharas*). The basic aspects of early Buddhism are mental cultivation, meditation, and contemplation, and are considered essential to realize the state of freedom. As stated above, one of the three major disciplines of the Buddhist path (as understood by some schools, at least) involves meditation. The belief is that it is difficult, if not impossible, to fathom reality-as-it-is without deep introspection and self-examination. And as we have seen, if we do not develop a penetrating understanding into things-as-they-are, our suffering will probably intensify. Thus, the importance of meditative and contemplative disciplines has been underscored by various schools.

The four foundations of mindfulness are: body (*rupa*), sensations (*vedana*), mental occurrences (*chitta*), and phenomena or events (*dhammas*). This pertains to meditation on breath, emotions, thoughts, and the interconnectedness of all phenomena. Mindfulness involves remembering to stay present in the here-and-now rather than giving in to distractibility, boredom, restlessness, and all the other forms of a wandering mind. When most people try to do this, they discover that staying present and alert takes practice. Since the nineteenth century, there has been a great revival of meditation programs based on the four foundations. This form of Buddhist meditation is often called *vipassana*, meaning "seeing" or "insight." Deep insight into the mind reveals the three marks of reality and the core of the Buddha's teaching: *dukkha* (suffering), *anicca* (impermanence) and *anatta* (no-self), as have been discussed earlier.

The *Brahmavihara* ("abodes of Brahma") are commonly known as the four immeasurables and usually considered to be complementary to the four foundations of mindfulness. The four immeasurables are loving kindness, compassion, sympathetic joy, and equanimity. These practices are called "unlimited" because through them the practitioner cultivates unlimited friendliness, compassion, and sympathetic joy for all beings, regarding everyone equally and with total equanimity, rather than picking and choosing favorites or directing these positive emotions solely to those with whom we are close or of whom we approve. Among other things, these practices cut away at the self-centeredness that is so endemic to the untrained mind and that intensifies suffering. Intriguingly similar lists of states of meditations are found across Hindu and Jain Dharma traditions. These have to do with meditation and contemplation.

In the centuries and millennia after the life, death, and teaching of the historical Buddha, a great efflorescence of teachings has developed, and has led to an emergence of many forms of Buddhist traditions. But no matter what else Buddhists may affirm, they tend to go for refuge to the *dhamma/dharma*, which would include the early teachings that are considered foundational: The Four Noble Truths, teachings about interdependence, impermanence, no-self, the practices of the four foundations of mindfulness, and the four immeasurables.

New Teachings and Developing Controversies

Some modern students who study the Buddha's teachings vis-à-vis the Pali discourses (*suttas*) might become frustrated and impatient because of their repetitive nature. Nevertheless, repetition is expected given that the Buddha's teachings were orally transmitted and he spoke to various audiences. Even though a definite timeline for the composition of these texts is debatable, they have been systematized into the Pali canon known as *Three Baskets* (*Tripitaka*) as it has three different components: basket of disciplines for monastics (*vinaya*), basket of discourses (*sutta*), and basket of special or higher doctrine (*abhidhamma*). The *sutta* texts are further divided into five *nikayas* (collections). It has been theorized that very early on Buddhists began to experience similar frustrations and tried to systematize what the Buddha had taught. Through this enterprise, they developed the third set of Buddhist canonical writings, the *Abhidhamma* (Sanskrit: *Abhidharma*). Though these texts are included in the canon, few scholars regard them as direct teachings of the Buddha. To support this idea, scholars note how two of the different schools that developed early in Buddhist history have two different sets of *Abhidhamma* texts in their collection.

However, no matter the specific context, the *Abhidhamma* enterprise of analysis is similar in all schools of Buddhism that engage in it. The term "*Abhidhamma*" is meant by proponents to connote that they were pulling the *dhamma* teachings, scattered throughout the *suttas*, into a coherent system and engaging in further analyses to clarify them. This form of analysis can be traced back to the two terms that were often used by the Buddha to describe how phenomena are beneath their superficial appearances: "composites" and "conditioned." *Abhidhamma* analysis strives to fully test all the implications of both these words in the most thoroughgoing, detailed manner imaginable. The logic can be traced thusly: things appear to be solid entities—complete in-and-of-themselves—and separate from one another. However, they are actually "composites" and therefore made up of many smaller units of, ultimately, infinitesimally small components. It is crucial to understand this because when things are believed to possess non-derivative existence we are inclined to think they are unconditioned and will endure. Thus, our later experience of impermanence will cause us suffering. In addition, apparent phenomena are thoroughly conditioned, meaning they are subject to interdependence and the laws of cause and effect. Therefore, to conclude, every phenomenon and every state of mind is in constant flux, ever-changing, evanescent, unreliable and unable to bring lasting peace and freedom. As this shows, *Abhidhamma* analysis is the relentless, uncompromising, painstaking search to break everything down into its component parts and to understand their causal connections.

Because phenomena are conditioned composites made up of many components, they are unstable and unreliable. Such thoroughgoing analysis, and a complete acceptance of its implications, would bring the practitioner to the understanding of *antiya* or *anicca* (impermanence). There, the Buddhist practitioner could cross over from *samsara*, where they continue to flail around in the perpetually repeated births and deaths of cyclic existence, to *nibbana*, the deathless state that extinguishes the notion of any false-self— a state without the negative aspects of grasping and ignorance. Many modern Buddhists might find *Abhidhamma* difficult and unappealing due to its complexity and the amount of tedious details, despite its obvious relevance to the understanding of the second Noble Truth (that is, the cause of suffering being the grasping and clinging to impermanent things). Nevertheless, Buddhist philosophers and disciplined Buddhist practitioners have engaged in such *Abhidhamma* analyses for centuries.

The deep analysis of *Abhidhamma* culminated in the creation of two major works. For the strand of Buddhism that came to be called "Theravada," this style of analysis reached its peak in the *Visuddhimagga*, or *The Path of Purification*, which was written by Buddhaghosa in Sri Lanka in the fifth century CE. The text is still regarded by many today as the foremost manual for this school of Buddhism. The other major school of *Abhidhamma* analysis belonged to the Sarvastivadin school, whose speculations about Buddhahood was discussed briefly in the previous section. Their *Abhidhamma* analysis culminated in a long work called the *Abhidhammakosa*, or *Verses on the Treasury of Abhidharma*, written by Vasubandhu in northwest India in the fourth century CE. Though the Sarvastivadin School eventually died out, this work remains important in the curriculum for modern Buddhist scholastic philosophy.

During the same period in Buddhist history in which people were absorbed in *Abhidhamma*, they were also quite concerned about questions of who the Buddha really was. These questions were also directly connected with other emerging questions about what path and goal the Buddhist practitioner should pursue. For instance, in the early Buddhist literature, there is no clear discussion on the distinction between *arahants*, Buddhas, and *bodhisattvas*. The Buddha of the Pali literature did not encourage, or even suggest, that his disciples should take the *bodhisattva* vow. Instead the emphasis was on the urgency of treading the path to *nibbana*. He encouraged them to strive for enlightenment and release from cyclic existence in this life. He proclaimed that his present life would be his last samsaric life, and he encouraged his students to take his last life as their model, not any of his previous lives.

Eventually, there emerged a shift in these ideas. Instead of unambiguously striving for enlightenment in their present lives, practitioners began to doubt whether that goal was the best choice, or even a possibility. For some centuries, Buddhists discussed three possible paths or goals for the practitioner. These were to be a *shavaka* (Sanskrit: *shravaka*, usually translated as "listener" or "student"), a *paccekabuddha* (Sanskrit: *pratyekabuddha*, "solitary Buddha"), or a *bodhisattva* ("being of wisdom") who makes eventual Buddhahood their goal. *Shavakas* could attain final realization in this life by being a student or a listener who followed a path already laid out by others. *Paccekabuddhas* are believed to attain enlightenment on their own but chose not to teach others or share their insights. *Bodhisattvas* chose to make a previous life of our age's Buddha their model by taking a *bodhisattva* vow, whereby they determined to someday discover the *dharma* unaided by a teacher and establish Buddha Dhamma in a universe in which it is unknown. Rather than striving to become an *arhant*, such a person aspires to the goal of Buddhahood itself, but sometime far in the future. Clearly, placing these three options before the practitioner is a significant innovation when compared to the teachings of the early Pali Buddhism. For some centuries, these three ideals co-existed in the Buddhist world, but eventually the *arahant* and the *bodhisattva* ideals came to be opposed to each other in some segments of the Buddhist world. However, many proponents of the *bodhisattva* ideal look to the Buddha's own life and teachings in order to justify the consistency between the ideals of the *arahant* and *bodhisattva*.

Mahayana Scriptures and Teachings in Historical Perspective

No argument in Buddhist history has been more divisive than disagreements over which of the myriad Buddhist texts are reliable and trustworthy. As one would expect, early Buddhists recorded their teacher's teachings for several hundred years (as memorized oral traditions rather than written texts). A legend that may hold historical validity claims that soon after the Buddha's death, his enlightened students, the *arahants*, met to affirm their agreement about his teachings. Several other councils (beginning *c.*400 BCE) were held in the next several hundred years to re-affirm these sets of teachings. However, people do not stop composing new, innovative religious texts in which they express their contemporary under-standings simply because a set of accepted authoritative texts is already in place. Therefore, Buddhists continued at the same time to compose texts in which they expressed their own understandings of the *dhamma*. In this case, the new texts used the same formula as the older ones. The oldest records of the Buddha's teachings often begin with the formula, "Thus have I heard. Once the Blessed One was dwelling at (name of the place) and he said the following ..." People continued to use that formula in these newer texts, as if the Buddha were still alive and teaching and as if they were equally *buddhavachana*, or "the words of the Buddha." But, historically, the authenticity of their status as *buddhavachana* was challenged possibly as early as the first century BCE. Those who accepted the newer texts as *buddhavachana* were eventually called "Mahayanists" and those who did not were often called "Hinayanists," or "adherents of the small vehicle," although this latter term is regarded as objectionable by many, including this author, in that it implies a narrow point of view. Therefore, the preferred name for "Hinayanist" is "Theravadins." This subject has been analyzed by various scholars in nuanced ways that is beyond the scope of this chapter.

Conflicts over the authenticity of these texts play a major role in the current situation of Buddhist sectarianism. For at least a millennium, there have been two major forms of Buddhism: Theravada, which prevails in Southeast Asia, and Mahayana, which prevails in East Asia and Tibet. (The Vajrayana Buddhism of Tibet is not always considered an independent form of Buddhism. Though unique, it requires a Mahayana foundation, according to its own self-understanding.) Historically, these forms of Buddhism originated in India and—though debates between them were common—they flourished side by side, mutually influencing each other, for most of the history of Indian Buddhism. In India, divisions between Buddhists involved different lineages of monastic ordination and not different views about Buddha Dharma. (It is important to note that from here on the Sanskrit term *dharma* will be used, as the Mahayana school's literature is primarily in Sanskrit rather than Pali language.) It is reported that monks of differing intellectual and spiritual persuasions routinely lived together in the same monasteries because they belonged to the same ordination lineage. Even as late as the seventh century at the great Buddhist university of Nalanda in the eastern part of India, Chinese pilgrims observed that there were few noticeable differences between Mahayana and Hinayana monks: "Those who read Mahayanist texts and worshipped *bodhisattvas* were Mahayanists, while those who did neither were Hinayanists."[45] Other than that difference, all observed the same monastic rules and practiced according to the Four Noble Truths.[46] Though some Mahayana texts contain polemical *anti-Hinayana* comments, mainstream Buddhist texts, which include Theravada texts, were barely concerned enough to reply to these criticisms. This led many scholars to conclude that, despite the volume of Mahayana writings in India, "very few monks [...] actually adopted the Mahayana vision, and those monks were just thought by their brethren to be a bit weird— but harmless."[47] In short, while the "Theravada-Mahayana" divide has featured prominently in both scholarly and popular Western understandings of Buddhism (as well as among some Mahayanists, especially Tibetan Buddhists), it simply does not hold for Indian Buddhism during Buddhism's golden age. As one scholar has put it, "The binary Hinayana/Mahayana model [is] ahistorical and [...] fundamentally inappropriate as a frame for the study of Buddhism."[48] In short, despite some differences, Buddhist schools at this time held to the shared essential teachings of the Buddha.

How did this framework of distinct Buddhist ideologies become so dominant in Western accounts of Buddhism? First of all, Buddhism largely disappeared from India by about 1200 CE, which meant the Indian model of an internally diverse Buddhism was simply lost. By then, Buddhism was well established outside India—in countries, including Sri Lanka, Tibet, China, Japan—but no area beyond India ever received and promoted all the diverse forms of Buddhism until twentieth-century Western Buddhism. In Southeast Asia, now a stronghold of the various forms of Theravada Buddhism, Mahayana and even Vajrayana forms of Buddhism once flourished but were eventually suppressed by local "reform" movements. In East Asia, now a stronghold of many kinds of Mahayana Buddhism, the earlier forms of Buddhism never really caught on even though the Pali texts were translated into Chinese. The Chinese always preferred Mahayana forms of Buddhism and used the Hinayana-Mahayana divide extensively in their own understandings of Buddhism, as is evident in the language used by Chinese travelers to India to describe the Buddhism they found there.[49] For instance, in his elaborate diaries, the seventh-century pilgrim Chinese philosopher and pilgrim Xuanzang shows reverence to the land of Buddha's birth and the teachings that he received from the Buddhist monks while in India.[50]

In Tibet, the Mahayana form of Buddhism known as Vajrayana (literally, "Diamond Vehicle," to imply strength and lucidity of the teachings) prevails. There is some evidence that Pali texts were transmitted to Tibet in the first transmission of Buddhism to Tibet during the eighth century CE, but much of that literature was lost during the suppression of Buddhism that followed in Tibet around the ninth century CE. When Buddhism was re-transmitted to Tibet in the tenth and eleventh centuries, Mahayana texts and Vajrayana practices were brought to Tibet but not, for the most part, the Pali texts or their Sanskrit counterparts. Thus, major strands of Tibetan Buddhism inherited a strong Mahayana bias from their beginnings, and with it a strong tendency to discount early Buddhism and regard Mahayana texts as literally *buddhavachana*. This occurs to the extent that many Tibetans vehemently claim even today that the historical Buddha himself taught the Mahayana sutras during his earthly life. They also routinely use a heuristic device called the "three-*yana* perspective" for organizing and understanding the various strands of Buddhism as the three *yanas* ("vehicles"), Hinayana, Mahayana, and Vajrayana. Hinayana, is often equated with pre-Mahayana Buddhism and thought to have been outdated by later developments, is considered a preliminary stage of development for individual practitioners—necessary, but also very preliminary. When serious Western scholarly study of Buddhism began in the nineteenth century, very little was known about Indian Buddhism and the

Hinayana-Mahayana divide. However, this polemic was then quickly incorporated into Western understandings of Buddhism, both scholarly and popular, as evidenced by scholarly emphasis on Mahayana teachings.

Hinayana-Mahayana Debate: Personal Reflections

As I suggested earlier, the term Hinayana simply must be given up, both because its literal meaning ("smaller vehicle," or even the "cast-off vehicle") was used in some Indian Mahayana texts as a derogatory label for those who did not follow the *bodhisattva* path or accept Mahayana scriptures as *buddhavachana*. Furthermore, it has never been used as a self-designation by the early school of Buddhism. Today, the term is often used casually by many who don't understand its historical origins and are not aware of its underlying connotations. But clearly, some Buddhists are being denigrated by the term, no matter what the intentions of those who use it may be, avoiding harmful speech has always been a mainstay of Buddhist ethics. Continuing to apply such guidelines to such a longstanding misusage of the older school of Buddhism is a cause for concern.

Next, it would be beneficial to establish a clearer understanding and appreciation for the Indian model of an internally diverse Buddhism. The modern Buddhist situation, for the first time in almost a millennium, is very similar to how it was in its golden age in India, when many forms of Buddhism flourished side-by-side and influenced each other's development. Finally, with the onset of globalization, Buddhists of all persuasions can interact with each other, thus making the Indian model of diversity, debate, and mutual influence not only possible, but a worthwhile option. Sectarianism and mutual disapproval have become outdated and inappropriate, according to modern Buddhists, although various forms of refuge and reverence to many representations of the Buddha continue to be found in various schools. For example, the Buddha may be revered as Amida (Shin Buddhism, also known as Jodo Shinshu, a school of Pure Land Buddhism in Japan) or Shakyamuni (Nichiren Buddhism, based on the teachings of the thirteenth-century Japanese monk, Nichiren). But in all forms of Buddhism, to my knowledge, going for refuge involves going for refuge to the Buddha, *dharma*, and *sangha*, as was taught by the Buddha himself.

Specific Mahayana Claims and *Bodhisattva-Arahant* Ideals

By the time a few centuries had passed after the Buddha's death, it had become common to claim that a Buddhist practitioner could pursue one of three paths: *shravaka*, *pratyekabuddha*, or *bodhisattva*. But rather early in Buddhist history, significant tension developed between those who advocated the *arahant* ideal and those who advocated the *bodhisattva* ideal. Rejection of the *arahant* ideal and the insistence that every Buddhist practitioner should take the *bodhisattva* vow, has become the most definitive and distinctive hallmark of Mahayana teachings. In fact, in Mahayana liturgical contexts the refuge vow is always coupled with the *bodhisattva* vow. Thus, for Mahayanists, it is not possible to take one vow without the other. In trying to understand this distinctive Mahayana requisite, it is helpful first to understand what is being asked of practitioners who take the *bodhisattva* vow, and then to discuss, or at least outline, why taking the *bodhisattva* vow became so important to Mahayanists.

Students of Mahayana traditions who are contemplating taking the *bodhisattva* vow are often told that they would be taking a vow to be compassionate, to put others before self, and to remain in *samsara* until they have first helped liberate all sentient beings. Sometimes, they are told that their vow is to attain "complete, perfect Buddhahood" rather than the "inferior enlightenment of an *arahant*." An illustrative example of the *bodhisattva* vow can be found in a verse, often spoken by the Dalai Lama, in a text of the seventh-century Mahayana Buddhist Shantideva: "As long as space abides and as long as the world abides, so long may I abide, destroying the sufferings of the world."[51] Thus, *bodhisattvas* are contrasted with *arahants* who they view as selfishly content with individual liberation instead of willing to remain in *samsara* until all beings are also free from cyclic existence.[52] They are also often told that they are giving up the lower goal of "individual liberation" in favor of "universal liberation." The emphasis throughout is on compassion: there is a strong implication that unless one is willing to take the *bodhisattva* vow, one is self-centered and not compassionate. In some contexts, students are encouraged to look down on Buddhists who don't take the *bodhisattva* vow, depicting Buddhism without the *bodhisattva* vow as unimaginable, unthinkable, and an oxymoron. Such students can be very shocked when they learn more about Buddhist history and discover that the historical Buddha did not teach his students to take a *bodhisattva* vow and emphasized individual liberation.

Implicit in the vow and its surrounding ethos is the understanding that enlightenment in this lifetime is unlikely, even undesirable, because it is not a worthy goal and reveals improper motivation. Thus, the vow is very future-oriented and presumes acceptance of rebirth as a fact, at least in more traditional settings. One is essentially saying that one is willing to put up with a very long, if not endless, series of deaths and rebirths because of the desire to be useful and helpful to others. That is quite a commitment if one is realistic, rather than romantic, about what rebirth entails.

What can contemporary Buddhists, especially Western Buddhists, make of such a proposition? In my long experience of listening to Buddhist teachers—both Asian and Western—discussing this vow, several things stand out. First, the emphasis is fundamentally on developing a caring, compassionate attitude and helping others, even if that involves personal discomfort, rather than on future rebirths. Such concern for the general well-being of others is the most crucial aspect of the vow. One dedicates oneself to the task, without calculating personal gain and loss. Second, some teachers who give the *bodhisattva* vow also encourage their students to nevertheless strive for enlightenment in this life, even though a general assumption is that the *bodhisattva* vow suggests it takes many lifetimes. One teacher said, "Don't worry that if you attain enlightenment and are not reborn, you will no longer be able to help others. Remember the example of the Buddha who was not reborn. Who has helped more people?" Finally, this same teacher took the unprecedented (at least in my experience) step of simply giving the *bodhisattva* vow to the whole audience attending a teaching session at which one student had asked to receive it. She said, "One should think about taking refuge vows, but why would anyone hesitate to take *bodhisattva* vows? It's just a vow to be more kind. So you're all getting it, whether you asked for it or not!" Thus, the *bodhisattva* vow has been taught variously by different teachers seeking to bridge the gap.

One question remains: how did the *bodhisattva* ideal come to replace the *arahant* ideal, despite the fact that the *arahant* ideal may be much closer to what the historical Buddha taught? This transition is one of the more obscure chapters in Buddhist history, and so very few books discuss it in any detail. Nevertheless, several factors seem crucial: One of them was a growing skepticism about the worthiness of an *arahant* (not so much those who were immediate disciples of the Buddha, but of those who claimed that status in later times). One theory hypothesizes that there must have been some failure of leadership or major scandal that weakened peoples' confidence in the leaders of the *sangha* of the time. Nevertheless, in Mahayana Buddhism in general, the *bodhisattva* ideal replaced the *arahant* ideal.

Even more unnerving was the fact that as time went by, according to the historical accounts, fewer and fewer people seemed to attain realization. In my view, this was partially due to the fact that people began to expect an *arahant* to perform miracles as proof of their enlightenment. Perhaps it was due to the Buddha's extraordinary tales that had been passed down by laity and monks, or that religious accomplishments are often associated with miracles. But because miracles are always much rarer in any contemporary time than in legends about the past, people began to conclude that it was no longer possible to attain enlightenment. As often happens after the death of important religious leaders, emphasis gradually shifted from the past Buddha to the future Buddha, Maitreya, and practitioners hope that they would be reborn when he would be on Earth. The term *maitreya* derives from the term *maitri*, meaning "loving-kindness" (one of the components of Brahamaviharas, as discussed earlier), which indicates a Buddha of compassion and friendliness who will bring *dharma* to the world.

But why wait for Maitreya? As stories about the Buddha's previous lives, and the *bodhisattva* vow he took many lifetimes ago, grew more prominent, people began to look to the Buddha's previous life (in which he took his *bodhisattva* vow) as their model and not his last earthly life (in which he attained enlightenment, deathlessness, and freedom from future samsaric existence). Thus, taking the *bodhisattva* vow became the prevalent norm of Mahayana Buddhists. Others rejected it based on the Buddha's own words. According to the followers of early Buddhism, the Buddha had not taught this practice. But Mahayanists reply that the Buddha is much more than one historical person, and that *dharma* can be greater than what he taught, even if it cannot conflict with what he taught.

Although both *arahant* and *bodhisattva* ideals can be justified, in their more polemical presentations, Mahayanists also claim that earlier forms of Buddhism were not simply different but were in fact mistaken and inadequate. Historically speaking, it is quite common for new religious movements to be extremely critical of what has come before, so this dimension of Mahayana thought is understandable as an historical phenomenon that has typified various reform movements. Mahayana's extremely critical stance toward earlier Buddhism is, in fact, one of the proofs that it was once a new religious movement in the Buddhist context. But because these Mahayana polemics concern the major Buddhist ideals of wisdom and compassion, it is important to examine whether these Mahayana claims hold up. A thorough analysis would require many pages of commentary, but for the current purposes an overview is necessary and sufficient.

Quite commonly, Mahayana polemical texts claim that earlier Buddhists were lacking in wisdom because they did not sufficiently understand emptiness or voidness (*shunyata*), a concept developed by the second-century Buddhist philosopher Nagarjuna. To help make sense of this discussion, it must be remembered that the oft-used term "emptiness" simply means that things exist interdependently; that is, they do not exist inherently, but only apparently. Mahayanist polemics claim that earlier Buddhists understood that the ego, or the self, is empty of inherent existence but did not sufficiently understand that phenomena are also empty of inherent, non-derivative, existence. This is a rather astonishing claim whose basis is not clear, for it simply is not born out by a reading of early Buddhist texts. Evidently those who make this claim are arguing with certain interpretations of *Abhidhamma*, and not with early Buddhist texts. Given that Tibetan Buddhists, who are prone to making this argument, do not have most of the early texts in their canon, but do study *Abhidhamma* extensively, this hypothesis has at least some cogency. One would have to concede that early Buddhist texts did not use the word "emptiness" very frequently, but that does not mean that the insight is lacking. They simply express the insight in other ways, such as the constant emphasis on the ideas of interdependence and impermanence in the Pali canon.

The other major Mahayana polemical claim against earlier Buddhists is even more problematic. As has already been discussed in part, their promotion of the *bodhisattva* ideal as the only relevant path for a Buddhist practitioner has led Mahayanists to claim that early Buddhists were deficient in their appreciation of kindness and compassion, despite the importance of the four immeasurables in early Buddhist teaching. But more critical is what the Buddha says very early in his teaching career when he sends his disciples out to teach others, telling them to go forth and teach "for the welfare and happiness of many, out of compassion for the world, for the benefit, welfare, and happiness of gods and men [sic]."[53] This refrain is repeated many times in the Pali texts. Nevertheless, in my conversations with Mahayanist students, when I have pointed out this passage, they have replied with reverence, "Oh, that sounds so Mahayana!" Another asked me if it was not possible that the phrase had been inserted into the text later on by a Mahayana commentator. This expectation that Mahayanists somehow have a monopoly on the Buddhist concept of compassion is very pejorative and really deserves to be eradicated from Mahayana self-representation.

Important Mahayana Thinkers and Movements

Though Indian Buddhism remained internally diverse until its disappearance from India, many of the newer intellectual and philosophical currents of Buddhist thought came from thinkers identified as Mahayanists. Perhaps the two most important of these thinkers are Nagarjuna (second century CE) and Asanga (fourth century CE). They are associated with the two major schools of Indian Mahayana philosophy, Madhyamaka ("Middle Way") and Yogachara ("Yoga Practice"), which is usually called the "mind-only" school.

Nagarjuna comes very early in the sequence of named authors of major Buddhist texts and is often considered the most important Buddhist teacher after the Buddha himself, sometimes even being referred to as "the second Buddha." His most famous text, and one he definitively authored out of the many attributed to him, is the *Mulamadhyamakakarika* ("Fundamental Verses on the Middle Way"). For Buddhists, finding the middle way between extremes has always been a central focus, and the main point of this work is to argue that emptiness—every phenomenon's lack of inherent existence—is the middle way between eternalism and nihilism. In other words, the middle way is against the view that persons exist eternally, and against the view that no person exists after death, which would mean that there are no consequences for your actions after this life.

Nagarjuna declared, in one of his most famous verses, that if one understands interdependence, then one understands that all things without exception are empty of inherent existence, though they do appear real to the senses. This distinction between appearance and existence is crucial to understanding what Nagarjuna is saying. Writing in the midst of the *Abhidhamma* debates, Nagarjuna apparently thought that declaring all phenomena empty of inherent existence would more effectively short-circuit the human tendency to rely on phenomena to satisfy us than the endless parsing of *Abhidhamma* analysis that reduces all existence to atomic units.[54] Nagarjuna grounds himself in the early Pali *suttas*, and though he often has been rejected by Theravadins and embraced by Mahayanists, I would claim that he is a pan-Buddhist thinker rather than a specifically Mahayana thinker. In his main text, he neither affirms the Mahayana *sutras* as *buddhavachana*, nor advocates the *bodhisattva* ideal against the *arahant* ideal. As we have seen, these are the two marks of a specifically Mahayana orientation concerning Buddhist sectarianism. However, his ideas were taken up by later thinkers who regarded themselves specifically as Mahayanists and ignored by those who did not.

The situation is quite different with Asanga, who might be considered the founder of Mahayana Buddhism as a specific orientation or denomination within Buddhism. As the author of at least five major treatises, he defended and advocated for Mahayana texts as the "true teaching" of the Buddha. His role in the emergence of fully realized Mahayana ideas about Buddhahood, the *Trikaya*, has already been presented. But what makes him specifically a Mahayanist is his allegiance to the future Buddha, Maitreya, combined with his assumption that enlightenment was no longer possible, and so his goal was to be reborn with Maitreya when he incarnated on earth as the next Buddha.

According to one interpretation of the four turnings of the *dharma* wheel, the Yogachara teachings (a prominent school of Mahayana Buddhism) are often regarded as the third turning of the wheel of *dharma*, playing off the image that the Buddha turned the *dharma* wheel the first time when he gave his first sermon. Nagarjuna's teachings on emptiness, often said to be explanations of the *Prajnaparamita sutras*, which Mahayanists claim were taught by the Buddha himself, are considered the second turning. As a third-turning teacher, Asanga more fully worked out some of the implications of interdependence and emptiness. He focused more on psychology and how the mind apprehends appearing—but empty—phenomena. How they appear is at least in part conditioned by the characteristics of the apprehending mind, especially by how confused or enlightened that mind is. What we know is what our minds apprehend, which is the meaning of the "mind-only," often mistakenly said to be a form of idealism. These teachings claim that there are no physical objects "out there," external to the mind. They claim that neither subject nor object can arise independently, but only interdependently upon each other. The fundamental mistake we make is to reify either or both. In fact, there is no independently existing subject or object of consciousness—there is just consciousness.

Finally, Asanga wrote a very famous text called the *Uttaratantra Shastra*, which is a treatise about *tathagatagarbha* (often translated as "Buddha Nature"). The treatise is said to have been dictated to Asanga by the Bodhisattva Maitreya.

The Tathagatagarbha School based its teachings around sutras such as the *Tathagatagarbha Sutra*, the *Shrimaladevi Simhanada Sutra*, and the *Lankavatara Sutra*, the last of which was also influential in the Yogachara School. These teachings work out more fully and explicitly the implicit assumption, found in most schools of Buddhism, that all beings have the potential to attain realization, transcend their confusion and ignorance, and truly understand things-as-they-are. Without this assumption, the whole Buddhist enterprise would not make much sense. Nevertheless, because these teachings are often phrased in substantialist language, as if some kind of real "self" or entity is being posited, not even all Mahayana schools agree with this teaching.[55]

With Asanga, Mahayana became a definitive denomination within Buddhism, whereas before him there had merely been many disparate tendencies or strains of thought. It is also about this same time that archeological findings include references specifically to Mahayana institutions in donations records for the first time.[56]

The Mahayana sutras and thinkers sought to solve many of the problems plaguing Buddhism at the time, especially those circling around the question of why one specific person, Siddhartha Gautama, had become the Buddha of our age, and how best to follow his example. For Mahayanists, the *bodhisattva* path was established as the only correct option for a Buddhist practitioner. But those solutions created almost as many problems as they solved. The consensus was that it had taken the person who became our Buddha countless lifetimes to achieve that goal, and it would therefore take each practitioner countless lifetimes—three incalculable eons—to attain complete, perfect Buddhahood. Essentially, the Mahayana considered enlightenment and freedom to be unimaginably far into the future.

Later, Mahayana Buddhism became extremely diverse, especially as Buddhism was adopted in East Asia where newer forms began to develop. It is impossible to survey all those forms of Buddhism in one chapter, but it is helpful to briefly discuss three later developments in Mahayana Buddhism, all of which are well-known in the West today. Furthermore, they all sought to solve the problem of how to speed up the enlightenment process and in effect return to the early Buddhist understanding that this could be one's final samsaric birth. These three schools are: Vajrayana, Pure Land, and Zen Buddhism. None of these schools undercut or eliminated the *bodhisattva* vow for their adherents, but they nevertheless also promised more immediate relief to the problem of perpetual rebirth.

Vajrayana Buddhism

Vajrayana Buddhism, today most characteristic of Tibetan Buddhist schools, developed in north India in the last centuries before Buddhism's demise in India. This is a very complex form of Buddhism that can be daunting, even unnerving, to outsiders. It is also subject to runaway misrepresentation because of its recent public presentations of sexual imagery, which can be alarming to the practitioners of the path. Vajrayana Buddhism often claims to be the "path of skillful means" that can lead to Buddhahood in this lifetime and in one's current body. Vajrayanists are very serious about their claim of enlightenment in a single lifetime through the use of their specific methods. The skillful means recommended in Vajrayana practice is to identify with an already enlightened being, meaning one of the innumerable *sambhogakaya* Buddhas and *bodhisattvas*. In its practice, this branch includes various elements of yoga, including chanting (*mantra*), ritual hand gestures (*mudra*), and visualization of the enlightened being (meditation). One recites a liturgy about this being, visualizes oneself as this being, and recites its *mantra* (a set of syllables that capture its essence). Through this process, one sheds one's conventional identity as a confused, unaware human being and gradually comes to more fully understand the core of one's self as an already enlightened being who has temporarily lost his or her way.[57] Because of the Tibetan leader, the fourteenth Dalai Lama, and his world-wide popularity, this tradition is becoming more widely known in the West.

Pure Land Buddhism

Pure Land Buddhism is one of the dominant forms of Buddhism in Japan, though it derives from the *Sukhavati-Vyuha Sutra*s composed in India. Despite the fact that it has Indian and Chinese antecedents, Pure Land Buddhism came into its own in twelfth- and thirteenth-century Japan under the leadership of Honen and Shinran. This Buddhism is oriented to the *sambhogakaya* Buddha Amitabha (Japanese: Amida)—the "Buddha of Infinite Light"—who used the immense merit earned during his long *bodhisattva* career to create a "Pure Land" located in the Western quarter of the cosmos, not on this Earth. His vow was to create a Pure Land in which enlightenment and rebirth would be easy, because he recognized how difficult, and even impossible, it was for ordinary human beings to meet the immense demands of a thorough-going Buddhist practice. According to Pure Land Buddhism, one needs only to rely on the power of Amitabha's vow, and on what he has already done for us to be reborn in his Pure Land. There, full enlightenment is only a step away and everything co-operates to teach the *dharma*. This might be interpreted as the most "faith-based" of all forms of Buddhism and therefore also one of the most easily misunderstood. Many Pure Land Buddhists claim that giving up self-reliance is the ultimate form of egoless-ness. Recognizing that there is no permanent abiding self beneath the flux of experience is one of Buddhism's most central ways of talking about interdependence and emptiness.[58] Nevertheless, some Mahayanist Buddhist sources describe the "Buddha-nature" in a way that appears to be something similar to the permanent abiding self.

Zen Buddhism

The form of Buddhism best known by its Japanese name "Zen" (Chinese: *Ch'an*) also has strong antecedents in India and China. Traditionally, the origins of the school are traced to Bodhidharma, an

Indian teacher who came to China from India in the sixth century CE, although accounts of his life are more legendary than historical. One of the most important of all Zen teachers is Dogen, who—along with his school of "Soto Zen"—flourished in thirteenth-century Japan and is regarded as perhaps one of the most brilliant Buddhist thinkers of all time. Rather than the complexity of Vajrayana Buddhism and some Buddhist philosophical schools, this form of Buddhism advocates simply sitting mindfully (*zazen*), also called Zen sitting, in the posture of enlightenment (cross-legged with erect back) that Buddhists often believed was the posture that Siddhartha assumed when he sat under the Bodhi Tree. The Zen tradition emphasizes regular face-to-face meeting (*dokusan*) with one's teacher or monastic leader, also known by the common name *roshi*. Dedicated practice of this exercise is believed to yield the same results for contemporary practitioners as it did for Siddhartha on that May, full moon night two and half millennia ago—an awakening which brings peace and freedom. This single practice alone is considered sufficient and one need not engage in the ritual and philosophical complexities that have developed in Buddhism in the intervening centuries.[59]

"I Go for Refuge to the *Sangha*": The Community of Those Who Practice Dhamma Together

The various schools of Buddhism are a testament to the fact that *dhamma*—as reliable teachings—has been interpreted variously over the centuries. This is to be expected, for the *dhamma* is the central theme of the Three Refuges. The Buddha himself is believed to have claimed that the *dhamma* he taught was far more important than his own historical personage. The *sangha* (community) exists only because there is a group of people who practice and rely on *dhamma*. Historians of religions tell us that living religions are constantly updating and changing, and that the only unchanging religion is a religion that no one practices any more. Thus, it should not be surprising that many variants on the refuge of *dhamma* are alive and flourishing today, although there is also always a conservative strain that resists, decries, and condemns change. Every new Buddhist movement that ever developed had its detractors who claimed that it was a perversion of the true *dhamma*.

Yet the old Buddhist text, the Pali *Mahaparinibbana Sutta*, either anticipated this development, or, perhaps, had the relevant episode inserted into the *sutta* after various versions of *dhamma* had already begun to develop. Almost on his deathbed, the Buddha instructed his disciples about what to do when, after his death, people would come forward with texts and teachings that they claimed to have heard from the Buddha himself. He instructed them to neither accept nor reject such teachings but to examine them thoroughly and determine whether or not they were in accord with established *dhamma/dharma*. If they were, they could be regarded as *buddhavachana* whether or not the historical Buddha had ever spoken such words during his earthly life.[60] Whatever is taught by any one of these well-established forms of Buddhism, its adherents regard those teachings as reliable teachings taught by the Buddha himself, even if they were taught by a disciple who had realized the reliable *dharma* on their own hundreds of years later or obtained through a vision of the Buddha.

From its very beginnings, the *sangha*, or the community of those who practice *dharma* together, has been crucial to Buddhist practice and self-understanding. As soon as there were disciples and students of the Buddha, the *sangha* became the third refuge. While Buddhist practice is essentially a matter of individual understanding and realization, it is very difficult to pursue alone. Most people who try to understand and practice Buddhism solely on their own become discouraged and lose heart. For starters, *dharma* teachers are considered essential because Buddhism's often counter-intuitive messages might be difficult to assimilate on one's own. People are encouraged and uplifted when they practice and study difficult materials together. Like-minded companions are very helpful on the spiritual path.

In most Buddhist settings, the *sangha* has consisted of monastics and laypeople in a symbiotic relationship of financial and spiritual support. However, how to structure that relationship so that it is of genuine and mutual benefit to both monastics and laypeople needs to be explored carefully. Certain basic understandings of whom or what the *sangha* is need to be established, before other issues and considerations can even be dealt with. For those guidelines, we should look at how *sangha* is discussed in the earlier texts attributed to the Buddha himself. Citing the *Mahaparinibbana Sutta*—though the same comments are frequently found in other texts as well—in this first layer of Buddhist understandings of *sangha*, it is understood to consist of four orders: monks, nuns, laymen, and laywomen. In the story told in the *Mahaparinibbana Sutta*, Mara comes to the Buddha and suggests that it is time for him to leave his mortal body. According to the legend, almost immediately after his enlightenment experience, Mara had come to Buddha with the same request, but Buddha had countered that he would not attain *parinibbana* ("final release," or physical death with no following samsaric rebirth) until there were realized disciples who could teach and transmit the *dharma* in all four divisions of the *sangha*. In the *sutta*, the criteria are laid out:

> monks and disciples who are accomplished, trained, skilled, learned, knowers of the Dhamma, trained in conformity with the Dhamma, correctly trained and walking in the path of Dhamma who will pass on what they have gained from their Teacher, teach it, declare it, establish it, expound it, analyze it, make it clear, till they shall be able by means of the Dhamma to refute false teachings that have arisen, and teach the Dhamma of wondrous effect.[61]

In the highly repetitive style of Pali canon this text then repeats exactly the same phrases regarding "nuns and female disciples," laymen followers, and laywomen followers.[62] These disciples are not only well trained themselves, but are also able to pass on the *dharma* that they have been taught. At this point in the narrative, which is toward the end of the Buddha's life, the Buddha accedes to Mara's request, replying that it is acceptable for him to end his work because there are now accomplished disciples and teachers in all four orders of the *sangha*.

Several points are crucial. Despite the clarity of this definition of *sangha*, throughout Buddhist history many other definitions have been proposed. In some of them, the *sangha* does not even consist of human followers of Buddha Dharma, but only of already enlightened beings and *bodhisattvas*. Other points about the *Mahaparinibbana Sutta's* definition of *sangha* need to be highlighted. First, both monastics and lay followers are given equal status and responsibility for realizing and teaching the *dharma*. Second, and very clearly, both women and men, whether as monastics or laypeople, are given equal status and responsibility for realizing and teaching the *dharma*. These points are so important because they have so often been violated throughout Buddhist history and in Buddhist discussions about who the "real" *sangha* is and who can realize and should teach the *dhamma*. Very often it is the male monastics who have been privileged to hold this role, as if they alone were the true followers of *dhamma* and the only spokespersons for the Buddha as *dharma* teachers. However, regarding both laypeople and women (as nuns or laywomen), this common traditional practice clearly violates what the Buddha is represented as having said in this *sutta*. Here, the Buddha states how it is essential that not only male monastics but women also become realizers of *dhamma* and capable teachers of *dharma*. Otherwise his mission has not been fulfilled. In most situations throughout Buddhist history, the evidence clearly demonstrates that, regarding this guideline, the Buddha's mission is far from having been fulfilled.

Monastic and Lay Buddhists in Various Forms of Asian Buddhism

The original model for the Buddhist community as set up by the Buddha during his lifetime clearly involved both division and symbiosis between monastic and lay Buddhists. This model—that has been followed by most Buddhist communities throughout history—is also somewhat unusual in world religions, although there are Hindu monastics and monasticism in Jain and Catholic communities to a similar extent.

Buddhist monasticism owes a great deal to the cultural norms of the Buddha's day, during a time of relative prosperity and peace in India which allowed for intellectual and spiritual exploration. Many people doubted whether the accepted, conventional ways of life and ritual practices, as taught in the Vedas, worked or brought lasting peace and satisfaction. One could say that a "countercultural" movement (or rather a parallel *sramana*, or ascetic movement) was occurring that led many to question what we might call "the establishment," especially regarding established religious practices and goals. The alternative renouncer lifestyle of those who rejected the establishment in India of the Buddha's time involved renouncing domestic life, social position, possessions, family, and career because it seemed clear to them that such pursuits could not bring deep satisfaction or spiritual liberation. Instead, they lived a life of homeless wandering, depending on local residents for food and shelter on a daily basis. They then spent their time in deep introspection, meditation, and various other spiritual disciplines, seeking freedom from the endless round of conventional samsaric rebirth and realization of deep serenity and joy in the meanwhile. Siddhartha was only one of many young men (and much fewer women) who opted out of the conventional system by choosing renunciation (*sannyasa*, the fourth stage of life) without fulfilling other *dharma*s (duties) as prescribed in Hindu Dharma (even though the Buddha is said to have "rebelled" against certain existing practices such as caste system, he often used the vocabulary of the Vedic system and remained in the Brahmanical cultural norms.) There were many orders of such homeless wanderers in Siddhartha's day. The one founded by Siddhartha Gautama was uniquely successful, but another contemporary order, the Jains, has also survived to the present day. Historically, the *sramana* movement was incorporated into the mainstream movement of Brahamanical traditions around the life of the Buddha, and it continues to the present day.

Traditionally in India's religious context, such renunciation of social position, responsibilities, and possessions has been accepted, even respected, in Indian society from ancient times all the way to the present. Indian culture and religion have a deep recognition of the fact that material pursuits do not satisfy our deepest spiritual longings and that radical renunciation may be required to achieve spiritual fulfillment. But the preferred alternative in Indian society is to take that step later in life, after having fulfilled family and social responsibilities, when the younger generation can take over and carry on the task of maintaining family, social, and political order, as outlined in the earlier chapter on Hindu Dharma. Generally, for young men to take that step was more radical and less appreciated. Often young women did not have the option of opting out from social constraints for the pursuit of individual liberation. Though Buddhists have always respected and often romanticize the young men who became the Buddha's followers, their fathers, mothers, wives, and children were often much less enthusiastic about having been abandoned by them.

In this model, monastics and laypeople are quite distinct from each other, though they are also interdependent. Monastics' appearances are completely distinctive—one can immediately identify monastics by their dress and demeanor. Buddhist monks and nuns shave their heads and wear identical robes supposed to be made out of cast-off rags, though these days they seldom are. If dietary rules are strictly followed, they eat one main meal a day and don't eat after the noonday. Their possessions are few, and according to the strictest rules they are not allowed to handle money or engage in trade and agriculture. Monastics gave up homeless wandering soon after the Buddha's lifetime; monastic dwellings were created separate from villages but also close enough for frequent interactions. In Indian and Southeast Asian contexts, though not in East Asian or Tibetan contexts, monastics often go to the village daily to "beg" for food in a ritualized exchange. Obviously, monastics—who traditionally did not have roles as merchants, farmers, or any other occupation of the day— were completely economically dependent on laypeople and that interdependence still holds in most Asian Buddhist contexts.

But what of laypeople in general? What's in this system for them? For despite the Buddha's oft-repeated guideline that the *sangha* consists of monks, nuns, laymen, and laywomen, we hear mainly about monks in most Buddhist records. Both monastics and laypeople regard the traditional division of labor as a mutually beneficial symbiotic system because to attain Buddhism's goals one needs to engage in the two accumulations: the accumulation of merit (through positive *karma*) and the accumulation of wisdom. Monastics gain the opportunity to find release through the accumulation of wisdom, and laypeople are enabled to accumulate merit through their generous support of monastics and religious institutions. The accumulation of wisdom depends on the study of Buddhist teachings and practice of Buddhist disciplines, such as keeping the vows, study of scriptures, and meditation. These take considerable time and effort. The accumulation of wisdom greatly facilitates realization, which is difficult, if not impossible, without it. Therefore, a lifestyle dedicated to the accumulation of wisdom is important, and the monastic lifestyle of renouncing family and career was thought to be the ideal way to dedicate oneself fully to it. But not everyone is emotionally or temperamentally suited to monasticism, or is so inclined to renounce sensory and societal needs. For such people, the accumulation of merit was the most relevant option. Merit is accumulated by an ethical lifestyle in general, and generosity towards those pursuing the accumulation of wisdom full time in particular. It is hard to overemphasize how important generosity is in traditional Buddhist ethics.

It is also hard to overemphasize how well this system that recognizes two paths works to support those pursuing scholarship, art, and spiritual realization. Those who provide the generous support also gain from this system. The belief in the Dharma traditions in general is that the accumulation of merit through generosity leads to a happy and successful life in the future. Equally, it is believed that stinginess, especially if one is wealthy, leads to a negative future. Thus, generally in Asia the wealthy have supported monastics in Buddhist and other religious institutions. If anything about traditional Buddhism provides relevant commentary on contemporary American society, surely this understanding of wealth and generosity manages.

But this symbiotic system also has its downside. For one, it presupposes that serious Buddhist practice and study will be done mainly by monastics. Laypeople were usually not taught deeper Buddhist principles because it was not thought that they would have the time or inclination to do such study and practice. Clearly, serious Buddhist practice can be difficult and time-consuming (it is not surprising that Mahayana Buddhist traditions, like Pure Land, seek to make the *dharma* accessible to all). But the problem of establishing a community of diligent lay practitioners has sometimes been unsuccessful on account of the fact that the system expects monastics to specialize in the accumulation of wisdom, and laypeople to specialize in the accumulation of merit. At times lay Buddhists move away from the *dhamma* taught by Buddhist teachers and resort to folk practices of magic that Buddha himself did not endorse. This specialization also makes it easier to undermine the Buddhist path because its specialists are so dependent on a group of political patrons or economic donors whose loyalties can shift. Historically, on more than one occasion, when the monasteries were destroyed and the monastics returned to lay life, Buddhist tradition as an independent practice either died out or never again returned to a high level of achievement, because lay Buddhists had not been sufficiently educated and had not developed deep loyalty to Buddhist principles and understandings. Such a story partially explains how Buddhist traditions became nearly extinct in the land of its origins. Additionally, the requirement for celibacy and other vows sometimes became a problem, observed more in the breach than in actuality.

In the sweep of Buddhist history, there has been some shift away from such heavy reliance on monastics, especially male monastics, as the main carriers of Buddhist tradition. In Vajrayana Buddhism, both in late North-Indian Buddhism and in Tibetan Buddhism, a third alternative gained popularity. Claiming to be neither monastic nor lay, some practitioners called themselves *yogis* (masculine), or *yoginis* (feminine). They did not join monasteries or nunneries and sometimes formed long-term partnerships with spiritual consorts. But Buddhist practice and realization was their top priority, not conventional family life or business success. They studied and practiced as seriously as was the norm for monastics, perhaps more seriously in many cases, and often became important teachers. Those practices that don't fit in the binary categories of lay and monastic have been termed as Tantric—they generally emphasized the spiritual efficacy of practices such as mantra recitation, meditative visualization, and ritualism.[63]

Japanese Buddhism also began to depend much less on celibate monastics as carriers of Buddhist tradition in the thirteenth century when Shinran—who, with his teacher Honen, co-founded Pure Land Buddhism—left monastic life, and married, but did not give up his role of religious leadership. Instead, he proclaimed a dedicated life style that was neither lay nor monastic. He had been trained at the great Tendai monastery on Mount Hei, northwest of Kyoto, which was then the leading Buddhist institution in Japan. But he was troubled by the fact that neither his philosophic studies and rituals nor his meditative practices brought him the peace and contentment that had been promised. He was equally troubled by the show of celibacy, which many found a difficult vow to keep. He finally decided to leave for good and turned to more devotional practices based on the Pure Land sutras. His teachings on the virtues of relying on "other-power" and the efficacy of Buddha Amida's Primal Vow, rather than an unreasonable expectation in this degenerate age of "self-power," resonated with the Japanese people. Thus, the emphasis is on the power of Amida Buddha's vow for the final release, not the self-effort. His school of Buddhism eventually became the dominant form of Buddhism in Japan. He also openly married, which was unprecedented for Japanese Buddhist leaders of the day. Due to some political factors and his successful example, celibate monasticism is almost non-existent in Japan today. Most Japanese temples are owned and run by a family lineage in which the priesthood is hereditary. Priests may go through a period of celibate monastic training in their youth, but they then return to take over their home temples and raise the next generation of religious leaders.

These two cases, and others such as Buddhism in Nepal, show how the more common Buddhist tendency to favor male monastics over laymen has been challenged in significant ways. The Buddha also set up a fourfold *sangha* that included realized nuns and laywomen who were competent to teach *dhamma*. Historically speaking, however, many Buddhist institutions have not fared well in meeting this criterion set up by its founder.[64]

The guideline for the fourfold *sangha* is found, among other places, in the *Mahaparinibbana Sutta*. However, a much more frequently cited comment is also found in the Pali *suttas*. In the Pali *Vinaya* (and other *Vinayas* as well), a story is told of how the Buddha's foster-mother, Mahaprajapati, requested ordination as a female monastic, which the Buddha finally granted, though reluctantly, and only after imposing eight special rules on nuns that completely subordinated them to male monastics.[65] Obviously, there is a conflict between how the Buddha is represented in this story and what he said at the end of his life in the *Mahaparinibbana Sutta*. Most scholars reject the ordination story as a later interpolation because it is so at odds with the other narratives of the Buddha's encounters with women like Sujata (who fed ascetic Siddhartha Gautama milk and rice before he sat under the Bodhi tree for meditation) and Visakha (an extremely affluent devout follower and supporter of the Buddha). Nevertheless, given a long history of Buddhist androcentrism and misogyny, the story of the Buddha not wanting to ordain women is much better known to most Buddhists, including relatively well-educated Buddhists, than the frequent repetition of his guidelines on the fourfold *sangha*. It is often quoted by those who oppose the revival of women's monastic ordinations.

Thus, it becomes clear that, whatever the historical Buddha may have taught, the culture of male dominance, combined with some misogyny, have been dominant in most parts of Asia throughout much of Buddhist history and have overwhelmed whatever egalitarian insights the Buddha may have brought into his *sangha*. A nuns' *sangha* was found in Indian Buddhism, which probably existed until Buddhism's disappearance from India, and was also transmitted to Sri Lanka with the rest of mainstream Buddhism, most likely during the reign of King Ashoka in the third century BCE. Historically, the Sri Lankan nuns' *sangha* was wiped out in the eleventh century and was not restored there until the twentieth century. Buddha Dharma spread to the rest of Southeast Asia, but the tradition of nuns' ordination did not spread with Buddhism, although various forms of women's renunciate lifestyle were introduced locally. Nevertheless, *bhikkhuni* (nun) ordination had been taken from Sri Lanka to China and from there to other parts of East Asia. Those ordination lineages have never died out, and today nuns in Korea, Vietnam, and all parts of the Chinese diaspora practice in these lineages. As for Tibet, nuns have been able to receive novice ordination for centuries, though until recently their levels of economic support and education were generally pitifully low.

Contemporary times in many parts of the Asian Buddhist world have seen enrollment in monks' *sanghas* declining, as men seek prosperity in the secular economy, while nuns' *sanghas* have increased in numbers. Socio-economic factors also affect women who seek to adopt the religious life of a nun. Women, who do not have the same opportunities in the secular economy, become nuns to avoid patriarchal marriages, to have a somewhat independent life, and to receive some education. Nuns are gradually receiving better economic support and more complete Buddhist educations. There are also vigorous movements to restore full *bhikkhuni* ordination to Tibetan and Theravada forms of Buddhism. These movements are on the verge of success as of this writing.

Laywomen, however, have been both the economic backbone of interdependent monastic/lay institutions and the most neglected segment of the fourfold *sangha*. For large financial donations, monastic institutions may be dependent on powerful, rich business leaders and other Buddhist laymen. But on a daily basis, monks depend on laywomen for their daily rations and taking care of the immediate needs for the care of the monasteries. Within a domestic unit, women traditionally have considerable power and independence in dispersing economic resources, and make all the daily decisions regarding such matters. Thus, when monks go on their early morning "begging" rounds, it is women and girls who ladle food into their empty bowls, which they then carry back to the monastery for a communal meal shared equally by all, no matter their individual success at "begging" on any specific day.

However, despite their economic centrality, the fate of most of these girls and women was to be allowed very little Buddhist education, to have very little chance for serious Buddhist practice, to marry young, and to be expected to spend their lives taking care of men and children. The freedom from domestic drudgery afforded by life as a monastic was never as widely available to women as to men. Having a son who became a monastic brought prestige to a family, but having a daughter who became a nun did not. It is no wonder that the view that rebirth as a woman was an unfortunate occurrence became widespread in the Buddhist world. And given the modern pursuit of gender equality, it is no wonder there is a rise of worldwide contemporary Buddhist women's movements. It is important to note that this phenomenon is not specific to Buddhist traditions, and can also be seen in various Hindu and Jain traditions.

Sangha in Contemporary Times: Issues and Recommendations

The monastic/lay division and symbiosis of traditional Asian Buddhism was rooted in the norms and values of Indian culture of the Buddha's day. It was also rooted in the practicalities of a labor-intensive agricultural economy as well as social and medical conditions which meant that people engaging in sexual activities were very likely to have children. Many of those children would die young and many women also died in childbirth. In addition, the modern conditions of individual choice to which we are so accustomed—of being able to live on one's own apart from family and society—were virtually impossible. People could not and did not survive as independent individuals and had to be part of a social unit, such as a family or clan. If one did not want to primarily belong to either a family or a clan, one needed the support of a different social aggregate such as a monastic community. To have monastics (mainly male) specialize in Buddhist study and practice, and laypeople specialize in accumulating merit by supporting them in their worthy endeavors, may have been the most adaptive solution possible, given those limits of economy and society. Even the gender roles, which seem so unpleasant to modern women, may have been all that was possible given the medical knowledge and social and economic factors, but women navigated those roles skillfully, with respect to women's contributions to the *sangha*. However, this does not mean there is any reason to regard traditional Buddhist gender roles and the monastic/lay division of labor as timelessly appropriate ideal, or as something by which we should be bound today. Various modern teachers in Dharma traditions are finding ways to interpret scriptures so that women can enjoy the right to dignity and autonomy.

In particular, there is no reason to equate the renunciation considered necessary for Buddhist monastics to have shaved heads and wear robes. Renunciation is often believed to be foundational in early Buddhism (although, as mentioned earlier, some East Asian Buddhism chose to reject this tradition), and so one needs to renounce a great number of conventional attitudes, desires, and habits because they are counter-productive and do not lead to the peace and freedom that are the goals of Buddhist practice. In many forms of Buddhism, the traditional criteria for renunciation were having neither family nor money-making occupations, and the markers of that renunciation were shaved heads and robes. However, the questions arise: is it inappropriate, given contemporary conditions, to assume that only those with shaved heads and who are wearing robes engage in renunciation, and to continue to privilege them above equally worthy and accomplished lay practitioners? Is it impossible for a layperson who has appropriately limited their reproduction and consumption to also be practicing renunciation and be highly accomplished regarding Buddhist study and practice? And should such a person automatically be ranked below monastics and considered less worthy, as has often been the practice in traditional Buddhist cultures? As Buddhism is spreading to all corners of the world, modern followers are asking these questions.

Issues in the Vow of Celibacy

In Buddha's day, the reasons for celibacy may have had little to do with shame about sexuality or the idea that it is "anti-spiritual." Nevertheless, India's culture has traditionally seen the renouncer committed to the spiritual goal of liberation as defined by the vow of celibacy (discussed in the chapter on Hindu Dharma). More practically, celibacy was necessary mainly because sexuality resulted in children, and children then required a great deal of economic support and caregiving, both of which affect the amount of time for Buddhist study and practice. Thus, celibacy was not just about renouncing sex but also about being free of the time-consuming demands of family and career. With birth control allowing modern Buddhist practitioners to have more options and to limit reproduction sensibly or avoid it altogether, as well as longer life spans, these reasons for celibacy may no longer apply to some contemporary practitioners, especially in the West. One can also limit career demands by choosing one that is less stressful, less time-consuming, and more in accord with Buddhist values. Many traditional Buddhists might consider this interpretation to be the "great experiment" as it apparently deviates from the Buddha's teachings that required a life of discipline and renunciation.

However, traditionally there was another, more urgent reason for renouncing sexual relations, family life, and pursuit of a career: without significant Buddhist training already in place, each of these factors might easily become a breeding ground for the many counterproductive attitudes that work against one's peace and freedom, such as desire, grasping, jealousy, competitiveness, hostility, and aggression. These may be the real problems for Buddhist realization, since the path of the Buddha warns against these temptations. The monastic path was meant to safeguard from such distractions. Ironically, such attitudes are not unknown among monastics either. Prestige and career advancement can also be part of a monastic life, and special relationships can be difficult to avoid or eliminate completely, especially considering the high value placed on the teacher–student relationship.

Issues in Religious Authority

Thus, we see from the one side that having a shaved head and wearing robes does not necessarily protect one from some of the most problematic attitudes associated with realization.[66] The Buddha warns against ostentatious display of the outward religious symbols. We see from the other side that under modern conditions, it may be possible that those who are technically laypeople—in that they have not taken vows to renounce sexuality and possessions—may nevertheless practice renunciation. There is another, highly practical reason for lessening the distinctions between those in robes and those not in robes under current conditions. At least in the Western world, there simply is not a significant economic basis for large-scale monasticism, although the economic basis for monasticism may remain in place in Asia. Traditional monasticism requires a large base of pious lay Buddhists, who are invested in the traditional attitude of accruing a stock of merit by serving monks and nuns, and are not concerned with attaining liberation in this life. This large base of pious lay Buddhists is simply non-existent in the West. Most of those who are interested in Buddhism and regard it in highly favorable terms want to engage in Buddhist practice themselves, and that takes considerable time and money. Though they do contribute for the upkeep of Western Buddhist meditation centers and other institutions, much of this support goes to less well-off lay practitioners, allowing them to occasionally attend a practice program, rather than to choose a life of full-time monasticism.

Though some Western monastics bemoan this situation, I do not think it is entirely negative. Some contemporary monks and nuns work as university professors teaching Buddhist studies in secular universities, work that is little different from the educational functions taken on by Buddhist monastic institutions in traditional societies. Their presence and influence could be very beneficial in lower levels of education as well. In traditional Buddhist societies, in which monasteries and nunneries also functioned as orphanages, what literacy existed was often mediated by monastic institutions. Though not as many monastics have as yet taken up such work, there is little reason why monastics should not also take up social service occupations and volunteer work as counselors, therapists, medical personnel, and even police officers—a role they filled in traditional monasteries. Many dedicated lay Buddhists already work in such occupations. One of the criticisms that can be brought against more traditional Buddhist monastic institutions is that they do little to alleviate the suffering so apparent in society all around them, especially when compared to their Christian counterparts, and so modern expressions of Buddhism might address this critique. However, traditional Buddhists may point to the Buddha's teachings to justify their lack of social involvement, which are oriented toward eradicating the existential suffering through the Eightfold Path, not simply eliminating social suffering.

One Buddhist institution in Taiwan is a notable exception to this generalization and may well prove to be a model for future Buddhist service-oriented monasticism. Tzu Chi, whose headquarters are in northeastern Taiwan, is the world's largest Buddhist relief organization. Founded by the female *dharma* master Cheng Yen in 1966, it consists of a small core of economically self-sufficient nuns and a large corps of full and part-time volunteers. It has a medical college at its headquarters and branches all over the world. It has founded, and supports, many hospitals and schools and is frequently involved in relief work after natural disasters everywhere in the world.

A blurring and blending of traditionally lay and traditionally monastic functions and specializations seems to be characteristic of Buddhism in most parts of the modern world. All over the world, including Asia, lay people are taking up serious meditation practice, once thought to be something that monastics primarily could or should engage in. Some scholars of Buddhism criticize this new emphasis on meditation as something "modern," or even artificial. They claim that throughout Buddhist history, most Buddhists have not meditated, which is certainly true, and that therefore there is something suspect about this sudden surge of interest in meditation. This establishment also says the same thing about the upsurge in more supposedly rational, "modern" understandings of Buddhism prevalent in both Asia and the West. Plenty of rote practices and magical ritualism are still found in the Buddhist world because of the integration of Buddhist teachings into the religiosities of local traditions and cultures. However, a growing interest in a deeper understanding of Buddhist texts and principles, as taught by Buddha, does seem to be on the rise all over the Buddhist world. Some scholars are troubled by Buddhist "modernism," as they call it, because it does not correspond with the traditional folk Buddhism, although they would be hard pressed to demonstrate that such "modern Buddhism" is less in accord with Buddhist classic canonical texts and the Buddhist principles put forth in this chapter than traditional "folk Buddhism."

One of the major characteristics of this modern Buddhism is that the Buddhism of monastics and the Buddhism of laypeople are no longer so different. Differences in dress and in lifestyle may remain to some extent. But differences in understanding, in practices, and in achievements are no longer so noticeable. Certainly this is something to be lauded and celebrated. Monasticism as renunciation of sexuality, family, and possessions should be thought of as a lifestyle choice appropriate for some Buddhists rather than something that makes monastics categorically superior to lay learned Buddhists, who are just as dedicated to Buddhism, devote just as much of their life energy to Buddhism, and are just as knowledgeable and well-practiced, but do not have the traditional shaved heads or wear robes. Thus, a well-educated Buddhist lay person should receive just as much authority and respect in the Buddhist *sangha* as a monastic of similar attainments. Due to the changing cultural and social landscape of religions taking roots in foreign lands, such debates are common and are giving rise to new ways to make the teachings relevant to common people.

Gender Equality

Another major characteristic of this modern *sangha* is its gender equality. Whether as nuns or as laywomen, women will equally take on all Buddhist roles, including that which is most important and central: the role of a *dharma* teacher who at long last fulfills the criteria set out by the historical Buddha in the Pali literature from two-and-a-half millennia ago. There is no doubt that eventually the barriers to women gaining full monastic ordination and Buddhist educations will soon be overcome in those *sanghas* that still do not ordain women or educate them equally with monks. Indeed, in other *sanghas*, especially among Western Buddhists, these barriers have already been largely overcome, with the result that about half the authorized *dharma* teachers are women, at least in North America. Some of these teachers are extremely popular, well-known, and influential: there are a number of very prominent Western scholars and teachers who are drawing attention to women's issues in Buddhism, such as Pema Chodron and Professor Karma Lekshe Tsomo. However, there is still a gap between the perceived higher prestige of male teachers over the female ones.

Additionally, modern *sanghas*, in both their monastic and lay manifestations, will be fully involved with the societies in which they live. Though I would claim that Western and non-Buddhist commentators have underestimated the nature and extent of Buddhist social engagement in Asia and exaggerated the extent of supposed traditional Buddhist passivity, there is still a plenty of room for contemporary "engaged Buddhism." This is an international movement with strong roots in Asia that seeks to bring Buddhist wisdom to bear on contemporary social issues. The phrase itself was coined by Thich Nhat Hanh, the famous Vietnamese social activist and *dharma* teacher, to describe the way in which he and his fellow Vietnamese monastics tried to be of service while not advocating for either side during the Vietnam War. In his work and in that of other commentators on engaged Buddhism, it becomes clear that the major contributions of Buddhism to social action include a deep understanding of how difficult, but how necessary, it is to engage in social action without ideological fixation or self-righteous anger.[67]

Engaged Buddhism

Engaged Buddhism deals with all the major issues of our day: economic injustice, war and peace, environmental degradation, and social discrimination of all forms, to name only some of its most obvious concerns. However, in terms of how engaged Buddhism intersects with traditional Buddha Dharma, the most potent understanding it brings to traditional Buddha Dharma is recognition of the role structural violence plays in suffering. Recognition of structural violence is a relatively modern discovery that explains how human self-interest is the cause of suffering of war, poverty, sexism, racism, or homophobia. Previously, most religions attributed such things to the will of God, natural law, cosmic order, or individual *karma* from distant past lives. But understandings of structural violence demonstrate how the power and influence of a few people can undermine a whole society and cause immense human suffering. Thus, for example, sexism is not the result of God's will or individual *karma* but is instead the creation of the self-interest of a few. In Buddhist Abhidharmic terms, structural violence is a conditioned composite, and, therefore, is inevitably subject to destruction, even if long-lived. Humans created this monster, and so the answer is to collectively choose to disassemble it. For example, rather than continue to regard women's suffering under sexism as the result of their individual *karma*, we use the Buddhist disciplines to confront this mindset. Likewise, for every other form of human suffering that is not the result of human embodiment in an impermanent body, the Buddhist teachings can assist in their eradication. Some prominent examples of engaged Buddhism include the introduction of Mindfulness techniques into the prison system (see the *Dhamma Brothers* program), and Buddhist 12-step recovery programs.[68] There has also been emergence of Buddhist environmental and ecological movements and neuroscientific projects which have focused on the salutary effects of meditation practice.[69] Buddhist feminism (led by

Buddhist nuns such as Professor Karma Lekshe Tsomo) and large-scale organizations such as the International Network of Engaged Buddhists are leading Buddhist social activism.[70] Because this understanding of structural violence is so completely consistent with Buddhist understandings of interdependence and emptiness, it could energize Buddhists to disassemble oppressions taken for granted by too many as the inevitabilities of *karma*. It would become clear that simply affirming the concept of *karma* does not entail ignoring the suffering inflicted by one human upon another, and that the Buddhist path emphasizes the value of taking personal responsibility for the elimination of the demons of greed, temptation, and selfish desire, and not overlooking the suffering of others.

Finally, in the modern *sangha*, there needs to be much less intra-Buddhist sectarianism than in the past. Many modern Buddhists posit the real existence of Theravada and Mahayana Buddhism as separate sects opposed to each other for most of the history of Buddhism. But we have seen that during Buddhism's golden age in India, in the early and middle post-Christian centuries, these movements, trends, or tendencies co-existed in relative peace and harmony. They influenced each other greatly and also debated their disagreements with each other.

But after Buddhism mostly disappeared from India, it was separated into largely Mahayana forms in Northeast Asia (i.e., Tibet, Japan, China, and Korea) and largely Theravada forms in Southeast Asia (i.e., Vietnam, Thailand, Sri Lanka, Laos, and Burma). These forms of Buddhism lost direct contact but nevertheless debated with each other in polemical texts. Now, due to globalization and the ease of communication, all forms of Buddhism can easily interact with one another again. At present in the United States, there are practitioners of most current forms of Buddhism, which is an unprecedented opportunity for interchange. However, the situation is complex in the communities where Buddhist lineages and traditions have continued for many generations. Now we find many small lineages and *sanghas* that remain largely confined to their familiar surroundings, refusing to interact with each other or listen to each other's teachers.

Conclusion

This chapter has systematized the Buddhist framework of *dhamma*, or reliable teachings, through the teaching and practice of the three refuges: Buddha, *dhamma*, and *sangha*. As we have seen, all these teachings go through transformations, with time and changing cultural contexts. Even though Buddhism disappeared from India around the twelfth century CE, it has nevertheless been very influential throughout history in the realms of Indian philosophical thought and Hindu theology. With the works of great Buddhist thinkers, Buddhism finds expression in various new sociocultural and historical forms. The new philosophical and religious ideas evolved from the Buddha Dharma, and these eventually led to various new groups and lineages of Buddhism. This continues to be the case in the modern globalized world as Buddhism has spread across the globe, and continues to be explored as a means of addressing new challenges and problems.

Notes

1. Editor's comment: Sadly, this chapter is being published posthumously as Rita Gross passed away in November 2015. She did not get a chance to see the final book, although she was eagerly waiting to see this piece in print. Given her lifetime's study of Buddhist history and teachings, this chapter at times conveys the strong personal reflections of the author on certain issues. As an editor, I choose to honor her voice and have made edits and additions where they were absolutely needed for clarity and coherence.

2. Rita Gross used the term Buddha Dharma, but, as the editor, I have added the Pali term Dhamma to reflect the language of the Buddha's teachings that have been recorded in the Pali canon.

3. I have chosen to minimize the use of Buddhist technical terms which are numerous and culled from many languages, as much as possible. But it is impossible to discuss Buddhism without some use of Sanskrit and Pali terms. Regarding whether to use the Sanskrit or Pali spellings of these terms—which are very similar—as much as possible, I chose to use the Pali spelling when dealing with early Buddhism and Theravada Buddhism and Sanskrit spellings when dealing with Mahayana Buddhism. I have, generally, not used Chinese, Japanese, or Tibetan terms.

4. Bhikkhu Bodhi, trans., *The Numerical Discourses of the Buddha: A Translation of the Anguttara Nikaya* (Massachusetts: Wisdom Publications, 2012), 1208. The original Pali formulation can be found In Edmund Hardy, trans., *The Anguttara Nikaya, Part V* (London: Oxford University Press Warehouse, 1900), 329–30. An alternate translation runs: "Well declared by the Exalted One is dhamma that is of this visible life, unhindered by time, that bids one come to see it, that leads onward, to be understood by the discerning, each for himself." F.L. Woodward, trans.,

The Book of Gradual Sayings (Anguttara Nikaya) or More Numbered Suttas, Vol. 5 (Oxford: Pali Text Society, 2003), 210.

5. The Garuda Purana lists the following incarnations (Avatars) of Vishnu: "The Fish, the Tortoise, the Boar, the Man-lion, the Dwarf, Parashurama, Rama, Krishna, Buddha, and also Kalki," 8:10–11. In Ernest Wood and S.V. Subrahmanyam, *The Garuda Purana* (Allahabad: Panini Office, 1911). In the Bhagavata Purana, the Buddha is listed as the twentieth Avatara of Vishnu. See: Canto 1.3:24. The full text of the Bhagavata Purana is available at http://bhagavata.org/downloads/bhagavata-compl.html (accessed July 20, 2016). See also Bhagavata Purana, Canto 11.4:22 wherein Vishnu, in the form of the Buddha, is proclaimed to be born in the Kali Age for the benefit of humanity.

6. Bodhi, *Anguttara Nikaya*, 425–6 (AN 4:36 *Dona Sutta*). In this *sutta*, the Buddha – when he is asked if he is a deity or a spirit – answers in the negative. He also denies that he is a human but qualifies all those negative claims by pointing out that he has cut off the taints that could have made him a deity, a spirit, or an ordinary being, rather than an enlightened, human being. He goes on to say, "though born in the world and grown up in the world, I have overcome the world … Remember me as a Buddha."

7. Bhikkhu Bodhi, trans., *Samyutta Nikaya* (22:87): *The Connected Discourses of the Buddha* (Boston, Massachusetts: Wisdom Publications, 2000), 939.

8. For more on miracles in Buddhism see: Rupert Gethin, *The Buddhist Path to Awakening* (Oxford: One World, 2001). Further: Phyllis Granoff, "Scholars and Wonder-Workers: Some Remarks on the Role of the Supernatural in Philosophical Contests in Vedanta Hagiographies," *Journal of the American Oriental Society*, 105(3) (1985), 459–67.

9. See: Asvagosha's *Buddhacarita*, 5:12, available at http://www.ancient-buddhist-texts.net/Texts-and-Translations/Buddhacarita/ (accessed January 5, 2017). Patrick Olivelle, trans., *Life of the Buddha by Ashvaghosha* (New York: New York University Press, 2008), 129.

10. For more on concept of the Wheel of Dharma (*Dharmachakra*), and the Three Turnings, see: Robert E. Buswell and Donald S. Lopez, *The Princeton Dictionary of Buddhism* (New Jersey: Princeton University Press, 2014), 243.

11. *Princeton Dictionary* defines a Buddha-field (Buddhakshetra) as follows: "[A] realm that constitutes the domain of a specific Buddha." For further information on Buddha-fields, see the "Buddhakshetra" entry in *The Princeton Dictionary of Buddhism*, 153.

12. There are a number of biographies written on the Buddha's life. For instance, the Mahavastu is a biographical text allegedly associated with the Mahasamghika school of Buddhism (see *Ibid.*, 512). Another text, called the Nidanakatha, ascribed to Buddhaghosha, depicts the Buddha's past lives and is embedded within what came to be called the Jataka Tales (see *Ibid.*, 583). There is another biography, known as the Abhinishkramana

which is ascribed to the early Buddhist Dharmaguptaka school. The reader is referred to *Ibid.*, 245–6.

13. http://www.animenewsnetwork.com/encyclopedia/manga.php?id=3569; http://en.wikipedia.org/wiki/Buddha_(TV_series); Thich Nhat Hahn, *Old Path, White Clouds: Walking in the Footsteps of the Buddha* (Berkeley, California: Parallax Press, 1991); Elizabeth Coatsworth, and Raoul Vitale, *The Cat Who Went to Heaven* (New York: Aladdin, 2008).

14. For a short informative post on this controversy, see Harvard University's Notes on the Dates of the Buddha Shakyamuni, available at http://isites. harvard.edu/fs/docs/icb.topic138396.files/Buddha-Dates.pdf. For a longer, much more detailed consideration see Charles Prebish, "Cooking the Buddhist Books: The Implications of the New Dating of the Buddha for the History of Early Indian Buddhism," *Journal of Buddhist Ethics* 15 (2008), available at http://blogs.dickinson.edu/buddhistethics/files/2010/05/ prebish-article.pdf (accessed January 15, 2017).

15. For more on Ashoka see: Etienne Lamotte, *History of Indian Buddhism* (Paris: L'Institut Orientaliste de Louvain, 1988), 223–58.

16. Olivelle, trans., *Life of the Buddha*, xxiii.

17. Maurice Walshe, trans., *Digha Nikaya: The Long Discourses of the Buddha* (Boston, Massachusetts: Wisdom, 1995), 245 (DN: 16: 2.26. *Mahaparinibbana Sutta*). Some translations use "lamp" rather than "island." It is unclear which is the more accurate translation.

18. Bhikku Nanamoli, *The Life of the Buddha According to the Pali Canon* (Washington: PBS Pariyatti Editions, 1972).

19. Dharmachakra Translation Committee, *A Play in Full: Lalitavistara* (2013), available at http://www.freesangha.com/forums/mahayana-buddhism-library/new-lalitavistara-sutra-translation/. Not available in print version.

20. The Bodhisattva Vow, as it became known in Mahayana Buddhism, appears early on in the texts attributed to Asanga. Asanga discusses this topic both in the Bodhisattvabhumi section of the larger Yogacharabhumi text, particularly in the tenth chapter, the "Shilapatala." For an English translation of this chapter see Mark Tatz, *Asanga's Chapter on Ethics with the Commentary of Tsong-Kha-pa, The Basic Path to Awakening, the Complete Bodhisattva*, 94–262. A collection of ten Bodhisattva Vows are delineated at some length in the *Flower Ornament Sutra*, in the 40th chapter. See: Thomas Cleary, *The Flower Ornament Scripture*, 704–7. A more eulogistic account of the general Bodhisattva Path can be found in the tenth chapter of Shantideva's Bodhicharyavatara. See Shantideva; Crosby and Skilton, trans., *The Bodhicharyavatara*, 133–43.

21. Often the English word "eon" is a translation of the Sanskrit term "Kalpa." Kalpa can also more generally be rendered as "(an) age." There are various types of Kalpas, each differentiated according to both quantitative and qualitative criteria. The reader is referred to Buswell and Lopez, *Princeton Dictionary*, 409, for a general introduction.

22. Walshe, *Long Discourses*, 246, 251–2 (DN 16: 3.3–6, 3.34–47. *Mahaparinibbana Sutta*).

23. For a more detailed account of the Sthavira Nikaya school, see Alex Warder, *Indian Buddhism* (India: Motilal Banarsidass, 2000), 283–304. And, for more detailed information on the Mahasamghika school, the reader is referred to: Charles Prebish and Jan Nattier, "Mahasamghika Origins: The Origins of Buddhist Sectarianism," in *History of Religions*, 16 (3), 237–72. For a detailed analysis of Mahasamghika and Sarvastivadin monasticism, the reader is referred to: Charles Prebish, *Buddhist Monastic Discipline: The Sanskrit Pratimoksha Sutras of the Mahasamghikas and Mulasarvastivadins* (Delhi: Motilal Bansarsidass Publishers Private Limited, 1996).

24. For a more detailed account of Sarvastivada philosophy, see: Collette Cox, *Disputed Dharmas: Early Buddhist Theories on Existence* (Tokyo: The International Institute for Buddhist Studies, 1995), 21–37.

25. For an extensive discussion on the concept of the Dharmakaya see: John Makransky, *Buddhahood Embodied: Sources of Controversy in India and Tibet*, 23–83. Further: Nagao and Kawamura, trans., *Madhyamika and Yogachara: A Study of Mahayana Philosophies*, 103–23.

26. Gunag Xing, *The Concept of the Buddha: Its Evolution from Early Buddhism to the Trikaya Theory* (New York: Routledge Critical Studies in Buddhism, 2005), 19–52.

27. For more on the Mahasamghikas theories of the Buddha-bodies, see Lamotte, *Indian Buddhism*, 622–5.

28. See Buswell and Lopez, *Princeton Dictionary*, 409.

29. The reader is referred to Walshe, *Long Discourses*, 59; and Buswell and Lopez, *Princeton Dictionary*, 503, 520.

30. According to Buswell and Lopez, *Princeton Dictionary*: "[T]he four cardinal directions (north, east, west, south), the four intermediate directions (northeast, southeast, southwest, northwest), plus the zenith and the nadir." See entry under "dashadish" (ten directions), 902.

31. Xing, *Concept of the Buddha*, 53–66.

32. For a detailed discussion of the Sambhogakaya and Nirmanakaya see Griffiths, *On Being Buddha: The Classical Doctrine of Buddhahood*, 128–46 and 90–7, respectively.

33. For a very helpful summary of the three kayas see http://www.kagyu.org/kagyulineage/buddhism/cul/cul02.php.

34. Xing, *The Concept of the Buddha*, 101 and 129.

35. Asanga discusses the concept of the *Sambhogakaya* in *Mahayanasutralamkara* 5:59. For more information see Makransky, *Buddhahood Embodied*, 55–6. See also Dr. (MRS.) Surekha Vijay Limaye, *Mahayanasutralamkara by Asanga* (Delhi: Sri Satguru Publications, 1992), 134. Asanga further discusses the *Sambhogakaya* in the 10th Chapter of the *Mahayanasamgraha*. For more information, see: Lamotte, *Indian Buddhism*, 363–453.

36. A notable example is the *Lankavatara Sutra*. For more information, the reader is referred to D.T. Suzuki, *Studies in the Lankavatara Sutra* (India: Motilal Banarsidass, 1999). See in particular page 334.
37. Xing, *Concept of the Buddha*, 145.
38. One example of the importance of lineage in Indian Buddhism is salient in the tendency of Zen masters to demonstrate their ancestral lines. These complex lattices of spiritual transmission from teacher to student are visually depicted in the following chart: http://dhamm adhatu.com/wp-content/uploads/2015/07/chan-lineage-master-lands cape-Copy.jpg.
39. See Buswell and Lopez, *Princeton Dictionary*, 143, for more information on the four immeasurables. The entry is listed under "Brahmavihāra."
40. For an excellent introduction to the Buddhist teaching of the Four Noble Truths in the Pali canon, see: Walpola Rahula, *What the Buddha Taught* (New York: Grove Press, 1959), 16–50. Also: Ainslie E. Embree, ed., *Sources of Indian Tradition Second Edition Volume One: From the Beginning to 1800* (New York: Columbia University Press, 1988), 100–13.
41. See: Rahula, *What the Buddha Taught*, 45–50, for an excellent discussion of the Buddhist Eightfold Path.
42. The Khandas were elaborately detailed in the Khandavagga section of the *Samyutta Nikaya*, an early canonical Buddhist text. A masterful exposition and translation of this chapter can be found in: Bodhi, *Samyutta Nikaya*, 827–1108.
43. For a detailed account of the khandhas in Pali Buddhism see: Rahula, *What the Buddha Taught*, 20–8.
44. Often this discourse is found under the title "The Questions of King Milinda." See Embree, *Sources*, 103–5 for discussions on the "parable of the chariot."
45. Akira Hirakawa, *A History of Indian Buddhism from Shakyamuni to Early Mahayana* (New Delhi: Motilal Banarsidass, 1993), 122.
46. *Ibid.*
47. Williams and Tribe, *Buddhist Thought: A Complete Introduction to the Indian Tradition*, 98.
48. Peter Skilling, "Vaidalya, Mahayana, and Bodhisattva in India: An Essay Towards Historical Understanding," in *The Bodhisattva Ideal: Essays on the Emergence of the Mahayana*, 71.
49. For an excellent overview of the interactions between both Indian and Chinese philosophers, translators, and pilgrims see Sally Wriggins, *Xuanzang: A Buddhist Pilgrim on the Silk Road* (1996).
50. *Ibid.*, 148.
51. Kate Crosby and Andrew Skilton, trans. *Bodhicharyavatara*, 143. See also: Shantideva's views on this topic. Bendall and Rouse, trans., *Siksha-Samuccaya: A Compendium of Buddhist Doctrine*, 15: "As long as the chain or births is endless from beginning to end, so long shall I live that holy life

for the well-being of all creatures [...]. I invite all the world; for I shall deliver it from poverty. No mind of malice and stubbornness, neither envy and grudging, will I cherish from this day as long as I have enlightenment. I will practise continence and avoid criminal lusts and imitate the self-restraint and morality of the Buddhas. Not as one that is hurried do I undertake to gain enlightenment. I will remain until the end of the chain of being for one living being's sake."

52. See Kate Crosby and Andrew Skilton, trans., *Bodhicharyavatara* of Santideva (Oxford: Oxford University Press, 2008), 138–43.

53. Bhikkhu Nanamoli, *The Life of the Buddha* (Seattle, Washington: PBS Pariyatti Editions, 2001), 52. This quotation is from the Mahavagga section of the Pali Vinaya 1.11.1.

54. For an analysis of Abhidharmika atomism and Nagarjuna's Madhyamaka response, see: Westerhoff, "Metaphysical Issues in Indian Buddhist Thought," in *A Companion to Buddhist Philosophy*, 129–39.

55. For a good introduction to the teachings of the Tathagatagarbha school, see: Paul Williams, *Mahayana Buddhism: The Doctrinal Foundations* (New York: Routledge, 2009), 103–28.

56. Andrew Skilton, *A Concise History of Buddhism* (Birmingham: Windhorse Publications, 1997), 94.

57. For a detailed account of Vajrayana Buddhism, the reader is referred to Embree, *Sources*, 188–200.

58. See: Williams, *Mahayana*, 238–59, for an account of the development of Pure Land Buddhism.

59. For general readings on Soto Zen see Bielefeldt, *Dogen's Manuals of Zen Meditation* (1988). Further: Tanahashi, ed., *Moon in a Dewdrop* (1985). For general materials on both Chinese and Japanese forms of Zen, the reader is referred to Suzuki, *An Introduction to Zen Buddhism* (1964). Further: Yamada and Habito, *Gateless Gate: The Classic Book of Zen Koans* (2004). And Cleary and Cleary, *The Blue Cliff Record* (1992).

60. Walshe, *Long Discourses*, 255–6 (DN 16: 4.7–12.)

61. *Ibid.*, 246–7 (DN 16: 3.7.)

62. *Ibid.*, 247 (DN 16: 3.8.)

63. For an introduction to Tantra, see Christopher Wallis, *Tantra Illuminated: The Philosophy, History, and Practice of a Timeless Tradition* (California: Mattamayura Press, 2013).

64. Editor's note: See: Gross, *Buddhism After Patriarchy* (1993).

65. Hermann Oldenberg, *Vinaya Texts*, Volumes 1–3, 521–4 (Cullavagga 10:1).

66. See: Radhakrishnan, *The Dhammapada*, §264, p. 142.

67. http://www.inebnetwork.org. See also: Christopher Queen, ed., *Engaged Buddhism: Buddhist Liberation Movements in Asia* (1996). Further: Susan Moon, ed., *Turning Away: The Practice of Engaged Buddhism* (2004), available at http://plumvillage.org/about/thich-nhat-hanh. See also Thich Naht Hanh, *The Heart of the Buddha's Teaching: Transforming Suffering into Peace,*

Joy, and Liberation (1998). Further: Thich Naht Hanh, *The Miracle of Mindfulness: An Introduction to the Practice of Meditation* (1975).

68. Prison Mindfulness Institute, available at http://www.prisonmindfulness. org. See also Whitney, *Sitting Inside: Buddhist Practice in American Prisons* (2002); The Dharma Brothers: The East meets West in the Deep South, available at http://www.dhammabrothers.com. See also Phillips, *Letters from the Dhamma Brothers* (2008); Buddhist Recovery Network, available at http://www.buddhistrecovery.org. See also Griffin, *One Breath at a Time: Buddhism and the Twelve Steps* (2004).

69. See: Alan Hunt Badiner, ed., *Dharma Gaia: A Harvest of Essays in Buddhism and Ecology* (1990). Also: Tucker and Williams, eds., *Buddhism and Ecology: The Interconnection of Dharma and Deeds* (1998); for illustrative examples of the interaction between cognitive science, neuroscience, and mediation see Thompson, *Waking, Dreaming, and Being: Self and Consciousness in Neuroscience, Meditation, and Philosophy* (2015). Also: Wallace, *Meditations of a Buddhist Skeptic: A Manifesto for the Mind Sciences and Contemplative Practice, A Radical Approach to Studying the Mind* (2012).

70. See Karma Lekshe Tsomo, ed., *Innovative Buddhist Women: Swimming Against the Stream* (2000). Also: Tsomo, *Buddhist Women and Social Justice: Ideals, Challenges, and Achievements* (2004).

Selected Bibliography

Badiner, Alan Hunt, ed. *Dharma Gaia: A Harvest of Essays in Buddhism and Ecology*. California: Parallax Press, 1990.

Buswell, Robert E. and Lopez, Donald S. *The Princeton Dictionary of Buddhism*. New Jersey: Princeton University Press, 2014.

Cleary, Thomas, *The Flower Ornament Scripture*. Massachusetts: Shambala Publications, 1993.

Cox, Collette, *Disputed Dharmas: Early Buddhist Theories on Existence*. Tokyo: The International Institute for Buddhist Studies, 1995.

Embree, Ainslie E., ed. *Sources of Indian Tradition Second Edition Volume One: From the Beginning to 1800*. New York: Columbia University Press, 1988.

Gethin, Rupert. *The Buddhist Path to Awakening*. Oxford: One World, 2001.

———. *The Foundations of Buddhism*. Oxford: Oxford University Press, 1998.

Gombrich, Richard. *What the Buddha Thought*. London: Equinox Publishing, 2009.

Griffin, Kevin. *One Breath at a Time: Buddhism and the Twelve Steps*. Rodale Inc., 2004.

Griffiths, Paul, *On Being Buddha: The Classical Doctrine of Buddhahood*. New York: The State University of New York Press, 1994.

Gross, Rita. *Buddhism After Patriarchy: A Feminist History, Analysis, and Reconstruction of Buddhism*. New York: State University of New York Press, 1993.

Hahn, Thich Nhat. *The Heart of the Buddha's Teaching: Transforming Suffering into Peace, Joy, and Liberation*. New York: Harmony Books, 1998.

———. *Old Path, White Clouds: Walking in the Footsteps of the Buddha*. Berkeley, California: Parallax Press, 1991.

———. *The Miracle of Mindfulness: An Introduction to the Practice of Meditation*. Boston, Massachusetts: Beacon Press, 1975.

Hirakawa, Akira. *A History of Indian Buddhism from Shakyamuni to Early Mahayana*. New Delhi: Motilal Banarsidass, 1993.

Johnston, E.H., trans. *Ashvaghosa's Buddhacharita or Acts of the Buddha* 1936. Reprint. New Delhi: Motilal Banarsidass, 2007.

Moon, Susan, ed. *Turning Away: The Practice of Engaged Buddhism*. Massachusetts: Shambala Publications Inc., 2004.

Nanamoli, Bhikkhu. *The Life of the Buddha According to the Pali Canon*. Seattle, Washington: PBS Pariyatti Editions, 2001.

Nyanatushita himi, Bhikkhu. *The Bodhisattva Ideal: Essays on the Emergence of Mahayana*. Kandy, Sri Lanka: Buddhist Publication Society, 2013.

Olivelle, Patrick, trans. *Life of the Buddha by Ashvaghosha*. New York: New York University Press, 2008.

Phillips, Jenny. *Letters from the Dhamma Brothers*. Washington: Pariyatti Press, 2008.

Prebish, Charles. *Buddhist Monastic Discipline: The Sanskrit Pratimoksha Sutras of the Mahasamghikas and Mulasarvastivadins*. Dehli: Motilal Bansarsidass Publishers Private Limited, 1996.

Prebish, Charles and Jan Nattier. "Mahasamghika Origins: The Origins of Buddhist Sectarianism." *History of Religions*, 16(3) (1977): 237–72.

Queen, Christopher S., ed. *Engaged Buddhism: Buddhist Liberation Movements in Asia*. Albany, New York: State University of New York Press, 1996.

Skilton, Andrew. *A Concise History of Buddhism*. Birmingham: Windhorse Publications, 1997.

Strong, John S. *The Buddha: A Short Biography*. Oxford: Oneworld, 2001.

Suzuki, D.T. *An Introduction to Zen Buddhism*. New York: Grove Press, 1964.

Thompson, Evan. *Waking, Dreaming, and Being: Self and Consciousness in Neuroscience, Meditation, and Philosophy*. New York: Columbia University Press, 2015.

Tsomo, Karma Lekshe. *Buddhist Women and Social Justice: Ideals, Challenges, and Achievements*. Albany, New York: State University of New York Press, 2004.

Tucker, Mary Evelyn and Duncan Ryuken Williams, eds. *Buddhism and Ecology: The Interconnection of Dharma and Deeds*. Massachusetts: Harvard University Press, 1998.

Wallace, Alan B. *Meditations of a Buddhist Skeptic: A Manifesto for the Mind Sciences and Contemplative Practice, A Radical Approach to Studying the Mind*. New York: Columbia University Press, 2012.

Walpola, Rahula. *What the Buddha Taught*. New York: Grove Press, 1959.

Warder, Alex. *Indian Buddhism*. Delhi: Motilal Banarsidass, 2000.

Westerhoff, Jan. "Metaphysical Issues in Indian Buddhist Thought." In Steven Emmanuel, ed., *A Companion to Buddhist Philosophy*. London: John Wiley & Sons, Inc., 2013.

Whitney, Kobai Scott. *Sitting Inside: Buddhist Practice in American Prisons*. Colorado: Prison Dharma Network, 2002.

Williams, Paul. *Mahayana Buddhism: The Doctrinal Foundations*. New York: Routledge, 2009.

Williams, Paul and Anthony Tribe. *Buddhist Thought: A Complete Introduction to the Indian Tradition*. London: Routledge, 2000.

5

Sikh Dharam: Path of the Seeker of Truth

Jagbir Jhutti-Johal[1]

This is my karma and my Dharma; this is my meditation. The Lord's Name is my immaculate, unstained way of life.

— Guru Granth Sahib

Introduction

The Sikh Dharam (more recently also known by the term "Sikhi") is one of the world's youngest religions. It originated on the Indian subcontinent in the fifteenth century. In the Sikh tradition, the term *dharam* (this is the Punjabi vernacular rendering of the term, but in the Gurmukhi it is spelled as *dharma*) has various meanings, including religion, righteousness, duty, virtue, merit, honesty, sect, justice, and faith.[2] For example, according to the *Guru Granth Sahib,* chanting the sacred name is *dharam*: "My Guru gives the Naam, the Name of the Lord, to those who have such karma written on their foreheads. He implants the Naam, and inspires us to chant the Naam; this is Dharma, true religion, in this world."[3] Sikh Dharam was founded by Guru Nanak, a charismatic leader considered a messenger of God, who was born in 1469 CE in the region of Punjab (literally "a land of five rivers"). This region is located in western India in what is now part of Pakistan. From a small movement of kindred spirits, the Sikh Dharam has grown into a religion of around twenty million people.[4] In their short and turbulent history, the Sikh people have been key players in many of the major events of Indian history, including the fall of the

Mughal Empire, the rise of the Sikh Empire under Ranjit Singh in Punjab, the rise and fall of the British Empire, and the Indian struggle for independence. Over the past century, Sikhs have migrated all over the world in substantial numbers. As a result of this diaspora, Sikhs are to be found in many countries outside India, primarily in the United Kingdom, United States of America, Canada, East Africa, and Malaysia.

The Sikh Dharam has its roots firmly embedded in the philosophy of its place of origin. It shares many Indic philosophical and theological concepts with traditions of Hinduism and Buddhism—such as *dharma*, moral duty; *samsara*, the cycle of birth and rebirth; *karma*, the law of action; and *moksha*, liberation—although its interpretations of these concepts may be different. Similar to Semitic faiths, it is an ardently monotheistic tradition and advocates the belief that God, beyond human comprehension and formless (*nirankar*), created the universe and everything that exists within it. Sikhs traditionally accept that the central figures of other religious traditions, such as Krishna, Moses, Jesus, and Mohammed, were messengers of God with a divine mission. However, the Sikh tradition does not believe that God takes a human form and hence rejects the idea of, for example, the divinity of Jesus Christ and the gods or *avatars* (incarnations such as Lord Krishna and Rama) of Hinduism.[5]

The *Dharma* Paradigm and the Guru–Sikh Perspective

In fifteenth-century India, the Sikh tradition emerges at the confluence of Abrahamic and Indic "religious" traditions, and at the transitional phase from "medieval" to "modern" times. As such, it is inherently comparative, inclusive, diverse, critical, and hetero-geneous. Its development constitutes a sort of Indic "Enlightenment" that invents new ways to speak and act beyond the "sacred" and "secular." That is, it is both "religious" and "secular," and neither. This "Enlightenment," thus espoused by the Sikh Gurus, is different from the European Enlightenment movement, which sought to move beyond "religion" and elevate reason to the highest status. The Sikh tradition offered an enlightened point of view that not only confronted many archaic, superstitious belief systems, but also provided a way for the *"guru–sikh"* relationship to lead to individual spiritual awakening and social harmony.

The Sanskrit word *guru* means "teacher," or literally "the one who dispels ignorance." The word *sikh* (a Punjabi vernacular expression) is derived from the Sanskrit *shishya*, meaning a "disciple" or "learner." The relationship between the *guru* and the *sikh* encompasses the core of Sikh tradition: a continual quest along the path to understanding Truth (*Sat*) and the Divine Name (*Naam*). *Satnaam* is the term for the all-pervasive Ultimate Reality (*Ek Onkar*), which is One. This experience generally involves the guidance of the Guru, which now is manifested in the form of the *Guru Granth Sahib*, the holy book of the Sikhs.

According to Sikh teachings, the term *dharam* refers to spiritual wisdom, righteous living, and responsibility towards God and creation. It is a term that expresses the sense of "duty" and "way of life" that a Sikh aspires towards. In the Sikh tradition, the term *dharam* has a specific meaning, different from the more common usage in the Brahmanical system of Hinduism. This understanding of *dharma* includes the duties of *varna* (caste) and obligations concerning different stages of life (*ashramas*), both of which systematized Hindu society of the time. To understand what the Sikh tradition is and what this means to its followers, I will look at the historical development of the faith and the three core teachings of its founder, Guru Nanak: *naam japna* (recitation of God's name), *dharam di kirat karni* (earning an honest living), and *vand chakana* (selfless service).

A Short History

Guru Nanak and the Formation of the Sikh Tradition

Sikhs derive tremendous strength from their history, which is one of spiritual re-invigoration, beautiful poetic literature, martyrdom, and struggle against persecution. Guru Nanak, the founder of the tradition, was born in the fifteenth century during a relatively peaceful period in Northern India, following waves of invasions from Turks and Afghans as well as upheavals due to internal political and social factions. The interface between the religious ideologies of the invaders and the native Hindus' own customs created political and social confusion. Despite this peace, the previous years of war and political and social turmoil had left an indelible mark on its people, making it a period of great uncertainty, ignorance, and moral disintegration. Society was fragmented by the political oppression of foreign rulers, the rivalry between the two main religions—Hinduism and Islam—and the various regional and religious conflicts. The caste system had led to religious and racial segregation, and the performance of rituals was considered by critics of the time to be merely perfunctory due to prevalent superstitions. Many *sants* (saints) of the medieval Bhakti movement also note in their poetry how Indian people at that time were following these sectarian and superstitious beliefs instead of religious ones. Guru Nanak was also disenchanted by the deterioration of human values, but most importantly, he believed that the world had entered a dark age—an age in which most people had become alienated from the goal of liberation, and religion had lost its true purpose as the path to truth. It is poetically stated in the *Guru Granth Sahib*:

> The Dark Age of Kali Yuga is the knife, and the kings are butchers;
> Righteousness has sprouted wings and flown away.
> In this dark night of falsehood,
> the moon of truth is nowhere visible.[6]

Historically, Guru Nanak's life (1469–1539) coincided with a period of religious renaissance in Europe—Martin Luther (1483–1546) and John Calvin (1509–64) being among his contemporaries.[7] In a similar and no less revolutionary way, Nanak challenged the current theologies and practices of his day (i.e., those of Hinduism and Islam) and propagated the message that the liberation of the soul was open to all, irrespective of race, sex, caste, or religion. Guru Nanak's life story itself is a tale of the quest for truth, the performance of miraculous deeds, and the ministry of a charismatic leader and teacher who sought to rescue the path to spiritual truth from the human entanglements of social inequality. He was a householder but lived a life devoted to the Divine Truth, both in external dealings and internal spiritual pursuit. Nanak's egalitarian message becomes particularly clear after he achieved divine revelation, or realization, sometime around the age of thirty. After disappearing into a river and meditating in the water for three days, Guru Nanak emerged having had a powerful vision of the nature of reality, divinity, and human existence. He recorded that vision in the *Japji Sahib*, "the Song of the Soul," which highlights a philosophy that recognizes the Divine Light (*jot*) dwelling within all of God's creation—from minute creatures to human beings. Miraculous events of Guru Nanak's life have been recorded in the *Janam Sakhi* narratives and continue to inspire the followers of the Sikh tradition.

Certain ideas that Guru Nanak had, as well as his choice of vocabulary, suggest that some of his teachings may have drawn inspiration from Sufism, a branch of Islamic mysticism, and the Bhakti or Sant devotional movements that had originated around the twelfth century in various parts of India. However, he ultimately fashioned his own philosophy, elevating "truth" to the highest status and recognizing God as being one with truth. In practical terms, Nanak taught that the Creator (*Karta Purakh*) was immanent and accessible to everyone, encouraged charitable works and selfless service, and promoted the advancement of the status of women. Many Hindus revere Nanak as an extraordinary *sant* who sought to restore the *dharma*, which had been degenerating in his time, by travelling throughout India and beyond to teach the path of Truth, unity, and humanity. Many great authorities of Hinduism and Islam were impressed by his clear message and teaching style that was accessible to all people from different castes, religions, and genders.

Guru Nanak and the Succession of Gurus

Before his death, Nanak appointed a successor, Angad, to continue his mission, which officially established the Sikh tradition. For the next 250 years this tradition continued, where each Guru appointed a successor to carry the tradition of Sikhi before leaving his mortal body. In all there were a consecutive series of ten human Gurus, commonly referred to as "the Golden Chain," and each are accorded equal status among Sikhs. In fact, for many Sikhs the Gurus are considered to be the spirit of Nanak assuming ten different forms. Therefore, Nanak and subsequent Gurus are referred to as Nanak I, Nanak II, and so on in the *Guru Granth Sahib*. Each Guru advanced the tradition by adding various facets to it. For example, in the sixteenth century Guru Angad collected Nanak's hymns into a book and added his own compositions. He also gave Sikhs a new script, Gurmukhi (literally "from the mouth of the Guru"). This gave the Sikhs a written language distinct from that of Hindus and Muslims that helped to foster a distinctive Sikh identity.[8]

As the number of Sikhs began to grow, the third Guru, Amar Das, began to institutionalize the Sikh faith. He accomplished this by appointing territorial ministers and creating the system of *langar*, or "Guru's free kitchen," an integral part of Sikh religion that continues to be an important feature of the Sikh Dharam. Guru Amar Das also introduced various social reforms such as the prohibition of *sati* (the widely known, but rarely practiced custom of self-immolation by *kshatriya* widows on their husband's funeral pyres) and sought to free women from archaic customs. He allowed remarriage of widows, advocated monogamy, denounced the veiling of women, and appointed women leaders. Guru Ram Das, the fourth Guru, established a village, which was eventually to become the city of Amritsar—the spiritual and political capital of the Sikhs in Punjab. The fifth Guru, Guru Arjan, oversaw the construction of the holiest shrine, the Harmandar Sahib, popularly known as the Golden Temple. The Golden Temple is located in Amritsar, India, and it is a popular pilgrimage site as thousands of people of different faiths frequent it daily. Guru Arjan was a prolific writer and composed more hymns than any of his predecessors. His most important achievement was the compilation of the *Adi Granth*, an authoritative collection of his work and the works of the first four Gurus. It also included the poetries of Hindu and Muslim saints whose views echoed those of the Gurus. In 1604, the *Adi Granth* was installed at the Harmandar Sahib in Amritsar, Punjab, India. It became the embodiment of Sikh thought that helped catapult Sikh teachings to the masses. The essential teachings of Guru Nanak emphasize Truth and the Name of Lord:

> Upon this Plate, three things have been placed: Truth, Contentment and Contemplation.
> The ambrosial Nectar of the Naam, the Name of our Lord and Master, has been placed upon it as well;
> It is the Support of all.
> One who eats it and enjoys it shall be saved.
> This thing can never be forsaken;
> keep this always and forever in your mind.[9]

The growing influence of Guru Arjan Dev consequently brought him into conflict with the Mughal rulers of Punjab as his presence and popularity became a threat to their power. The Mughal Emperor Jahangir had Arjan arrested, and while in custody Guru Arjan was put to death. Guru Arjan is seen by Sikhs as their first martyr, and his death marked a turning point for the Sikh community which began to feel a real and physical threat to their principles and way of life.

The sixth Guru, Guru Hargobind, in reaction to this, added a militaristic dimension to the Sikh faith. He introduced the concept that the Guru has both spiritual authority (*piri*) as well as a worldly and temporal role (*miri*). *Miri-Piri* requires one to be a saint first and a soldier second. This means that a Sikh's saintliness and spirituality should come first and foremost, and that spirituality should guide them in their worldly and temporal matters. It was a concept central to the Sikh Dharam from the very outset of Guru Nanak's time right through to the tenth Guru, Guru Gobind Singh. Guru Nanak was a saint, but he was also a family man. He was both an enlightened being and socially concerned—unlike the yogis who renounce society completely—and he actively defied social and political ills of his times. Furthermore, none of the Gurus endorsed the ascetic lifestyle prevalent in Hinduism and other Dharma traditions, and instead promoted the sanctity of the householder lifestyle. However, Guru Hargbind took the concept of worldly concern to a different level. This concept is further symbolized through the creation of the Akal Takht (Throne of the Timeless) by Guru Hargobind at Harmandar Sahib, as the Sikh Dharam's seat of temporal affairs. It is one of the five seats of authority in the Sikh Dharam.[10] The Akal Takht is the highest seat of authority, created to address issues of justice and order in the *Panth*. The Sikhs are asked to embody heroism that is grounded in the Guru's Word:

> He alone is a spiritual hero, who believes in the Word of the Guru's Shabad (Naam). He alone obtains a true seat in the True Court of the Lord, who surrenders to the Command of the Commander.[11]

Thus in terms of action, Sikhs must first be attached to the love of God, and they must have the qualities of a saint in order to be a soldier ready to confront this-worldly battles against injustices. Through this unique model of Saint-Soldier, Guru Hargobind sanctified actions for the protection of the faith and human dignity. By prioritizing saintly qualities and affairs, politics becomes purified and spiritualized, rather than spirituality becoming politicized.

The period of Guruship between the seventh (Guru Har Rai) and eighth Gurus (Guru Har Krishan) was generally one of peace and the continual spread of Sikh teachings. This peace was shattered during the tenure of the ninth Guru, Guru Tegh Bahadur, who died

defending *dharam* and the rights of other religious traditions to
practice their faiths. Like the fifth Guru, Guru Tegh Bahadur was
executed by the order of the Mughal emperor. Guru Tegh Bahadur
also composed many hymns that were later added to the *Adi Granth*
by the tenth Guru, Gobind Singh, who also renamed it as the *Guru
Granth Sahib*. Guru Gobind Singh gave the Sikh community a
unique external identity and passed the Guruship to the Holy
Scripture, the *Guru Granth Sahib*, which is the Eternal Living Guru for
the Sikhs today.

Formation of Khalsa

In 1699, the tenth Guru, Guru Gobind Singh, was instrumental in
creating the Khalsa (the community of the "pure"), which established
the Sikh Dharam as a distinct religious movement—with a unique
and separate Sikh identity and code of conduct. This was achieved
through both the institution of an initiation ceremony called the
Amrit Sanskar/Amrit Pahul, which is performed in the presence of the
Guru Granth Sahib, and the adoption of the five articles of faith,
which are commonly known as the Five Ks. The principles of the
faith and other key instructions on how a baptized Sikh must
live were imparted to the initiates; for example, principles such as
devotion to God, service to mankind, fighting against injustice, and
defense of the weak. The ceremonious receiving of *Amrit* involves
various sacraments:

> On acceptance of these instructions, *Amrit* (nectar of immortality) is
> prepared by pouring water and sugar in a steel bowl and stirring the
> mixture with a double-edged dagger while selected verses from the *Guru
> Granth Sahib* and *Dasam Granth* (collected works attributed to the tenth
> Guru) are read out aloud. Five handfuls of *Amrit* are drunk by the
> initiate and five handfuls are sprinkled over their hair and eyes. Further
> prayers are then offered followed by a random reading of a verse from
> the GGS.[12]

Once initiated into the Khalsa, membership of this sacred order
requires the Khalsa Sikh to adopt the *panj kakar* (Five Ks). These are
five articles of faith whose name in Punjabi begins with a "K": *kesh*
(unshorn hair),[13] *kangha* (a wooden comb), *kara* (a simple steel
bracelet), *kachera* (special cotton underwear) and *kirpan* (a short
sword). These articles of faith are symbols of commitment to both
spirituality and the defense of justice. Furthermore, to emphasize

equality Khalsa Sikhs were required to use a caste-neutral last name: Singh (Lion) for men and Kaur (Princess) for women. These spiritual last names signify the dignity of both male and female genders, and unite Sikhs within the family of Sikh tradition. Finally, it also requires the adoption of a code of conduct, which prohibits Sikhs from consuming alcohol, tobacco, drugs, and animal products (such as meat, fish, and eggs). Through the institution of *Amrit* and the tenth Guru's role in creating a distinct Sikh identity, we can see how the sixth Guru's ideology of *Miri-Piri* began to take concrete form. The adoption of the Five Ks symbolizes both the embrace of a spiritual shared identity and the restoration of human dignity.

It is this order of Saint-Soldier, as instituted by Guru Gobind Singh, which has become the model of the devout Sikh. This model has been stressed by the Shiromani Gurdwara Parbandhak Committee (SGPC), established in 1920, and is responsible for overseeing and managing the *Gurdwaras* (Sikh places of worship). It is the distinct religious identity, expressed through external symbols (the "Five Ks"), that is defined in the *Rehat Maryada* and the various Gurdwara Acts. In considering the history of the Gurus and their teachings, it is evident that with each Guru the emphasis of the Sikh movement shifted, in part as a natural evolution of the religious movement but also as a response to changing political and cultural circumstances. However, it is quite clear from the *Guru Granth Sahib* that the core spiritual or religious ideology of Guru Nanak did not change.

The *Guru Granth Sahib*

The *Guru Granth Sahib* is the repository of the spiritual teachings of the Sikh Dharam. It is the Sikhs' perpetual guide and contains the main doctrines of the Sikhs concerning God, God's nature and attributes, and the means by which the divine realization may be attained.[14] Sikhs view it as the revelation of God's word transmitted through His messengers, the Gurus. As Nanak stated, "When I have spoken, I spoke as You made me speak."[15] Thus, the Guru is the spokesperson for the Divine Being.

Guru Gobind Singh, in one of his famous sayings, commands that the Sikhs consider *Guru Granth Sahib* as the Guru:

It is a Divine Order for every Sikh to obey the *Granth* as the Guru. Have faith in the *Holy Granth* as your Master, and consider it the visible manifestation of the Guru. He who hath a pure heart will seek guidance from its Holy Word.[16]

This might appear to be a new teaching, but Guru Ram Das and Guru Arjan Dev had also stressed the inseparable relationship between the word of the Guru (*Bani*) and the Guru himself:

> The Word, the Bani is Guru, and Guru is the Bani. Within the Bani, the Ambrosial Nectar is contained. If His humble servant believes, and acts according to the Words of the Guru's Bani, then the Guru, in person, emancipates him.[17]
>
> The mortal came to hear and chant the Word of the Guru's Bani.[18]

Guru Amar Das also explained how *Gurbani* (the words of the Guru) was a guiding force: "Gurbani is the light to illuminate this world; by His Grace, it comes to abide within the mind."[19]

Since the word of the Gurus is considered the Word of God, it carries complete authority for Sikhs. The Divine Word (also termed *Shabad Guru*) is embodied within the *Guru Granth Sahib* and revered as the "living" Eternal Guru. The first Guru, Guru Nanak Dev, explained the divine origin of *Gurbani* as the divine *logos*, or the spiritual Naam that is revealed through the Guru:

> From the Word, comes the Naam; from the Word, comes Your Praise. From the Word, comes spiritual wisdom, singing the songs of Your glory. From the Word, come the written and spoken words and hymns. From the Word, comes destiny, written on one's forehead. But the One who wrote these Words of destiny—no words are written on His forehead. As He ordains, so do we receive. The created universe is the manifestation of Your Name. Without Your Name, there is no place at all.[20]

What is clear is that the *Guru Granth Sahib* is not a record of history—it is a document of spiritual wisdom of—the Divine Eternal revealed to Sikhs by the human Gurus. The paucity of references within the *Guru Granth Sahib* describing contemporary historical events is an indication that the Gurus wished it to transcend these superficial issues and focus on the timeless and eternal creator. Indeed, many would argue that the entirety of the *Guru Granth Sahib* is simply an attempt to explain the first phrase in it: *Ek Onkar*, "there is but one God." The below is an excerpt from the document describing the uniqueness of the *Guru Granth Sahib* as a scripture and a testament of its appeal to all who seek wisdom.

A description of the Guru Granth Sahib given by Pearl S. Buck, winner of the Nobel Prize for literature, 1938:

Shri Guru Granth Sahib is a source book, an expression of man's loneliness, his aspiration, his longings, his cry to God and his hunger for communication with that being. I have studied the scriptures of other great religions, but I do not find elsewhere the same power of appeal to the heart and mind as I feel here in these volumes. They are compact in spite of their length, and are a revelation of the vast reach of the human heart varying from the most noble concept of God to the recognition and indeed the insistence upon the practical needs of the human body. There is something strangely modern about these scriptures and this puzzled me until I learnt that they are in fact comparatively modern, compiled as late as the sixteenth century, when explorers were beginning to discover the globe upon which we all live as a single entity divided only by arbitrary lines of our own making.

Perhaps this sense of unity is a source of power I find in these volumes. They speak to persons of any religion or of none. They speak for the human heart and the searching mind ...[21]

The *Guru Granth Sahib* confirms a unique feature of the Sikh Dharam: that the word of the Guru—*Gurbani*—is the key to the experience of the Divine and not the Guru himself. The Guru is the instrument that God uses to spread His Word. Insofar as *Gurbani* is a Divine Order, and the Word is doctrine, the teachings are not only illuminative but prescriptive, and the teachings contained within *Gurbani* are timeless, relevant, and applicable now. Hence, the *Guru Granth Sahib* is not just a sacred scripture, but a "living and eternal" Guru continuing to teach a way of life for the present. The text is comprised of 1,430 pages known as *Angs* (limbs) and is revered and attended to as the living Guru. Any mishandling of the *Granth* is strictly prohibited. Its language is Gurmukhi (literally "from the mouth of the Guru") and is composed in verse. Moreover, it is structured by various *ragas* (melodies) of classical Indian music. It not only includes the hymns of the Sikh Gurus, but also the poetry from the saints of Hindu and Sufi traditions. The scripture is unique because it was compiled by the Gurus themselves, not by their later adherents.

Sikh Theological Concepts

The Ultimate Reality

The central statement of the Sikh faith about God is given in the opening lines of the *Guru Granth Sahib*. They provide a succinct summary of the very essence of Sikh beliefs about God.

> One Universal Creator God.
> The Name Is Truth.
> Creative Being Personified.
> No Fear.
> No Hatred.
> Image Of The Undying,
> Beyond Birth,
> Self-Existent.
> By Guru's Grace.[22]

The unity and oneness of God is a theme continually repeated throughout the text. God is also described as formless, without gender, common to many religions, and beyond human comprehension. God is the creator and the cause of creation. He does not incarnate in human form. The essence of God is known as *Naam* and this pervades all creation. Sikhs believe that every soul is a divine spark of the eternal flame of the creator and the ultimate aim is for each spark to obtain union with its divine source.

The Human Condition and Spiritual Liberation

The *Guru Granth Sahib* is replete with instructions on how Sikhs (this term is broad in its definition so that it can include all seekers of Truth) should live as human beings within the world if they wish to achieve the ultimate goal, which, in the Sikh Dharam, is to attain liberation (*moksha*) from the cycle of birth, death, and rebirth, and unite with God (*Sahaj*). According to Guru Nanak, a life-cycle may encompass 8.4 million life forms, from a microscopic creature to a human being. The human birth is considered as the only opportunity to break this cycle and to fulfil one's destiny. Human beings are thought to be blessed with reason, wisdom, and the potential to have an awareness of God. What one does on Earth will determine what happens when one dies, and therefore the performance of good deeds and remembering God's name is vital to break the cycle of reincarnation: "As one acts, so does he receive. As he plants, so does he eat."[23]

Guru Nanak preached that liberation was open to all, irrespective of caste, creed, or sex. However, the goal of liberation is not an easy one to achieve due to the numerous distractions put in front of us, and because it ultimately depends upon God's grace. Guru Nanak was conscious that family life had degenerated,[24] that corruption and dishonesty was rife in society, and that religious worship had descended into meaningless rituals of fasting, bathing at religious sites, religious penances, and pilgrimages.[25] Instead of elaborate rituals, Gurus provide detailed guidelines for connecting oneself to the Divine. The *Guru Granth Sahib* is replete with instructions on how to achieve ultimate union with God. Many of these teachings focus on performing good deeds that center on the three fundamental principles: *naam japna* (recitation of God's name; *kirat karna,* or *dharam di kirat karni* (earning an honest living); and *vand chakana* (selfless service involving giving to those in need). We will look at each of them briefly.

Naam Japna, or *Naam-Simran:* "Recitation of the Divine Name"

This concept represents a quest to connect with the Creator, overriding all else, and should be coupled with a life dedicated to truth and service to others. Guru Arjan Dev, the fifth Guru, who sacrificed his life for *dharam*, emphasized the true treasure of *Naam*:

> Those who deal in the Naam, God's Name, are wealthy. So become a partner with them, and earn the wealth of the Naam. Contemplate the Word of the Guru's Shabad. Abandon your deception, and go beyond vengeance; see God who is always with you. Deal only in this true wealth and gather in this true wealth, and you shall never suffer loss. Eating and consuming it, it is never exhausted; God's treasures are overflowing. Says Nanak, you shall go home to the Court of Supreme God with honour and respect.[26]

Naam simran should be performed three times a day. There are specific instructions for reciting the *Gurbani*: Sikhs should wake before dawn and purify themselves by taking a bath. While there are no required ritual ablutions before prayer, bathing is seen as essential for personal hygiene and to help reinvigorate the mind and body for meditation. There are three set prayers to aid meditation. First, at dawn Sikhs meditate by reciting a selection of hymns composed by Guru Nanak and Guru Gobind Singh (namely *Japji Sahib and Jaap Sahib*). Next, at sunset they recite the *Rehras* (evening prayer), and finally, before going to bed they will repeat a prayer called *Kirtan Sohilla*. However, a Sikh's thoughts should not be directed to God only during these designated times. The remembrance of God's name should be practiced at all times while committed to charity and honest living, irrespective of whether one is officially initiated or not. This means that by following this practice one evolves and becomes transformed through the control over (not eradication of) all tendencies which keep one away from the ultimate goal. The daily prayers can be performed by oneself, collectively as a family, or at the *Gurdwara*.

Dharma di Kirat Karani: "To Earn An Honest, Truthful Living"

According to Guru Nanak, the decay within society during his time was a result of declining spiritual awareness. He spoke of an "ideal" society free of crime, dishonesty, and tyranny, and grounded in morality and ethical living. He emphasized the importance of practicing truth in daily affairs. He did not stress meditations on abstract Truth, but rather taught the value of applying truth in one's daily life. He was aware of those learned men in his time who were dedicated to the study of scriptures, but were oblivious to the significance of practicing truth in worldly affairs:

> There are so many stubborn-minded intelligent people, and so many who contemplate the Vedas.
> There are so many entanglements for the soul.
> Only as Gurmukh do we find the Gate of Liberation.
> Truth is higher than everything; but higher still is truthful living.[27]

Guru Nanak's sermon to his fellow Muslims encapsulates his teachings on ethical living:

> There are five prayers and five times of day for prayer; the five have five names. Let the first be truthfulness, the second honest living, and the third charity in the Name of God. Let the fourth be good will to all, and the fifth the praise of the Lord. Repeat the prayer of good deeds, and then, you may call yourself a Muslim. O Nanak, the false obtain falsehood and only falsehood.[28]

He reinterprets the five daily prayers central to Islam as instructions to transform human conduct so that daily life itself becomes a prayer.

Furthermore, he connected virtues to God and thus established an inseparable relationship between a virtuous life and worship of God: "All virtues are Yours, Lord, I have none at all. Without virtue, there is no devotional worship."[29]

Guru Nanak gives an analogy of a goldsmith's furnace whereby self-control, understanding, love, and *Naam* are enlisted as tools. Our soul has to be purified and made luminous by these tools. Once spiritual qualities have been cultivated, one ceases to lead a self-centered life and instead proceeds to lead a God-centered one that demands constant accountability in order to produce one's spiritual endeavor. This can be explained in how practicing selfless service (which makes one humble) and prayer (which makes one wise) leads one to the constant realization of God's presence.[30] Once one is aware of the Immortal Divine presence of God within everything, one becomes spiritually focused and this is reflected through actions which demonstrate humility and a sense of accountability to God.[31] In turn, although this benefits the individual in that it conduces to spiritual liberation, it also benefits society as a whole by creating good citizens. Thus, the Sikh Dharam seeks to reform the world by spiritualizing the human and provides principles that can be followed by any individual—man or woman. The Gurus also recognized that while engaged in these worldly matters one should not become attached to worldly possessions and relationships.

Maya (delusion) pulls the individual away from the one God, *Waheguru*. The concept of *maya* is found in various Indian philosophical traditions. The specific way that Sikh Dharam uses the term is to connote the attachment humans have to ephemeral, material things that distract the mind from God. The individual is instructed to worship and pray to *Waheguru*, and remember *Waheguru* at all times because if one wants to end the cycle of rebirth and achieve union with God (*mukti*), the individual has to recognize that only the Lord's name can save a Sikh from the process of transmigration.

> Your Name is the Fearless Lord; chanting Your Name, one does not have to go to hell.[32]

This instruction to pray to God, advocated by the Gurus, could be interpreted as prescribing renunciation from the world, but this is not the case. Although Sikhs are instructed to pray to God, Guru Nanak rejected asceticism, the renunciation of worldly life, celibacy, and the separation from one's family or home to achieve true holiness and union with God. Instead, *grihasthi* (married life) was celebrated and encouraged.

Vand Chakana: "Eat After Sharing with Others"

This principle encompasses acts of *sewa* (selfless service) and compassion. Sikhs are encouraged to work hard and honestly for a living and to share the fruits of their labor.[33] As we saw earlier, the highest objective of human life is the remembrance of God's name, so there is a great emphasis on *sewa* and the concept of selflessness (*nishkamta*). Although the concept of selflessness is present in Hinduism and other religions of India, the Sikh Gurus make selfless service the central tenet of the Sikh Dharam and link it to the ideal of God-realization. *Sewa* mandates a complete dedication to giving without expecting any material or spiritual reward in return. Such service cultivates qualities such as altruism, commitment, and sincerity. It is those individuals who serve without any desire for reward who achieve liberation because they destroy their ego by cultivating humility and the ultimate union with God. Furthermore, there are many references in the Sikh Sacred Scripture that illustrate the importance of service to one's Guru—service which can be interpreted as service to the eternal Guru by following the teachings presented in the *Guru Granth Sahib*. It is emphasized that through this service, one can become closer to God and gain peace.

There are other qualities required of a Sikh which are explained in the sacred scriptures. Wisdom, truthfulness, justice, temperance, courage, humility, contentment, and love for humanity,[34] are essential for moral living and spirituality. The quality of humility is synonymous with surrendering one's ego to the Guru and to God.

> He is true Sikh who surrenders before the Guru and bows his head; Who puts his mind and forehead on the feet of Guru; who holding dear to his heart the teachings of the Guru expels ego from his self.[35]

There is a paradox implicit in this terminology. Although a Sikh says he or she is surrendering to God, they are not in fact losing anything, but rather gaining "the whole world."[36] Furthermore, despite being "dead" to one's worldly self, the Sikh is very much spiritually alive.[37] Bhai Gurdas was an influential Sikh historian and writer and he elaborates this in many hymns that he composed.[38] Thus, losing oneself in the service of others yields great results:

Truth and contentment govern this body-village.
Chastity, truth and self-control are in the Sanctuary of the Lord.
O Nanak, one intuitively meets the Lord, the Life of the World; the
Word of the Guru's Shabad brings honour.[39]

Along with the virtues of chastity, truth, and self-control, values of
forgiveness, compassion, and refrainment from blaming others are
also considered essential. The level of unconditional, wholehearted
forgiveness and compassion that Sikhs are required to exercise is
extraordinary. Baba Sheikh Farid, a Sufi mystic, whose poetry is
recorded in the *Guru Granth Sahib*, teaches the message of returning
good for evil, and love for hate.[40] The Gurus emphasized that Sikhs
should not see fault in or blame others, and instead look to recognize
the faults and weaknesses within oneself?[41] Other qualities referred to
are those of self-control, freedom from desire, restraint, modesty and
continence, patience and understanding, spiritual wisdom and divine
knowledge, love and compassion, contemplation of *Naam* and
communion with God, contentment, truth and good deeds, and
calmness. Guru Nanak provided a symbolic depiction of the Hindu
sacred thread that had traditionally represented the higher castes: "Make
compassion the cotton, contentment the thread, modesty the knot, and
truth the twist. This is the sacred thread of the soul."[42] Guru Gobind
Singh eloquently provided a metaphoric meaning of Hindu ascetic
practices and elevated the virtuous household life to a higher status:

> O man, lose your shackles thus: Treat your home as a forest retreat and
> have the heart of a hermit, make continence your matted hair,
> communion with God your ritual bath, and righteous living your ritual
> long nails. Make divine knowledge your center and smear your body with
> ashes of God's Name (*Naam*). Eat little and sleep little; love the practice of
> compassion and forbearance. Be calm and contented and you will be in
> control of three states (desire; ignorance and laziness; good living).
> Keep lust, anger, pride, greed, obstinacy and worldly attachments at bay.
> Thus will you see your own essence and reach the highest level.[43]

Principles such as *naam japna* (recitation of God's name), *kirat karna*
(earning an honest living) and *vand chakana* (selfless service) are both
internal and external practices that enable spiritual growth and
facilitate moral and ethical living. They emphasize an individual's
social responsibility to ensure the well-being of society.[44] Thus the
practice of religion has been simplified by the Gurus who emphasize

devotion and pure conduct over dogma: "Of all religions, the best religion is to chant the Name of the Lord and maintain pure conduct."[45]

Guru Nanak teaches that to achieve liberation of the soul and ultimate union with God the true seekers have to live according to the teachings as set out in the *Guru Granth Sahib*. As discussed earlier, there is an emphasis on sincere worship, and serving God (*sewa*) through altruism, both of which are difficult to achieve due to ego and self-centeredness (*haumai*). The external action of *sewa* is essential for "those who search for a seat in God's court."[46] Throughout the *Guru Granth Sahib* and in the *Ardas* (concluding prayer) the importance of good deeds, conduct, and service to mankind is stressed. Guru Nanak stated that no *achar* (true moral character) can be built without the sincere worship of the *Ek Onkar* (One God) and His Name while living within this world. He rejected the ideal of *yogis* who make their living by begging alms, and upheld the sanctity of self-sufficiency and hard work:

> The lazy unemployed has his ears pierced to look like a Yogi.
> Someone else becomes a pan-handler, and loses his social status.
> One who calls himself a guru or a spiritual teacher, while he goes around begging—don't ever touch his feet.
> One who works for what he eats, and gives some of what he has
> —O Nanak, he knows the Path.[47]

All the Gurus were married, apart from the eighth Guru, Guru Har Krishan, who died when he was eight years old from smallpox. The Gurus emphasized the renunciation of the five vices through living a householder's life of service. The Gurus demonstrated this by fully contributing to the social, political and economic well-being of society because they realized that the world and all that was in it was God's creation. Two Gurus sacrificed their lives to defend the religious freedoms and the dignity of human life. This is uniquely different from the Hindu, Buddhist, and Jain Dharma traditions in which the choice of renunciation for spiritual liberation is held in high regard.

Haumai and the Five Vices

Although the qualities for ethical living are highlighted, the *Guru Granth Sahib* elucidates the difficulties that one encounters in attempting to achieve the state of *achar*, or true moral living.

A Sikh must overcome *haumai* (selfish ego) to achieve liberation. Any English translation of the term is inexact, but it can be generally interpreted as an inner, egoistic, self-centeredness. According to the Gurus, all people are born with *haumai,* which is God-created. It acts like a veil obfuscating the presence and vision of the divine that pervades everything around and within each person. It is the great disease of humanity and leads the mind and soul into delusion and worldly attachment.[48] Thus *haumai* can be compared to the concept of *ahankar* in Hinduism, as it is similar to the veil of ego that separates the divine and the soul. The Sikh Dharam recognizes *ahankar* within the five vices and considers *haumai* to be the sum of all egotistic tendencies.

According to Guru Nanak, detachment from worldly possessions is essential to the spiritual process.[49] When individuals become attached to worldly possessions they become *manmukh* (self-centered) because *haumai* and the accompanying five vices of *Kam* (Lust or Desire), *Krodh* (Anger), *Lobh* (Greed/Covetousness), *Moh* (Attachment), and *Ahankar* (Ego or Pride) encourage unethical behavior and prevent individuals from realizing God, which in turn prevents release from the cycle of rebirth.[50]

The Gurus argued that internal actions such as *naam simran* are essential in the quest to overcome *haumai.*[51] Devotion to the Divine helps in the control of selfish desires or vices, and if *sat* (truth) and *nimrata* (humility) are practiced then one can become virtuous and achieve spiritual liberation. The goal is to turn the gaze from self-centeredness to Guru-centeredness: "One who becomes Gurmukh knows only the One. Serving the One, peace is obtained."[52] The practitioner recognizes that in the end they will have to face God on their own, and a morally good person rises above *haumai* to consider only the greater good.[53] Overall, when one is not attached to material or worldly possessions and lives a good life guided by dedication to *naam simran* ("meditation of the True Name") then "lust, anger, egotism, jealousy and desires are eliminated by chanting the Name of the Lord."[54]

Individuals are encouraged to perform *sewa* and to be concerned with the welfare of all because of the universality of humanity. Service to others engenders humility in the heart of a Sikh. Notions of superiority and inferiority become meaningless because *all* human beings are viewed as equal. By controlling the five vices and focusing on good actions, individuals contribute to their spiritual progression and the well-being of their community. However, one must perform these deeds selflessly and without any expectation of reward.

Gurmukh and *Manmukh*

These two concepts literally mean, "Guru-centered" and "self-centered." As discussed earlier, *haumai* and the five vices make an individual a *manmukh* because they are self-centered. However, an individual who has overcome and controlled *haumai* (ego) and the five vices by following the Guru's teachings and *naam simran* becomes a *gurmukh* (God-centered) and attains spiritual liberation. The *Guru Granth Sahib* elucidates how liberation requires that a self-centered approach be replaced by a God-centered approach in life so that one may achieve a new state of consciousness and realize God within. Therefore, there is an intricate connection between self: If you conquer your own mind, you will conquer the world.[55]

For turning toward Guru and Truth, the most important practice is *naam simran*: "meditation on the True Name." This goes well beyond the concept of constantly repeating God's name. The mind must be wholly tuned to the essence of God so that the person becomes totally absorbed in Him and every thought and action are imbued with God's devotion. Ultimately this is done without any mental effort or any conscious awareness, and the result is a natural dedication of one's life to God and the service of others. *Naam simran* is not something to be done alone or away from society, and it certainly does not necessitate withdrawal from daily life. It should be accompanied by participation in the life of *sangat*, or the fellowship of believers, as an active member of the community.[56] The way that Sikh Dharam elevates the company of spiritual community members to a high status is one of its unique aspects.

Nanak describes five realms, or levels, of spiritual experience as one traverses the path towards union with God.[57] The final level is the realm of Truth, which leads to the realization of the Truth and absolute harmony with God. In contrast to many religious traditions—in which salvation is achieved after death—Sikhs do not have to wait for death to achieve this state of being. Liberation is available in this present life. Death only marks the final release of the body, which is a concept shared with other Hindu traditions of India, especially that of *Jivanmukti* (liberation during this life, also espoused by some of the sub-schools of Advaita Vedanta).

The discipline of *naam simran* and working to attain union with God, the ultimate goal, are certainly not easy tasks, and many Sikhs accept that they will not easily reach the realm of truth. However, the goal is certainly one worth striving for and sincere efforts through *sangat* and *pangat* can make it achievable.

Sangat and *Pangat*

Guru Nanak established the *sadh sangat* (holy congregation) to worship and sing devotional hymns in praise of the Creator. The concept and institutions of *sadh sangat* and *pangat* (sitting together in rows with fellow Truth-seekers)[58] allow Sikhs to associate with saints or other religious-oriented people in collective worship as a means to help the individual in *naam simran* and in overcoming worldly desires. The company of saints is an antidote to worldly temptations: "The world is drunk, engrossed in sexual desire, anger and egotism. Seek the sanctuary of the saints, and fall at their feet; your suffering and darkness shall be removed."[59] In practice of the *sangat-pangat,* all Sikhs—irrespective of caste, gender, or wealth—sit together to worship and sing in praise of the creator, as children of the same God, and they recognize that "No one is my enemy, and I am no one's enemy,"[60] and "I am not good; no one is bad."[61] Such teaching is not only directed toward nourishing humility in an individual's heart but also toward creating a deep sense of community.

Sikhs also partake in *langar*: a free community kitchen, in which men and women of any caste or background sit together and share a meal collectively prepared by volunteers. The *langar* requires active participation from all members of the community and this participation can be through the following two types of selfless *sewa*: physical *sewa* (*tan*), or monetary *sewa* (*dhaswandh*—one tenth of one's earnings), which should be performed without desire (*nishkam*), and with complete humility (*nimrata*).

Sangat and *pangat* are therefore two important institutions in the Sikh Dharam which promote equality and *sewa* among followers. The association with holy people aids worship and concentrates the mind so that it is "God-centered." It also enables members to live within society both ethically and morally. Such individuals become imbued with the qualities of humility and selflessness, and work for the betterment of society.[62] The Sikh congregation serves as a physical place that promotes the gathering of seekers who partake in the *sewa* of the Guru and communion with other Sikhs.

Gurdwara and *Dharamsal*

When discussing places of worship one must consider the following two concepts: *Gurdwara* and *Dharamsal*. *Dharamsals* were prominent at the time of the first five Gurus; the emergence of *Gurdwaras* happened from the time of the sixth Guru. *Gurdwaras* ("the door to the Guru") today are the very nucleus of the Sikh community. The word *Gurdwara* is comprised of two words: *Guru* and *dwara*. The Guru is one who leads a seeker from spiritual ignorance (*Gu*, "darkness") into spiritual enlightenment (*ru*, "light"). The *dwara* is the "abode" or "gateway" to the Guru (God).

In the initial stages of Sikh history, everywhere Guru Nanak went he founded a *Dharamsal*—a place of religious gathering where people would congregate and sing the Guru's hymns together. They became centers for propagating and disseminating Guru Nanak's teachings, anchoring Sikh faith to the Gurus.

Dharamsals were established at the headquarters of the earlier Gurus—such as Kartarpur, Khadoor Sahib, and Goindwal Sahib—and functioned as the centers of the Sikh faith under the personal supervision and direct control of the Gurus themselves. The *Guru Granth Sahib* likens this earth to a *Dharamsal*, which was created by God for humans to practice *dharam*.[63] It implies that as travelers find shelter in *Dharamsals* during their travels, we too find shelter on the earth only for a short time. The objective is to use this time on earth wisely. There are numerous passages in the teachings of the Guru that use this analogy to motivate Sikhs to consider the temporality of this world and the true objective of human life. Bhai Gurdas says, "Earth is the abode for the conduct of Dharam."[64]

At the time of the sixth Guru there was a version of the *Adi Granth*, literally "the first book." The Sikh religious scripture was compiled by the fifth Guru, Arjan, who installed it at Harmandar Sahib in 1604. The emergence of *Gurdwaras* in connection with episodes in the Gurus' lives explains the revered connection that Sikhs observe between the personalities of the Guru and the historical *Gurdwaras*.

The *Gurdwara* became even more important when Guru Gobind Singh bestowed the Guruship to the *Guru Granth Sahib* in 1708.[65] At this point, they became the house of the eternal Guru and a place of worship. In this holy place devotees are in the presence of their Guru to receive spiritual grace and blessings, and to benefit from the holy company for spiritual advancement. In his writings, Bhai Gurudas notes the relationship between Sikh *Gurudwaras* and Sikh religiosity. The prolific *Gurdwaras* provide a place for the Sikhs to congregate, to learn about prayer and how to live a virtuous life through selfless service, but also serve as a space wherein the Sikh Dharam can be put into action.[66] Life at the *Gurdwara* is intended to create human beings who are as virtuous as saints. Furthermore, the function of the *Gurdwara* extends to spiritual instruction and schooling; hospitality, shelter, and charity; and the provision of *langar* (free, blessed vegetarian food prepared and served by means of voluntary service and contributions).[67]

Inside the *Gurdwara*, worshippers approach the *Guru Granth Sahib* and genuflect or prostate before sitting down on the ground. This should not be confused with idol worship—this act is performed to accept the authority of the *Guru Granth Sahib* and its teachings. Traditionally, all traditions of India revere great saints and *gurus*, and followers show respect by bowing down to them. The general convention is to sit on the floor, but chairs are provided for those who cannot. Men and women usually sit on separate sides of the *Guru Granth Sahib*, which is more in line with Indian culture than with any aspect of Sikh belief. There is no fixed day for worship as dictated in the scripture, but in the West Sikh congregations usually gather in large numbers on Sunday to reflect the diasporic context in which Sikhs live. Since hymns of the scripture are set in classical melodies (*ragas*), music and the singing of hymns are integral to meditation and worship. Music is seen as a way of lifting hearts and minds and facilitating one's contemplation of God.

The Sikh Dharam has no priesthood or ordained ministers. Any initiated lay member of the congregation may lead the worship, male or female. In practice, many *Gurdwaras*, especially in the West, employ a *granthi* (reader)—usually male—whose responsibilities include reading the scriptures, performing ceremonies, and maintaining the upkeep of the *Gurdwara*. However, his role should not be confused with that of a priest. He does not have any special religious authority above that of an ordinary lay member, but he will invariably be well-versed in the scriptures.

In keeping with the principle of equality, the *Gurdwara* is open to all religious (and non-religious) people of any nationality, caste, gender, and so on. This openness is extended to the *langar* as well: all partakers will sit together on the floor and eat—another expression of equality. In the contemporary context we see young members of the community taking *langar* out of the *Gurdwara* to feed the homeless. When David Cameron became Prime Minister in the United Kingdom in 2010 he called for a "Big Society" in which citizens help their fellow beings. Given the Sikh Dharam's emphasis on *sewa* and feeding the poor and needy, it is not surprising that the Prime Minister and other UK politicians have also recognized the importance of *langar* and *sewa* in his Vaisakhi speeches.

Gurdwaras are intimately associated with the spiritual, social, and political practices of Sikhs today, having come to symbolize the spiritual and worldly identity and authority of the Sikh Dharam. They are central to the lives of the Sikh people and a testament to the continuing tradition and practical embodiment of Sikh teachings by defining Sikhs as a distinct, separate, and independent community.

Sikh Dharam in Contemporary Society

If they are to last, religious movements tend to develop a set of rules and practices to give permanency to the message of their founders. They likewise promote a tight knit community of followers. In this regard, most of the practices that are followed today emanate from the time of the Gurus, but have been formalized only in the last two centuries. They are a systematic reinforcement of the teachings of the Gurus.

It is important to note too that the Sikh community is not homogeneous. Sikhs, like any other religious group, have followers who are orthodox in their practices and those who are more liberal. Some are cultural Sikhs and may not follow the traditional rules exactingly. The diversity within the Sikh tradition is reflected in the degrees of its practitioners' adherence to the faith. For example, Amritdhari or Khalsa Sikhs are practitioners who are initiated through an official ceremony. The Keshdhari—who keep their hair unshorn and wear the outward symbols of the Sikh faith (i.e., the turban)—are born into the tradition, but are not initiates. Lastly, the Sehajdhari/Mona Sikhs retain an affiliation to the Khalsa but choose to remove the outward symbols of the Five Ks.[68] However, to affiliate oneself with the Sikh Dharam is to simply believe in the one eternal God, the ten Gurus, to accept the *Guru Granth Sahib* as their eternal Guru, and to practice the essential core teachings of *naam japna, kirat karna*, and *vand chakana*.

Being born into the Sikh Dharam—a religion based equally upon actions and beliefs—requires this of Sikhs so that they can break the endless cycle of death and rebirth and return to God. This can be achieved by following the teachings of the Gurus, having control over the five vices, eradicating the ego, and by putting an end to living life as a *manmukh* (one who is self-centered). Nevertheless, the Sikh Dharam honors religious pluralism, as the Sikh scripture contains voices from the saints of traditions other than their own. Some ethnographers like Nicola Mooney note the existence of some "religiously hybrid" Hindu and Sikh families in India who culturally follow mixed tradition. Some Sikhs participate in the festivals and pilgrimages of other religions. Some Sikhs can culturally participate in the religious practices of other traditions, although their affiliation with the Sikh Dharam requires them to only follow the principles and practices of their own tradition.

The tradition passed on by the Gurus to Sikhs is upheld and guarded by the Shiromani Gurdwara Prabandhak Committee (SGPC). This committee systematically defined the practice of Sikh Dharam in 1950 by publishing Sikh *Rehat Maryada* (Sikh Code of Conduct and Conventions), which defined a Sikh as any human being who faithfully believes in the following:

1. One immortal being
2. Ten Gurus, from Guru Nanak Sahib to Guru Gobind Singh Sahib
3. The *Guru Granth Sahib*
4. The utterances and teachings of the ten Gurus
5. Finally, a belief in the Amrit ceremony (baptism) bequeathed by the tenth Guru, and the non-allegiance to any other religion

Thus, it is clear that "initiation" is considered to be a requirement for practicing Sikh Dharam. Sikh scholar Dr. W. Hew McLeod contends that a "true Sikh will normally be a Sikh of the Khalsa."[69] This could be regarded as an orthodox view echoing those of the *Panth's* hierarchy, and the Khalsa identity as the "Sikh ideal." However, the implications for accepting the Khalsa model as the unequivocally definitive archetype of Sikh identity are clear. If one is to accept that the Khalsa Sikh is the "true" Sikh, one is basing that conclusion on a strict interpretation of what a Sikh should be—that a Sikh should adhere vehemently to the teachings of the Gurus, which the SGPC promote. By doing this, a significant portion of the Sikh community would be both marginalized and ignored, a portion that embodies the "spirit" of Sikh teachings but who do not necessarily feel the need to strictly cultivate the outward images which are associated with Sikh "orthodoxy." This view seeks support from the teachings of its founder, who confronted the orthodoxy of his time and emphasized the spirit of devotion for a true disciple or seeker.

While Khalsa observance may provide immediate answers for identity, it is evident that today one archetypal Sikh identity does not exist and cannot be argued for. Not all Sikhs are the same. Like many faiths, there are several groups within the *Panth* due to differing observances of the Five Ks.[70] Today, the level of observance has resulted in the creation of "rankings" or "categories" of Sikhs.[71] In the Sikh literature these are revealed as:

1. *Amritdhari–Khalsa*: initiated Sikhs, or "pure or proper Sikhs"
2. *Keshdhari*: those who keep the *kesh* (unshorn hair) because they were born in the Sikh families, but who are not initiated
3. *Mona/Sehajdhari*: clean-shaven Sikhs who do not keep unshorn hair
4. *Gora Sikhs*: Western converts who are mostly followers of Yogi Bhajan, a modern teacher who established an organization called 3HO (Happy, Healthy, Holy)[72]
5. *Patit*: someone who may have taken *Amrit* but has lapsed[73]

It is clear that all Sikhs pick and choose how they practice their *dharam*. Ethnically Punjabi, Sikhs in Punjab practice the Sikh Dharam through their own cultural lens. Whether initiated or not, many Sikhs are still engaging in practices which the Gurus had tried to eradicate. For example, the *Guru Granth Sahib* contains many teachings of equality, but socially and culturally there is still gender discrimination and a cultural caste hierarchy which has seeped into the realm of Sikh religion, substantiated by the fact that caste names are defining *Gurdwaras*. This is not surprising as most religious people often deviate from the teachings put forth by the prophets or leaders of their traditions, despite their allegiance to their respective religious traditions. There is one group of Sikhs who do follow the Sikh Dharam according to the teachings as set out by the Gurus, and they are the convert Sikhs. However, it must be noted that this group reinterpret the teachings of the Gurus for modern times and to allow women to be *panj pyare* (traditionally only a male prerogative).

Convert Sikhs and Sikhs in Diaspora

Sikhs began migrating to the United States in the early twentieth century. One of the major developments of the Sikh Dharam in the United States is known as the "Happy, Healthy, Holy" (3HO) movement.[74] The movement was started by a Sikh immigrant, Harbhajan Singh Puri (1929–2004), later known as Yogi Bhajan. Its main centers are located in Espanola, New Mexico, and Los Angeles, California. The 3HO movement is a synthesis of elements of Hindu Tantra, the Sikh Dharam, and New Age spiritualties.[75] This development has created both interest and anxiety about the question of Sikh identity. The majority of convert Sikhs are Gora (literally "white," referring to Caucasian Sikhs) although some 3HO members are also from other racial groups, including African Americans. These members have converted voluntarily to the Sikh Dharam by taking *Amrit,* as Sikhi is not a missionary religion. In fact, many Sikhs believe that one should live within the religion that they are born into. To convert to another religion or to try to convert someone means questioning God's Will (*hukam).*

Convert Sikhs place a strong emphasis on the Khalsa identity (both men and women wear white turbans and clothes) and the *Rehat Maryada* (Sikh code of conduct). As some argue, their identity is pure and true to Guru Gobind Singh's Khalsa identity. This includes avoiding the consumption of animal products and adhering diligently to the disciplines. This raises problems for the Punjabi Sikhs, who might not be as stringent in following the principles and teachings of the Sikh Dharam. Punjabi heritage is perceived to be a fundamental criterion of the Sikh identity by many Punjabi Sikhs.[76] Furthermore, many Punjabi Sikhs, especially those who have taken *Amrit,* may observe cultural practices that the Gurus had tried to eradicate (e.g., caste surnames, gender hierarchy, and the custom of dowry). Convert Sikhs may not follow any of these culturally sanctioned practices, and some Punjabi Sikhs are known to admire the observance of the Khalsa discipline by the Westerners (of various ethnicities). However, there continue to exist some tensions between the two groups. Most Punjabi Sikhs do not see them as "real" Sikhs because they have not been born into the tradition and perform certain practices that seem closer to Hindu yoga traditions.[77] Many scholars have explored this tension.[78] It is for these reasons that many Punjabi Sikhs will not marry their children to a Sikh convert. Such tensions are natural when a tradition faces new developments and interfaces a new sociocultural context.

Notably, Sikh communities can be found in various regions of India and in many countries all over the globe. Although the Sikh migration to the West began in the nineteenth century, large numbers of Sikhs have migrated since the 1960s to countries including Thailand, Australia, East Africa, the United Kingdom, Canada, and the United States. Sikhs are emerging as important players in many fields, including business, academics, and politics. Simultaneously, the Sikh Dharam's second-generation leadership is addressing the challenges of preserving a distinct identity in diasporic communities, questioning gender hierarchy and cultural customs of caste and dowry, as well as re-defining identity for a global context. Furthermore, as a response to post-9/11 incidents of hate crimes against Sikhs—in large part due to the mainstream media's projection of the image of terrorists with turbans and beards—young Sikh leadership and community members are making efforts to bring the unique Sikh identity to the attention of political leaders, law-enforcement officers, and the Global society. This is particularly evident in the United States and the United Kingdom.

Modern Developments: Activism and Education in the United States and the United Kingdom

In the United States, Sikh students have formed many organizations to ensure that the rights of Sikhs in the diasporic communities are safeguarded, including the Sikh Mediawatch and Resource Task Force (SMART) and the Sikh American Legal Defense and Education Fund

(SALDEF), the latter being a fund dedicated to educating the public about the Sikh Dharam. Sikh leaders are also utilizing various media tools such as documentaries, stories, and films in order to bring awareness to Sikh traditions and practices. Films such as *Bend It Like Beckham* and *Ocean of Pearls* underscore the challenges that Sikhs with cultural and religious values face living in Western countries, as well as their struggle to assimilate into the society and avoid racial discrimination. In addition, many works of fiction and stories (e.g., *What the Body Remembers* by Shauna Singh Baldwin and *Dear Takuya . . . Letters of a Sikh Boy* by Jessi Kaur) reckon with not only their history and heritage in India but also the modern struggles of youths living in the United States. The recent attacks on a Sikh *Gurdwara* in Oak Creek, Wisconsin, once again energized the Sikh base to educate the community at large. A documentary, *Waking in Oak Creek*,[79] is an emotional tribute to those killed in the massacre, but it also depicts how the Sikh community found inspiration in faith and addresses a larger goal—the end of violence and bigotry. Such experiences in diaspora have motivated Sikhs to organize and educate Westerners about their distinct identity and express pride in their religion and culture.

In the United Kingdom, Sikh students have formed many organizations, such as the British Organisation of Sikh Students (BOSS) and Basics of Sikhi, to ensure that both young Sikhs and those outside the religion are informed about the faith. To guarantee that Sikhs are represented correctly in the media, we have the recent establishment in 2015 of SikhPA—Sikh Press Association. UK Sikhs have also been utilizing the media of broadcasting to teach about the Sikh faith, but also to bring global Sikh news to Sikhs in the diaspora, examples of channels include: Sikh Channel, Sangat TV, Khalsa TV, and Akaal Channel. They all have a global reach.

In addition to increasing awareness of other international Sikh groups within the general Sikh community, we also see an increase in political, civic, and social action engagement. In the United Kingdom and in the Diaspora, political engagement by Sikh organizations is on the rise, raising issues with the government that are affecting them back home in Punjab.[80] Examples include the Network of Sikh Organisations (1997), and then post-9/11 there was a proliferation of organisations, such as the British Sikh Consultative Forum, established in 2002, Sikh Federation UK, established in 2003, and the Sikh Council UK, established in 2010. One of the most significant contributions of these organizations was the establishment of the All Party Parliamentary Group for British Sikhs, which officially launched on July 12, 2005, chaired by Rob Marris, Labour MP for Wolverhampton South West.[81]

CitySikhs represents a new development in the Sikh community to establish apolitical organizations that engage with the wider community on interfaith activities. CitySikhs is an organization of young professional Sikhs who aim to provide a voice for professional Sikhs whilst empowering people to create positive change within society as a whole. They have researched issues that affect Sikhs in the United Kingdom and have published data annually since 2013. There have been five British Sikh Reports to date, which have been endorsed by politicians. Another organization is the Sikh Network, which published the Sikh Manifesto 2015–20, January 2015, and the UK Sikh Survey in November 2016.

The Sikh community has also engaged in social action in the United Kingdom. The theological teaching of *sewa* (selfless service) has always encouraged the notion of "Big Society" and social engagement. As a result, all Sikh *Gurdwaras* have used this ethical requirement as a means of bolstering local communities through civic engagement, whether it be "inward civic engagement" aimed at improving the wellbeing of the Sikh community or "outreach or outward civic engagement" service for the good of the wider community. It was noted in the 2016 British Sikh Report that "Sikhs in the UK are estimated to donate about £125 million to charity per annum and spend over 65 million hours each year on voluntary activities."[82]

Examples of social engagement by Sikh organizations, such as The British Sikh Doctors Organisation (BSDO), Nishkam Healthcare Trust and Sikh Awareness Society include working with specific groups, such as young people, the elderly and the homeless, providing counselling and support for people with learning difficulties and mental health needs, community development and educational projects, and social campaigning in favour of local and community needs.

A distinctive Sikh activity of social action is *langar*. *Gurdwaras* in the Diaspora serve *langar* to non-Sikhs, performing a function analogous to food banks and soup kitchens who support homeless people and those working in low-paid jobs.[83] In the United Kingdom, however, we are seeing a new role for *langar* in response to welfare cuts: *langar* is now being taken out of the *Gurdwara* by young Sikhs to feed the homeless. One organization that has done this is Midland Langar Seva, which feeds the homeless in Birmingham. Their activity has branched out into other areas, such as Coventry and Leicester. In London, there is the Sikh Welfare and Awareness Team (SWAT) who have a bus they park at the same spot every week in Central London to feed the homeless. Both organizations cater overwhelmingly to individuals who are not Sikh.[84] Such groups work with humility and the absence of ego, hence a lack of self-promotion or engagement in politics, because to do so would be take away from the religious element of the activity, which is selfless service.

While we see this activity in the United Kingdom on a national level, there is simultaneously an emerging wave of these young Sikhs addressing global who are establishing international organizations, such as KhalsaAid, which address global issues such as the refugee crisis in Greece, supporting Yezidi refugee families in Iraq, and installing water pumps in Malawi. They have also helped in national disasters, such as the flooding in the UK in December 2015, and recently in January 2016 a food and water project for 200 Yezidi refugees in northern Iraq.[85]

Another method Sikhs have developed to contribute to the well-being of society is the advancement of the Sikh Faith Schools, particularly since 2010. The first Sikh Faith School in the United Kingdom was called Guru Nanak Sikh Primary and Secondary School, which was founded by Sant Baba Amar Singh in 1999 in Hayes, in the London Borough of Hillingdon. Since the Conservative government came to power in 2010 more Sikh Faith Schools have opened in cities with a high population of Sikhs: Khalsa Primary School, Slough; Seva School, Coventry; Nishkam Primary and Secondary School, Birmingham. These faith schools aim to provide an education based on the Sikh Dharam, for Sikh and non-Sikh children, to educate and nurture young people and allow them to be comfortable with their religious identity, but also to be inspired by faith-values which will help them become good citizens. The Niskham Trust advocates the Sikh ethos and values, such as humility, service, compassion, self-discipline and forgiveness, for their primary school for example.

Contemporary Issues

The *Guru Granth Sahib* provides a methodology for achieving liberation, salvation, and how one should live a moral life as a "householder." However, while there is a blind acceptance of the *Guru Granth Sahib*, this does not mean that the interpretation of teachings has remained fixed in stone in modern-day society. Instead, it is evident that the Sikh community—in India as well as in the other transnational areas of Sikh settlement—is having to accommodate advances in a dynamic and ever-changing world. Like all religious communities, the Sikh community and religious leadership also needs to address controversial ethical issues—such as gender equality in religious leadership, abortion, euthanasia, IVF, the family, homosexuality, same-sex and interfaith marriages—and be open to a range of alternative approaches concerning these ethical issues. Two important issues that the Sikh community need to address in a multi-faith, global and modern world are gender equality and homosexuality.

Gender Equality

Respect for women, along with caste, class, and religious equality, is one of the central tenets of the Sikh Dharam. The patriarchal polarization that existed—women and nature on the one side against men and culture on the other—was repudiated by the Gurus who gave women greater equality, both social and religious. The Gurus taught that men and women are equal in the eyes of God, and both are born to complement one another. This is distinct from some of the other religious traditions that believe women came to exist only as part of a man and could therefore only achieve salvation through men. Instead, Sikh scripture outlines that women are to be regarded as equal to men and have the same right to grow spiritually, and that they are essential for the continuance of society and the preservation of its ethical structure:

> From woman, man is born; within woman, man is conceived; to woman he is engaged and married.
> Woman becomes his friend; through woman, the future generations come.
> When his woman dies, he seeks another woman; to woman he is bound.
> So why call her bad? From her, kings are born. From woman, woman is born; without woman, there would be no one at all.

O Nanak, only the True Lord is without a woman.That mouth which
praises the Lord continually is blessed and beautiful.
O Nanak, those faces shall be radiant in the Court of the True Lord.[86]

While gender equality was advocated by the Gurus, it is also
important to note that the Sikh Scripture uses predominately
masculine terminology and symbolism that has been interpreted to
reinforce male dominance and patriarchy; for example, God is
portrayed through male imagery, including terms such as *Akal Purakh*
("the Eternal Man"), *Karta Purakh* (the "Creator Man"). Furthermore,
there is a dearth of women role models in the scripture—one only
finds the symbolic depiction of the devotee as a bride yearning for
the Male God in the form of a bridegroom, or as a mother giving
birth to "kings."[87]

Although the Gurus preached what some people might call a
revolutionary message, which accorded women equality and
recognized their importance in the society, this belief was not always
translated into practice. Social and cultural traditions that have been
part of India's society for centuries have taken prominence today
instead of the theological teachings taught by the Gurus. As a result,
in a similar vein as women in other religious communities dominated
by patriarchal structures, some would argue that Sikh women still
have not achieved the gender equality socially and culturally that the
Gurus advocated. This inequality is demonstrated by the cultural
preference for a male child, which had led to a gender discrepancy in
the male–female sex ratio in Punjab for example. While this does
reflect that full equality has not been achieved, it is evident that in
the West Sikh women have achieved equality through education and
employment. Today, globally there are prominent Sikh women in
senior positions as academics, artists, and social activists.[88] What is
important to note is that while Sikh women, who draw inspiration
from their Sikh faith, have worldwide achieved equality through
education and employment in the wider society, within their own
religious institutions Sikh women still have not achieved the gender
equality that many Sikhs would interpret the Sikh teachings
advocate. Gender inequality is demonstrated by the lack of women
in roles of religious authority, and the prevention of female
participation in certain religious activities and ceremonies. For
example, women traditionally have not been allowed to be one of the
panj pyare (five beloved ones),[89] and nor can they take part in *sewa* in

the sanctum sanctorum of the Sikh holiest of holies at Harmandar Sahib in Amritsar, or during the Sukhasan ceremony at Harmandar Sahib, when the Guru Granth Sahib is removed from the Darbar Sahib and taken to rest in the Akal Takht.[90]

Women becoming part of the *panj pyare* is a contentious issue related to history and tradition: religious Sikhs argue that in 1699, when called upon by the tenth Guru, it was only five men who were prepared to sacrifice their lives; therefore, women cannot join the tradition of the five. However, what is interesting is that organisations that represent non-Punjabi Sikh converts do allow women to be part of the *panj pyare*.

Despite these limitations imposed on women, recently there have been landmark achievements of women being elected to run *Gurdwaras*. For example, in the United Kingdom Bibi Paramjit Kaur was elected president of the committee for Sri Guru Singh Sabha Gurdwara Bristol, Rajinder Kaur Lard was elected president of Harley Grove Gurdwara in Bow, East London, and Mandeep Kaur was appointed the Sikh Civilian Chaplain to the Military (UK). These achievements remind one of how Guru Amar Das appointed women to be missionaries, and of the 22 *manjis* (or dioceses) he established, four were run by women. Their position was equivalent to an Anglican bishop. Thus, because of education and recognizing the Sikh ethic of equality as demonstrated in the Guru Granth Sahib and the historical accounts of the Gurus, Sikh women are standing up for themselves and exerting their influence slowly but surely to reclaim their place within the religious realm.

Homosexuality

Like many other religions, homosexuality and same-sex marriages are problematic issues in Sikh Dharam. I will discuss how the Sikh community—particularly the diasporic community, which is bound to follow the constitutions of the lands they are in—has confronted this issue. Like many religious texts, homosexuality is not mentioned in the *Guru Granth Sahib*, nor does the solemnization of any same-sex marriage or relationship appear in the history of the Ten Gurus' historical period.

Many in the Sikh community say that Sikhs are not homophobic— as evidenced by scriptural sayings such as "[the Sikhs] recognise the human race as one,"[91] and from the fact that Sikhs pray every day for *Sarbat da bhalla* (the prosperity of all humanity). Nonetheless, it is clear that this is not entirely the case based on discussions suggesting that if Sikhs lived according to the teachings of *Gurbani* ("the words of the Gurus"), their same-sex inclinations could be controlled. Furthermore, as a Sikh one is required to live a life of restraint, transcending both physical and psychological temptations, as it is said in the *Guru Granth Sahib*: "[In the world] everyone acts according to the inclinations of the mind. Attuned to the Creator Lord, one remains free of fear."[92]

What is clear is that the influence of Western culture and education has encouraged two schools of thought in the diaspora: Conservative/Orthodox and Liberal. For example, Conservative/Orthodox Sikhs may argue that homosexuality goes against God's commandments because the *Guru Granth Sahib* stresses the importance of a monogamous relationship between husband and wife. This is probably the justification used in January 2005 by the Akal Takht when it issued an edict in response to a call from Canadian Members of the Parliament, who had to vote on government proposals to legalise gay marriage in Canada, for clarification on what the Sikh view on homosexuality and same-sex marriages was. The Akal Takht issued an edict (*Sandesh*) that same-sex marriages should be opposed and could not take place in *Gurdwaras*. This same ruling guided the Sikh response during the consultation with the UK government on the introduction of the Marriage (Same Sex Couples) Act.

The opposition to this controversial issue was also evident during a discussion show on a Sikh channel in the United Kingdom, on May 25, 2011. The "Sikh Ethics" series concerning the issue of homophobia and homosexuality within the Sikh community was cancelled after a short time on the air due to the fierce reactions from callers. However, some online sites like "gaysikhs.com" aim to dispel the myths about homosexuality and encourage open conversations with the followers of the tradition.[93]

Liberal Sikhs, on the other hand, argue that the *Guru Granth Sahib* stresses the importance of respect for all individuals, and if God created people to be homosexual then those people should be accorded the same respect and equality as any other person.

What is clear is that the Sikh community is addressing this new cultural reality through community conversations and various forms of media, like the popular film *Bend it like Beckham*. Contentious contemporary issues are also being challenged and readdressed through critical engagements with the Sikh religious texts, as evidenced by the multitude of voices being expressed in many popular and scholarly works.[94] Teachings are being analysed and reinterpreted from various perspectives, and it is only through this process that the religion will be able to manage and tackle modern-day issues. This will not lead to a new Sikh identity or a new way of being Sikh, per se, but it will guide Sikhs, who are dedicated to deal with modern issues according to the *Guru Granth Sahib,* and to live according to the Sikh Dharam.

Conclusion

Even though the Sikh Dharam is one of the youngest of the major religions of the world, it has come a long way in a short space of time with respect to its evolution into a distinct identity. From the message that Guru Nanak preached—on the nature of reality, divinity, and human existence—over five hundred years ago, it has now sprung into a cohesive and powerful religion that retains a diverse following as a global religion. Theologically, all humans retain a spark of the divine—the human body is itself a gift given by God to experience the divine light in oneself and in creation. Thus, for most Sikhs, religion is a journey in which one experiences the Divine in everything within and around oneself. This journey leads Sikhs on a search for truth and represents an opportunity to connect with the Creator to achieve liberation through a life that follows the path of *dharam* (ethical/ righteous living). It includes controlling and overcoming the five vices of lust, anger, greed, and selfishness, while remaining engaged in the world. Thus, service to one's fellow beings is considered an important part of the faith because it is so intrinsically linked to achieving union with God. Socially and politically, Sikhs continue to assert their unique identity that is rooted in the teachings of the ten Gurus and the *Guru Granth Sahib.* Sikhs in the diaspora are seeking to challenge stereotypes and address the issues of violence, inequality, identity, and justice. Sikh tradition, like other world religions, is comprised of multivalent voices and pluralistic viewpoints, and it continues to evolve in the land of its origin and beyond.

Notes

1. Some parts of this chapter have appeared in: A.R. Gatrad *et al.,* eds., *Palliative Care for South Asians, Hindus, Muslims, and Sikhs* (London: Quay

Books, 2006); and Jagbir Jhutti-Johal, *Sikhism Today* (New York: Continuum, 2011). The use of this content is with the permission of Quay Books and Continuum.

2. A common distinction among Abrahamic faith and Dharmic religions is explained in the following document: "The broad distinction between Abrahamic faiths (Christianity, Islam and Judaism) and Dharmic faiths (generally considered to include Buddhism, Hinduism, Jainism and Sikhism) is widespread throughout the world in both academic and popular usage. It is open to a range of objections and criticisms, however, and is not universally accepted. Sikhism, for example, is considered a Dharmic religion by many Sikhs but not by all." Quoted in "Living with Difference: Community, Diversity, and the Common Good," 30. Available at https://corablivingwithdifference.files.wordpress.com/2015/12/living-with-difference-online.pdf.

3. *Guru Granth Sahib*, 680. The translations of the *Guru Granth Sahib* (also known as *Sri Guru Granth Sahib*) are voluminous and difficult to locate. Therefore, since the page numbers of the hard copy correspond with a digitized version, I have chosen to use all citations from the following digital version: http://www.srigranth.org/servlet/gurbani.gurbani (accessed July 14, 2016).

4. "Sikhism," available at www.Sikhs.org (accessed April 23, 2016).

5. Sikhs also do not accept the authority of any of the scriptures from other religions. Jagbir Jhutti-Johal, *Sikhism Today* (London: Continuum, 2011), 1.

6. *Guru Granth Sahib*, 145.

7. Patwant Singh, *The Sikhs* (London: John Murray Publishers, 1999), 28.

8. Khushwant Singh, *A History of the Sikhs*, Vol. 1 (New Delhi: Oxford University Press, 1977), 52.

9. *Guru Granth Sahib*, 1429.

10. Akal Takht, Amritsar; Takht Keshghar Sahib, Anandpur Sahib; Takht Patna Sahib; Takht Damdama Sahib, Batinda; Takht Sachkhand, Hazur Sahib.

11. *Guru Granth Sahib*, 1023.

12. A. R Gatrad, "Sikh Birth Customs," *Archives of Disease in Childhood* 90(6) (2005): 560–3.

13. W.H. Mcleod, "Discord in the Sikh Panth," in *Journal of the American Oriental Society*, 119(3) (1999), 381–9. Also: "Chapter X – Beliefs, Observances, Duties, and Ceremonies," in *Rehat Maryada* (Amritsar: Shiromani Gurdwara Prabandhak Committee). Lastly, http://sgpc.net/sikh-rehat-maryada-in-english. *Kesh* is also, in the case of men, normally accompanied by the wearing of a turban or, if the hair is not particularly long (such as for young boys), a top-knot. The turban is considered of vital importance to men for a variety of reasons (e.g., hygiene) but mostly because of the importance placed upon tying the *kesh* in a top knot and keeping it neat and tidy; the turban is the best practical method of

achieving this. Women are not expected to wear the turban; but some particularly devout Sikh women have chosen to wear it.

14. Dorothy Field, *The Religion of the Sikhs* (London: J. McLeod, 2000).

15. *Guru Granth Sahib*, 566.

16. Quoted in: Surinder Singh Johar, *Guru Gobind Singh: A Multi-Faceted Personality* (New Delhi: M.D. Publications, 1999), 64.

17. *Guru Granth Sahib*, 982.

18. *Ibid.*, 1219.

19. *Ibid.*, 67.

20. *Ibid.*, 4.

21. P.S. Buck and Gopal Singh, trans., *Introduction to Translation of Guru Granth Sahib*, 7th ed. (New Delhi: Allied, 1987), xix.

22. *Guru Granth Sahib*, 1.

23. *Ibid.*, 662.

24. Anil Chandra Banerjee, *The Sikh Gurus and the Sikh Religion* (Delhi: Munshiram Manoharlal, 1983); W.H. McLeod, *Guru Nanak and the Sikh Religion* (Oxford: Clarendon Press, 1968); W.H. McLeod, *Sikhism* (London: Penguin, 1997).

25. "The true cleansing bath is service to the Guru. If salvation can be obtained by bathing in water, then what about the frog, which is always bathing in water?" *Guru Granth Sahib*, 484.

26. *Guru Granth Sahib*, 1219–20.

27. *Idid.*, 62.

28. *Ibid.*, 141.

29. *Ibid.*, 4.

30. "Let self-control be the furnace, and patience the goldsmith. Let understanding be the anvil, and spiritual wisdom the tools. With the fear of God as the bellows, fan the flames of the body's inner heat. In the crucible of love, melt the nectar of the Name, and mint the True Coin of the Shabad, the Word of God." *Ibid.*, 8.

31. "Truth is higher than everything, but higher still is truthful living." *Ibid.*, 62.

32. *Ibid.*, 465.

33. "One who works for what he eats, and gives some of what he has – O Nanak, he knows the Path." *Ibid.*, 1245.

34. H.S. Soch and Madanjit Kaur, eds., *Guru Nanak: Ideals and Institutions* (Amritsar: Guru Nanek Dev University, 1998). The *Guru* Granth Sahib emphasizes: "Truth and contentment govern this body-village. Chastity, truth and self-control are in the Sanctuary of the Lord. O Nanak, one intuitively meets the Lord, the Life of the World; the Word of the Guru's Shabad brings honour." *Guru Granth Sahib*, 1037.

35. Bhai Gurdas, Vaar 3, Pauri 20 of 20. All the cited references are from the digital version of the text, available at https://www.searchgurbani.com/bhai_gurdas_vaaran/pauri_by_pauri (accessed July 15, 2016).

36. "O Fareed, if you will be mine, the whole world will be yours." Stated by Sheikh Farid in the *Guru Granth Sahib*, 1382. Also, according to Bhai Gurudas, "The Sikh with his capital of devotion falls at the feet of Guru and the whole world bows at his feet." Vaar 11, Pauri 3 of 31.

37. Guru Arjna Dev says, "Remain dead while yet alive, and you shall be welcomed in God's Court." *Guru Granth Sahib*, 176.

38. "Only by becoming dead in life, i.e. totally detached, and not through mere verbal jargon one can become a true disciple. One could be such a person only after getting sacrificed for truth and contentment and by eschewing delusions and fears." Bhai Gurdas, Vaar 3 Pauri 18 or 20. Further, "Becoming an avid suitor of the form (Word) of the Guru and being dead to greed, infatuation and other relational propensities, he should remain alive in the world." *Bhai Gurdas*, Vaar 3, Pauri 19 or 20.

39. *Guru Granth Sahib*, 1037.

40. "Fareed, do not turn around and strike those who strike you with their fists. Kiss their feet, and return to your own home." In *Guru Granth Sahib*, 1378. Furthermore, "Fareed, answer evil with goodness; do not fill your mind with anger. Your body shall not suffer from any disease, and you shall obtain everything." *Guru Granth Sahib*, 1381.

41. According to Guru Ram Das, "Great is the greatness of God; He does not hear the words of the back-biters." *Guru Granth Sahib*, 84. In the words of Guru Arjan Dev, "The spiritually blind place the blame on others." *Guru Granth Sahib*, 258.

42. "Make compassion the cotton, contentment the thread, modesty the knot, and truth the twist. This is the sacred thread of the soul." *Guru Granth Sahib*, 471. Similarly, there are many references in the *Guru Grant Sahib* that emphasize the power of love and compassion over rituals. "Upon this plate, three things have been placed: Truth, Contentment and Contemplation. The Ambrosial Nectar of the Naam – the Name of God our Master, has been placed upon it as well; it is the support of all. One who eats it and enjoys it shall be saved." *Guru Granth Sahib*, 1429. Also, "Please bless me with the rice of truth and self-restraint, the wheat of compassion, and the leaf-plate of meditation. Bless me with the milk of good karma, the ghee, of compassion. Such are the gifts I beg of You, Lord. Let forgiveness and patience be my milk-cows, and the let the calf of my mind intuitively drink in this milk. I beg for the clothes of modesty and the Lord's Praise; Nanak chants the Glorious Praises of God." *Guru Granth Sahib*, 1329.

43. Guru Gobind Singh, *Dasam Granth*, 709. Quoted in http://sikhseverywhere.com/wp-content/uploads/2013/05/sikhinnerwarrior.pdf, 5 (accessed December 20, 2016).

44. "Of all religions, the best religion is to chant the Name of the Lord and maintain pure conduct." *Guru Arjan Dev, Guru Granth Sahib*, 266. Guru

Nanak further wrote, "All virtues are Yours, Lord, I have none at all. Without virtue, there is no devotional worship." *Guru Granth Sahib*, 54.

45. *Guru Granth Sahib*, 266.

46. *Ibid.*, 26.

47. *Ibid.*, 1245.

48. Daljeet Singh, *Sikhism: A Comparative Study of its Theology and Mysticism*, 2nd ed. (Amritsar: Singh Brothers, 1994), 206.

49. "Your attachment to your family, your attachment to all your affairs-renounce all your attachments, for they are all corrupt. Renounce your attachments and doubts, O brother, and dwell upon the True Name within your heart and body." *Guru Granth Sahib*, 356.

50. According to Guru Arjan Dev, "Acting in egotism, selfishness and conceit, the foolish, ignorant, faithless cynic wastes his life. He dies in agony, like one dying of thirst; O Nanak, this is because of the deeds he has done." *Guru Granth Sahib*, 260.

51. "Remembering the True Lord in meditation, one is enlightened. Then, in the midst of Maya, he remains detached. Such is the Glory of the True Guru; in the midst of children and spouses, they attain emancipation. Such is the service which the Lord's servant performs, that he dedicates his soul to the Lord, to whom it belongs." *Guru Granth Sahib*, 661.

52. "Those who have the Treasure of the Naam within emancipate others as well as themselves." *Guru Granth Sahib*, 52.

53. "The Gurmukh, while remaining dead, is respected and approved. He realizes that coming and going are according to God's Will. He does not die, he is not reborn, and he does not suffer in pain; his mind merges in the Mind of God. Very fortunate are those who find the True Guru. They eradicate egotism and attachment from within. Their minds are immaculate, and they are never again stained with filth. They are honoured at the Door of the True Court. He Himself acts, and inspires all to act." Guru Amar Das, *Guru Granth Sahib*, 1059.

54. *Guru Granth Sahib*, 1389.

55. *Ibid.*, 6.

56. W. Owen Cole and P.S. Sambhi, *The Sikhs: Their Religious Beliefs and Practices* (London: Routledge & Keegan Paul, 1978), 88.

57. The five Khands (realms) described in the *Guru Granth Sahib* (*Japji Sahib*) are:

   1. *Dharam Khand*: the realm of righteous action (pauri, 35)
   2. *Gian Khand*: the realm of knowledge (pauri, 36)
   3. *Saram Khand*: the realm of spiritual endeavor (pauri, 36)
   4. *Karam Khand*: the realm of grace (pauri, 37)
   5. *Sach Khand*: the realm of Truth (pauri, 37)

58. Nikky-Guninder Singh, *Sikhism: An Introduction* (London: I.B.Tauris, 2011), 46–50.
59. *Guru Granth Sahib*, 51.
60. *Ibid.*, 671.
61. *Ibid.*, 728. Further, "Kabeer, I am the worst of all. Everyone else is good. Whoever understands this is a friend of mine." Guru Nanak Dev, *Guru Granth Sahib*, 1364.
62. "By becoming the dust of the feet, the disciple is required to be near the feet of the Guru." *Bhai Gurdas*, Vaar 3, Pauri 19.
63. Pritpal Kaur Riat, *A Historical and Theological Evaluation of the Sikh Gurdwaras Act, 1925* (Doctoral dissertation, University of Birmingham). 2013. Accessible at Proquest.
64. *Bhai Gurdas*, Vaar 25, Pauri 13 of 20.
65. The *Adi Granth* was added to by Guru Gobind Singh to contain the teachings of the ninth Guru, Guru Tegh Bahadur. The revised book, which is in its contemporary form, became known as *Guru Granth Sahib*.
66. Bhai Gurudas in various verses underscores the importance of Sikh congregation and *Gurdwaras*, "[...] [S]adhus in the form of the Sikhs of Guru Nanak are innumerable because the Dharamsals flourish everywhere;" "The glimpse of the Sikh life can be holy had in the holy congregation and the Gurudvara, the door of the Lord;" and, "At the Dharamsals, they celebrate anniversaries of the Gurus and thus sow the seeds of virtuous actions." Bhai Gurdas, Vaar 23, Pauri 2; Vaar 28, Pauri 7; and Vaar 29, Pauri 5.
67. Riat, *Theological Evaluation*, 2013.
68. A.R. Gatrad *et al.*, "Sikh Birth Customs," *Archives of Disease in Childhood*, Vol. 90(6) (June 20, 2005), 560.
69. Quoted in Jhutti-Johal, *Sikhism Today*, 95.
70. The outward symbols of Sikh faith are the most publically recognizable aspects of an Amridhari and Keshdhari Sikh.
71. E. Nesbitt, *The Religious Lives of Sikh Children: A Coventry-Based Study* (University of Leeds, 2000).
72. Some Sikhs would not put the Gora Sikhs into this hierarchy as they are not seen as "true" Sikhs because they have no Punjabi connection.
73. Opinderjit Kaur Takhar, *Sikh Identity: An Exploration of Groups among Sikhs* (Hants: Ashgate Publishing Limited, 2005).
74. *Ibid.*, 161–4. Takhar argues that the Sikh Dharam of the Western Hemisphere and the 3HO, both established by Yogi Bhajan, are at times two different groups and at other times one group. She argues that 3HO places an emphasis on Kundalini yoga, while the Sikh Dharma of the Western Hemisphere also practices Kundalini yoga, but also practice and follow the Sikh teachings. Notably, there are no real figures about the exact numbers of Gora Sikhs.

75. For a detailed discussion on this topic see N. Singh, *Sikhism*, Chapter IV.
76. Takhar, *Sikh Identity*, 172–6; Doris Jakobsh, "3HO/Sikh Dharma of the Western Hemisphere: The "Forgotten" New Religious Movement?" *Religious Compass*, 2(3) (2008): 385–408.
77. V.A. Dusenbery, "Punjabi Sikhs and Gora Sikhs: Conflicting Assertion of Sikh Identity in North America," in Joseph T. O'Connell *et al.*, eds., *Sikh History and Religion in the Twentieth Century* (Toronto: University of Toronto: 1988).
78. S.S. Kalsi, *The Evolution of the Sikh Community in Britain: Religious and Social Change Among the Sikhs of Leeds and Bradford* (Leeds: University of Leeds, 1992).
79. https://www.niot.org/cops/wakinginoakcreek.
80. Jasjit Singh, "Who speaks for British Sikhs," available at http://www.publicspirit.org.uk/who-speaks-for-british-sikhs/ (accessed June 11, 2016).
81. Gurharpal Singh and Darshan Singh Tatla, *Sikhs in Britain: The Making of a Community* (London: Zed Books, 2006), 120.
82. http://www.britishsikhreport.org/wp-content/uploads/2016/03/British-Sikh-Report-2016.pdf, 20 (accessed July 26, 2016).
83. *Commission on Religion and Belief in British Public Life: Living with Difference: Community, Diversity and the Common Good* (Cambridge: Woolf Institute, 2015), 62.
84. "Sikh Organization for Prisoner Welfare," available at http://www.prisonerwelfare.org/news-media/510-midland-langar-seva-society.html; "Sikh Welfare and Awareness Team," available at http://www.swatlondon.com/ (accessed December 20, 2016).
85. "KHALSAAIDl," available at http://www.khalsaaid.org/ (accessed December 20, 2016).
86. *Guru Granth Sahib*, 473.
87. Jhutti-Johal, *Sikhism Today*, 28–55.
88. Prominent Sikh Women from the US and UK: Sikh female academics: Professor Nikky-Guninder Kaur Singh (US), Professor Parminder Bhachu (US), Professor Kulwant Bhopal (UK). Sikh Actor: Parminder Nagra (UK); Film Director: Gurinder Chadha (UK); Artists: Amrit Kaur Singh and Rabindra Kaur Singh, otherwise known as The Singh Twins (UK); Law: Mejinderpal Kaur (US), Amrit Singh (US); Model, Harnaam Kaur (UK); and Social Activist: Valerie Kaur (US).
89. American convert Sikhs do allow women to make up the *panj pyare*.
90. D.R. Jakobsh, "Sikhism, interfaith dialogue, and women: Transformation and identity," *Journal of Contemporary Religion*, 21(2) (2006), 183–99.
91. Paraphrase of *Dasam Granth*, 47, available at http://www.sridasam.org/dasam?Action=Page&p = 51.
92. *Guru Granth Sahib*, 1167.
93. "Gay Sikh: Homosexuality Within Sikhism," available at http://www.gaysikh.com (accessed July 18, 2016).
94. Jhutti-Johal, *Sikhism Today*.

Selected Bibliography

Banerjee, Anil Chandra. *The Sikh Gurus and the Sikh Religion*. Delhi: Munshiram Manoharlal Publishers, 1983.

Bhachu, Parminder. *Twice Migrants: East African Sikh Settlers in Britain*. London; New York: Tavistock Publications, 1985.

Buck, P.S. and Gopal Sigh, trans. *Introduction to Translation of Guru Granth Sahib*. 7th ed. New Delhi: Allied, 1987.

Cole, W.O. and P.S. Sambhi. *The Sikhs: Their Religious Beliefs and Practices*. London: Sussex Academic Press, 1978.

Dusenbery, V.A. "The Poetics and Politics of Recognition: Diasporan Sikhs in Pluralist Politics." *American Ethnologist*, 24(4) (1997): 738–62.

———. "Punjabi Sikhs and Gora Sikhs: Conflicting Assertion of Sikh Identity in North America." In Joseph T. O'Connell, *et al.*, eds. *Sikh History and Religion in the Twentieth Century*. Toronto: University of Toronto, 1988.

Field, Dorothy. *The Religion of the Sikhs*. London: J. Murray, 1914.

Gatrad, A.R., *et al.* "Sikh Birth Customs." *Archives of Disease in Childhood*, 90(6) (2005): 560–3.

Jakobsh, Doris. "3HO/Sikh Dharma of the Western Hemisphere: The 'Forgotten' New Religious Movement?" *Religious Compass*, 2(3) (2008): 385–408.

———. "Sikhism, Interfaith Dialogue, and Women: Transformation and Identity." *Journal of Contemporary Religion*, 21(2) (2006): 183–99.

Jhutti-Johal, Jagbir. *Sikhism Today*. London: Continuum, 2011.

Jhutti-Johal, Jagbir and Sukhvinder Singh Johal. "The Sikh Grand Narrative." In A.R. Gatrad *et al*, eds., *Palliative Care amongst South Asians*. London: Quay Books, 2005, 83–94.

Johar, Surinder Singh. *Guru Gobind Singh: A Multi-Faceted Personality*. New Delhi: M.D. Publications, 1999.

Kalsi, S.S. *The Evolution of the Sikh Community in Britain: Religious and Social Change Among the Sikhs of Leeds and Bradford*. Leeds: University of Leeds, 1992.

McLeod, W.H. *Exploring Sikhism: Aspects of Sikh Identity, Culture and Thought*. Oxford: Oxford University Press, 2000.

———. "Discord in the Sikh Panth." In *Journal of the American Oriental Society*, 119(3) (1999): 381–9.

———. *Sikhism*. London: Penguin Books, 1997.

———. *Who Is a Sikh? The Problem of Sikh Identity*. Oxford: Clarendon Press, 1989.

———. *The Sikhs: History, Religion and Society*. New York: Columbia University Press, 1989.

———. *Guru Nanak and the Sikh Religion*. Oxford: Clarendon Press, 1968.

Mooney, Nicola. *Rural Nostalgia and Transnational Dreams: Identity and Modernity Among Jat Sikhs*. Toronto: University of Toronto Press, 2011.

Nesbitt, E. *The Religious Lives of Sikh Children: A Coventry-Based Study*. Leeds: University of Leeds, 2000.

Riat, P.K. *A Historical and Theological Evaluation of the Sikh Gurdwaras Act, 1925.* Doctoral dissertation, University of Birmingham, 2013.

Soch, H.S. and Madanjit Kaur, eds. *Guru Nanak: Ideals and Institutions.* Amritsar: Guru Nanak Dev University, 1998.

Singh, Daljeet. *Sikhism: A Comparative Study of its Theology and Mysticism,* 2nd ed. Amritsar: Singh Brothers, 1994.

Singh, Gurharpal and Darshan Singh Tatla. *Sikhs in Britain: The Making of a Community.* London: Zed Books, 2006.

Singh, Khushwant. *A History of the Sikhs, Vol. 1.* Oxford: Oxford University Press, 1977.

Singh, Nikky-Guninder Kaur. *Sikhism: An Introduction.* London: I.B.Tauris, 2011.

Singh, Patwant. *The Sikhs.* London: J. Murray, 1999.

Takhar, Opinderjit Kaur. *Sikh Identity: An Exploration of Groups Among Sikhs.* Hants: Ashgate Publishing Limited, 2005.

Woolf Institute, *Commission on Religion and Belief in British Public Life: Living with Difference: Community, Diversity and the Common Good.* Cambridge: 2015.

Sufism in India

Arthur F. Buehler

Human beings are members of a whole,
Created of one essence and soul.

If one member is troubled by pain,
Others suffer severe strain.

You who have no sympathy for human pain,
Deserve not the name human to retain.

– Saadi of Shiraz

Introduction

The cross-fertilization of religious, philosophical, mythical, ethical, and spiritual ideas did not only occur among the Dharma traditions; significant interactions have also occurred with Abrahamic traditions. For example, Islam (translated as "submission") arrived in India around the eighth century CE and became an important part of the religious dialogue. On the Indian subcontinent, a large population of the followers of Islam, known as Muslims, continues to flourish. Islam differs from the Dharma traditions in some fundamental aspects: Islam is monotheistic and holds the belief in one all-powerful, omniscient God, known as Allah. The prophet Muhammad is the Messenger of God who received the Divine revelation, which is considered the direct word of Allah, over a period of twenty-three years. This word has been recorded in the holy Qur'an. In practice, the Qur'an mandates that Muslims follow the

Five Pillars, which are the foundational acts a Muslim must complete to live a good life: *shahadah* (reciting the Muslim declaration of faith), *salat* (ritual prayers five times a day), *zakat* (paying alms to benefit the poor), *sawm* (fasting during the month of Ramadan), and *hajj* (at least one pilgrimage to Mecca). In sharing the Indian subcontinent with followers of the Dharma traditions, Islam both influenced and was influenced *by* those traditions. Here we focus on Sufism, commonly known as the mystical aspect of Islam, which has continued to be a part of the shared religious landscape of India since it gained significance in South Asia in the early part of the second millennia.

Sufism contains devotional elements similar to those found in the Hindu Bhakti movement of the medieval era, as has been discussed in the Hindu Dharma chapter. Indeed, one of the most significant results of this interaction was the formation of the Sikh tradition, which became a prominent religious movement in its own right. This historical analysis does not seek to suggest the deliberate borrowing of the terms and ideas, but rather to substantiate the reality of a more organic system of interactions between the religious and philosophical movements on the Indian subcontinent.

Origins and Characteristics of Sufism

The word *Sufi*, derived from the lexical root of the Arabic word *suf,* meaning "wool" and denoting how the early Sufis wore humble cloaks, was first used in an eighth-century Islamic context to describe Muslim ascetics who focused on the inner experience to become closer to God. Ascetics wearing woolen clothes in the deserts of the Near East drew on the inner experiences of the prophet Muhammad and Qur'anic verses to describe their own supra-rational experiences. By the tenth century, this activity developed into a branch of the Islamic religious sciences, which has become known as Sufism in the West. The English term Sufism conflates the two ideas of *tasawwuf* ("the process of becoming a Sufi") in the Sunni world and *'irfan* ("theoretical mysticism") in the Iranian Shi'i world. Sufi activities are generally acknowledged by historians to be responsible for the spread of Islam in the eastern Islamic world, including present-day India. The Sufi message is more expansive and yet remains inclusive of the doctrinal, orthopraxic religion known as Islam. That is, although

Sufism around the world has historically been practiced almost exclusively by Muslims, it has also gone beyond the human-created boundaries of Islam. It includes anyone who seeks to submit to God, and thus it remains true to the technical meaning of Muslim ("submission") in Arabic. On the Indian subcontinent, the outer expression of Sufi practice is most often seen around the shrines of dead Sufi masters—who are nevertheless still considered *alive* insofar as people go to them for healing and grace.

The Sufis trace their mystical tradition to the prophet Muhammad himself, and Sufi practices in many ways involve one's direct experience of God. While the Sufi tradition originated from a different religious umbrella, its practices share several of the same qualities as many of devotional paths in Dharma traditions. Some of these practices include the devotional remembrance of God (*dhikr*), meditation (*muraqabah*), concentrating on the subtle spiritual centers of consciousness (*lata'if*), and the annihilation of the ego-self (*fana*). On the Indian subcontinent, the Sufi traditions included a component of devotional music within their practices. The most important dimension of Sufi practice is the commitment on behalf of a student to place him or herself under the tutelage of a Sufi *shaykh*. The *shaykh* is the spiritual teacher who guides the student on the path to attain the direct experience of the Divine.

The *Shaykh*–Seeker Relationship: Transformation and Transmission

There are many ways in which these traditions parallel, but there is one main element that serves as the focus of this analysis: the teacher-student relationship. One of the central tenets of Sufi and Dharma traditions is the transfer of knowledge from teacher to student (i.e., Hindu Sants, Sikh Gurus, Buddhist Masters, and Sufi Shaykhs). This chain of teachers is known as a lineage; Sufis refer to it as *silsilah*.

> Choose a shaykh, for without a shaykh the journey is one of sadness, fear, and danger. Without a guide you are bewildered so do not travel alone on a road you have never seen nor turn away from the guide.[1]

Mainstream Indian forms of spiritual practice follow the same basic principles of Sufi transformative practice. In Sufism, the locus of transformation is the *shaykh*–seeker relationship. Sufis become teachers by first developing an intimate spiritual relationship with an authentic *shaykh*, and the *shaykh* then authorizes a student to teach once they have reached a certain stage of spiritual development. This authorization serves as the conduit that allows Sufi knowledge to be transferred from one generation to the next, creating an ongoing chain of knowledge that is referred to as a lineage. For Sufis, the highest value is placed on lineages that can be traced all the way back to the Prophet Mohammad. The sacredness of the teacher–student relationship is also seen in various Sant traditions of Hinduism, the intricate lineages of the Sikh tradition, as well as in the Buddhist and Jain traditions. On the Indian subcontinent, the lineages of the Sufi orders—Naqshbandi-Mujaddidi, Chishti, Shadhili, and Qadiri—continue to the present day.

The principal pedagogical focus on radical ego transformation that underlies the *shaykh*–seeker relationship functions as a crucial element for inner spiritual development. In the secular world, the nuance and context of this methodology has been lost or distorted as these societies struggle to understand the value of submitting to a spiritual authority. From a contemplative Sufi perspective, non-discerning skepticism of Sufi *shaykhs* in the modern world can become a cover for an ego ruse that prevents humanity from seeing the most precious pearl of the teaching, even if it is right in front of us. As Rumi, the well-known planetary poet, asks:

> How long will you run around in circles? One needs a master to learn a trade and to do business. When you seek knowledge in China [referring to a Prophetic saying] do not disgrace yourself. Seek a shaykh and keep company with him. Whatever the Plato of the age tells you to do, give up your ego-self and act accordingly.[2]

Rumi reminds us that obedience and respect for one's teacher is essential for any trade or art. At the same time, one must beware of questionable *shaykhs*. It is not the outward appearance or smooth words that mark a true teacher, but the sincerity of their inner struggle with the ego. Rumi writes of this in a prelude to a section of poetry:

> [This is] a description of the cowardice and weakness of a spoiled Sufi who has never struggled with the ego-self or experienced the pain and anguish of divine love. He has been deluded by the homage and hand-kissing of people who venerate him, declaring that he is the most famous contemporary Sufi.[3]

Rumi emphasized, as have many other traditions, that the struggle with one's ego is an essential part of any experience of divine love and therefore warns against the outward show of religiosity and succumbing to the desire for popularity. Many modern, educated people are at a great disadvantage when it comes to understanding other types of knowledge outside their familiar, comfortable world-view or education. For Sufis, the work to train one's character and inner self is considered essential to the development of the human being. To the Sufi, there is no way for transformation to manifest from the external to the internal. It is only by changing the internal self that the external world undergoes change automatically. Alas, this is not the domain of modern, educational institutions, but Sufism as a spiritual tradition is still seen in other parts of the world as a simultaneously valuable path to developing the person as an ethically aware and socially responsible human being. In fact, facilitating these kinds of transformations is the primary activity of a practicing Sufi.

Educating the inner self does not stop at the personal; for Sufis, internal character development is only the beginning. It is expected that this beauty of character be communicated harmoniously through one's behavior in society. The training of one's heart becomes translated into compassionate behavior toward others. Just as we have seen in the Sikh tradition, it is the emphasis on service (e.g., acts of service, devotion, and dedication to the welfare of the community) that defines a "true" Sikh. The more intimate the realization of God, the greater the extension of one's compassion towards all of God's creations. Mahatma Gandhi also made a similar connection between love for God and service for humanity, and one of the great Persian poets Saadi Shirazi noted, "there is no worship without service to humanity."

Some might dismiss the idea of an external teacher and look towards the wisdom within. This is the epistemological difference between authoritative and intuitive knowledge. Is one's inner teacher a sufficient guide and therefore an external *shaykh* is unnecessary? But many think that the inner teacher is most likely the ego "in robes and a turban." There is such a thing as an inner teacher—in my personal understanding and experience—but only spiritual Einsteins are able to access this inner guide and dispense with a living *shaykh*. There are only a few who have access to the path of spiritual knowledge without the guidance of a teacher, and so to the Sufi most people are instead burdened with an ego masquerading as an internal teacher. They do in fact have need of an external teacher to give them feedback on their progress, often in ways that can take the form of uncomfortable and sudden wake-up calls. For example, the Sufi *shaykh* will confront the seeker's ego by presenting actual life trials if need be. However, Sufism is an internally and culturally diverse tradition and thus the term "Sufism" should not refer to a monolithic tradition. Rather, the Sufis have developed into various forms within different cultural contexts throughout the Middle East and Asia.

Sufi Traditions in India and Sufi–Sant Interactions

Sufism in India is a confluence of (1) the Islamic religious inheritance from the Arabic tradition, (2) the government, law, dress, and culinary habits characteristic of many of the Turkish rulers and aristocracy, (3) the pervasive influence of Persian literature, fine arts, mysticism, and philosophy, and (4) the indigenous Indian religious philosophy and practices and social environment in which Islamic culture thrived. Broadly speaking, Indian Sufis originated from various regions such as Arabia, Iran, and Central Asia. Subsequent generations of these immigrants grew up in India and increasingly took on the customs and languages of the people around them.

Although it is difficult to trace any exact historical records, it is believed that Sufis arrived in India around the thirteenth century, a time when Nath and Kanphata *yogis* were propagating their practices. The Naths were the *yogis* associated with the Hindu Shaiva tradition, which came to prominence around the thirteenth century, and the Kanpatha *yogis* who worshipped Shiva and can be identified by the large earrings they wear. The practices of both these groups did not fit into the Hindu orthodoxy. For example, since nomadic Naths did not observe the restrictions of Brahmanical ritual, they thought nothing of eating in the free public kitchens sponsored by Sufi lodges. (Generally, orthodox Hindus avoided eating food not prepared by Brahmins in Brahmin kitchens because of their very strict purity laws.) While hardly representative of "Hindu" culture as a whole, the *yogis* were one of the few Indian religious groups who shared interests in psychophysical contemplative methodologies with the Sufis. Both groups competed to some extent for popular recognition as wonder-workers and healers. In early Indian Sufism it was common to read Sufi accounts of winning miraculous bouts with *yogis*. At the same time, Sufi interest in yoga was limited to its practical, physical value and did not usually include serious engagement with the philosophical texts of Vedanta or other Sanskritic schools of thought.

The Hindi romance *Padmavat* by Muhammad Ja'isi, a Chishti Sufi, extensively discusses yogic physiology and states. Like many other Bengali Muslim authors, he gives a detailed account of the *chakras*, nerves, drinking nectar, and other yogic themes, all of which are integrated into an Islamic vocabulary and worldview.[4] The 1891 Indian census, which listed *yogis* under the rubric of "miscellaneous and disreputable vagrants," indicated that over seventeen per cent of *yogis* were Muslims, although by 1921 the proportion of Muslims had fallen to less than five per cent.[5] Census categories can be skewed and inconclusive, but such data does indicate that there were probably Muslim *yogis* existing right up to the twentieth century.[6] Historically, the boundaries between religious communities in India were much more permeable than they are today. Referring to this fluidity between religious communities, Carl Ernst remarks that,

> the long history of Muslim interest in the philosophy and practice of yoga is a helpful corrective to the blinders that we often bring to the understanding of religion today, which is frequently defined in purely scriptural terms without reference to history and sociology [...] The transmission of yoga—in Arabic, Persian, Turkish, and Urdu translations and through images—is an important reminder that the history of Indian religions needs to take account of a wide range of sources, including those Muslim interpreters who were so fascinated by yoga.[7]

Historically, many Muslims were fascinated by yoga, since at least the eleventh century when the famous scholar Al-Biruni translated a version of Patanjali's *Yoga Sutras*, the foundational text of yoga, into Arabic.[8] In terms of textual evidence, we find an excerpt from *The Fifty Verses of Kamarupa* in a Persian encyclopedia compiled in Shiraz by Sharaf al-Din Amuli that discusses breath control and *chakras* practices.[9] A Mughal prince Darashikuh, who followed his Qadiri *shaykh* Miyan Mir, also had great knowledge of Hindu yogic vocabulary and practices. Due to these confluences, certain similarities between the practices of Sufi and Indian spiritual traditions, as well as interactions between Sufis and yogis, have been interpreted as compatibilities between yoga and Sufism.

Baba Farid: A Legacy of Interreligious Exchange

The vast majority of Muslims were from native Indian families, so the customs, culture, and mentalities of Indian society infused a constantly increasing Indo-Muslim society. Before modernist, fundamentalist, and nationalist agendas attempted to create impermeable and fixed religious boundaries, many Indians of different traditions freely interacted with one another. One such example of these porous boundaries is the poetry of Baba Farid, which is revered even in modern times throughout the Indian subcontinent.

Shaykh Fariduddin Ganj-i Shakar ("Sugar Treasure"), more popularly known as Baba Farid of Punjab, was from the Chishti Order. His shrine is located on the right bank of Sutlej, near the town of Pakpattan ("the holy ferry"), and is frequented by followers of various faith traditions.[10] Baba Farid was a poet like those of Sant Kabir and Sant Ravidas of the Hindu Bhakti tradition. He was famous for his supernatural powers, and stories of his miracles circulate in religious circles. In the Indian tradition, the evil eye is the idea that an ill-wisher's feelings can affect another person negatively. Writing amulets were very common because they were thought to protect people from the "evil eye." Therefore, many Indians still go to a Sufi for amulets to protect one from a variety of unseen dangers.[11] According to one account, when Nizamuddin Auliya went to see his master Baba Farid, his neighbor asked him to bring an amulet back. Baba Farid had Nizamuddin write some names of God on a piece of paper, and then Nizamuddin went back and handed the paper to his neighbor. This news spread, and soon crowds of people began requesting amulets from Baba Farid. People receiving the amulets offered gifts, which Baba Farid distributed. He continues to be revered among Muslims, Hindus, and Sikhs, and many frequent his shrine and offer gifts.

When Baba Farid died, a vast shrine complex that included a mosque, public kitchen, and houses for his family was developed. Baba Farid's successor was his son, Badruddin Sulayman, also called the Diwan ("treasury official"). The Diwan was seen as Baba Farid's living representative, and so both he and the shrine itself could transfer Baba Farid's spiritual power (*baraka*) to the believers. Descendants of Baba Farid then started to build subsidiary shrines in the Punjab area because people believed the *baraka* came from Baba Farid's descendants rather than from his tomb.[12] "The spirit of Baba Farid was there like a beacon" along with his subsidiary, inspiring teachers and followers throughout the Punjab region.[13] When many of these people of Punjab became Sikhs, they did not forget the teachings, legacy, and inspiration of Baba Farid.

Baba Farid and the Sikh Tradition

The Sikh Scripture *Guru Granth Sahib* (earlier known as the *Adi Granth*) contains over hundred compositions attributed to Baba Farid. If they were all put together, found in three different places in the text, they would comprise about 8 of the 1430 pages of the *Guru Granth Sahib*. It is the only substantial collection of vernacular verses attributed to a Sufi during this early period in India. Instead of Persian, the lingua franca of the eastern Islamic world, the verses are written in a southwest Punjabi dialect, now called Siraiki. Most of the verses associated with Baba Farid are in the format of the *doha*, which is the classic teaching couplet of medieval India that succinctly conveys images and messages. This *doha* style is found in the writings and poetry of many Hindu Sants of the time. The following passages from the text evoke a powerful image of the love God has for humanity:

> Night ends, but still you sleep; you die while living yet. Though you forget the Lord, still He does not forget.[14]
> Do not utter even a single harsh word; your True Lord and Master abides in all.
> Do no break anyone's heart; these are all the priceless jewels.
> The minds of all are like precious jewels; to harm them is not good at all.
> If you desire your beloved, then do not break anyone's heart.[15]

The interactions among Sufis and Sikhs have not always been filled with amity. For instance, when the Sikhs under Mahraja Ranjit Singh (1780–1839) conquered Punjab and Kashmir in the nineteenth century, they deliberately desecrated the most treasured mosques of Lahore by killing pigs and converting their courtyards into stables. Mosques were the center of the Islamic governments, open only to Muslims, and so trashing the defeated army's religious sites has been a common practice among various warring tribes throughout the world.[16]

However, Ranjit Singh also contributed to the upkeep of major Sufi shrines in Lahore that are open to all. Even today one can find many examples of how Sufism is integrated with other Indic traditions: Sikhs join audiences of Chishti Sufi musical performances around the world. In 2006, for example, many Sikhs were in the audience when the Sabri Brothers (Sufi qawwali musicians) played informally in Jakarta. The late Nusrat Fateh Ali Khan also found it quite natural to sing his Punjabi, Persian, and Siraiki odes inside Sikh *Gurdwaras*. Sikhs in the Punjab did not hesitate to join the ecstatic Sufi Chishti lineage's musical sessions, and the Sufis thought nothing of initiating Sikhs and Hindus into their lineages even though they were non-Muslims. Furthermore, as a pan-Indian phenomenon, vernacular Sufi poetry was one of the ways Sufi ideas spread among the common people.

The Development of Sufism in India

Sufism is not a monolithic tradition, as evidenced by the variety of Sufi orders that exist. The Sufism found on the Indian subcontinent is expressed through the practices of the following orders:

1. *Qadriyya*: The Persian Arab, Abdul Qadir Jilani, is more popular in South Asia than any other part of the world except for his native land of Iraq. He is the founder-figure of the Qadiri Sufi lineage, which is the most widespread lineage in the world. South Asian Muslims visiting Abdul Qadir's tomb outnumber non-Iraqi pilgrims from any other country.[17] Abdul Qadir's rise to popularity in South Asia most likely stems from the supernatural legends associated with him, legends which preceded the arrival of his descendants in India.[18]

    Devotion to Abdul Qadir has been widely expressed in popular culture through ritual. At this level of popular ritual, Abdul Qadir's death anniversary is celebrated each eleventh of Rabi' al-thani (the fourth Islamic month). In Sind, where many big trees are named after Abdul Qadir, the entire month is called eleven (*yarhin*) because of this day that commemorates Abdul Qadir.[19] It is evident that Abdul Qadir has captured the imaginations of individuals from a wide range of geographic locations and social classes of the South Asian community.

    The Qadiri tradition continued near Lahore, in Qasur. It was here that one of the greatest Punjabi Sufis, Bulleh Shah Qadiri (1680–1757), graced the world with his moving poetry. Bulleh Shah did not outwardly conform to societal demands, whether it is in his choice of a spiritual master, who came from a low caste, or in his decision to live a celibate life, which is contrary to the traditional Islamic views. His writings expressed concern for social problems of his time. In many respects, he seems to have a spiritual affinity to the Hindu's Sant Kabir and the Sikh's Guru Nanak. His poetry expressed a daring vision of unity that would not necessarily have been harmonious with the worldview of many sharia-minded Muslims:

> Neither Hindu nor Mussulman, let us sit to spin, abandoning the pride (of religion). Neither a *sunni* nor a *shi'a*, I have taken the path of complete peace and unity ... I am not walking in the way of either sin or virtue. Bulleh, in all hearts I feel the Lord (therefore) Hindu and Mussulmans both have I abandoned.[20]

Bulleh Shah's poetry is mystical but it also inspired painters and singers alike. His legacy is revered by many contemporary Hindu and Sikh Sants.

2. *Naqshbandiyya*: Unlike the Qadiris, Naqshbandi Sufis came mostly from Central Asia. This order traces its spiritual lineage to the Prophet Muhammad. The Naqshbandiyya became established on the Indian subcontinent during the great Mughal emperor Akbar's reign (1556–1605) when dozens of Naqshbandi Sufis had important positions in his government. The Naqshbandi Order was a prominent order for two hundred years in the lives of Indo-Muslims. Mirza Mazhar Jan-i Janan, a well-known Naqshbandi *shaykh*, accepted the Hindu deities Rama and Krishna as prophets of God. He even argued that the Hindu practice of venerating images was different from that of the pre-Islamic Arabs. To him, the Hindu practice of *darshan* was similar to concentrating on the mental image of the Sufi *shaykh* as a means of getting closer to God. After Mirza's death, some of his authorized teachers associated closely with "Hindu" mystics, particularly those connected with the Nanakpanth or the sect of Guru Nanak (later known as Sikh Dharam) and the Kabirpanth sect of Sant Kabir. The practices of these two groups transcended narrow, religious boundaries. Focusing on *bhakti* (devotion), they kept their distance from the ritualism of both Brahmin priests and orthodox Muslim religious scholars.[21] This trend is seen in the Hindu Sant tradition and the teachings of the Gurus of the Sikh tradition. However, Emperor

Akbar patronized the Indian Chishti Sufi lineage, an order that used the Hindi language.

3. *Chistiya*: Historically, the early development of the Chishtis in India began with Mu'inuddin Chishti. He introduced the Chishti Order in Punjab and Rajasthan. Ernst and Lawrence in their book, *Sufi Martyrs of Love: The Chishti Order in South Asia and Beyond*, provide a comprehensive account of the Chishti Order. Emperor Akbar visited Mu'inuddin Chishti's tomb many times, having performed his first pilgrimage on foot to the mausoleum in 1564. Like his father, Humayun, Akbar also visited the Sufi saint Salim Chishti, whose holy intercession and prayer Akbar believed had expedited the birth of his first surviving son and heir.

Expressing Sufism in an Indian Manner: The Chishti Sufi Order

The Chishti Order expressed itself in a distinctly Indian manner, and as such it requires a brief elaboration. The foremost Indian Chishti is Nizamuddin Auliya, whose shrine is located in Delhi. The shrine has been frequently visited by people of all traditions. Nizamuddin, the main successor to the poet Baba Farid, set up a Sufi lodge near the seat of power in Delhi and saw twelve rulers come and go in his lifetime. As other Chishtis after him, Nizamuddin allowed Hindus to take part in the *sama* (the hearing of chanted verse) and initiated them into the Chishtiyya without formal conversion to Islam. Muslim religious leaders tried to prohibit these sacred musical sessions, but to no avail. The Chishtis generally (and wisely) refused stipends offered by rulers, but did accept unsolicited gifts. When Chishtis moved to the provinces, the rulers generally gave them lucrative land grants, which helped fund the glorious Sufi shrines still in existence today.

Like all Sufi lineages, Chishtis love and worship the arts, including music. On Thursday evenings these Sufi shrines usually held a musical assembly where everyone was welcome to join and experience an ecstatic state brought on by the poetry and music. At some point, this devotional music (songs accompanied by small musical instruments) came to be called *qawwali* and have continued to be performed on the Indian subcontinent to this day.

The Chishti practice of listening to chanted verse and music has traditionally been circumscribed by a strict set of rules and accompanied by the discipline of ego training. In the case of Nizamuddin Auliya, each listening session began and ended with recitation of the Qur'an; everyone had to be in a state of ritual purity (a requirement before Islamic prayer); and there was no chewing of betel nut allowed (chewing betel nut with tobacco can be addicting). Listening with a pure heart becomes a gateway to mystical experiences. One of Nizamuddin's pupils, Burhanuddin Gharib, described the altered states of consciousness he experienced while listening to chanted verses of Qur'an and Sufi music. If the listener longs totally for God with little to no longing for the world, then listening to music in Sufi assemblies is permitted. If there is more longing for the world than for God, then listening to music is not permitted (although like other religious establishments, the rules were likely to be broken regularly). Thus, devotional music comprises an essential part of Chishti mystical path and continues to be a part of Indian culture. Chishti Shrine, Dargah of Chishti, in Ajmer, India, marks the symbol of interreligious interactions among Islam and Dharma traditions and is frequented annually by both male and female followers of various religions.

Conclusion

Sufism is inextricably linked to the monotheistic tradition of Islam; however, although it does not immediately present itself as an Indian tradition (if geographical origin is to be the defining factor of an Indian religion), its mystical path and approaches parallel those of many Indian Sants and devotional traditions. Similar to the way that most *yogis* lived and practiced outside the Brahmanic caste system, most Indian Sufi practices occurred outside the mosque and official Islamic institutions. Hence, without the oversight of Islamic institutions, it comes as no surprise to find Sufis and *yogis* sharing their similar techniques, and, at times, competing with each other upon Sufism's arrival in India.

An excellent example of how this relates to the Dharma traditions is the Sants in northern India, where Kabir (a north Indian *bhakti* poet) is one of the most well-known and revered by Hindus, Muslims, and Sikhs. When Sufis became widespread in India, we have found that vernacular Indian languages began to flourish. Just like the Sikhs and Hindus had their specific rituals, Muslims had theirs. But this did not prevent almost all Sufis from opening their doors to the entire

Indian community—from outcasts to Brahmins—and inviting them to share a very Indian meal.

This historical analysis of Sufism in India should further demonstrate the diversity and interconnectedness of India's spiritual traditions. Taking the melting pot of India's various cultural and religious traditions into account, it has hopefully created a clearer understanding of how Sufism, an apparent outlier, has become such an integral part of Indian culture. Since its beginnings in India in the thirteenth century, the open, devotional, and mystical framework of yoga and spiritual practices of followers of Sikh, Hindu, and Sufi traditions has allowed much of these interactions to take place. Sufi poetry found in the Sikh *Guru Granth Sahib* and Sufi shrines strewn across Indian landscapes are testament to the ways in which this organic system of interactions between the religious and philosophical movements has propagated and flourished.

Notes

1. Quoted in Arthur F. Buehler, *Recognizing Sufism: Contemplation in the Islamic Tradition* (London: I.B.Tauris, 2016), 141.
2. Mawlana Jalaluddin Rumi's *Mathnawi* are from the Nicholson translation, easily available as a PDF online. The translations are by author of this chapter. A reliable physical copy of Nicholson's translation can be found in Reynold A. Nicholson, *The Mathnawi of Jalalu'ddin Rumi, Edited from the Oldest Manuscripts Available with Critical Notes, Translation, & Commentary* (Lahore: Islamic Book Service, 1989). Nicholson, *Rumi* Vol. V and VI, 486.
3. *Ibid.*, 464.
4. See Carl Ernst, "Muslim Interpreters of Yoga," in *Yoga: The Art of Transformation*, ed. Debra Diamond (Washington, DC: Smithsonian Books, 2013), and http://www.unc.edu/~cernst/pdf/Smithsonian.pdf (accessed December 5, 2016).
5. General Report on the Census of India, 1891, available at https://archive.org/details/cu31924023177268 (accessed January 15, 2017).
6. *Ibid.*, 38.
7. Ernst, "Muslim Interpreters of Yoga," in *Yoga: The Art of Transformation*, 68, available at http://www.unc.edu/~cernst/pdf/Smithsonian.pdf.
8. Andrey Safronov, "Arabic Translation of Patanjali's Yoga Sutras made by Al-Biruni. The Problem of Yoga Impact on Sufism," *Yoga-sutra.org*, 2014, available at http://en.yoga-sutra.org/2014/02/the-arabic-translation-of-patanjalis.html.
9. Ernst, "Muslim Interpreters of Yoga," 59–68.

10. See Richard M. Eaton, "The Political and Religious Authority of the Shrine of Baba Farid," in *Moral Conduct and Authority: The Place of Adab in South Asian Islam*, ed. Barbara Daly Metcalf (Berkeley, California: University of California Press, 1984), 333–56.

11. For a scientific eye-opener on the reality of the "evil eye" and parallel phenomena in the animal world, see Rupert Sheldrake, *The Sense of Being Stared at and Other Unexplained Powers of Human Minds* (Rochester, Vermont: Park Street Press, 2013).

12. Eaton, "Religious Authority," 340.

13. *Ibid.*, 345.

14. Christopher Shackle, "Sikh and Muslim Understandings of Baba Farid," lecture, Amrit Kaur Ahluwalia Memorial Lecture, UC Berkeley, Berkeley, California, April 19, 2008.

15. Shaykh Baba Farid, *Guru Granth Sahib*, 1384.

16. Arthur F. Buehler, *Sufi Heirs of the Prophet: The Indian Naqshbandiyya and the Rise of the Mediating Shaykh* (Columbia, South Carolina: University of South Carolina Press, 1998), 215.

17. D.S. Margoliouth, "Kadiriyya" in P. Bearman, Th. Bianquis, C.E. Bosworth, E. van Donzel, W.P. Heinrichs, eds., *Encyclopedia of Islam, Second Edition* (2012) 4:382. Pakistani contributions are the main source of revenue for the caretakers of the tomb, who find it useful to learn Urdu, available at http://dx.doi.org/10.1163/1573-3912_islam_COM_0411.

18. Probably on the basis of al-Shattanawfi's thirteenth-century hagiography, *Bahjat al-asrar*.

19. Annemarie Schimmel, *Islam in the Indian Subcontinent* (Leiden: E.J. Brill, 1980), 121.

20. L.R. Krishna, *Punjabi Sufi Poets* (Bombay: Oxford University Press, 1938), 75. Passage translated by L. Rama Krishna.

21. For a further exposition of this Hindu Naqshbandi lineage, see: Thomas Dahnhardt, *Change and Continuity in Indian Sufism: A Naqshbandi-Mujaddidi Branch in the Hindu Environment* (Delhi: DK Printworld, 2002).

Selected Bibliography

Buehler, Arthur F. *Recognizing Sufism: Contemplation in the Islamic Tradition.* London: I.B.Tauris, 2016.

———. *Sufi Heirs of the Prophet: The Indian Naqshbandiyya and the Rise of the Mediating Shaykh.* Columbia, South Carolina: University of South Carolina Press, 1998.

Dahnhardt, Thomas. *Change and Continuity in Indian Sufism: A Naqshbandi-Mujaddidi Branch in the Hindu Environment.* Delhi: DK Printworld, 2002.

Dale, Stephen Frederic. "The Legacy of the Timurids." *Journal of the Royal Asiatic Society*, 8(1) (1998): 43–58.

Eaton, Richard M. "The Political and Religious Authority of the Shrine of Baba Farid." In Barbara Daly Metcalf, ed., *Moral Conduct and Authority: The Place of Adab in South Asian Islam*, 333–56. Berkeley, California: University of California Press, 1984.

Ernst, Carl. *Refractions of Islam in India: Situating Sufism and Yoga*. New Delhi: Sage Publications Private Ltd, 2016.

———. "Muslim Interpreters of Yoga." In Debra Diamond, ed., *Yoga: The Art of Transformation*. Washington, DC: Smithsonian Books, 2013. Available at http://www.unc.edu/~cernst/pdf/Smithsonian.pdf (accessed January 15, 2017).

———. *Sufism: An Introduction to the Mystical Tradition of Islam*. Boulder, Colorado: Shambala, 2011.

———. "Situating Sufism and Yoga." *Journal of the Royal Asiatic Society*, 15(1) (April 2005).

Krishna, L.R. *Punjabi Sufi Poets*. Bombay: Oxford University Press, 1938.

Margoliouth, D.S. "Kadiriyya." In P. Bearman, Th. Bianquis, C.E. Bosworth, E. van Donzel and W.P. Heinrichs, eds., *Encyclopedia of Islam, Second Edition*. Leiden: E.J. Brill, 1960–2005.

Nicholson, Reynold A. *The Mathwani of Jalalu'ddin Rumi. Edited from the Oldest Manuscripts Available with Critical Notes, Translation, & Commentary*, Vol. I–V. Lahore: Islamic Book Service, 1989.

Schimmel, Annemarie. *Islam in the Indian Subcontinent*. Leiden: E.J. Brill, 1980.

Shackle, Christopher. "Sikh and Muslim Understandings of Baba Farid." Lecture at the 2008 Amrit Kaur Ahluwalia Memorial Lecture, UC Berkeley, California, April 19, 2008. Available at http://southasia.berkeley.edu/sites/default/files/Sikh%20and%20Muslim%20Understandings%20of%20Baba%20Farid%20.pdf (accessed January 15, 2017).

Sheldrake, Rupert. *The Sense of Being Stared at and Other Unexplained Powers of Human Minds*. Rochester, Vermont: Park Street Press, 2013.

Glossary of Terms

Abhidhamma (Sanskrit: *Abhidharma*): Third-century BCE Buddhist texts; contain scholastic analysis of doctrinal teachings.

Achar: Moral character.

Adharma: The opposite of *dharma* (virtue, duty, cosmic order); evil; vice; chaos.

Adi Granth: The name for the original version of the *Guru Granth Sahib*. It was compiled by the fifth Guru, Guru Arjan Dev, and installed at the Harmandar Sahib in 1604.

Ahankar: Pride.

Ahimsa: Nonviolence; absence of even the desire to harm any living being in thought, word, or deed; the one of the five *yamas*, or moral restraints.

Akal Takht: Throne of the Timeless, located in Amritsar, India.

Amrit: Water consecrated by the *granthi* and used in *Amrit Sanskar/ Amrit Pahul* (initiation/baptism) ceremony. It is the Sikh counterpart to Holy Water used in Christian ceremonies of baptism.

Anatta (Sanskrit: *anatman*): "No-self" or "non-self." A core Buddhist belief that there is no substantial self or soul; one of the three marks of existence (*trilakshana*).

Anicca (Sanskrit: *anitya*): "Non-eternal." Impermanence; transitory; one of the three marks of existence (*trilakshana*).

Aparigraha: Non-grasping; non-attachment; one of the *yamas*, or moral restraints.

Ardas: Sikh prayer that forms the culmination of any religious service.

Artha: Wealth; power; one of the four goals of human life according to the Hindu religious system.

Asa di var: Guru Nanak's prayer, consisting of *Shlokas* and twenty-four *Pauris*. It contains verses by Guru Nanak, Guru Angad, Guru Ram Das, and Guru Arjan.

Asanga: Fourth-century Mahayana Buddhist thinker and author of *Uttaratantra Shastra,* a treatise about "Buddha Nature." Often considered the founder of Mahayana Buddhism as a specific orientation or denomination within Buddhism.

Ashrama: A stage of life in Hindu Dharma. The four stages of life are *brahmacharya* (being a student), *grihastha* (being a householder), *vanaprastha* (retiring from worldly affairs), and *sannyasa* (renunciation of the world).

Asteya: Non-stealing; one of the *yamas*, or moral restraints.

Atman: Self; the core of one's being; identical to *Brahman* according to the non-dualistic Advaita tradition of Vedanta.

Avatara (Hindi: *avatar*): Lit., "descent;" incarnation of a deity, usually Vishnu, in a physical form. Avataras appear for the purpose of re-establishing *dharma* when it is endangered.

Avijja (Sanskrit: *avidya*): "ignorance." Although it can mean mere incomprehension, in Buddhist philosophy it often signifies the root cause of the cycle of *samsara*.

Bhagavad Gita: "Song of the Blessed One;" a section of the *Mahabharata*, one of the two major epics of Hindu sacred literature (the other being the *Ramayana*). This text contains the dialogue between Lord Krishna and a warrior, Arjuna, who is facing the dilemma of doing his duty of waging war against his cousins. The book is a crystallization of various strands of Indian philosophy and yogas. This text has come to be greatly revered as an independent scripture and has been the object of many commentaries, including one by Mahatma Gandhi.

Bhagavan: The Blessed One; God; the Supreme Being; usually applied to the deity Vishnu.

Bhakti: Devotion; profound loving connection with the Supreme Being; seen by many Hindu traditions as the pre-eminent means of achieving liberation from the cycle of rebirth.

Bhakti movement: A popular theistic devotional movement in India that cut across all sections of society and includes many prominent female exponents. This movement emerged in the first millennium CE (though on the basis of earlier traditions), but reached its zenith around the sixteenth century. Also known as the Sant tradition, it emphasizes devotion as the pre-eminent path to liberation from the cycle of death and rebirth.

Bhikkhu/Bhikkhuni: "Monk" and "nun," respectively. Ordained Buddhist monks and nuns.

Bodhisattva: "Being set upon enlightenment" or "Being of Wisdom." The goal of Mahayana Buddhism, while *arahant* (most worthy or perfected person) is the goal of Theravada Buddhism. In taking the *bodhisattva* vow, a Buddhist practitioner is asked to take a vow of compassion for all sentient beings.

Brahma: The deity who brings the universe into existence at the start of each cosmic cycle; the creator god in Hindu Dharma.

Brahmacharya: "Divine Conduct" but is generally translated as "celibacy"; one of the *yamas*, or moral restraints; also the first *ashrama*, or student stage of life. The vow of celibacy defines an unmarried (and thus chaste) student preparing for adult life.

Brahman: The ground of all being; infinite being, consciousness, and bliss.

Brahmana: Priestly text; portion of the *Veda* composed after the original *samhitas*, and intended to explain the Vedic rituals to Brahmins, or priests.

Brahmin: A member of the community, or "caste," of religious specialists and intellectuals; actually spelled *brahmana*, but the spelling as Brahmin differentiates the members of this community from the texts of the same name; one of the four *varnas*.

Buddhavachana: "The Words of the Buddha." The accepted teachings of the Buddha within a Buddhist tradition.

Caste: Contemporary term, derived from the Portuguese *casta*, or "color," for the system of hereditary occupations practiced by many communities in India (including, but not limited to, Hindus). The term conflates two distinct concepts: *varna* and *jati*. There are four *varnas*: *Brahmin*, Vedic priest; *Kshatriya*, warrior, administrator; *Vaishya*, trader; and *Shudra*, laborer.

Chakras: Lit., "circle." Points or areas in the body considered to be a node or center of spiritual energy and power.

Charvaka: Alternative name for the Lokayata system of Hindu materialist philosophy.

Chisthiyya: Chishti Sufi Lineage. An Afghan Sufi lineage, technically originating in Chisht.

Dalit: Lit., "The oppressed;" a term coined by B.R. Ambedkar by which many members of the "lower" castes or the "untouchables" refer to themselves to highlight the marginalization they have experienced. Gandhi used the term "Harijan" or "People of God" for the "untouchables."

Darshana: View, worldview; the preferred term for an Indian system of philosophy. Also, the phenomenon of seeing and being seen by the holy being, and the image or *murti* of a deity, usually in a temple setting. It is an experience of great religious significance for most Hindus and people of Dharma traditions.

Dasam Granth: A book containing the writings of the tenth Sikh Guru, Guru Gobind Singh; compiled by Bhai Mani Singh.

Daswandh: a Sikh term for giving one-tenth of one's income to the service of the community.

Dhammapada: Lit., "the Verses of Dhamma." A compendium of popular maxims attributed to the Buddha.

Dharma (Pali: *dhamma;* Gurmukhi: *dharam*): moral duty; righteousness; virtue; law; and teachings.

Dharmanirpekshata: Generally translated as "secularism." Indian principle of democracy dictates equality of all religions.

Dhikr: "Remembrance." A form of devotional Sufi practice in which the name of God is repeated either silently or verbally.

Digambara: Literally, "'sky-clad." Monks of this sect of Jain Dharma seek to shed attachment to all bonds, including clothes.

Doha: An Indian vernacular term for a poem in the medieval Bhakti tradition of India. These were often sung and accompanied by music.

Dukkha (Sanskrit: *duhkha*): "Suffering," "unsatisfactoriness." One of the three marks of existence in Buddha Dhamma (*trilakshana*).

Ek Onkar: One God; the basis of Sikh theology.

Faqir (*fakir*): An ascetic in Sufism.

Five Ks: Symbols of Khalsa identity; each begins with the letter "K." The Five Ks are: *kesh* (uncut hair), *kara* (a steel bracelet), *kangha* (a wooden comb), *kirpan* (sword or dagger), and *kachera* (pair of shorts).

Granthi/giani: A Sikh priest, a ceremonial reader of the *Guru Granth Sahib*.

Gurdwara: A Sikh temple, "Door to the Guru."

Gurmukh: A Sikh term for someone who has realized God and overcome his/her ego to walk the Gurus' path.

Guru: A teacher or spiritual preceptor. In the Sikh tradition, there were ten human Gurus responsible for the founding and propagation of Sikh Dharam, beginning with Guru Nanak and ending with Guru Gobind Singh.

Guru Granth Sahib: The tenth Guru—Guru Gobind Singh—added Guru Tegh Bahadur's (ninth Guru) verses to the *Adi Granth* and renamed the revised volume the *Guru Granth Sahib*. It contains the compositions of six Sikh Gurus: Guru Nanak, Guru Angad, Guru Amar Das, Guru Ram Das, Guru Arjan and Guru Tegh Bahadur. It also contains teachings of Hindu religious leaders, such as Ramananda and Namdev, and Muslim saints (Kabir and the Sufi Shaykh Farid). It is the Eternal Living Guru for Sikhs.

Hindutva: Lit., "Hinduness;" a term coined by Vinayak Damodar Savarkar to define who is a Hindu. The term has also become a synonym for Hindu nationalism.

Haumai: Ego—I; Self-centeredness, which prevents an individual from becoming a *Gurmukh*.

Hinayana Buddhism: Lit., "Smaller Vehicle." The preferred term is Theravada Buddhism or the "Way of the Elders," implying the earliest school of the Buddhist tradition.

Hukam: The will of God.

Ishtadevata: Preferred or chosen deity; the form of divinity through devotion to whom one seeks liberation from the cycle of rebirth.

Ishvara: Lord; God; the Supreme Being; often applied either to the deity Shiva or Vishnu.

Jati: Lit., "birth"; the community into which one is born, as defined by the pursuit of a hereditary occupation and ranked hierarchically based on the perceived purity of the work involved.

Jiva: Living being; life force; soul; that which undergoes the process of *karma* and rebirth.

Jot: Divine light.

Kama: Desire, longing, or sensory enjoyment; one of the four aims of human life in Hindu Dharma.

Kanphata Yogi: Worshiper of the God Shiva. Associated with the Tantric movement of Hindu Dharma. They are followers of Goraknath and are distinguished by their large earrings.

Karah Parshad: A sacrament in the Sikh tradition. The sweet mixture is made of equal amounts of flour, sugar, water and butter. It is placed in the cupped palms of the members of the congregation at the end of any religious service.

Karma: Work; action; the law of cause and effect according to which any thought, word, or deed will result in a corresponding effect concerning the one who thinks, speaks, or does it.

Karta Purakh: Creator, a term for God in Sikh Dharam.

Kaur: Lit., "princess." The surname given to all Sikh women of the Khalsa; introduced by Guru Gobind Singh to eliminate caste distinctions.

Keshdhari: A Sikh who does not cut their hair, but is not initiated.

Kevala Jnanin: Term for a liberated being in the Jain tradition.

Kevalam: Lit., "aloneness"; used as a term for spiritual liberation, especially in Jainism.

Khalsa: Lit., "pure ones." The community of initated Sikhs founded by Gobind Singh, the tenth Guru, in 1699.

Kirat Karna: Honest work.

Kirtan: Religious singing.

Kirtan Sohalia: Night-time prayer said before Sikhs go to bed.

Krishna: Lit., "dark one"; "attractive one"; popular Hindu deity; a character in the *Mahabharata* and narrator of the teachings in the *Bhagavad Gita*; an *avatara* or incarnation of Vishnu, though seen in some Vaishnava traditions not simply as an incarnation, but as the Supreme Being.

Krodh: Anger.

Langar: The community kitchen in the *Gurdwara*, where free food is prepared, cooked and served to all. Food is prepared and served by both men and women who are volunteers. Men and women eat separately: men sit on one side of the room, while the women sit on the other side.

Lata'if: Subtle centers of consciousness located in the body; very roughly equivalent to yogic *chakras* and Chinese traditions' *dan tiens*.

Leshya: Mental reactions caused by the effects of a particular food, mental state, environment, and so on. They are classified using various colors. For example, emotions of hatred and malice are considered black or grey and benevolence is signified as red.

Lobh: Greed; covetousness.

Lokayata: Ancient Indian system of materialist philosophy. Unlike mainstream Hindus, the adherents of this system rejected the belief in *karma* and rebirth, typically viewing ritual activity and spiritual practice of any kind as a means of duping the ignorant.

Madhyamaka: Lit., "Middle Way"; Major school of Indian Mahayana philosophy. A follower of this school is called a Madhyamika.

Mahabharata: Lit., "Great Tale of the Bharata Dynasty"; one of the two major Hindu epics. It is the longest epic of the world, which contains the story of an ancient war between two branches of a royal family in northern India. The *Bhagavad Gita* is a small portion of this massive text.

Mahayana Buddhism: "Great Vehicle." Emerged in first century CE and is considered a more accessible path as it is open to laypeople who seek to become *bodhisattvas*. Also known as Northern Buddhism.

Manmukh: An individual who is ego oriented.

Mantra: Lit., "instrument of thought;" a set of syllables that are recited or reflected upon in order to bring about spiritually prosperous results.

Maya: Greed, wealth, or delusion.

Miri-Piri: Temporal and spiritual authority.

Moh: Attachment.

Moksha: A Sanskrit term for liberation from the cycle of rebirth; the highest of the four aims of human life; the pursuit of liberation often involves taking up a yoga, or spiritual discipline. In epistemological sense, it is the state of self-realization. In the Sikh tradition, for the freedom from the cycle of death and rebirth, the term *mukti* is used.

Muraqabah: A Sufi practice that is roughly equivalent to meditation/contemplation.

Murti: Image; usually a sculpted image of a deity. *Murtis* (commonly known as idols) are typically found in temples but can also be found in home shrines.

Naam: God's name or Divine essence in the Sikh tradition.

Naam simran/japna: Meditation on God's name.

Namokara: Most widely used prayer of the Jain tradition. Also known as the *Namaskar Mantra* and the *Mahamantra*, it involves reverence and supplication to Jain teachers. The mantra is believed to yield miraculous powers.

Naqshibandis: The Sufi lineage founded by Bahauddin Naqshband (d. 1389 in Buhkhara).

Nath Yogi: A member of a group of *yogis* who are associated with Shaivism and are thought to have emerged in the thirteenth century.

Nibbana (Sanskrit: *nirvana*): Lit., "to blow out." In Buddhism, refers to a state beyond desire and delusion. This state marks the end of rebirths in *samsara*.

Nirankar: Formless Divine.

Nirmanakaya: Lit., "body of apparent manifestation."

Nishkamta: Selflessness.

Niyama: "Restraint," or injunction; one of a set of five moral virtues: purity, contentment, asceticism, self-study or inquiry, and contemplation of God.

Paccekabuddha (Sanskrit: *Pratyekabuddha*): "Solitary Buddha."

Panj kakar: see Five Ks.

Panj pyare: The "five beloved ones." The designation given to the five men who were prepared to sacrifice their lives for the faith when called upon by the tenth Guru in Sikh Dharam. They were the first five members of the Khalsa.

Pahul: Initiation ceremony, or baptism.

Pangat: People sitting together in rows to show a communal meal, that is, *langar*.

Parinibbana: "Final release." The physical death with no following samsaric rebirth.

Paryushan: An important holy week of repentance and fasting in the Jain tradition.

Patit: An initiated Sikh who has lapsed in his/her observations; today this term is also used to refer to Sikhs who are not initiated and do not live according to the *Rehat Maryada*.

Pinjrapole: Animal shelters.

Prasad: "Grace." Usually refers to God's grace and food offering to a deity.

Praticcasamupada (Sanskrit: *pratityasamutpada*): "Dependent co-origination" or "dependent origination." The Buddhist belief that all entities (*dhammas/dharma*) arise and exist in dependence on other entities.

Puja: Worship; primary mode of interaction with Hindu deities.

Punya: Good *karma*; merit; results of good actions that one has previously committed.

Puranas: "Ancient lore"; Hindu texts composed in the first millennium of the Common Era and detailing the deeds of the major deities, including Vishnu and Shiva.

Pure Land Buddhism: Primarily popular in Japan. A central practice is the worship of Amitabha Buddha in order to be reborn in the Pure Land of Sukhavati.

Purusha: The divine being whose body is sacrificed, according to the *Rig Veda*, to create the cosmos; also the principle of spirit in the *Samkhya* system of philosophy, roughly similar to the concepts of *jiva* and *atman*.

Purushartha: Aim or goal of human life, according to Hindu Dharma. There are four such aims: *dharma* (duty, virtue), *artha* (wealth, power), *kama* (fulfillment of desires, including sensory enjoyment), and *moksha* (liberation from the cycle of rebirth).

Qadiri Sufi: Member of the Qadiri lineage whose founder is considered to be Abdulqadir al-Jilani (1077–1166).

Qawwali: Type of Chishti devotional music prevalent in South Asia. Usually it is in Urdu and Punjabi languages.

Qur'an: The holy scripture of Islam. It is considered to have been revealed directly by God to the Prophet Muhammad.

Rab'al-thani: Fourth month in the Islamic Calendar.

Ramayana: "Life of Rama"; one of the two major Hindu epics, the other being the *Mahabharata*; narration of the adventures of the hero Rama, who is considered an incarnation of Lord Vishnu, and his wife, Sita. It is the most popular text of Hindu literature.

Rehat Maryada: Sikh Code of Conduct.

Rig Veda: The most ancient of Hindu texts; the oldest of the *Vedas*. It consists primarily of hymns to the *devas*—deities embodying various natural phenomena.

Rishi: Sage; wise person through whom the *Veda* was revealed; any sage or wise person in the Hindu tradition.

Sadharana dharma: Universal duties; moral virtues required of all persons, consisting of the *yamas* and *niyamas* in Hindu Dharma.

Sahaj: State of mind in which one unites with the divine.

Samadhi: Absorption in the object of one's meditation; separation from *prakriti*, or material nature; the aim of the Yoga system of Patanjali, as outlined in his *Yoga Sutra*. It is also the last step of the Buddhist eightfold path.

Samhita: Hymn; the oldest portion of each *Veda*, which provides hymns for Vedic rituals.

Samkhya: One of the six systems of Vedic philosophy; often paired with the Yoga system of Patanjali. It emphasizes the duality of spirit (*purusha*) and material nature (*prakriti*).

Sampradaya: Hindu sect or denomination.

Samsara: The cycle of birth, death, and rebirth; perpetuated by the law of *karma*; at the time of physical death, actions whose results have not yet manifested will cause a birth to occur in circumstances that will enable this manifestation to take place.

Sangha: Lit., "association" or "community"; Third Refuge of Buddhism, consisting of those dedicated to Buddha's Dhamma in monastic communities.

Sannyasa/sannyasin: Stage of life in which one becomes a renunciant. A *sannyasin* is an individual who has renounced the world.

Santosha: Contentment; one of the *niyamas*, or moral injunctions.

Sant: A term used interchangeably with saints; however, they are etymologically different. *Sant* is associated with *Sat* or Truth; thus, *sants* are those who have realized the Truth or Divine Reality. *Sants* are not canonized by any religious authority. The Bhakti movement of India is also known as Sant tradition.

Sat: Truth; Divine Reality.

Satya: Truth; as one of the *yamas*, or moral restraints, it refers to honesty and veracity.

Sehajdhari: Sikhs who are not baptized and cut their hair.

Sewa: Selfless service.

Shabad: Divine Word.

Shaiva/Shaivism: Tradition based on worship of Shiva as the supreme deity.

Shakta/Shaktism: Tradition based on worship of Shakti as the supreme deity.

Shakti: Lit., "power"; mother goddess; the creative power behind creation. The consorts of deities are known as their *Shakti*; also one of the proper names of the goddess married to Shiva.

Shauca: Purity; one of the *niyamas*, or moral injunctions.

Shavaka (Sanskrit: *shravaka*): Lit., "listener" or "student."

Shaykh: Lit., "elder"; usually used for high-level teachers of religious knowledge in Sufism.

Shramana movement: Lit., "striver movement"; emerged in the first millennium BCE (though possibly drawing upon older traditions) in reaction to the claim of the Brahmins to spiritual authority based on birth (*jati*).

Shruti: Lit., "that which is heard"; the *Veda*; the most authoritative Hindu texts.

Shunnata (Sanskrit: *shunyata*): Lit., "emptiness" or "voidness"; a central Buddhist concept related to the doctrine of interdependence.

Siddha Loka: Realm of perfection.

Smriti: "That which is remembered"; Hindu texts of derivative authority, including the epics.

Sukha: "Happiness," "pleasure."

Sunni Islam: The majority sect of Islam, which agrees that Abu Bakr, the actual successor to Muhammad, was the best person to follow the Prophet.

Suttas (Sanskrit: *sutras*): Pali and Sanskrit discourses attributed to the Buddha.

Svadharma: One's own duty; in contrast with universal *dharma* (*sadharana dharma*), this refers to the responsibilities specific to a particular station in life or situation.

Svadhyaya: Self-study; study of scripture and wise teaching; one of the *niyamas*, or moral injunctions.

Swami: Master; title by which many Hindu monks, or *sannyasins*, are known.

Svetambara: "White-clad." A sect of Jains found mainly in western and northern India.

Tanha: "Thirst" or "craving"; the Buddha speaks of it as the selfish craving that perpetuates samsaric existence.

Tantra: Style of spirituality that utilizes the senses to go beyond them, and that seeks to tap into powers latent in the physical and subtle bodies of its practitioners to accelerate the process of spiritual liberation. Tantric thought emphasizes the non-duality of the sensory and spiritual realms.

Tapas: Asceticism; ascetic practice; one of the *niyamas*, or moral injunctions.

Tasawwuf: The original Arabic term for Sufism; considered to be the inner mystical aspect of Islamic religion.

Tathata: "Suchness"; aspect of *nirvana*.

Tattvartha Sutra: Considered one of the most authoritative texts of Jain philosophy (*c.*200–450 CE). It is written in Sanskrit.

Theravada Buddhism: "Way of the Elders." Founded on the earliest schools of Buddhism that emphasize the Buddha's teachings preserved in the Pali canon. Found primarily in Southeast Asia.

Three Refuges: The three main components of the Buddha's teachings, including Buddha (Teacher), *dharma/dhamma* (Teachings) and *sangha* (Community). Also known as the Three Jewels.

Tirthankara: "Ford-Maker," also called, "Jina" (Victor). Twenty-four great Jain spiritual teachers. Lord Mahavira, who was the contemporary of the Buddha, is considered to be the last Tirthankara.

Trikaya: "Three Bodies"; the Mahayana concept referring to the three states in which the Buddha manifests: *Dharmakaya* "true body," abstract, impersonal and ever-present Buddha; *Nirmanakaya*, body of apparent manifestation; *Sambhogakaya*, "bliss body" or "enjoyment body".

Upanishad: Mystical teachings of Hindu Dharma; the final portion of the *Vedas* that marks the movement from the emphasis on ritual to philosophy. These texts were composed in the mid to late first millennium BCE and form the basis of Vedanta philosophy.

Vaishnava/Vaishnavism: Tradition based on worship of Vishnu as the supreme deity. The majority of Hindus are Vaishnavas, though Shaivas and Shaktas are also prominent.

Vajrayana Buddhism: "Diamond Vehicle"; developed in Northern India and Tibet.

Vand chakana: Giving to those in need; an important teaching of Guru Nanak.

Varna: One of four divisions of society based on the type of work that one does for the social organism. Though there are indications that *varna* may at one time have been a matter of choice or aptitude, certainly by the middle of the first millennium BCE it was a hereditary hierarchical, patriarchal system of occupation based on the duties performed by one's father. Today called caste, attempts have been made to reform the injustices seen to be part of this system (inasmuch as it has involved marginalization of those seen as members of "lower" castes), or to eliminate it altogether. Also see: caste.

Veda: Wisdom; the oldest and most authoritative Hindu scriptures; composed, according to mainstream scholarship, from 1700 to 200 BCE, but some say they are much earlier. The four Vedas are: *Rig Veda*

(Veda of adoration); *Sama Veda* (melody for the hymns); *Yajur Veda* (instructions for Vedic sacrifices), and *Atharva Veda* (Veda of magic and healing formulas).

Vedanta: "End of the Veda." One of the six systems of Vedic philosophy, focused upon the interpretation of the *Upanishads*. This system has gradually become the dominant system of Hindu thought as various commentators through the centuries have assimilated aspects of other systems into it.

Vinaya: Lit., "education" or "discipline"; rules for Buddhist monastic communities. Based on the *Vinaya Pitaka* of the Pali canon.

Vipassana (Sanskrit: *vipashyana*) "Insight Meditation."

Waheguru: Name by which Sikhs refer to God—Wonderful Lord.

Yana: "Vehicle"; often used to contrast earlier (Hinayana) from later (Mahayana) Buddhist schools of thought. Vajrayana (Diamond Vehicle) was developed later.

Yama: Lit., "restraint"; name of the Vedic deity who presides over death, so called because he carries a noose with which to restrain unruly souls; also, a set of five moral virtues: nonviolence, truth, non-stealing, chastity, and non-attachment.

Yoga: Lit., "to yoke," implying the "union" with the Divine. Spiritual discipline; a practice or way of life pursued for the purpose of achieving liberation from the cycle of rebirth. Also one of the six systems of Vedic philosophy, as articulated in the *Yoga Sutra* of Patanjali and the various commentaries thereon. Hindu Dharma broadly considers four yogas. (1) Bhakti yoga: the spiritual discipline of devotion; (2) Jnana yoga: the spiritual discipline of knowledge, using the intellect to discern between truth and falsehood, the real and the unreal; (3) Karma yoga: the spiritual discipline of action; pursuing work without attachment to its results (*karma-phala-vairagya*) as a means of purifying the mind of egotism; and (4) Raja yoga: royal spiritual discipline; a popular term for Dhyana yoga, or meditation.

Yogachara: One of two major schools of Indian Mahayana philosophy. Also known as the "mind-only" school.

Yogis/yoginis: Masculine and feminine terms for independent Buddhist practitioners in Vajrayana Buddhism.

Yoga Sutra: Authoritative text of the Yoga system of Vedic philosophy. Its authorship is attributed to Patanjali, a figure of the mid to late first millennium BCE, though the text in its present form may date to a later period (up to about 500 CE).

Zen Buddhism: Form of Buddhism in India, China, and Japan. Founded in the sixth century in China. Zen advocates the simple act of mindful sitting as Siddhartha did under the Bodhi Tree.

Index

www.ingramcontent.com/pod-product-compliance
Ingram Content Group UK Ltd.
Pitfield, Milton Keynes, MK11 3LW, UK
UKHW020732280225
455688UK00012B/607